Writing for Professional Publication

By William Van Til

AUTOBIOGRAPHY	*My Way of Looking at It*
TRADE BOOKS	*The Danube Flows Through Fascism* *Foldboat Holidays* (contributor)
TEXTBOOKS	*Modern Education for the Junior High School Years* (collaborator) *Education: A Beginning* *Secondary Education: School and Community*
EL-HI BOOKS	*Economic Roads for American Democracy* *Time on Your Hands* *Education in American Life* (co-editor)
ANTHOLOGIES	*The High School of the Future* (contributor) *Curriculum: Quest for Relevance* (editor and contributor)
UNITS MONOGRAPHS	*Democracy Demands It* (collaborator) *The Work of the Bureau for Intercultural Education* *The Development of Education for Desegregation and Integration* *Widening Cultural Horizons* (collaborator)
ENCYCLOPEDIA ENTRIES	*Encyclopedia of Educational Research* *American Educator*
YEARBOOKS (EDITOR)	*Democratic Human Relations* *Intercultural Attitudes in the Making* *Forces Affecting American Education* *Issues in Secondary Education* (contributor to eight other yearbooks)
SELECTIONS	*The Making of a Modern Educator* *One Way of Looking at It* *Another Way of Looking at It* *Van Til on Education*

Plus various pamphlets, columns, magazine and journal articles, book reviews.

Writing for Professional Publication

SECOND EDITION

William Van Til

Coffman Distinguished
Professor Emeritus
of Education

Indiana State University

Allyn and Bacon, Inc.

Boston   London   Sydney   Toronto

Once again, for Bee

Library of Congress Cataloging in Publication Data

Van Til, William.
  Writing for professional publication.

  Bibliography: p.
  Includes index.
  1. Authorship. I. Title.
PN146.V38 1986   808′.02   85-15793
ISBN 0-205-08467-2

Printed in the United States of America

10 9 8 7 6 5 4 3 2 1 90 89 88 87 86 85

Contents

Supplements

Part Four   **How About . . . ?**

Preface

The book in your hands is called *Writing for Professional Publication.* It is a second edition, updated, revised, and containing new content while retaining useful material from the well-received earlier edition.

By writing, we mean producing material to be read, such as books and articles.

By professional, we mean pertaining to an occupation requiring special knowledge and training in some field of learning.

By publication, we mean the act or process of publishing.

So by writing for professional publication, we mean producing material to be read in published form, by people in occupations requiring special knowledge and training in a field of learning.

Writing for Professional Publication is a book for anyone who writes or plans to write about the concerns of people in a profession. Most of those who write for professional publication are themselves people who are engaged in the professions. Many, though not all of these practicing professionals, are teachers, largely in colleges and universities.

Many writers for professional publication need advice on how to begin. Consequently, *Writing for Professional Publication* begins with chapters on why people write, breaking into print, and publishing a first book.

Opportunities for professional publication are wider than most of us realize. Broadly interpreted, writing for professional publication includes writing for professional magazines, publishing in scholarly journals, book reviewing, writing columns, writing and editing yearbooks, developing anthologies, writing textbooks, writing nonfiction trade books, and writing specialized books (including monographs and scholarly, technical, medical, business, and reference books). Part One, "Publishing Opportunities," includes a chapter on each of these possibilities.

Writers for professional publication face problems of finding time, getting ideas, using tools of the trade, working with word processors, developing style and using manuals, finding a publisher, and contracting for a book. Once launched, they must cope with developing a manuscript; reading edited manuscripts, galleys, and page proofs; and preparing indexes. Part Two, "The Writer at Work," devotes a chapter to each of these aspects of writing.

Writers should know what happens to their manuscripts after their work is submitted. They need to understand the roles of editors, the functions of outside readers and referees, the work of copyeditors, the production process, the copyright rules, the economics of publishing, and marketing procedures. Through chapters on each topic, Part Three, "In the Editorial Offices," deals in broad terms with what the writer needs to know about the editing and publishing process.

In my workshops on writing for professional publication held for faculties of many universities, I have been asked many questions. Most have been answered in Parts One through Three. Some unanswered questions are discussed in Part Four, "How About . . . ?"

Writing for Professional Publication is an informal, relaxed, and personalized book. I believe that writing for professionals need not be pompous; scholarship and readability can be reconciled. So I have adopted dialogues to communicate ideas throughout twenty-nine chapters. The dialogues in "Publishing Opportunities" place relatively inexperienced professionals in interaction with an experienced writer for professional publication. In "The Writer at Work," experienced writers from different academic fields converse. "In the Editorial Offices" brings together a textbook editor, an editor of a journal, and an experienced writer, who is a continuing protagonist throughout the book. The dialogues draw freely upon my participation in varied publications over many years.

Supplements follow each chapter of dialogue. Though the supplements are highly varied, each supplement has a common purpose—to provide the reader with concrete illustrations of what has been talked about in the preceding chapter. The supplements include comments by well-established authors, queries to periodicals and publishers, forms used by journal and book publishers, directories, editorial policies, listings of authors' guides, bibliographies (reporting dates of recent printings or editions), excerpts from articles, contractual arrangements, sample pages and galleys and page proofs, reviews by manuscript readers, production sequences, copyright forms, indexing procedures, etc. See the Table of Contents of Supplements for specific titles.

Thus, *Writing for Professional Publication* is in part a narration in dialogue form, and in part an anthology of illustrative material for the writer. Consequently, the book can be read in various ways. Some readers may wish to proceed from cover to cover, reading a dialogue followed by a supplement, then reading the next dialogue and supplement, and so on. Other readers may wish to begin by reading only the dialogues. Some may zero in on the supplements alone. Still others may wish to concentrate on special topics of interest to them, through reading selected chapters and supplements at any point in the book. The book has been organized to enable readers to adapt the content to their own needs and interests as writers for professional publication.

The goal I have had in mind is to help you write for professional publication. Good luck!

William Van Til
Lake Lure
Terre Haute, Indiana

Acknowledgments

This is a book based on a lifetime of writing. How can I possibly thank all who have contributed? I can't. My thanks would have to begin with my mother and Miss Emily Curry, principal of P.S. 15, who had faith in my writing when I was a child. I would have to thank scores of teachers, not just the poet and critic Mark Van Doren, who was my undergraduate adviser at Columbia College. I would have to thank dozens of editors, not just Maxwell Perkins of Charles Scribner's Sons, who accepted my first book. I would have to thank all members of my family who have learned to live with a writer in the house, not just my wife Bee who has edited almost all of my writing—and when she hasn't I have rued the day! Yet I still would not have named an incalculable number of authors I have read, thousands of my former students, hundreds of colleagues, a score of administrators, a dozen or two secretaries, and a flock of graduate assistants. Fortunately I had the opportunity to thank many of them through my autobiography, *My Way of Looking at It* (Lake Lure Press, RR 32 Box 316, Terre Haute, Indiana, 47803), which was published in 1983, midway between the first edition of *Writing for Professional Publication* and this revised edition.

Even if I limited my thanks to those who have shaped my thinking on writing for professional publication, I could not adequately express my appreciation. These people would include nearly half of the staff of the School of Education of Indiana State University, who enrolled in my course in writing for publication during my decade at ISU, and the professors at universities from Minnesota to Alabama and from Maine to Arizona, who have participated in the Writing for Professional Publication workshops that I now conduct on the road.

So I must limit myself to thanking those closely related to the making of the first edition of this book: Bee Van Til, my wife and editor; my son, Roy Van Til, who helped develop the supplements; Ruan Fougerousse, my secretary, who can read my handwriting; the staff of Allyn and Bacon, who granted me full cooperation and tape-recorded interviews; the nationally known authors who commented expressly for this book on why they write; the workshop participants who allowed me to reproduce their query letters; the authors, editors, and publishers who gave me permission to carry their ideas in the supplements to my chapters; the readers of first drafts of my manuscript, Stanley Elam of *Phi Delta Kappan*, John F. Ohles of Kent State University, Richard D. Kimpston of the University of Minnesota, and Jean Grambs of the University of Maryland; and the readers of my completed manuscript, Stanley Elam, Roy Van Til, Jean Grambs, Robert R. Leeper, former editor of Association for Supervision and Curriculum Development publications, and Virgil A. Clift, emeritus, New York University.

My thanks for help on the second edition go again to Bee Van Til; Allyn and Bacon; workshop participants and permission grantors; those who suggested changes from the first edition for consideration, my son Jon Van Til of Rutgers University, Harold G. Shane of Indiana University, Alice Denham of Texas Tech University, and Richard D. Kimpston; those who reviewed the chapter on word processing, William Linville of Indiana State University, and Thomas Estes of the University of Virginia.

PART I

PUBLISHING
OPPORTUNITIES

1

Why Write?

Writing to communicate
Writing for enjoyment
Self-impelled to write
Achieving professional recognition
Money as a factor
Rewards through tenure, promotion, and salary increments
Publish-or-perish policies

The setting is an office that resembles thousands of similar offices of professors across the country—filing cabinets, typewriter, shelves crowded with books, desk, a desk chair, a guest's chair. The characters include Bill, an experienced professor who remarkably resembles the author of this book. Talking with Bill is Charlie, an assistant professor in his early thirties who is a composite of graduate students and graduate assistants whom the author has known throughout his career. Like all of us, Charlie has some questions and doubts. Charlie speaks first.

Charlie. But why *should* a person write for professional publication anyway? Take me, for instance. I breathed a deep sigh of relief after I completed my doctoral dissertation. Now I'm just beginning to get used to students calling me professor instead of Charlie. I like the college—even though they don't pay me what I immodestly know I'm really worth. I enjoy my students, at least most of them, and I get along all right with the faculty. The dean does his thing and I do mine and we don't bother each other. I like my lifestyle. Why should a person write?

Bill. Many possible reasons, Charlie. You'll have to decide whether any of them apply to you. A major reason why some of us write is to communicate with a wider audience than we can reach with our voices. We think we've got something to say, something that's worth hearing, and we want to put it down in writing and share it with other people. Somewhere along the way we've tried or experienced or thought or found out something that we want to communicate to others. Communication is a real urge, whether it takes the form of the scholar's pursuit of knowledge, or the practitioner's explanation of know-how—or even the rooster's daily proclamation that morning has come again! We want to make ourselves heard; we want to make a difference.

Charlie. I don't know. I can identify my biological urges more easily than my writing urge. On the other hand, when I read the junk that some in my field are writing, I think that I ought to—

Bill. That's what I mean. The urge to communicate. Even to communicate with oneself.

Charlie. I don't understand what you're saying.

Bill. Writers not only want to communicate with others. Sometimes they write to clarify their own ideas, to assemble and organize data, and to arrive at defensible positions. Writing helps people clarify competing arguments, see details in perspective, and understand matters on which they would otherwise be vague. Writing can be a form of talking to yourself, finding out what you really think—in effect, writing can be a form of communicating with yourself.

Charlie. Maybe we would have better books and articles if authors wrote first drafts to communicate their ideas to themselves and then wrote later drafts to communicate their views to the profession. Some authors mistake preliminary gropings for polished publications.

Bill. A good point. Writing shouldn't be regarded as a chore to be rushed through.

Another reason some write is for enjoyment. Some people enjoy tennis or bowling and proudly exhibit their trophies. Writers often enjoy writing and proudly exhibit their publications. Some of us find writing satisfying. We like to create. Words are our medium, not paint or clay. So we write and rewrite, and the act of publication itself is a curious anticlimax.

I think some of us write because we have to, because our lives would not be complete without writing. We convince ourselves that our writing, necessary to us, is also helpful to others. And, happily, sometimes it is. Some people write because they want to add to knowledge in a field of study, perhaps through organizing and reporting on their own research or their projects. Some write because they feel an obligation to their discipline.

Charlie. Any less noble reasons to write for professional publication?

Bill. Recognition. In professional work, writers are usually recognized by their colleagues and are looked up to. The professional who writes is seen by others as a leader. Not all may agree with the views expressed, but none can deny that here is a person willing to enter into professional discussion, to express views and report findings, to stand up and be counted. When a profession looks for leaders, it turns to its writers. How else do you learn about fellow professionals save through their writing?

Charlie. How about hearing them at conventions?

Bill. You hear them at conventions because they have written and published previously. Program planners are readers. They invite writers to deliver papers, take part in panels, and make addresses. Even the lowly chairperson, limited to introducing the speaker, and the humble recorder who summarizes the proceedings are usually invited because somebody has read their previous writing.

Charlie. This leads to job offers and new opportunities?

Bill. Sometimes. Professionals come home from conventions and suggest that Dr. Doakes would be a good local consultant or speaker or colleague or teacher. Recognition has set in.

Charlie. I begin to sniff the fresh aroma of green stuff settling into this conversation. How about another reason for writing—writing for money? Payment for articles? Royalties?

Bill. I hate to disappoint you, but the large majority of academics do not receive income for their publications. Indeed, publication sometimes costs them money. A study of journals, half of them in the business field, reported that 9 percent charge an author a "submission fee" (usually $10–$15) simply for *consideration* of a manuscript. In some fields, authors sometimes pay part of the cost of publishing their articles. When the articles are published, authors often buy reprints and send them to colleagues at the authors' expense. Very few writers for professional publications grow rich. Just as in Hollywood, for every star there are hundreds of extras.

Charlie. I'm from Missouri. Show me.

Bill. Book reviews for professional periodicals: You get the book. Articles: The overwhelming majority of scholarly journals pay nothing to professors who write for the profession; a few magazines, sometimes among the less prestigious in the profession, may pay a small fee for an article. Yearbooks of professional organizations: Expenses incurred by committee members in coming to one or two planning meetings may be paid; however, all income from the yearbook goes to the sponsoring professional association. Monographs: The sincere thanks of the scholars in the discipline. Textbooks for college students and other professional books: Royalties range from peanuts to a fortune; royalty payments for most people who write in their professional fields are heavily weighted toward the low end of the continuum. Textbooks for students in elementary and secondary schools: The proverbial exception proving the rule. Willie Sutton, the eminent bank robber, was once asked why he robbed banks; he replied, "Because that's where the money is." This is also the case with textbooks for elementary and secondary school students.

Charlie. How about articles on education in magazines for homemakers? How about best-selling books for the general public—I think you call them trade books?

Bill. The competition from freelance writers who are not members of your scholarly group is intense and fierce. We will now have a moment of silence while you try to name for me any professors who have recently appeared in *McCall's* or *Ladies' Home Journal* or who were interviewed on their recent best seller on NBC's *Today Show.* You may be able to come up with a very few. Maybe on ABC's *Good Morning, America* or NBC's *Tonight Show* or CBS's *60 Minutes*?

Charlie. So my fresh aroma of green stuff is rapidly disappearing?

Bill. Not quite. How about the financial rewards for professional writing that are built into the academic tenure, promotion, and salary system? A great many of the authors of books written for university presses, scholarly houses, and textbooks firms are professors. A strong minority of authors of nonfiction books for the general public are also engaged in college and university teaching.

Residents of academia often write because publication leads toward permanent appointments, promotion through the academic ranks, and salary increments. Unfortunately, no one seems able to evaluate objectively good teaching or counseling. But publications are tangible, visible, and numerable—indeed they sometimes seem innumerable! So publications count heavily in personnel decisions.

Charlie. Publish-or-perish?

Bill. I seem to have heard the phrase somewhere. But don't forget that the most deeply satisfying reason for professional publication is to communicate, to try your damnedest to make a difference in this imperiled world through sharing the best of your insights with others.

Charlie. You always were a romantic, weren't you?

Bill. Not guilty. In the long run, I'm the realist. And don't bother to remind me that in the long run we are all dead. While I am alive, I will still try to make a difference through writing.

Charlie. Bill, what do you really think of the publish-or-perish policy?

Bill. If publish-or-perish is interpreted as requiring every professor and administrator to publish scholarly work regularly, I oppose the policy. Forcing all university staff members into the same mold ignores individual differences and violates respect for individual personality, one of the fundamental democratic values. Staff members should be given the opportunity to emphasize brilliant teaching, skillful administration, sensitive counseling, active community participation, productive research, able writing, or whatever combination of these contributes most to the staff member's personal growth and the institution's mission.

A college or university should certainly include a substantial number of people who emphasize writing and/or research, and they should be encouraged and compensated. Yet staff members who emphasize teaching, administration, guidance, or community participation should also be recognized and rewarded. An institution of higher learning that is out of balance through a relative lack of writing and research activity should correct the imbalance by employing new staff members who emphasize writing and research in their work patterns.

Publish-or-perish policies which deny individuality too often lead to mediocrity. That's not good for the growth of the individual or the achievement of the institution's mission. Under the pressure of publish-or-perish, what is apt to perish is high-quality publication.

Charlie. Some degree of publish-or-perish policy prevails in many colleges and universities. It's another reason why some academics write.

Bill. People write for many reasons, Charlie—to communicate with others or with themselves, for enjoyment, because they are self-impelled to write. They also write to achieve recognition, to attain tenure, promotion, and salary increments. Some write in settings where publish-or-perish is the rule; others write in settings where indifference to writing is apparent. Some write for one particular reason or other; some write for a combination of reasons. You might want to consider what some experienced writers have said about why they write.

WHY I WRITE

Why do I write? Persons have an inner urge to make sense of their worlds and to communicate that sense–making to others. As part of the human situation I can give and receive, care and be cared for, stimulate and be stimulated. I write in order to share my searchings, to show I care, and to stimulate and be stimulated. I feel best about writing when I have ideas to which I must give birth.

Louise M. Berman
College of Education
University of Maryland,
College Park, Maryland

I have been motivated to take the time and invest the effort required for writing for professional publications by my interest in the subject, my instinct toward some kind of creative activity, and by need to make a living.

James MacGregor Burns
Department of Political Science
Williams College
Williamstown, Massachusetts

I write for many reasons. The earliest, and perhaps the strongest, is to share my work with others who might find it useful—researchers, scholars, teachers, and parents. Another reason, which came later, is to collect myself—my ideas, thoughts, and reactions. Thus writing has become a way of keeping in touch with others and with myself.

Jeanne S. Chall
Harvard University
Graduate School of Education
Cambridge, Massachusetts

As an undergraduate, I began to observe that my professors of extraordinary diligence and depth were those who published. By the time I reached graduate school, I had learned to avoid those popular professors who engaged in rhetorical exercises—in excessive empty sloganeering. Rather, I selected those who published in their fields. Thus, from the beginning of my career as a college professor, I operated on the principle that excellent college instruction depended on excellent scholarship. I was convinced then, and am now even more sure, that the best way to achieve excellence in scholarship and teaching is to write.

The second reason for writing was my desire to clarify and to give more valid interpretations and meanings to ideas and issues than some of my colleagues. Yet I was cautious in this because I was sure that the wisdom of the Western world could be reduced to a few small volumes. I have always been distressed by the fact that the shelves of the libraries groan under the weight of too much shabby scholarship.

A third reason was that academic respectability demanded it.

Virgil A. Clift
Professor Emeritus of Social
Science Education
New York University
New York, New York

Ideas are never fully crystallized until they have been channeled from my mind down into my arms and then
Rushed into my hands toward my fingers and flown through their tips out onto the little black and white keys of my typewriter
Where, somehow, they emerge as words on a previously stark, blank piece of bond paper which immediately becomes
Transformed from *nothing* into an intricate part of what came before and then will follow—
The exciting research, the newest understanding, the breakthrough manuscript, the best book . . .
And from that simple act all Life can seethe.
You asked me why I write. That's how I *breathe*.

Rita Dunn
Professor
St. John's University's
Center for the Study
of Learning and
Teaching Styles
Jamaica, New York

I write for several reasons. Among them is the fact that I work in a segment of United States history (history of the South and Afro-American history) where there has been so much distortion and misrepresentation that the need to correct the record is urgent. Secondly, as a professor in a university I believe it is important that I contribute to the fund of available knowledge as well as set an example for future scholars. Finally, there are few things that are as satisfying and rewarding as discovering some new truth and imparting it to others.

John Hope Franklin
John Matthews Manly Distinguished
Service Professor of History
The University of Chicago
Chicago, Illinois

I started to write when I was about 14, and have never stopped. I enjoy writing but also do it because I can express myself better on paper than by talking. Indeed, I chose academic life partly because it encouraged and rewarded writing. Although my publications are generally considered professional, I have sought, particularly in the books I have written so far, to transcend my professional field: to write both for sociologists and for "general" readers. For example, *Deciding What's News* (Pantheon Books, 1979), a sociological study of the national news media, was written as much for journalists and "news buffs" as for my colleagues in sociology. I try hard to keep sociological jargon to a minimum, and to write clearly, which often requires many drafts, but I would like to make my own research, and sociology itself, meaningful and comprehensible to people other than sociologists.

Herbert J. Gans
Professor of Sociology,
Columbia University;
and Senior Research Associate,
Center for Policy Research
New York, New York

Why do I write? I have always wanted to write—first fiction, then (when I found out I could not be a Melville or Woolf or Flaubert) essays and articles and books. I suppose I do so because that is one of the ways in which I can define myself as a person in the world, one of the ways in which I can try (as Sartre says) to address others "in their freedom." I do so because it is one of my ways of ordering my own experience, my own ideas, integrating what I learn with what I discover. Also I write because I love to shape the medium of language, to see what it can do, how it can express and describe and report. And, I suspect, I write in order to find out what I think. I am always to some degree surprised when I read a page or two that I have written. Now and then I am thrust into despair or boredom and embarrassment; but I am usually startled, surprised by what I have said.

I like to speak as well as write, of course; but there is something privileged, something distinctive about writing that enables me to say (I think) what I probably cannot say when I am lecturing—unless I write the lecture (as I sometimes do) first. But even then, the "message" of the spoken word seems to be different. I suppose I think that writing addresses people closer to their centers, unless the writing is purely descriptive or analytic (which my writing is not).

Am I asked to say that I publish because I am afraid of perishing? No, that is not why I write; but I suspect I may have been rewarded overmuch for something I so like to do.

In conclusion, I must assert that I can never say that I have learned to write or fully created myself as a writer, any more than as a teacher. If I ever say that, I shall realize I am ready to call it quits.

Maxine Greene
William F. Russell Professor
in Foundations of Education
Teachers College,
Columbia University
New York, New York

Apart from technical papers my writing has been devoted to exposition in the area of mathematics. The mathematics texts have been concerned entirely with technical results and with theorem and proof. But mathematics proper has little meaning and, I would dare to say, little value for almost all students of mathematics. Hence I have tried to show in my books, *Mathematics in Western Culture, Mathematics and the Physical World, Mathematical Thought from Ancient to Modern Times,* and other writings why and where mathematics has been significant.

In my more technical books and papers, writing has a totally different value. It forces me to clarify for myself the details of a mathematical argument that one tends to accept as understandable but which one finds, when writing for others, is not so clear and must be clarified.

I do believe, too, that mathematics education at all levels suffers from failing to present the significance of the subject, and I hope more writing will be done on this aspect of mathematics.

Morris Kline
Professor Emeritus of Mathematics
New York University
New York, New York

My reasons for professional writings are multiple. It would be an oversimplification to state otherwise. The motivations include the following:

1. To further the use of one's ideas, concepts, or methods by others.
2. To gain acceptance of peers.
3. For ego satisfaction in seeing one's words in print.
4. To cope with one's own mortality. To leave something behind as a contribution to the future.
5. To help discipline one's self to put ideas and creativity into an organized and readable form.

In writing over 200 articles, 6 pamphlets, and 8 books, I find as I continue to write that impressing peers or my ego becomes less important and a desire to contribute something useful to solving human problems becomes a more dominant motivation.

Gordon L. Lippitt
School of Government
and Business Administration
The George Washington University
Washington, D.C.

I write to share my thoughts, discoveries of insights, and concerns with others. I want to communicate, to persuade, to influence, sometimes to challenge. Writing with me is talking with others—and it can be done by letter, speech, article, informal lecture, or even poetry. Often my writing has followed research embarked upon because I could not find any published information bearing upon the topic of my particular interest. Where that has been true I feel impelled to write and share my findings so that others will not have to travel the same uncharted ground I had to travel. Or I may write on a controversial subject to offer a point of view which has not been expressed by others and which may offer a different perspective.

The Rev. Dr. Pauli Murray
Episcopalian minister,
lawyer, educator
Baltimore, Maryland

I write to communicate my discoveries to other scientists, my opinions to people who might be interested in them, and my knowledge to students.

Linus Pauling
Linus Pauling Institute of Science
and Medicine
Menlo Park, California

Why write? Is it an irresistible inner compulsion, the desire to share what one learns through work, or a search for an immortality of sorts?

At times, when the going is lonely in professional efforts, writing offers the opportunity to reach out to other professionals or to larger groups. It forces one to clarify in order to share one's thinking. At times, it provides momentary relief against daily frustration and a sense of impotence.

Writing also offers an opportunity to move from and to build on the small mosaics of daily work. It helps one to discover and portray the larger designs that represent underlying convictions and beliefs.

Hon. Justine Wise Polier
Retired Judge
Domestic Relations Court
New York and New York
State Family Court

I think the bulk of what I have written falls into two categories. Some of it, especially my earlier work, has often been an effort to call attention to some ill or danger to which I thought people insufficiently alerted. It is for this reason that I wrote twenty years ago of the dangers to public education of the political right wing—and why more recently I have written about the fact that today's school criticism is confined to no *single* portion of the political spectrum.

The second major purpose that prompts me to write is the desire to work out and fully clarify a question or problem or situation for myself. I find that committing myself to do a paper on some topic is the best way I know of learning about it. (For some material, assumption of the responsibility for *teaching* it may seem an equal or superior guarantor of learning. But the topics and questions which make for good papers are not always the topics and questions most pertinent for classes.) By the time the paper is completed, I have dealt with its topic far more carefully and systematically than I would otherwise have done—and, at least sometimes, I am able to feel satisfied that I've got the issue straight.

Mary Anne Raywid
Professor of Education
Hofstra University
Hempstead, New York

I write for several reasons. First, I have a deep conviction that those who have the privilege of doing research are working with new data and have an obligation to feed back into the system—hopefully to contribute new knowledge that will make the world a better place. Second, I find writing is one of the most demanding and effective ways of clarifying my own thinking. Third, I find it one of the most creative (albeit frustrating) forms of human intellectual activity.

Writing is the most difficult work that I do, and anyone who feels that writing comes easily is, I believe, destined to fail as a writer. It requires enormous discipline, blocking out all of the more pressing immediate problems and getting down to it. There are no shortcuts—all whom I know who write well suffer enormously to develop a product they are willing to share with others—and they are rarely satisfied with it even then.

David E. Rogers, M.D.
President
The Robert Wood Johnson Foundation
Princeton, New Jersey

I think the greatest motivation for writing for professional publications is the feeling that one has deep insight and certain knowledge or experience that one would like to share with his fellows, hoping that this will be helpful in the spreading of new knowledge, and the critical evaluation of the tremendous mass of knowledge in the scientific literature today.

Howard A. Rusk, M.D.
Distinguished University Professor
New York University
School of Medicine
New York, New York

I have always believed that those who want to lead in the development of any profession should write where there is a need. Edward Thorndike followed this principle in the first quarter of this century, and he acquitted himself admirably. His work had far-reaching effects on all aspects of instruction in the public schools. In my case, a book on curriculum, written from the vantage points of history, was needed, so I co-authored one. Classroom discipline was a leading, but neglected, problem (not considered a fit subject for inquiry by university scholars), so I wrote in response to that need. The curriculum of the home is enormously important for school learning, and parents need help in "curriculum development." I have attempted to meet this need by writing a book for parents. (I believe that this is a "professional" book in every sense of the word.) Everything I write is an attempt to contribute to the solution of some critical but neglected problem in education. My personal pleasures are in the work itself, and in the knowledge that a need for it really exists.

Laurel N. Tanner
Department of Urban Education
Temple University
Philadelphia, Pennsylvania

2

Breaking into Print

After thinking over why members of the professions write for publication, Charlie returns to Bill's office the next day. He wants advice on how to break into print. Bill suggests two channels for beginners. He also acquaints Charlie with his First Law and Second Law. Bill is obviously fonder of his First Law than of his Second Law.

Charlie.   I'm back again, Bill. I've decided that I want to write for professional publication. Never mind my reasons.

Where do I go from here? What's your advice for the beginner? I've done the customary papers in the graduate seminars, and I've written my doctoral dissertation. I have some drafts of things I've tried to write, and I recently threw away two rejection slips. What now?

Bill.   For a neophyte writer for professional publication the two most accessible channels are book reviews and certain kinds of articles. These are a beginner's most promising possibilities for breaking into print.

Take book reviewing, for instance. Choose some brand-new books in your field that you intend to read and that you think you're competent to review—

Charlie.   Hold on. If the books are brand-new, how do I know they exist?

Bill. Go to your bookshelves in your office and jot down the names of the most frequent publishers in your area of specialization. Drop a postcard to the sales manager asking for the catalog that includes books in your broad field and for information on the latest publications. If a book salesperson comes by your office, ask what's new.

Then write a letter to the editor of a professional journal that you read regularly. Ask the editor whether the publication would consider a review of any of the books you have chosen. Tell the editor why you think these books should be reviewed in the journal.

Charlie. Why should anybody say yes? The editor doesn't know me from Adam.

Bill. Editors of professional publications are almost always in need of good book reviews. The old hands are often too busy writing their own books, doing research, consulting, working with national organizations, or doing whatever else old hands do (even teaching and advising, I hope!). As an unpublished writer for professional publications you can boldly enter the province of book reviewing. Though some book reviews are solicited from old reliables by editors, the opportunities for neophytes to volunteer are substantial.

Charlie. Suppose the editor doesn't send me a book for review. I suppose I could wangle one from the publisher.

Bill. With your ingenuity, I'm confident that you could beg, borrow, or steal one. Write a thoughtful review. Send it off, reminding the editor that you wrote earlier about this book. There's a good chance the editor will use your review.

Charlie. Sounds promising. How about articles? Certain kinds, you said.

Bill. Articles based on their own teaching or other professional experiences are good bets for the beginners who want to write for professional publication. For instance, maybe you've carried on a community study with your students. Great! Maybe you've tried out a special approach for the gifted, or a particular ethnic group, or handicapped students, or whatever. Fine! Perhaps you've developed some laboratory techniques or supervised a new type of internship. Bravo!

Charlie. Editors go for experiences?

Bill. Editors are hungry for accounts of teaching and administrative and other professional experiences, especially editors whose magazines have a varied readership. Mildred S. Fenner, who edited the journal published by the National Education Association, once told me, "Bill, tell your students in your classes in writing for educational publication to send us realistic descriptions of their experiences rather than highly abstract discussions of educational theories or issues. We are flooded with the latter. But we never get enough of the former."

Don't misinterpret this. Any account of a personal experience should be related to some intellectually tenable hypothesis. But editors and readers welcome relief from the flood of "think pieces" ground out by upwardly mobile faculty members as they lurch toward the higher academic ranks, needled by the publish-or-perish syndrome. If editors want an abstract or highly theoretical treatment of a problem, they will probably turn to a recognized specialist whose name and work are already familiar to them.

Charlie. How about articles based on a person's doctoral dissertation?

Bill. If you intend to go this route, begin writing soon. It may be later than you think. Dissertations, like unrefrigerated fish, don't keep. They say that only tobacco and whiskey improve with age.

Unless you are writing for a highly unusual periodical, don't submit to the editor the summary that has been duly approved by your doctoral committee. Instead, talk directly to the readers of the periodical that is your outlet. Tell them what your study was all about, what you found out, what you didn't find. Rewrite. If the dissertation-based report is for a specialized scholarly journal, try the article on an intelligent colleague. If you are sharing your generalizations in a more general, more widely read magazine, try it also on a friend or neighbor or your long-suffering spouse. They don't understand it? Rewrite it again. Keep your article scholarly, but make it readable. Write for your specific audience.

A good dissertation can be the basis for more than one article. For instance, an article that reviews the literature related to the subject of the dissertation. Or a research article, with tables or figures, that reviews related studies and emphasizes methodology, findings, and discussion. Or a popularized article, de-emphasizing methodology and numbers and stressing the findings and their implications for practitioners.

Some periodicals prefer practical field-oriented articles; others use discussions of current issues; still others report on research—and some run all three. Select with care the magazines and journals that are to be your targets. Though there may be a half-dozen or more wide-circulation professional magazines appropriate for your more general articles, there are probably only a very few scholarly journals open to specialized reports on your research procedures and conclusions.

Charlie. I am beginning to get worried about that latter group of beginners who don't want to report experiences in teaching or to popularize their dissertations in the more general magazines. What about the theorist? The speculative writer? The researcher who writes for a few fellow specialists?

Bill. Admittedly, breaking into print is more difficult for them. The possible outlets are fewer, and the competition for publication in scholarly journals is often intense. But research journals do exist, both general and in specialized fields. And there are some journals that are hospitable to theory.

Study the content of the periodicals, whether general professional magazines or scholarly journals. Incidentally, Charlie, I often use "magazine" for general professional periodicals and "journal" for more specialized scholarly periodicals. The categories seem to help writers in differentiating among readerships. However, you may prefer, as many people do, to use "journal" to describe all professional outlets for articles.

Regardless of categorizations, recognize that one editor's meat is another editor's poison. An incredible number of authors send inappropriate manuscripts to magazines and journals they obviously have never read—else they would not have sent *that* manuscript to *that* particular periodical.

State and regional magazines and journals afford many opportunities for publication. These are frequently minimized by the new author, dewy fresh from graduate school and from enforced reading of the most prestigious journals. Yet many state and regional periodicals are well edited and highly useful. New authors gain both expertise and confidence through contributions that are read by professionals in the state and region, including colleagues. A state magazine or journal often gives preference to members of the sponsoring state association.

The advantage of writing for periodicals published by the professional organizations to which the author belongs are obvious, Charlie. Presumably these are periodicals with which the author is fully familiar through regular reading. Editors often favor contributions from members; indeed, some organizations require membership as a condition of publication.

Speaking of professional organizations reminds me of an effective approach to developing a scholarly article—presenting a paper at the meeting of your professional organization.

Charlie.   I recently answered a call for papers. But my organization doesn't publish the papers presented at the conference.

Bill.   A clearinghouse such as Educational Resources Information Center (ERIC) might request a copy, or you might submit a copy to them directly. Your paper, if accepted, would be stored, put on microfiche, and abstracted and indexed in *Resources in Education*. In the *Journal of Education*, August Fruge proposed a two-level system for *all* scholarly writing, one for publishing manuscripts that are useful quality publications and one for easy access to unpublished articles and books through a national supplementary library. The latter would be similar to education's ERIC system; in response to requests, copies would be made available to scholars through copying or microfilm.

Charlie.   That's a good step forward, but I'm more interested in journal publication.

Bill.   To receive an invitation to deliver a paper, a scholar must submit at least an abstract; to present a paper orally, a scholar must write a paper. The prospective author gets the benefit of questions and comments from fellow scholars in the audience and from informal feedback in the lobbies and the hotel rooms. Consequently, ideas and approaches are often reshaped as the scholar later writes the paper for submission to a journal. By all means tell the editor that the article is based on a paper presented at a specific conference; this never harms and often helps.

After you have determined the outlets that you think might carry your article, you should query.

Charlie.   What does that mean?

Bill.   A while ago you mentioned that you had received two rejection slips. What's your approach to submitting an article?

Charlie.   I write something and I send it to the editor. God knows what the editor does with it. Maybe he or she adds it to that stack of things intended for reading some day, like the stack on my own desk. Anyway, the editor just sits on it. Weeks or months later, I receive a form letter. The editor says no.

Bill.   The time has come for me to acquaint you with Van Til's First Law: "Query, always query." Before you set pencil to pad, or fingers to typewriter, determine the specific publication outlet or outlets in which you would like your writing to appear. Study your proposed outlet as to style, length, content, and even such editorial practices as footnoting. Only then write to the editor. Describe specifically and persuasively what you have in mind. Address the editor by name, rather than as "Dear Editor," thus helping to indicate your familiarity with the periodical. Enclose a self-addressed stamped envelope—the acronym is SASE—to expedite a response.

Charlie.   Can I send out more than one query at a time?

Bill.   You can. I know of no ethical reason why you should not. After all, you are simply inquiring whether or not the editor might be interested in your article.

Querying is different from sending photocopies of your completed manuscript to several publications. Some editors frown grimly on this practice of multiple submissions. They regard it as unethical. Those who send copies of completed manuscripts to several editors often end up in editorial doghouses. In all fairness, I must add that some editors are quite willing to consider unsolicited manuscripts sent simultaneously to a number of periodicals. However, always tell them as gently as you can that you are sending your manuscript to other editors.

Charlie.   What's the advantage of querying?

Bill.   Querying saves you a great deal of time. Suppose you send several query letters concerning an article. Editor A may respond that the journal has already run several articles of the type you contemplate. Editor B may tell you that the journal already ran a special issue on this topic. Editor C may tell you that your article "does not meet our editorial needs.'' This can mean anything, but it always adds up to no and the editor is not going to tell you why.

Charlie.   Let's hope there is an Editor D.

Bill.   Editor D may send you a warm, vibrant, passionate, enthusiastic, and loving response.

Charlie.   Blessings on Editor D. And what is a warm, passionate, loving, etc., response?

Bill.   Editor D may say, ''We will read your article with care if you send it to us,'' or ''We will send your proposal to readers and let you know later.'' If you are lucky enough to get such a rapturous response, you may rightly celebrate. You have placed your foot firmly in the door.

Charlie.   Does querying apply to books too?

Bill.   Yes, but you're getting a bit beyond the question of breaking into print. It is a brave beginner whose first publication is a book. But if it is a book you have in mind, give the editor an ample description, a comparison with existing books, and some biographical data. If interested, the editor will ask for a prospectus and/or sample chapters. I'll tell you about the prospectus later, if you wish.

Charlie.   I'm still hung up on why an author should query rather than send in a manuscript.

Bill.   Because otherwise your manuscript is one in a zillion to come in ''over the transom.'' That's an archaic term dating back to the nineteenth century when publishers' offices had transoms over which unsolicited manuscripts presumably were heaved by the postal service. Many, many times more unsolicited manuscripts are received than query letters. An editor of a professional periodical with a circulation of 130,000 told me that, for every query, he receives 25 unsolicited manuscripts not preceded by a query.

Your unsolicited manuscript will be read by someone one of these days. But if you query, the editor is likely to respond soon; editors like to keep their desks clean too.

I don't deny that some unsolicited manuscripts are published. But I do urge you to increase your chances of acceptance by adopting the query procedure.

Charlie.   Suppose I'm lucky enough to know someone on the editorial board. Should I send the query to that individual, rather than to the editor? Or suppose I could get my major professor in my doctoral program to put in a good word for me. Should a newcomer to writing seek endorsement from a known scholar or an experienced author?

Bill.   Better tread softly, because feelings and sensitivities are involved. Some editors might regard intervention by others on your behalf as an undesirable pressure on them and might conclude that you were brash. Still other editors might welcome supportive letters and regard endorsements or interventions as part of the data they should take into account in decision-making. Some editorial board members or major professors might willingly accept your asking them to call your manuscript to the attention of editors; others might resent your request as presumption and hard-selling on your part.

If you are uncertain of the reactions of the various personalities involved, you might accompany your query to the editor with a personal letter or phone call to the board member or major professor, in which you mention that you have submitted a query to the periodical. The old pro, familiar with the editor's ways, can then follow up or not, as the individual sees fit. At any rate, don't try to make intervention by members of your network serve as a substitute for Van Til's First Law, "Query, always query."

Charlie.   Does Van Til's Second Law exist?

Bill.   Certainly. Van Til's Second Law is "Feel free to pay no attention to Van Til's First Law." My own first book was completely unsolicited; my manuscript went in over the transom. I was twenty-six and known only to my mother and my wife. My manuscript was personally read and accepted by one of the greatest of all editors, Maxwell Perkins of Scribner's, who also edited (ahem) Ernest Hemingway, F. Scott Fitzgerald, and Thomas Wolfe.

As for my own first article, it was theoretical, a contribution to what was then a vigorous debate over whether or not educators should indoctrinate. The article quarreled vigorously with the views of the eminent social reconstructionist George S. Counts, then at the peak of his career after publishing *Dare the School Build a New Social Order?* I opposed indoctrination.

Phi Delta Kappan published my article, and *Educational Method* reprinted it. To beard the lion in his den, I sent a reprint to the great George S. Counts. I will never forget the last sentence of his reply. He thanked me; then he added, "When you are more mature, I think you will think differently." You might want to take into account this perverse experience in breaking into print when you consider my advice to begin not with theory but with your teaching or administrative or other professional experiences!

Any other questions for this session?

Charlie.   Yes. Do all editors endorse your First Law?

Bill.   Some do and some don't. Editors of nonfiction trade books, of scholarly and other professional books, strongly approve of the query approach. Almost all College Department and School Department editors who work with college textbooks and with elementary and high school textbooks want to think with an author about the nature of the book, rather than be presented a supposedly finished manuscript. They want to participate in developing the publication so that it becomes the best possible book.

As to periodicals, the editors of professional magazines with a wide and varied readership often appreciate a preliminary query. A number of editors of journals for a specialized group of readers also see advantages to them in queries. However, many editors of scholarly journals prefer their first contact with an author to be the completed manuscript.

Charlie.   Why?

Bill.   Some editors claim that over-the-transom submissions save them time and effort. They find them more convenient. Scholarly journal editors often receive only a small amount of released time from teaching for their editorial chores: circulating manuscripts to reviewers, selecting articles, working with authors on revisions, copyediting, marking typescripts for the printer, proofreading, and so on. They may regard queries as an additional and unnecessary burden. It seems to me, though, that editorial time and effort saved through any reduction in correspondence is more than offset by the time and effort invested in conscientious reading of unsolicited manuscripts, most of which prove to be unacceptable.

Frankly, Charlie, I'm not greatly concerned with editorial convenience. I am more concerned about the welfare of authors who wait months and even years before learning whether a journal article will be accepted, and then experience rejection. They then submit the article to another journal, which again takes an unconscionably long time to decide. The process continues toward infinity. Eventually, many promising authors give up.

A more valid defense of submitting a completed article without preliminary querying is advanced by many editors of research journals. They say they can determine the possibility of publication of research only through consideration of the complete report or paper, not from a query describing the topic and conclusions. They have a good point.

Many editors of scholarly journals carry general descriptions in their publications of the nature of articles they will consider and the procedures that they will follow. Some have a fuller description of editorial needs and procedures available to prospective authors on request. These editors may regard queries as unnecessary, possibly even as irritating. So beware.

On the other hand, a tactfully worded query to a research journal or scholarly periodical may elicit information on whether or not the proposed article is within the scope of the journal as the editor sees it. The author might receive more detailed information on the journal's style or criteria for evaluation of manuscripts. A sympathetic editor might even warn the author of the existence of a substantial backlog of accepted manuscripts that would prohibit publication of additional articles for the next two years.

If you decide to send an editor an article without a preliminary query, choose your outlet with special care to avoid rejection for inappropriate subject matter. Be aware of such factors as frequency and speed of publication, as well as circulation and readership. When you follow the Second Law, the responsibility to make sure your unsolicited article is right for that particular journal rests squarely with you and you alone. If you judge wrongly, you will be in for formidable delays.

Charlie. Suppose I send three queries to three different journals. Let's suppose I receive a positive response from the least prestigious of the three and indications of interest with suggestions of modifications from the other two—or any other combination of possible acceptances. Where should I send the article?

Bill. When this particular situation arises, only you can decide where to send the article. Write the article for whatever responsive journal you have chosen, and send it off as soon as possible.

Charlie. Won't other editors who may have indicated interest be troubled?

Bill. I doubt that they will lose much sleep about it. They are much more likely to be troubled if they had accepted an unsolicited manuscript of yours only to find that another journal to which you had sent the same unsolicited manuscript also planned to publish it. In that case, your letter of withdrawal in which you explain why you have chosen to give the manuscript to the other journal might not sit well with the rejected editor.

However, in the case of more than one favorable response to a query, you submit your article to the journal you have chosen. If it is rejected, then send it, with appropriate modifications, to the journal next in line, along with a pleasant letter referring to the editor's earlier correspondence. "I appreciated very much your letter of (date) in which you said, '———.' Since then I have written the enclosed article, which I am submitting to you for your consideration. . . ." By the way, Charlie, you might be overly optimistic in assuming that so many editors will express interest. This doesn't happen to most authors.

Charlie. Should the query approach or the approach of submitting an unsolicited manuscript be used by the writer whose manuscript is appropriate for only one journal in the entire universe of publications? Or the researcher who wants the findings to appear in one journal and only that journal? Or authors who are convinced that the golden words of their manuscript will persuade an editor to publish, whereas their leaden-worded query will not make the editor's pulse beat fast? Or the masochist completely acceptant of and resigned to long waits, repeated rejections, and hopeful resubmissions? Should authors skip the query and simply submit their unsolicited articles to editors whom they have reason to believe won't welcome queries—editors who wish people like you would stop advising would-be authors to query?

Bill. For them we have developed the Second Law, "Feel free to pay no attention to Van Til's First Law."

However, for most writers for professional publication, I still recommend a query to a magazine or journal. The query should take one or two pages to accomplish three things. It should inform the editor of the central ideas and conclusions in the prospective article. It should persuade the editor that what you have to offer is worth reading. The inquiry should tell who you are and why you are equipped to write this particular article. Along the way there is no harm in mentioning comparable articles published by the magazine or journal. Any editor likes to hear that somebody has been reading the publication.

Participants in my university workshops on writing for professional publication have prepared queries to periodicals concerning their prospective publications. You might want to look over a sampling and judge which you think are most effective. Some of these queries were mailed to editors by workshop participants and some were not. Since writers are often mobile, some of those who developed queries may now have different titles or may have accepted new positions elsewhere.

Bear in mind that editors sometimes move on to new posts. So don't assume that the individual addressed in these queries is necessarily the current editor. A writer should always check with the latest issues for the names of the current editors.

QUERIES TO MAGAZINES AND JOURNALS

Dr. Beeman N. Phillips, Editor
Journal of School Psychology
College of Education
Department of Educational Psychology
The University of Texas
Austin, TX 78712

Dear Dr. Phillips:
    I am writing to inquire if an article based on my
dissertation study may be suitable for publication in the
Journal of School Psychology. The title of my dissertation
is Psychological Education: A High School Mini-Course
Utilizing Peer Counseling to Teach Helping and Problem-
Solving Skills and Decrease Feelings of Alienation.
    In response to the great numbers of adolescents with
emotional problems and the inadequacy of our present delivery
system in meeting their needs, and also the problem of feelings of school alienation by adolescents, I determined that a
course based on the training of adolescent peer counselors
might be a way of meeting these needs. Accordingly, I
developed, taught, and evaluated a course entitled "Psychology
of Helping" to two ninth-grade classes for three weeks.
The goals of the course were
      1. to increase students' helping and problem-solving
          skills;
      2. to develop a refined curriculum for other profes-
          sionals to build on;
      3. to decrease feelings of school alienation;
      4. to examine the role of the psychologist in this
          kind of involvement.
    The article will deal with the steps taken in developing
and implementing such a course, the process involved in teaching the course, and the results. There are many elements
involved in such an undertaking that I can discuss and that
can be helpful to school psychologists in considering a similar
project.
    I want to tell you how helpful it has been to me to
have your fine Journal of School Psychology to keep me abreast
of our field.
    I look forward to hearing from you.

                        Sincerely,

                        Joan P. Gillespie, Ed.D.
                        Psychologist
                        Weld Mental Health Center, Inc.
                        Greeley, Colorado
                        80639

Dr. Gerald M. Senf
Editor-in-Chief
The Journal of Learning Disabilities
1331 E. Thunderhead Drive
Tucson, Arizona 85718

Dear Dr. Senf:

I am writing to solicit your response to an idea that I have for a potential article in The Journal of Learning Disabilities. I have recently completed a research project that has yielded some fascinating findings which may well add significantly to the professional deposit of knowledge about children with learning disabilities.

The article, as I have developed it to this point, could appropriately be titled ''Dyslogic Syndrome and Dysocialization.'' The notion for this paper was an outgrowth of my tutorial work with several dozen college, high school, and junior high school students who had been classified as learning disabled, but who were also very bright or intellectually gifted. Much as I had suspected, the characteristics of dyslogia were exhibited to some meaningful extent by each of my subjects. My original reaction was that I had identified a syndrome which was unique to the gifted-learning disabled student. My subsequent research yielded some surprises.

I developed two questionnaires that were circulated to teachers of the learning disabled, chapter I students, the nonhandicapped, and the gifted. I then interviewed a selected number of teachers and observed a sample of students who appeared to be high-risk dyslogics.

There are three major observations that I believe would be of considerable interest to special education teachers, university faculty, school psychologists, and other readers of The Journal of Learning Disabilities. First of all, the dyslogic syndrome is a paramount, but neglected diagnostic and treatment concept in learning disabilities. Secondly, dyslogia appears to be very prevalent among the learning disabled population. Finally, it seems that the notion of dyslogia exists independently of a syndrome which I have called ''dysocialization.'' To my knowledge, the observation that dyslogia exists independently of severe disabilities in socialization among the learning disabled is original with my research.

The article that I propose will be based in part on institutional research supported by Northern Arizona State University and a paper presented to the Arizona Association for Children with Learning Disabilities. It is my aspiration that the information contained within such an article in The Journal of Learning Disabilities will provide fresh insights into the nature of learning disabilities, which might in turn lead to modest improvements in selected diagnostic and intervention practices.

I know that you receive many queries about possible articles, so I am especially appreciative of any consideration given this proposal. Regardless of your interest in my writings, be assured of my sustained appreciation of the excellent contribution your journal makes to our field.

Sincerely,

Daniel L. Peterson, Ed.D.
Professor of Special Education
Northern Arizona University
Flagstaff, Arizona
86011

Dr. Samuel Ball, Editor
Journal of Educational Psychology
Educational Testing Service
Princeton, NJ 08541

Re: Inquiry

Dear Editor:

We are in the process of completing a manuscript entitled "Student Variables as Related to Answer Changing" in which we are predicting that age, sex, grades, and some personality variables (dominance, depression, introversion, and anxiety) affect answer-changing patterns in college students. Such an article would be appropriate for students, teachers, and administrators.

We have a total of eleven years' teaching experience with backgrounds in clinical psychology, statistics, and program evaluation.

Any comments, suggestions, or recommendations from you would be greatly appreciated.

Respectfully,

Lillian Range Sitton

Ira Adams

Howard Anderson
University of Southern
Mississippi
Hattiesburg, Mississippi
39401

James J. Muro, Editor
The Humanist Educator
College of Education
North Texas State University
Denton, Texas 76203

Dear Dr. Muro:
    I am writing to solicit your reaction to an idea I have
for a possible article in The Humanist Educator. At this
point I have only developed an outline for this piece. As
it has developed, however, it seems to be emerging as the
type of paper which would interest your readers.
    The article, as I envision it, would be titled "Adversar-
ialism in Education." The notion for the paper grew from my
work as Chief Hearing Officer for the Maine Commission of
Educational and Cultural Services. In this work, I serve as
an Administrative Judge, resolving disputes between parents
and school systems statewide in matters of special education.
In the resolution of these disputes I have been increasingly
concerned about the bitterness, strife, and general polemic
orientation of the process. The effect of this disharmony on
the parent-school relationship and on the child appears
serious to me. This article would serve as a vehicle to get
this issue into the professional literature in hopes that an
increased awareness of the potential dangers in highly
adversarial proceedings may encourage an increasingly humanistic approach to the process.
    The article may be divided into four major areas:
  I.   Background in special education law focusing on due
       process mechanism
  II. Discussion of what occurs in hearings
  III. Discussion of the implications for school, parents,
       children of II above
  IV. Recommendations for improving the process.
       1) Increased reaching out to parents
       2) Offering independent evaluation of the child
       3) Increased efforts at external mediation
       4) Changes in the hearing procedure
       5) Summary
    I had considered several of the journals in special ed-
ucation as possible sources of publication. However, I chose
The Humanist Educator because of the journal's orientation
to changing educational systems into organizations which are
more responsive to people. Your readers are likely to be key
people in effecting the changes I am proposing.
    Thank you for your consideration of my query. I look
forward to your response.

                              Sincerely,

                              Charles M. Lyons, Ed.D.
                              Assistant Professor of
                              Special Education
                              University of Southern Maine
                              Gorham, Maine
                              04038

Mr. Robert P. McIntosh
The American Midland Naturalist
University of Notre Dame
Notre Dame, Indiana 46556

Dear Mr. McIntosh:
    I have recently compiled the results of two research
projects into an article which I would like to submit to you
for consideration for publication.
    For the last twelve years I have been working with the
flood plain vegetation within Colorado. My Ph.D. research,
completed in 1970, was concerned with the vegetative communities along the Arkansas River in eastern Colorado. Since
that time I have completed three other flood plain projects
on the South Platte River, which is located approximately
200 miles north of the Arkansas River and is a similar flood
plain at the same elevation. These studies were summarized
in a major report to the Bureau of Reclamation, which had
supported such research in preparation primarily for the
construction of a reservoir.
    Upon examining the results of studies of these two
major drainages, I have found that the South Platte vegetative communities are relatively stable, while those of the
Arkansas River are undergoing a major change. This change is
primarily the result of the introduction of a Mediterranean
species, salt cedar (<u>Tamarix ramosissima</u>), which today makes
approximately one-third of the total acreage of woody
vegetation found along the Arkansas River.
    The article that I have prepared was recently presented
at a wildlife symposium concerning riparian habitat and
communities sponsored by the Wilderness Society and the
Colorado Division of Wildlife. It would be my hope that the
information within this article would provide your readers
information concerning the impact of introduced species on
flood plains and also serve as base-line information on
the nature of the riparian vegetation found along the flood
plains of these two drainages.

                            Sincerely,

                            Ivo E. Lindauer
                            Assistant Dean
                            College of Arts and Sciences
                            University of Northern
                            Colorado
                            Greeley, Colorado
                            80639

Robert D. Brown
University of Nebraska-Lincoln
Educational Psychology and Social Foundations
26 Teachers College
Lincoln, Nebraska 68588-0440

Dear Dr. Brown:
    I am writing to solicit your reaction to an article which I am in
the process of writing that deals with a comparative analysis of
characteristics and needs of reentry women enrolled at The University of
Texas at El Paso. The literature review has been completed; the survey
instrument has been designed, field tested and revised; and the
questionnaires have been mailed to 1,000 randomly selected female
students over the age of 25 who were enrolled during the Spring 1984
semester. My plans are to have the data analyzed and the article
completed by mid-October.
    The Journal of College Student Personnel has carried several
articles on the subject of the reentry female student. Thus, I need not
emphasize the importance of the topic in higher education today. What
makes my paper unique, however, is the focus on the Hispanic reentry
woman, and the comparative analysis of Anglos and Hispanics. My
institution, located on the U.S./Mexican border, enrolls an approximate
50 percent Hispanic student population. The campus environment is an
interesting blend of two separate cultures.
    In the Spring 1984 semester, the University enrolled an approximate
2,900 women over age 25. A large number of these women are Hispanics who,
for many reasons, may be experiencing their return to school in a way
different from that of their Anglo counterparts. The literature on
minorities has frequently asserted that the range of problems is great
for minorities, even greater for minority females, and they may be even
more complex for minority females over the age of 25.
    Through my roles as faculty member, Departmental Chair, student
adviser and counselor, I have had rich opportunities to observe, and to
relate to, college students of all ages. My degree in Higher Education
(Indiana University) with emphasis on Student Personnel Services, has
sensitized me to be aware of student characteristics and needs. During
the past five years I have become acutely aware of the older female
students, whom I have come to admire and respect.
    The information gained from this study will certainly be important
to the administration, faculty, and staff at my University. I believe
that it will also be an important contribution to the literature, and I
would be pleased if it could reach an audience as extensive as the
readership of your journal.
    Thank you for your consideration of my query. I look forward to your
response.

                              Sincerely,

                              Bonnie S. Brooks, Ed.D.
                              Chair
                              Department of Educational
                              Psychology and Counseling
                              The University of Texas at El Paso
                              79968

Dr. Gene V. Glass, Editor
American Educational Research Journal
Laboratory of Educational Research
University of Colorado
Boulder, CO 80309

Dear Dr. Glass:
  I am writing to inquire about the possibility of submitting an
article to you for the American Educational Research Journal.
  The current thrust in public education to foster and promote
educational excellence has resulted in several new studies. I recently
completed a national study entitled ''Teachers of the Year 1978-1982: A
Profile and Analysis.'' This doctoral research, completed in 1983,
identified characteristics of ''successful'' teachers and determined
their attitudes on relevant educational issues. The criterion of success
was receipt of the prestigious Teacher of the Year (TOY) award for the
years 1978-1982.
  To determine which attributes and attitudes are characteristic of
outstanding educators, I compared and contrasted these TOY
characteristics and conceptions with those of ''typical'' or ''average''
teachers. In 1981 the National Education Association (NEA) conducted a
national survey of America's teachers and developed a report entitled
STATUS OF THE AMERICAN PUBLIC SCHOOL TEACHER. Many of the measures
utilized in the Teacher of the Year study paralleled those of the NEA
study and lent themselves to direct statistical and substantive
comparison.
  The results of comparing ''award-winning'' and ''average''
teachers from the NEA and TOY studies determined significant factors or
dimensions which differentiated these two types of teachers and provided
an empirically based means for identifying excellence in education.
Teachers of the Year excel well beyond their peers in terms of
background, training, experience, professional attitudes, and behavior.
These characteristics should be encouraged and fostered to promote
teaching excellence. In order to achieve a greater degree of excellence
in education, increased attention and resolution must be brought to the
basic issues of teacher morale, prestige, compensation, and job
satisfaction, not only for exceptional teachers like TOYs but for all
teachers. In short, this article will demonstrate that the expertise and
talent of exceptional teachers warrant recognition, require
utilization, and deserve reward as crucial first steps in America's
elusive quest for educational excellence.
  A preliminary version of the article that I anticipate was
presented at the AERA Annual Meeting in New Orleans in April 1984. I had
considered several of the research journals in education as possible
sources of publication but chose the American Educational Research
Journal because of its orientation toward empirical studies in education
which enhance educational practice.
  I have a total of thirteen years' teaching experience ranging from
first grade through university level with a background in elementary
education, administration, curriculum, instruction, and supervision. I
sincerely believe that this article would be of interest and use to your
readers for they are the individuals who are likely to be key people in
promoting and implementing the recognition and rewards which are called
for in the quest for educational excellence.

I realize that you are very busy but please be assured that any comments, suggestions, or recommendations would be greatly appreciated. I look forward with interest to your reply.

Sincerely,

Terry L. Wiedmer, Ed.D.
Adjunct Professor
School of Education
University of Montana
Missoula, Montana
59812

Editor
Journal of American Indian Education
Center for Indian Education
302 Farmer Building
Arizona State University
Tempe, AZ 85287

Dear Editor:
    I have an article, ''Successful Teaching Techniques for Freshman American Indian Students in Community College,'' which I believe you will be interested in reviewing for publication. As you know, statistics show that 85 percent of all American Indian students entering community colleges for the first time will drop out before the completion of the freshman year. Based on my experience as a teacher of five years' duration at Navajo Community College, Shiprock, New Mexico, campus, I have compiled a list of common student problems. Some of these are lack of study skills, unwillingness to ''speak out'' in class, and inability to accept responsibility for buying books, attending class regularly, and turning in assignments on time. Short courses can be developed to teach study skills; discussion opportunities can be built into every class; orientation seminars required for all freshmen can help the students develop a sense of personal responsibility.
    By sharing these techniques and several others with your readers, I can help make teaching these students a rewarding experience for teachers and students.
    My article adheres to your suggested reference manual, the University of Chicago publication, and is approximately 1,000 words long.
    Thank you for considering my article.

               Sincerely,

               Kay B. Edwards
               Graduate Student
               Northern Arizona University
               Flagstaff, Arizona
               86011

James Betchkal, Editor
The American School Board Journal
1055 Thomas Jefferson Street, NW
Washington, D.C. 20007

Dear Mr. Betchkal:
    I am completing a manuscript entitled, ''An Analysis of Career
Ladders for Career Teachers'' in which state-adopted career ladder plans
are analyzed for decision makers in education.
    The purpose of this article is to provide an objective analysis of
the structure, criteria, responsibilities, salary increments, and
evaluation requirements in a format to facilitate detailed study. The
information should be of interest to teachers, administrators and school
board members designing salary programs to provide career alternatives
and monetary rewards to outstanding teachers.
    I have just completed a comprehensive survey of alternative salary
plans for our school district which includes a section on career ladders.
This concept is rather complex, and I believe your readers would
appreciate having an analysis of each component available for study.
    If you are interested, I would be happy to submit the manuscript to
you for possible publication in The American School Board Journal. I look
forward to your response.

                              Sincerely,

                              Margret A. Montgomery
                              Director of Research and Development
                              Tyler Independent School District
                              Tyler, Texas
                              75701

3

Publishing a First Book

Bill's advice on breaking into print does not suffice for Charlie, who is newly fired with ambition. So Charlie extends the conversation beyond articles and book reviews and into the realm of breaking into print through publishing his first book. Bill acquaints Charlie with the nature of both the book query and the prospectus.

Charlie. I know you told me the question was premature, Bill, but I want to ask it anyway. I always did believe in starting at the top and working my way down. How about publishing a book? How does a member of a profession bring a book proposal to the commercial publisher's attention?

Bill. By seeking to meet editors. By writing for advice to friends in the profession who have already published books. By tying in with a published author. By being recommended by an established writer.

Professionals who are professors like yourself have an additional entree. Major publishers have sales representatives, sometimes called travelers. When they call on you in your office to acquaint you with their list, they are likely to say casually, "And what are you yourself writing these days, professor?" They may include your response in their report to the national office.

Important as they are, don't depend entirely upon these "reps." Tell published friends about your aspirations. Make a point of talking to some of the editors at national conferences you attend. Indicate your interest and expertise in your specialized field and ask whether they need any reviewers of their unsolicited manuscripts. Maybe they have a project already underway on which they could use your expertise.

If you have influential friends, use your network. However, since most first-book authors don't move in circles with access to publishers, the usual approach of the beginner is to write queries to College Departments or to still more specialized divisions within the publishing companies.

Charlie. Same query as to a journal? You said that an effective query to a book publisher consists of a description of your proposed book, a comparison with similar books, and something about yourself. Isn't this similar to the query you recommended as an approach to a periodical?

Bill. Similar yet different. For one thing, your query should give book editors a clear picture of the content of the book as a *whole*. An outline is particularly helpful if it is carefully subdivided and well detailed. But don't submit a detailed outline if you haven't as yet thoroughly thought through the entire structure for the book.

The comparison of your book with other books not only informs the editorial staff on what has been published in the field and by whom. Your comparisons also give the publisher's staff the opportunity to judge how well you are acquainted with the field, how knowledgeable you are about books and publishing.

Your self-description identifies your expertise in the chosen field. It resembles the biographical material in a query to a periodical.

The comprehensive description, the comparisons, and the biographical material all contribute to answering the initial question that the publishing house asks, "Is this manuscript worth publishing?"

Charlie. Why initial? You mean there is another question that has more of a ring of finality about it?

Bill. Yes. The basic question a commercial book publisher asks is "Will it sell?" Editors of journals and magazines worry less about sales. They almost always have a built-in audience, frequently the membership of the sponsoring organization. On the other hand, editors of periodicals hope that readers like their publications and that their circulations will grow. For many people, receiving the journal or professional magazine is the basic reason for joining the organization and renewing their membership. Sales are important to editors of professional periodicals, but not as important as they are to book publishers.

The commercial companies that publish books have to believe that their product, in this case your book, will sell. Not as much as a fiction best seller—though the company certainly would not mind if it did—but enough to compete and preferably outstrip the competitors in its category. A book company can afford to be wrong occasionally in its belief that an individual book will sell sufficiently. After all, a widely distributed book can make up for several "dogs." But the commercial book publisher who wants to stay in business cannot be wrong too often. The bottom line is the moment of truth for the commercial publishing company. Even publishers of scholarly books and monographs have to make realistic estimates of the potential market. Even editors at university presses, squeezed by governmental and university economy drives, must take volume of sales into careful account in decisions.

Charlie.   How do my query materials relate to a decision concerning sales?

Bill.   Important in a market decision are your description of the book and your discussion of what the company will call "the competition"—though you may prefer to think of your fellow authors as your colleagues. Does the description cover the ground? Is the content right for a book of this nature? Is it sufficiently like the competition—yet sufficiently different? There are a host of similar questions the publisher must ask.

Charlie.   Does a query to a book publisher have to be extensive?

Bill.   One or two pages will do, unless you are already well along on the book and think it best to include a detailed outline and a chapter or section of the manuscript. Usually a page or two will enable editors to decide whether they are interested in the possibility. Your query has served your purpose if the editor wants to learn more about the project. If interested, an editor will ask for sample chapters and/or a prospectus.

On the other hand, some advise writers to combine a query and a prospectus in a weighty initial mailing to a book publisher. They argue that if editors have more to go on, they may make more thoughtful preliminary decisions. If interested, editors will almost always ask for a prospectus anyway. So why not bypass an introductory query unaccompanied by a prospectus?

I still think a good query is enough as an *initial* approach to a busy editor. An expanded proposal that includes sample chapters can be sent after editorial interest is aroused. Your prospectus can then be tailored to the requirements and needs of a specific publishing enterprise. Maybe you will want to give yourself more time in order to develop a highly appropriate, effective, and lengthy prospectus.

Charlie.   A prospectus? Good Lord, I thought I could concentrate on my writing after I got some expression of interest in response to a query.

Bill.   You could have once upon a time when publishing of professional books was more informal and education at all levels was a growth industry. In the late 1960s I wrote to an editor for whom I had scouted and recruited authors and told him a bit about a textbook I wanted to write. He said, "Fine," and we moved directly into a contract. But that doesn't happen anymore.

Now, after a publishing company indicates interest in response to your query, the staff will ask for much more information before reaching a decision. This applies even to experienced authors who have what editors like to call "a track record." And you are talking about writers who haven't published books as yet.

Charlie. So I send a prospectus to an editor who has expressed interest in my book.

Bill. In writing the prospectus, bear in mind that you are writing not only to the editor with whom you have been corresponding. You are writing the prospectus for the consideration of a group of people, several in editoral work, others in promotion, sales, art, and management in general. You are also writing for advisers or readers to whom the prospectus will be sent. You are attempting to persuade people with a variety of backgrounds that your book will be a good risk for the publishing company. Feel free to incorporate into your prospectus some materials, ideas, and even good phrases that you have already included in your query. Most of the people who will see the prospectus will not have seen the query.

Charlie. But much more goes into the proposal that you call a prospectus than into a query?

Bill. Right. If you haven't done so already, prepare a detailed outline with abundant subheadings. Draft a tentative table of contents. Include in your proposal at least one and preferably several chapters. Update and enclose the résumé you used in obtaining your most recent academic post. Develop a cover letter, and send the whole batch off to the editor, always with a self-addressed stamped envelope.

Charlie. A cover letter?

Bill. A cover letter should include a description of the book: what is unusual, important, significant about it; your own special qualifications and expertise; who is going to read your book; the nature of the competition; the proposed length and delivery date of the book; and the types of proposed illustrations and graphs and special features.

Your description should be plain and clear, a paragraph or two that supersynthesizes the entire book. Your comments as to new aspects, significance, and so on, are to persuade any reader that the book is needed, should be published, and should and will be read.

The biographical material is a humanization of your résumé and a statement of your special qualifications to write this particular book. What do you do now? What is your background? How are you qualified? What are your strengths? What unusual contribution can you make to the treatment? There is no prescribed form for your personal self-description. Level with your reader. Don't hide your light under a bushel; this is no time for undue modesty.

Your indication of who will read the book is of high importance to the publisher. Your projection will be especially impressive to the staff of the publishing house if you can name courses for which the book could be adopted. In the case of a textbook, describing specific courses is understandably essential. At the very least, be specific as to the groups that will constitute your market. Recognize that an editor may be wary of a book simply described as "supplemental."

Draw and expand upon your query when you write of the strengths and weaknesses of the competition. When you honestly believe your book will be better, tell your prospectus reader why. If other books have virtues, admit it. You may want to compare your proposed book with other books in the field as to number of pages, format, organization, and emphasis. If your book happens to parallel another in the structure of the chapters, show why your new book is worth publishing; perhaps the earlier book is outdated or sketchy or unnecessarily complex and complicated, while yours is contemporary, comprehensive, and crystal clear—at least we hope so.

As to length, make your best estimate. If you err, let it be on the side of brevity, for publishers are skittish of very lengthy books. Be realistic as to completion date.

As to features, such as illustrations, charts, maps, graphs, and other niceties that publishers lump together as artwork, beware again of the publisher's fiscal caution, for artwork is costly. On the other hand, textbook publishers in particular will welcome sale-oriented features such as questions for discussion, bibliographies, study guides, and so on.

And no typographical errors, please. A book editor of my acquaintance encircles all typos in queries and proposals. When he reaches a magic number—which he hasn't revealed to me—that's all, brother!

Charlie. So far we have been talking about books for the general public and about College Department textbooks primarily for college and university students and about books for specialized scholars. How about books for elementary and high school students? Does the query approach apply here too?

Bill. That depends on what type of book for the young reader you are talking about. If you are referring to books for children and youth sold in regular bookstores and ranging from children's picture books to fiction and nonfiction for young adults, you don't query. You send such a book to a publishing house that specializes in children's books or to the Juvenile editor of a house that has a Juvenile Division or Department. A query or even a prospectus doesn't suffice for appraising the potential of literature for children or young adults. However, I assume that you were thinking of writing a textbook for elementary or secondary school students in your capacity as a professional educator. In that case you turn to the School Department or Division, colloquially called El-Hi.

Charlie. I was thinking of textbook writing.

Bill. If the el-hi reader is your prospective audience for a textbook, by all means query the School Department of a commercial publishing house. Emphasize the specific student population that is your target population. Tell anything that you know or can find out about the potential market. Remember that the editor is asking, "What is so distinctive and remarkable about this proposed textbook in a field in which many competing books for elementary or secondary school students presently exist?" Recognize that the odds are heavily against you as an unknown; in most cases the El-Hi editor has a needed book in mind, has gathered leads as to possible authors, and has approached an experienced individual with an invitation to consider writing a textbook.

Charlie.   What happens then, Bill, in the case of the experienced author, or the newcomer like me if I manage to attract the editor's attention?

Bill.   The editor is likely to share with the prospective author of an elementary or high school textbook some realistic limitations and considerations, such as suggestions as to reading level, inclusion of minority groups, avoidance of sexism, and problems involved in widespread adoption. The prospective author prepares a prospectus somewhat along the lines I have already indicated and always includes several sample chapters. In many publishing houses, the acquisitions editor (so called because the editor is attempting to acquire a book) gets in-house reactions from an executive editor and a colleague who is most familiar with the subject matter on the elementary or high school level. If the in-house opinion is somewhat negative, the El-Hi editor may promptly reject the proposal or may tell the author what the in-house staff suggests as needed improvements. Maybe the reading level is somewhat inappropriate. Maybe the scholarship is faulty or dated. On the other hand, the editors may conclude that the proposal and the chapters seem promising and inform the author accordingly.

Charlie.   Wait a minute, Bill. It just occurred to me—how are the editors in a position to know that this is a promising book? How can editors keep up-to-date in my field when, as a specialist, I myself have so much trouble staying with the pack?

Bill.   Usually book editors are not specialists in your field. They are professionals in publishing. Often they are long-term career people with publishing houses; many have been successful sales representatives, marketing people, copyeditors, advertising writers, and the like. A few of them have moved from academia into editorial work, but this may have happened some years ago. So, if as an author you are an expert on child psychology or the Middle Ages or the ways of the Tibetan yak, it is highly unlikely that your editor will have a degree in that field. The book editor for a textbook publisher is a different breed of cat from the journal editor, who is often a professional in the field in which the magazine specializes. Journal editors usually rely heavily on their own expertise, even when they use other experts from professional fields to appraise and judge manuscripts.

Charlie. So?

Bill. So book editors who publish on professional subjects always use readers, even when an editor does happen to have some expertise in the subject matter of the manuscript.

A few publishers retain advisory editors or members of editorial advisory boards to whom they turn for advice. These advisers are well-established academics who read and react to proposals that survive preliminary editorial screening. Sometimes they may even read a query that the editorial staff passes on to them for an opinion. These readers are paid an honorarium or an annual payment. Occasionally, they receive a percentage of royalties if the proposal eventuates in a publication.

However, most publishing houses turn to some of your national colleagues in your specialized field. These "outside readers" or "manuscript reviewers," unaffiliated with the company, are paid about $50 to $150, sometimes more, for their appraisals of a prospectus, and more if they read an entire manuscript. A publishing house will not reach a decision to go ahead with a book without considering the advice of outside experts. Usually the reader does not know who wrote the proposal, and the author is not told who reviewed the proposal. Incidentally, Charlie, you too can volunteer to be an outside reader for a publishing house in your field of expertise. Serving as a reader is one way of breaking into book publishing.

Charlie. So the editor will send my prospectus to readers somewhere across the nation?

Bill. And you will wait for their response for what seems an eternity. You'll worry and watch for the mail.

Charlie. Eventually, I'll hear.

Bill. Eventually, you'll hear—from the editor, not directly from the anonymous outside readers.

Charlie. The editor might say yes?

Bill. And the editor might say no. Editors have a variety of ways of saying no. The odds against you are heavy.

But whether the ultimate answer is yes or no, you'll save yourself a great deal of time and misdirected effort by writing a preliminary query letter before you develop an extensive prospectus. You might want to appraise the following queries, drafted by workshop participants.

QUERIES TO BOOK PUBLISHERS

Dear Editor:

Your publishing company has an exceptional track record in publishing books in the field of biological sciences. However, I do not see in any of your lists of your publications a text for genetics.

I have an idea for a genetics text for sophomore classes in universities and colleges. The title will be something like Genetics, A Human Approach. The book will be addressed to a wide range of students with both professional and personal interests in learning genetics.

The major point of departure of my book from others in the field is that while my book will teach the basic principles of genetics, the illustrative material will be drawn almost solely from human genetics examples.

The knowledge now available in human genetics makes such a text possible. Such an emphasis on human genetics departs from the traditional patterns of genetics texts by deemphasizing plant, animal, and microorganismal genetics. However, this approach will aid the teacher in teaching the basics of genetics and the student in retaining this information for later professional or personal use.

There are genetics texts available giving basic genetics principles, and there are also academic and clinical human genetics texts available, but none that I know of which attempt to incorporate human genetics to the extent proposed in the first college course in genetics.

This book will be completed in two years. I have excellent sources and advisers at the University of Colorado Medical School in Denver and the Biological Sciences Curriculum Study in Boulder.

E. Edward Peeples
Associate Professor Bio-
logical Sciences-Genetics
University of Northern
Colorado
Greeley, Colorado
80639

Dear Editor:

The purpose of this letter is to inquire concerning publication of a phonics handbook I am in the process of developing. Since the book covers phonics from a linguistic perspective, I have considered the title Phonics with a Linguistic Slant.

The content of the book includes an extensive introduction to phonics as the subject relates to the linguistic field of phonology. Basic linguistic terms are defined and examples are included for each. Phonemes and graphemes are given major attention, as the relationship between those two terms is fundamental in the teaching of phonics. The most lengthy division includes approximately seventy phonics generalizations with numerous examples to clarify them. The generalizations, arranged in order of difficulty, include both major and minor generalizations. The minor generalizations are proposed as regular exceptions to the major generalizations. Ending material includes charts, such as one showing the various dictionary/glossary symbols used to represent the phonemes (sounds) of the English language, and a glossary of terms used in teaching phonics.

The book would be used by students in the reading skills methods courses at teacher education institutions, as well as teachers in the field and parents. There are several good programmed phonics books on the market; however, there is a dearth of handbooks of the type I am preparing. Dolores Durkin, Alta Mellin, and Arthur Heilman are authors of widely used phonics handbooks, but their works do not have the contemporary linguistic base that my book has. Albert Mazurkiewicz's book is linguistically oriented; however, it is quite theoretical for teachers. My book takes a simple, practical approach.

I taught elementary school for eight years before entering graduate school at the University of Southern Mississippi, where my M.S. and Ph.D. degrees were earned in Elementary Education with emphasis in reading. I have tutored many children in remedial reading utilizing a reading program I have developed, which encompasses the phonics principles my proposed book enumerates. Presently, I am a faculty member at the University of Southern Mississippi, where I teach elementary education methods courses.

I shall be looking forward to hearing from you concerning prospects for publication of my book.

Sincerely,

Janie A. Allen
Associate Professor
University of Southern Mississippi
Hattiesburg, Mississippi
39406

Dear Editor:
    I am currently seeking a publisher for a practical
humanities book on classroom management. More and more books
dealing with interpersonal relationships of all kinds, from
marriage to industrial management, are concerned with increasing effectiveness in two areas:
    1) communication skills
    2) conflict-solving skills
    There are still few books specifically for teachers in
this area. The market is potentially quite large, as indicated
by some of the more popular books in the area, such as <u>Teacher
Effectiveness Training</u> by Thomas Gordon or <u>Psychology in the
Classroom</u> by Rudolf Dreikurs.
    I worked with Dr. Dreikurs and have been interested in
writing a book integrating his approach with the approaches
of other humanistic approaches. Unique features of this book
will include brief case studies from elementary, junior high,
and high school. Many of my students who are secondary teachers
have expressed concern that many books which would be competitive with mine concentrate mainly on examples from the elementary school. Illustrating how the principles discussed in
the book apply to all three levels would give the book a
wider potential market among teachers. The book would also
be appropriate as a textbook for in-service teachers in courses
such as Educational Psychology or Classroom Management and
in undergraduate classes such as courses dealing with the
psychology of education.
    A prospectus giving more specific information is enclosed.
Please let me know if you would be interested in such a book.

                            Sincerely,

                            Robert J. Martin
                            Educational Psychology
                            Northeast Missouri State
                            University
                            Kirksville, Missouri
                            63501

Dear Editor:

I am interested in writing a book that consists of vignettes of children's problems as they relate to a theoretical base such as Piaget's cognitive development, Erikson's psychosocial development, or Bandura's modeling theory. This book would look at the typical problems of the elementary school child in the area of family, school, and crisis situations (see skeleton outline). In each of these areas, a number of vignettes would be written, with discussion questions following.

The target audience for this book would be teacher education students who had previously taken a developmental psychology course where a number of basic theories had been studied. This book could be used as a text in an upper-level child psychology class or a student-teaching seminar in which education students are attempting to solve day-to-day classroom problems by utilizing recognized developmental theories. It could also provide vicarious examples in an initial developmental psychology class, as students attempt to transfer theory to real-life situations.

As a person who has been involved in teacher education for the past eleven years, I have often searched for a book with examples such as this. As yet, I have never found one. In the past two years I have inquired from several book representatives of various publishing companies if such a vignette or case study book is available. In all instances the answer has been "no." Colleagues at my university, as well as other professionals involved in teacher education, often mention this lack of realistic examples for students to read, analyze, and, hopefully, transfer to problems as they begin their teaching.

Although I have been involved in elementary education for three and one-half years and teacher education for eleven years, I have only been doing educational writing since I completed my Ph.D. Since that time, I have published one article based on research concerning Kohlberg's theory of moral development, one article on how Kohlberg's theory can be applied in an elementary school, and one that deals with utilizing a problems approach to teaching child psychology. I am a strong advocate of direct experience in teacher education, but I also feel that vicarious experiences could be used more advantageously. If I could publish a book such as I have previously discussed, I feel I would not only enhance my own child psychology class but offer a text to professional educators who are trying to bridge the gap between theory and practice.

Would you please consider my proposal for such a book and give me feedback concerning the possibility of getting it published?

Thank you.

Beverly W. Taylor
Associate Professor of
Educational Psychology
University of Northern Iowa
Cedar Falls, Iowa
50614

I. FAMILY PROBLEMS

    A. Sibling Relationships

    B. Parental Friction and Divorce

    C. Child from One-Parent Family

    D. Stepchild

    E. Foster Child

    F. Adopted Child

    G. Extended Family

II. School Problems

    A. New Students

    B. Acting-Out Child

    C. Shy, Withdrawn Child

    D. Picked-On and Ridiculed Child

    E. Minority Child

    F. Sex Stereotypes

III. Crisis Situation

    A. Child Abuse and Neglect

    B. Life and Death

    C. Onset of Puberty

    D. Physical and Health Problems

    E. When to Refer

LETTER OF INTEREST

Leading Educational Publishers since 1868

Professor Wanda B. Writer
1400 Public Street
Somewhere, U.S.A.

Dear Professor Writer:
    Thank you for your letter concerning your proposed book, Introduction to Psychology.
    The book proposal is an exciting one, and it appears to be directed at a fast-growing market.
    Allyn and Bacon, Inc. has been a leader in educational publishing for over 100 years. We have built our reputation by (1) extensive market analysis to develop a limited number of quality books, (2) very high editorial standards for manuscript development and book production, and (3) energetic marketing programs for maximizing sales.
    Your book is a prospect for our Longwood Division program, which sells literally hundreds of thousands of books to the in-service teaching market as well as the college pre-service market. The principal promotion medium for the Longwood Division is direct mail.
    I would appreciate receiving any additional material that you have prepared on the text. Do you have any sample chapters?
    I would like to have this additional material and your book outline reviewed by our editorial board. Based on their favorable appraisal of the book and its market prospects, we will be in a position to discuss a publishing agreement.
    I look forward to hearing from you. Thank you for allowing Allyn and Bacon the opportunity to consider your manuscript for future publication.

                          Cordially,

                          Ann Typographical

REJECTION LETTER

Leading Educational Publishers since 1868

Allyn and Bacon, Inc.
7 Wells Avenue, Newton, MA 02159
617/964-5530

Professor John B. Professional
Elsewhere, U.S.A.

Dear Professor Professional:
    Thank you very much for allowing us the opportunity to consider your proposed book, <u>Introduction to Education.</u>
    We found the proposal to be very interesting, but unfortunately we do not feel that it would fit our publishing program at the present time. I am sorry that we have reached this decision, and I hope you understand that this is no reflection on the quality of your work.
    We appreciate your thinking of Allyn and Bacon in connection with the publication of your work, and wish you success with your project.

                          Sincerely,

                          Ann Typographical
P.S. We are forwarding your material under separate cover.

SUGGESTIONS FOR A BOOK PROSPECTUS

Leading Educational Publishers since 1868

Allyn and Bacon, Inc.
7 Wells Avenue, Newton, MA 02159
617/964-5530

     The prospectus for a book focuses the author's thoughts and helps guide the publisher on several topics described below. While an outline deals with the contents and organization of a book, a prospectus emphasizes its rationale-- why it is being written, and for whom.

     <u>Object</u>: What does the book try to do? Develop the theory of the field, present information, describe tools and information methods?

     <u>Subject</u>: What does the book cover? Instructions in systems analysis and design; how to apply the available tools and methods; why the theory of the field is what it is and how it can be expanded, improved, and implemented?

     <u>Market</u>: Who will find the book useful? Students (graduate and undergraduate), researchers, consultants? Why will it appeal to each group? How can each group be reached economically? Text or trade appeal? For which courses is the book designed?

     <u>Competition</u>: What are the book's unique features? Differences between the proposed book and competitive books; relationship of this book to other books that might either precede or follow it; differences in breadth and depth of coverage from other books; amount of new material?

     <u>Approach</u>: How is the subject treated? Elementary or advanced treatment, simplicity of writing style, text or case treatment, mathematical or intuitive, new material or merely restatement of available literature, number and quality of questions and problems, tables and illustrations, photographs?

     <u>Size</u>: What is the length of the manuscript? Number of chapters, number of pages (double-spaced, typewritten on 8½ by 11-inch pages with adequate margins); number and type of illustrations, figures, and tables full-page or smaller; page format (if an ordinary book page is not suitable).

4

Writing for Professional Magazines

Charlie passes the word along that the veteran professor is amenable to helping young writers for professional publication. So Mary stops by Bill's office. Mary has been an assistant professor of education for several years. With her dissertation and a research article behind her, she wants help on writing for a broader audience through general professional magazines. Bill overviews magazines and suggests some guides to periodicals in the field of education. They talk of what she might write and discuss the pros and cons of collaborating with others.

Mary. Charlie told me about his conversations with you and said you might be willing to help me, Bill. I have published one article based on my dissertation. Now I would like to publish something in professional periodicals with a wider and more varied audience than that of the research journals.

Bill. That certainly widens your opportunities for publication. There are many professional magazines as well as highly specialized journals.

Let's take your own field of education, for instance. There are magazines that deal with education as a whole. Others are devoted to subdivisions of education, such as elementary education, secondary education, higher education, supervision, guidance, and so on. Still other periodicals are edited for those who teach in subject matter areas such as English, the social sciences, the sciences, and the various arts. Then there are the still more highly specialized journals on particular interests of educators.

Mary.   What's the distinction between magazines and journals?

Bill.   The distinction I use is necessarily somewhat shaky. Both professional magazines and scholarly journals are periodicals, "published at regular intervals of more than one day," unlike daily newspapers. In general, a professional magazine is edited for a wide/varied readership and a scholarly journal for a limited/specialized readership. But, in practice, the differentiation blurs. The two types often overlap. Some widely read professional magazines with varied readers are titled journals. Some scholarly journals have a remarkably wide and varied readership. And certainly the professional magazines are not unscholarly, nor are the scholarly journals unprofessional. Unfortunately, the distinctions are unclear. Yet, if not interpreted too rigidly, the differentiation can be useful to us. For your purposes, let's assume that professional magazines usually have a more general and varied readership than do most of the scholarly journals. Else we may get lost in semantics and subtle differentiations.

Another way of categorizing periodicals related to a profession is to divide them into four groupings. For instance, Robert J. Silverman, editor of the *Journal of Higher Education*, categorizes education periodicals as research journals, scholarly journals, professional journals, and association journals.[1] He perceptively describes how editorial requirements for each type of article differ. For instance, editorial requirements for a research article stress appropriate use of statistics, appropriateness of the total organization, validity of logic, and clarity and conciseness of writing. Editors of scholarly articles value clarity, conciseness, spirited writing style, and use of literature. They are less concerned than are research editors for use of statistics, replicability of the studies, and the emotional neutrality of their authors. Editorial requirements for a typical article in professional or association periodicals agree on the importance of writing style and organization but do not stress statistics and use of literature. Though the editors of all four types of articles value content of interest to readers, applicability to problems, and appropriate content, the editors of typical articles in professional and association periodicals are particularly concerned with reader interest, practicality, and timeliness. In deciding where to send queries or manuscripts, writers should take into account the requirements of journal editors and of associations.

However, education periodicals often use a mix of articles. For in-

[1]Robert J. Silverman, *Getting Published in Education Journals* (Springfield, Ill.: Charles C Thomas, 1982).

stance, professional and association periodicals may carry research articles; research and scholarly periodicals may be published by associations; and professional and association periodicals may carry scholarly articles. So keep in mind editorial requirements for the particular type of article you are writing.

Some writers make a practice of writing for both professional/association magazines and scholarly/research journals. They may write an article based on their new research findings for a journal read by a relatively limited number of their scholarly colleagues, and also write an article that applies the research to the broader audience of a more widely read professional magazine. Thus, two publications grow out of one significant research study..

Mary. Which of the education periodicals do you classify as professional magazines, edited for a wide/varied readership?

Bill. I can cite some, if you'll risk my being arbitrary. For instance, there are the American Federation of Teachers' *American Educator* and the American Council on Education's *Educational Record*. *Educational Forum* is published by Kappa Delta Pi, and *Phi Delta Kappan* by Phi Delta Kappa. These are organization-published magazines.

A few magazines that also deal with education as a whole are published by governmental agencies, such as *American Education* published by the Department of Education. Some are published by commercial concerns, such as *Education Digest, Learning,* and *Change.*

A great many professional magazines for a wide and varied educator audience are sponsored by universities or university subgroups. Among them are *Peabody Journal of Education,* Indiana State University's *Contemporary Education,* University of Hawaii's *Educational Perspectives,* Boston University's *Journal of Education,* University of Chicago's *American Journal of Education* (formerly *School Review*), Ohio State's *Theory into Practice,* Indiana University's *Viewpoints in Teaching and Learning,* and still others.

Mary. Why so many published by universities?

Bill. Publication of a periodical is a way to foster scholarship and to disseminate knowledge, two roles universities cherish. Professors are often proud to edit a publication with recompense in the form of status and reduced teaching load rather than money. The universities turn up office space, provide secretarial services, and sometimes make up operational deficits.

Mary. What about magazines in the subdivisions of education? And in the subject matter fields?

Bill. There the situation is reversed. Only a few universities sponsor magazines in subdivisions of education, such as the University of Chicago Press's *Elementary School Journal* or Ohio State University Press's *Journal of Higher Education* with the American Association for Higher Education. The great majority are published by educational organizations. For instance, the organization of high school principals publishes the *National Association of Secondary School Principals Bulletin;* the elementary principals, *National Elementary Principal;* the supervisors and curriculum directors, *Educational Leadership;* the school administrators, *School Administrator;* the school board members, *American School Board Journal;* the college professors, *Academe;* the adult educators, *Adult Education*—and that's only a sampling.

As to periodicals in the subject fields, I read in *Change* that in the field of language and literature in 1983 there were 3,024 periodicals in the world, of which 877 were published in the United States. Most of the language and literature journals are small; two out of three have a circulation below 1,500, and the vast majority report that they publish fewer than thirty articles a year. Modern Language Association has created a computerized data base to keep track of them.

Mary. I'm beginning to feel staggered.

Bill. Many professionals often have specialized interests that they share with others. They want to transmit their current thinking and research on that specialized interest to those who share their specific concerns. They find they can do this only in part through the more general magazines in their professional field, or through the magazines and journals dealing with a broad subdivision or a subject area. After all, editors can carry articles on high specializations only occasionally if they are to satisfy their range of readers. Too, the specialized articles have to be intelligible to readers who are not of the in-group. This hampers the scholar who wants to communicate to the knowledgeable without excess verbiage. So when the number of adherents and the state of finances permit, specialists launch their own journals.

Mary. How many subscribers are needed?

Bill. Circulation may be as low as several hundred, or even less if the faithful few settle for mimeographing or photocopying. But, paradoxically, some of the specialized journals have circulations that compare favorably to magazines appealing to more varied readers.

All in all, there are literally hundreds of periodicals, Mary, in your field of education. The *Guide to Periodicals in Education and Its Academic Disciplines* by William L. Camp and Bryan L. Schwark lists and describes 602 education and education-related magazines and journals—and reminds its readers that some editors didn't respond! And *Education/Psychology Journals: A Scholar's Guide* by Darlene B. Arnold and Kenneth O. Doyle, Jr., lists and describes more than 120 journals. Both are published by the colorfully titled Scarecrow Press, Inc., Metuchen, New Jersey. EdPress's *America's Education Press* is a useful directory of journals and newsletters compiled for the Educational Press Association of America. *Annotated Writer's Guide to Professional Educational Journals* by Elizabeth S. Manera and Robert E. Wright, published in 1982 by Bobets Publishing Company, Scottsdale, Arizona, is an excellent source for you. Overviews of 162 education and psychology periodicals include the periodical's address, clientele, style guide, design (including content), editorial policy, and other information.

Mary. Is there a manuscript marketing newsletter for academicians to help writers learn of editorial needs and requirements?

Bill. Not to my knowledge. In general, editors are not optimistic about the potentiality of a marketing newsletter. They recommend reading their editorial guidelines and consulting recent issues of their particular magazine or journal. However, there is an annual publication, *Magazine Industry Market Place* (Bowker), that describes needs and requirements of periodicals in some of the professions.

Mary. My question now may seem silly to you. But it's honest anyway. What should I write about? Does that seem like a foolish thing to ask?

Bill. Not at all. Fred T. Wilhelms once told me that there were two types of writers for professional publications whom he had encountered as a professor, editor, columnist, and organization executive secretary. One type constantly went deeper and deeper into specialization with every publication; the other type preferred a broader scope, shifting interests occasionally.

Your question "What should I write about?" would never occur to the first type, the deep probers. Inevitably they write in specialized journals about their latest finding or idea in their deep but narrow field. Their general topic is predetermined. The only decisions they have to make about content concern the aspects to report this time, the angles of approach, the limitations they intend to impose on themselves.

The second type of author covers a wider range of subjects. These writers study some aspect of a field for a while, write about it, decide that this is as far as they now want to go, take up some new aspect or even new field, then write about that. They often write for the broader audience that reads the more general professional magazines. To them, variety is the spice of writing.

For instance, Harold G. Shane of Indiana University has been published more than 500 times. He wrote to me:

> The desire to understand or internalize something of interest is not the sole explanation of why I write. Frankly, I very much enjoy trying to capture ideas in language and to express my thoughts in as interesting a fashion as possible to other people. I might also mention that it does not matter too much to me what I deal with in a manuscript. This is why I have written dozens of children's books and stories, technical manuscripts on boat handling, science fiction (in which realm my first published story appeared), or books and articles in the field of professional education. A well-known author once was asked, "How can you write so much when it is such a painful process?" Her response was, "It would be much more

painful not to write." I find this answer a very satisfying one since it reflects my own viewpoint, too.

Mary.   Are there dangers for writers less versatile and less scholarly than Shane?

Bill.   Yes. Writers who are skillful with words may be tempted to write on matters they know little about. However, a few letters to the editor from the knowledgeable specialists is the best cure for the ill-informed generalist. What was the subject of your research article based on your doctoral dissertation?

Mary.   Children of divorced parents.

Bill.   You might take a cue from the three key words. You might want to write more broadly about the problems of children. Or about parents. Or about divorce. Or about the combination.

Ask yourself what the mass media are saying about these topics. Ask what professional and lay magazines with broad readership are reporting—such as *Childhood Education* or *Parents'*, for instance. (If there isn't a magazine titled *Divorce* as yet, I suspect one will be published soon.)

Then join the ongoing debate. Lean heavily on your specialized knowledge. Yet be willing to go into broader controversial issues. Take a position on something concerning children, parents, or divorce. Select an aspect that moves you.

Recognize that your chosen outlet is a more general professional magazine than a specialized journal. Talk to a wider group of readers. Communicate. Don't be ashamed to popularize your findings and ideas. Take some suggestions from freelance writers and books of advice on writing articles.

Mary.   Such as?

Bill.   It's not enough to have a topic; a writer must find a theme. An article must say something. It must contend, demonstrate, attempt to prove.

A general reader must learn early what the article is about. If the general reader doesn't, he or she will soon stop being your reader. You and I have both read articles that meandered aimlessly and apparently endlessly. Even when we endured to the end, we couldn't identify the author's thesis. Such as article might well have been titled "What Professor X Happens to Know About—."

Don't expect to publish a general essay on children, or parents, or divorce in a professional magazine. You are writing an article, not an entry for an encyclopedia or a summary of a field. Ask yourself what you want to demonstrate. That children are resilient and don't suffer as much from divorce as is commonly thought? Or that the trauma of divorce cannot be shaken throughout the child's life? That both divorced parents can retain relatively good relationships with the child or that this usually doesn't happen? Should divorce be made easier/harder or should marrying be made easier/harder? Build the article around your contention, whatever it might be. Of course you will recognize the opposing view in your article and will proceed in a fair-minded way. But make the case for your own view.

Within the theme, find a focus. Rather than being content with global generalizations, can you find individuals, organizations, groups that reflect and support your contentions? Is there a population that you have studied? Is a person or group trying out possible approaches? Is there an episode that you can describe?

There are more professional magazines than you thought there were. So don't be troubled if your initial queries are received coolly or flatly turned down.

Mary. I hope I won't receive too many rejections of my queries.

Bill. Everyone does; you're not alone. Don't send the same query to periodical after periodical without taking the time to adapt the query to the special interests and requirements of the periodical to which it is newly being directed. Otherwise the sensitive editor may detect that a shopworn form letter was originally intended for other editorial eyes. If you prefer to submit an unsolicited manuscript, make sure you don't send off a copy that has been dog-eared from earlier rough receptions.

As to how many rejections a writer has to experience before abandoning an idea, no magic number exists. An authors' agent specializing in books written by members of professions once told me that it took him an average of eight submissions of a book manuscript before acceptance was achieved. If the author follows the query route, yet is rejected by a periodical, only the hours devoted to developing the query are lost, not the months that otherwise would have gone into writing the article.

We all hate to receive rejection letters. However, resist the temptation to crumple them and chuck them angrily in the general direction of the wastebasket. Some rejection letters tell you why your query or manuscript is being rejected. Some periodical editors will even respond to a follow-up letter from you asking why your material was rejected. A second reading of a rejection letter may turn up some suggestions for improvement. Smooth out that crumpled paper ball and take another look. Has the editor left the door open? Even a slight crack?

Mary. I have been thinking about the possibility of collaborating on articles. What are the advantages and disadvantages of coauthorship?

Bill. Like so many things in life, a great deal depends upon the collaborators themselves. In general, coauthorship is supposed to reduce the time needed to produce an article or, indeed, a book. Coauthorship is a way of using the varied knowledge and insights of the collaborators. It reduces the loneliness of authorship. The collaborators join resources, divide the labor, and help each other maintain motivation.

The possible disadvantages are that much time may be spent in discussion and even argumentation and little time in writing. If the collaborators are separated geographically, the exchange of ideas and eventually of pages of the manuscript may become burdensome.

Sometimes the joint product satisfies each of the authors. On the other hand, the end product may not fully please all members of the writing combination. Individual egos may get in the way..

Mary.   Do editors prefer collaborations on articles?

Bill.   Not necessarily. They may favor coauthorship or multiple authorship if one of the collaborators is well known to the periodical's readership. Some journal editors like collaborations in which at least one of the contributors has a doctoral degree.

Mary.   If the collaboration is between an experienced and an inexperienced writer, who gains most?

Bill.   There are situations in which the inexperienced writer gains through association with the veteran. The new writer may learn from the experienced writer and may gain an entree into publication that might otherwise be closed. The veteran writer may also benefit, possibly from having the newcomer do the library legwork and check details. The veteran may also receive new insights from the collaborator.

Mary.   What should a person take into account in choosing partners?

Bill.   Collaborators Fox and Faber in the June 1982 *Scholarly Publishing* suggest considering intellectual factors such as interests, theoretical perspectives, skills, and competencies. They advise also taking into account personal factors such as work habits, emotional dispositions, acceptance of commitments, work pace, and energy level. They suggest that both similarity and complementariness are important in collaboration.

Much depends on the individuals. A collaboration is like a marriage; it may be happy or unhappy. It may even end in divorce, in some cases relatively harmonious, in others acrimonious. Better stop me here, Mary, or I'll be making some wild analogies between your article theme, Children of Divorced Parents, and the offspring of your prospective collaboration!

Mary.   My next step is to develop a theme and a possible structure for my article. Then I'll query.

Bill.   Meanwhile, you might gather additional needed data. Some general magazines in the field of education have prepared advice sheets for their authors. You might write for them. You might also familiarize yourself with the acceptance and rejection rate of periodicals in your field. Admittedly, that's often a discouraging experience. But knowing the odds is preferable to blind plunging.

I have some notes here on a talk Larry A. Fass made to a writing for publication conference in Phoenix in 1982 and published in the writer's guide by Manera and Wright that I mentioned. His study of 98 periodicals in education and psychology found that authors of unsolicited articles had 17 percent of their submissions accepted for publication. (In contrast, *all* authors specifically invited by the editors to write were published.) Half of the periodicals accepted one-fourth or less of the unsolicited articles received. The magazine with the lowest acceptance rate received 3,728 unsolicited articles and published only 8 of them, about two-tenths of 1 percent.

One-third of the unsolicited manuscripts submitted to the 98 periodicals were received by only 6 magazines/journals. How about trying the other 92? According to Fass, some periodicals published almost 100 percent of unsolicited articles submitted. So don't give up too readily. Persist and publish!

SUGGESTIONS FOR AUTHORS
FROM *PHI DELTA KAPPAN*

Dear Author:
 This letter is designed to answer very briefly the more common questions asked by persons interested in being published in the Phi Delta Kappan.

1. What makes an article acceptable to the editors?
 We look primarily for two qualities: educational significance and readability. There is no easy formula for achieving these goals, since there are many kinds of significance and many different styles that are readable. However, we believe that to be significant an article must in some way be usable by the reader--to enlarge his knowledge, to improve his practice, to influence his decisions. We want it to deal with real problems. We want it to be factual, logical, and well focused. To be readable, it should use jargon sparingly, it should be concrete (an example for every principle or generalization), journalistic (first things first, no wasted words), and it should display--if at all possible--some wit and erudition. We don't like pedantic, dissertation, or textbook style. In particular, we don't like to see conclusions reported last; the first paragraph should state the major point of the article. Finally, a manuscript should in some way contribute to the purposes of Phi Delta Kappa: the promotion of research, service and leadership in the profession.

2. What are the procedures for submission of manuscripts?
 Very simple: Type your article, double-spaced, and send two copies to the editor. If you want them to be returned if the article cannot be published, enclose a stamped, self-addressed envelope. Tell us in a covering letter what you consider the main reasons why we should publish. Give us sufficient information about yourself for a standard author-identification paragraph.

 If you wish, send a letter of inquiry first, describing the article and perhaps including an outline. We must balance our coverage; sometimes we can tell you, on the basis of an outline, whether an article will fit in with our editorial plans.

3. Who makes the publication decision?
 The editor. Sometimes, if he is undecided, he will submit a manuscript to one or more of the editorial consultants listed on the Kappan masthead for their opinion. But few Kappan articles are juried.

4. What is the ideal length?
 We like some very short pieces, particularly the reports we use in Research Notes and the "light" or humorous pieces. Most of these are ideally 1,000 words or less in length. Feature articles vary between 1,500 and 4,000 words. We consider 2,500 an ideal length for the typical article. Book reviews (usually solicited, but welcome unsolicited) are generally from 350 to 750 words in length.

5. What editorial style is used?
   Kappan editors have drafted their own stylebook, based
   largely upon the University of Chicago Manual of Style.
   For footnote style, see past issues of the Kappan; do not
   use APA style. Since we copy edit all material to agree
   with our style, it is not essential to re-work your manuscript for Kappan submission, except for footnotes that
   have been prepared in APA style.

6. What about charts, graphs, photographs?
   We can use a limited amount of graphic material to illustrate an article. Statistical charts will be re-set
   to our specifications. Photographs will generally be
   black and white and must be of high quality for reproduction; amateur photography is seldom usable. Sometimes we
   can use a photo of the author, formal or informal.

7. Do you reprint material that has appeared in other journals
   of smaller or more specialized circulation?
   Ordinarily, no. But if a piece is of particular interest,
   if it has gained favorable notice and deserves wider
   dissemination, we will consider it.

8. Do you pay for manuscripts?
   Very seldom. Usually it is only when we solicit an article
   from a well-known authority who is not a Phi Delta Kappan,
   or from a professional author whose livelihood depends
   largely on the sale of his work, that we pay honoraria.

9. How can I contribute to one of the special issues?
   Special Kappans are generally planned by guest editors
   many months in advance, and most of the articles are
   solicited from persons who have published original work
   on the topic. We seldom announce specials in advance,
   largely because we wish to preserve some flexibility
   (postponing an issue if solicited material is delayed,
   for example). But a letter or phone inquiry to the Kappan
   editor will get you some information about specials.

10. Who holds copyright on Kappan articles?
    Generally, Phi Delta Kappa, Inc., does. Each issue is
    fully copyrighted. But an author may give permission
    for only one-time use and retain all other rights if he
    so desires.

11. How long does it take for the editors to make a decision?
    We acknowledge all unsolicited articles immediately upon
    receipt. We try not to hold a manuscript longer than two
    months without returning it, accepting it, or in some way
    communicating with the author. But in the months when
    more than 100 unsolicited pieces come in, we can fall
    behind schedule.

That's about all we can say until we see your manuscript.

                                    The Editors

Taking Criticism—and Using It

Here are eight constructive comments so frequently made that they might constitute a guideline for the critic, with accompanying advice to authors on how to read the comments and how to react.

The reader says:

1. *Not appropriate for this journal. Too specialized. Too general.* This is a problem of audience identification. The subject matter is wrong for the journal. The approach is wrong for it. The style is wrong. You're writing for another group of readers. Look at copies of the journal, comparing the article with those its editors have accepted as appropriate. A scholarly, detailed, heavily footnoted article will not be appropriate for a popular journal, nor will a breezy, undocumented one for a scholarly journal. Know the journal you are submitting to. Sometimes an editor, feeling that an article is not right for his journal, will suggest where else to send it. Thank him and follow the suggestion.

2. *Author has not done his homework.* The reader is saying that you have not done enough research. Presumably he knows of something you have missed, and he may tell you where to look. If you have already looked there and have chosen not to use that material, you may have neglected some of the scholarly conventions. The reader may in effect be asking for an opening review of relevant literature, or for a more exact demonstration by footnotes or references that you have covered the literature. Go back to the bibliographies to check, especially if you are charged with having ignored recent work.

3. *Excellent talk. An introductory lecture.* You probably got the idea for the paper while preparing a class presentation. You are still talking to students. Again, it is a matter of audience. The one you have submitted the article to is made up of scholars. Perhaps you should submit the article to a journal that emphasizes instruction in your field.

4. *The writer has nothing new to say.* What is a revelation to you may be an old lecture note to someone else. Hold with your discovery until you get three or four readers saying the same thing. Then accept it: you don't have a bonanza, only a worked-out mine. Start on something else. This time check the literature and make sure no one else has published the essence of your article, making the same point and using the same material.

5. *This is wrong, misleading, inaccurate, questionable.* If the comment refers to a matter of fact, like a date or a name, check it again and be

From Murray F. Markland, "Taking Criticism—and Using It," *Scholarly Publishing*, University of Toronto Press, February 1983, pp. 140–41. Reprinted from *Scholarly Publishing: A Journal for Authors and Publishers.* February 1983, by permission of the author and University of Toronto Press.

grateful. If it refers to an opinion, interpretation, or analysis, consider the possibility that you are wrong and reconstruct your argument. Apparently it was not convincing. Perhaps you need a supporting authority, additional evidence, a clearer statement of the argument, or an open and positive assertion of a disagreement with what is widely thought.

6. *This passage is not clear.* Reading it now, is it still clear to you? Are you sure you thought it through to start with? Is the difficulty in the language: a tripping inversion, a failing attempt at irony or humour, long, complicated sentences, punctuation? Have you, assuming that the point is obvious, not bothered to state it? Try saying the whole thing differently.

7. *Too brief, lacks detail. Too long, too much detail.* Both comments are to the same end: proportion, balance, support. Why did you put in the details you did? Why no more? Why no fewer? Do you intend to illustrate for clarification? To persuade as evidence? To impress with how much you know? One detail may illustrate. It takes more to persuade. One is too many if all that is intended is to impress. If the paper is called too brief, the task may be too large for a ten-page article and so you have skimped on details and depended too much on generalizations. If the article is called too long, you may be belabouring the obvious, enjoying the sound of your own voice, or still writing for a dissertation committee. There is always something that can be left out. If it can, it should be.

8. *This is badly written. Lumpy, long paragraphs lacking transitions, inexact language, pretentious words, and so on.* Some of what such comment speaks of is objective; sentence and paragraph length can be measured. But in general this criticism is difficult for an author to handle by himself. Look for help among colleagues who are writers. Editors on your campus. Even English faculty. Or read, and digest, some of the books that talk about writing style.

Figure 4-1 Characteristics of a Selected Sample of Education Journals

	Acceptance Rate (%)	Preferred Length (in Ms. Pages)	Min./Max. Pages	Refereed	Research Articles (%)	Articles per Year (Est.)	Issues per Year	Theme Issues per Year	Contributors Who Are University Personnel (%)	Prefer Query Letters	Days to Answer Queries (Avg.)	Days to Acknowledge Receipt of Ms. (Avg.)	Weeks Required for Decision	Effect of Photos on Acceptance
Action in Teacher Education	25	6	1–12	Yes	25	35	4	2	80	No	7	14	12	Possible
American Biology Teacher	30	12–15	*–20	Yes	10	*	8	3–4	60	Yes	5	7	15	Likely
American Journal of Education	13	*	*–20	Yes	90	11	4	1	100	No	14	14	12	None
Capstone Journal of Education	25	15	*–20	Yes	25	13	2	0	98	Yes	7	14	12–16	None
Child Development	*	15	2–50	Yes	96	*	6	1	95	No	2	1	6	None
Comparative Education Review	20	30	15–38	Yes	90	35	4	0	70	No	5	7	8	None
Computers and Education	25	20	**	Yes	100	*	4	1	100	No	**	1	12	Possible
Contemporary Education	5	10–12	1–25	Yes	10	48	4	3	75	No	2	7	2	None
Computing Teacher	30	**	1/2–3	Yes	10	135	9	2–3	30	Yes	10–21	7	6–12	Possible
Creative Child & Adult Quarterly	50	10	**	Yes	50	55+	4	Varies	50	No	7	21	4	Possible
Curriculum Inquiry	10	35	**	Yes	50	18	4	0	100	No	*	16	13	None
Curriculum Review	15	10–12	6–15	No	10	35	5	All	60	Yes	7–14	7	10–12	Possible
Delta Pi Epsilon	33.3	*	*	Yes	100	15	4	0	100	No	2	2	8–12	None
Early Child Development & Care	33.3	20	10–30	Yes	70	38	6	2	90	Yes	2	7	3	Possible
Early Years	2	*	*	No	0	200	9	9	*	No	*	14	2	None
Educational Forum	10	15–20	*–35	Yes	5	45	4	0	85	No	7	7	12–16	Possible
Educational Horizons	7.5	10–15	1–20	No	75	55	4	3	75	Yes	5	7	6	None
Educational Leadership	7.5	8–10	1–25	Yes	20	150	8	6–7	60	No	3	7	2–3	None

64

Educational Record	5.5	15-20	12-30	Yes	20	50	4	2	95	No	10	14	6	Possible
Educational Research	15	15	5-30	Yes	80	30	10	1	90	No	7-14	7-14	8-9	None
Educational Studies	*	*	*	Yes	0	7	4	0	90	Yes	5-7	7-14	*	None
Educational Technology Systems	60		10-30	Yes	50	30	4	1	50	Yes	10	7	10-15	Likely
High School Journal	10	8-10	2-20	Yes	60	40+	4	1-2	95	Yes	3	14	10	Possible
Instructional Innovator	33	10-12	5-30	Yes	10	80	8	8	45	No	7	21	26	Possible
International Journal of Early Childhood	*	8-12	6-12	*	*	12	2	0	50+	No	28	7	26	Likely
Journal for Research in Mathematics Education	20	20-30	*	Yes	90	25	5	1	80	No	5	7	12	None
Journal of Industrial Teacher Education	40	18-20	None	Yes	50	24	4	1	90	No	2	7	8	None
Journal of Reading	25	10-15	1-20	Yes	30	85	8	*	85	No	7	7	6	None
Journal of Reading Behavior	12.5	30	1-50	Yes	100	30	4	0	80	No	**	7	16	None
Journal of Research in Science Teaching	40	20	5-40	Yes	90	75	9	0-1	80	No	3	7	12	Likely
Journal of Teacher Education	13.1	12	6-15	Yes	35	144	6	Varies	85	No	*	7-8	5-8	None
NASSP Bulletin	18.2	8-12	7-15	No	15	180	9	9	55	Yes	3-5	2-3	4	None
Phi Delta Kappan	5	12	2-20	No	*	120	10	0	54	Yes	7	2	7	None
Reading Teacher	25	10-15	1-20	Yes	30	85	8	*	85	No	7	7	6	None
School and Community	25	5	1-15	No	25	88	6	4	27	No	5	14	2	Likely
School Science and Mathematics	10	16	*-16	Yes	20	52	8	0	50	No	2	*	3	Possible
Science Education	45	15-20	1-30	Yes	60	46	5	0	93	No	3	7	22	Possible
Social Studies	40	10	8-15	Yes	25	60	6	1	78	No	*	7	14	Possible
Teacher Educator	40	12	6-15	Yes	40	22	4	0	80	No	2	2	5-6	None
Vocational Education	5	6-8	4-10	No	**	80	8	8	50	Yes	60	60	12	Likely

* = don't know.

** = not answered.

Reprinted with permission, *Phi Delta Kappan*, Kenneth T. Henson, "Writing for Professional Publication: Ways to Increase Your Success," May 1984, p. 636.

5

Publishing in Scholarly Journals

Talking the language of scholars
The case for clarity
The major style manuals
Instructions from journals on manuscript preparation
Why journal publication takes so long
The roles of referees
Obtaining reprints
Directories of publishing opportunities

*A few days later Mary returns with her good friend Abe, an associate pro-
fessor of economics. Abe has pointed out to Mary some of the differences
between writing for a broad audience and writing for scholarly journals in
fields such as economics. They interact with Bill on improving communication to fellow scholars through refereed journals. Bill acquaints them with
the wide variety of authors' guides to journals which scholars might use as
they decide where to publish their findings.*

Mary. Bill, can you help us in our attempts to publish in scholarly
journals? All I learned from preparing the article based on my dissertation was that getting an article published takes a long long time.

I brought Abe with me this time. He is an economist. The journals
he wants to write for report primarily on research; the style is different
from that of the more general professional magazines and especially different from that of the popular magazines for the general public.

Bill. Mary and Abe, good to see you both. I agree that there are
marked differences. Whether you are writing for the general public, a
wide and varied professional readership, or the specialists who read the
scholarly journals, write to your audience. In the case of the scholarly
journals, your readers are specialists. Talk their language. Use the words
commonly found in their taxonomies—

Abe. To say nothing of their lexicons—

Bill. —even if your reader has to go to the dictionary to check the meaning of taxonomy or lexicon. You do have to write for an audience extensive enough to warrant publication. Yet don't be overly troubled if the lay reader can't completely understand you. Don't even be disturbed if a proportion of your profession as a whole doesn't completely comprehend your article. Your target audience is not the lay reader and sometimes not the entire profession.

At the same time, be sure that you are writing clearly, crisply, and comprehensively for your fellow specialists. If *they* can't understand you, there is something wrong. If a person proposes to write for scholarly journals, that person should be a highly competent researcher who has mastered both the methodology and the language of his or her field.

The author of Ecclesiastes once remarked, "Of making many books there is no end; and much study is a weariness of the flesh." Today this ancient wisdom could be updated: "Of making many scholarly articles there is no end; and much reading of them is a weariness of the flesh." The demands made on scholars to stay abreast of their fields through reading the findings of others are well nigh impossible to meet. Don't contribute to wasting your colleagues' precious time.

Abe. What most often goes wrong in communicating with specialists through scholarly journals?

Bill. Sometimes the purpose of the article is unclear. One can read on and on, yet never learn what the researcher had in mind.

Sometimes the conclusions are buried in the body of the article. Or the scope of the article is so wide that the context wanders aimlessly.

Sometimes important information is left out. The author makes the assumption that readers already know certain facts about which they are actually uninformed.

Sometimes vagueness is the enemy. If a word used in the trade has several meanings, make plain the meaning intended. If possible ambiguity exists, be willing to define terms. Don't use an elaborate word when a simple one will do. A careful reader will not be impressed by complex phrasing or vocabulary. Word-dropping the current "in" phrase is a form of pretentiousness that is readily recognized.

Remember that jargon has a dual definition, one reputable, the other discreditable. The reputable definition is "the specialized or technical language of a trade, profession, class, or fellowship." The discreditable definition is "nonsensical, incoherent, or meaningless utterance; gibberish." I'm afraid that some academics combine both in their writing.

It makes good sense to be careful with generalizations and to avoid oversimplified conclusions. A good scholar qualifies with cautious modifiers. Yet sometimes researchers become overly timid. In their stress on inconclusiveness, they convince their readers that there is nothing or very little to be learned from their studies.

If you really want to communicate, take the space for illustrations and examples. Use freely that blessed phrase "for instance." Occasionally summarize as you go along, rather than save all summary for final paragraphs.

Abe. Some journals facilitate communication by specifying particular style manuals.

Bill. They do. For instance—to use the blessed phrase—psychological journals often specify the *Publication Manual of the American Psychological Association.* In your own field of economics, Abe, the journals usually prefer the *Modern Language Association Style Sheet* or *The Chicago Manual of Style.* In addition, style instructions are often available upon request to the editor. Sometimes instructions are included in the front matter of a journal. Obtaining these well in advance of writing makes good sense, for periodicals have their idiosyncracies.

So save yourself time by studying the publication, by obtaining the journal's style sheet, if available, and by following the recommended style manual. If there are conventions in reporting your particular kind of research, even to editorial preference for graphs prepared in India ink, respect the ground rules.

Mary. I assume that the ground rules differ not only from journal to journal but from field to field. For instance, an article for a literary journal would differ from an article for a journal in the field of physics. Authors of scientific papers face problems of high cost of charts and graphs, along with the necessity for fast dissemination to offset early obsolescence of findings. The ground rules for a scholarly journal reporting research in my field of education may differ from those in Abe's field of economics.

Bill. As an illustration, let's take a scientific paper in biology or chemistry. Such a paper is a published report that describes original research results. The scientific community believes that a scientific paper can be regarded as a primary scientific publication when it is the first publication of original research results. That publication should carry enough information so that other able scientists in the field can appraise the observations, repeat the experiments, consider the processes followed, and test the conclusions. The experiment that the original researcher describes is not complete until published in a journal or some other outlet that is available to members of the scientific community. Therefore, the scientific paper must carry certain specific kinds of information. It requires an introduction, a section on materials and methods, a statement of results, and a discussion of findings, preferably in just that order. The introduction describes the problem. The section on materials and methods describes how the researcher studied the problem. The assessment of results describes what the researcher finds. The discussion of findings considers what the findings mean.

Abe. A paper of this sort is accompanied by an abstract.

Bill.   An abstract is a summary of the longer document; it stresses the problem and the solution. Editors of primary journals prefer an abstract of about 250 words or less. More people will read the abstract in the primary journal or in a collection of abstracts than will read the entire scientific paper. When the entire paper is being considered for publication, reviewers usually read the abstract first. Therefore the writer of the scientific paper should prepare the abstract with care, stressing clarity and simplicity yet still trying to state objectives, scope, methodology, results, and principal conclusions. Even though the abstract comes first, most experienced scientists write the abstract after writing the full paper.

Mary.   Just as most authors decide on the final title after the article is written.

Bill.   In the introduction to a scientific paper the author should define the problem, review the literature, and overview the methods. Specialized terms are also defined in the introduction. A good introduction will even summarize the major results of the study. The materials and methods section should be detailed. This is the place for necessary tables, references, technical specifications, and measurements. The idea is to include sufficient information so that a colleague would be able to reproduce the experiments. The next section on results presents the data; the section should be kept short, clear, and meaningful. The discussion presents principles and theoretical implications, compares and contrasts the findings with previous work, restates conclusions, and almost inevitably calls for still further research. Here is the place to tell what is significant about the study.

By the way, I owe many of these ideas to R. A. Day's useful *How to Write and Publish a Scientific Paper.*[1] For insights into how scientific papers are edited, authors in scientific fields should read Claude T. Bishop's *How to Edit a Scientific Journal.*[2]

Abe.   Mary told me about your query approach. Should research scientists use it in publishing the kind of scientific paper you have described?

Bill.   Only to a limited degree and then mostly to determine whether the manuscript is suited for the journal. Editors of scientific journals usually encourage contributors simply to submit their manuscripts. Consequently, the author must take special care in deciding upon the most likely journal. Authors should read with special care any general information carried by the journal, descriptions as to the scope of the journal in instructions to the authors, and the characteristic content of recent issues. Since it may be a long time until a manuscript is accepted or returned, authors should take into careful account the factors

[1]Philadelphia: iSi Press, 1983.
[2]Philadelphia: iSi Press, 1984.

of selection that are most important to them. Some may value prestige; others may opt for wide circulation; still others may be interested in how often the journal is published, since they wish to avoid lag in publication time. Still others are concerned about some combination of factors.

Mary. Bill, why does publishing in scholarly journals take so long? The article based on my dissertation took a full year from completion to acceptance, and a research article Abe wrote took seventeen months to appear in print. I hear horror stories of even longer delays.

Bill. Several factors, Mary. For one thing, the competition is intense. Take the category of professors alone. It seems that all of them are being urged, whether gently or harshly, to publish, and especially to publish in scholarly journals. Tenure committees often play the numbers game, and countless assistant professors are forced to play along, cranking out articles.

The large majority of American professors have written doctoral dissertations and would like to share their findings. An unknown proportion are actually carrying on research beyond their original doctoral studies. So even though the number of journals increases steadily, the opportunities for publication can't keep pace with the volume of potential contributors. To cite one of the oldest truisms of Abe's profession, factors of supply and demand must be taken into account.

To increase the opportunities to appear in print, service publishing has developed, essentially the printing of small editions of largely unedited camera-ready manuscripts by authors. New journals edited as a labor of love for a few subscribers often spring up when editors have available a typewriter and about $500. Reproductions of typed manuscripts are also made available on demand through microfilming and photocopying. Yet for numerous would-be contributors the road to publication is long and rough. Competition for space is keen.

Another reason for time lag is that the people who conduct the scholarly journals are often part-time editors. Some of them proceed in the leisurely way attributed to academics. Few of them resemble the stereotype of the hyperactive city editor of a newspaper or the harried staffer of a newsweekly. And—don't tell anybody—not all of them are highly competent editors. All this contributes to delay.

Even if the editor is a workaholic or a competent full-time professional, the scholarly journal is almost always refereed.

Mary. When I hear the word "referee," I think of boxing or football.

Bill. But, as you well know, in professional publication refereeing indicates that an article competing for space in the journal is read by outside readers. The referees may be members of the journal's editorial board. They may be chosen from a panel of names accumulated by the editor and advisers. They may be individuals to whom the editor turns occasionally for help on a specialized topic. Their role is to advise the editor whether the article advances and contributes to knowledge, is based on good scholarship, is free from errors in its facts, and arrives at legitimate and logical conclusions. A good referee can contribute to maintaining high editorial standards.

Referees for journals are usually highly experienced professionals. This means that they are busy with their own teaching, counseling, research, consultation, conferences, and writing. Naturally, your article isn't their highest priority. Result—delay. Perhaps two readers get their reports in on time. But everything may be suspended while awaiting a third reader's report. Even when that is received, all may not be smooth sailing. The referees may disagree; the editor may turn to other readers or may temporize. Sometimes a new editor takes over, and when that happens the journal may change policies.

Mary. Referees, like authors, should accept their responsibilities. They ought to hold to schedules agreed upon with editors. They should decline offers to referee if they are short of time or if they lack expertise on the specific topic of the manuscript. They should be willing to give new ideas the hearing they deserve. When referees reject an article, an author would appreciate receiving helpful suggestions from them via the editor.

Bill. Many professional periodicals are also refereed. Most of the editors of refereed journals refer *all* manuscripts received to their referees. On receiving manuscripts, the editors of nonrefereed periodicals judge for themselves or use their staffs as boards of editorial consultants; they also may turn occasionally to outside readers for an opinion.

A national survey of institutional representatives of the American Association of Colleges for Teacher Education, largely deans and chairpersons, concluded that 89 percent of the respondents regarded articles in refereed journals as significant data in making decisions on promotion and tenure. Only 52 percent thought publishing in nonrefereed journals significant evidence for promotion and tenure decisions. Yet 53 percent gave more weight to publishing in nonrefereed national magazines or journals than to publishing in refereed state or regional journals.[3]

Mary. So for the person concerned about tenure and promotion, publication in refereed national journals would be most desirable. It may be a long time though before one's article appears.

Bill. Many manuscripts are neither immediately accepted nor rejected. Especially in scientific fields, authors receive suggestions for modifications from editors and referees. Someone may have caught some fundamental defects that necessitate rethinking on the part of the

[3]Robert J. Suppa and Perry A. Zirkel, "The Importance of Referred Journals: A National Survey," *Phi Delta Kappan,* June 1983, pp. 79–80.

author. Someone may criticize relatively small points that involve rewriting by the author. Or someone may have criticized unjustly, leading the author to engage in further correspondence with the editor in defense of the author's view. Modifications take time. You may have a better article when the modifications are made.

So, all in all, expect delays in decision-making and in publication dates when you contribute to scholarly journals.

Abe. But what a great day for scholarship when your publication finally appears!

Bill. Celebrate by making sure that the right people read it.

Abe. How?

Bill. During the publication process, the journal will probably offer you the opportunity to obtain reprints. Take advantage of it, despite your tight budget and the formidable cost of reprints. Send copies not only to your mother and your favorite aunt but also to those professionals who should read your article.

Abe. I assume I wouldn't include those who regularly receive the magazine through their membership in the sponsoring organization.

Bill. You might even include some members, if you particularly want your ideas to reach them. An old spiritual advises, "Everybody talkin' 'bout heaven ain't goin' there." Everybody receiving a scholarly journal—

Mary. Cynic!

Abe. How about resources to help writers find publication outlets for their efforts?

Bill. Comprehensive directories of journals include *Ulrich's International Periodicals Directory,* a whopping listing of over 64,800 periodicals across the world; *Irregular Serials and Annuals,* an international directory that lists 34,000 publications issued irregularly or less than twice a year; and *Standard Periodical Directory,* more than 68,000 names and addresses. For a listing by states, writers can refer to *Ayer Directory of Publications.* Librarians frequently consult *Magazines for Libraries,* over 6,500 titles. *Directory of Small Magazine/Press Editors and Publishers* annually lists 3,500 small magazines and presses.

My own favorite among the directories is *Directory of Publishing Opportunities in Journals and Periodicals* by Marquis Academic Media, which contains in the 1981 edition thousands of entries extensively described in a multisubject directory. Freelance writers prefer the *Writer's Market* published by Writer's Digest Books, or *The Writer's Handbook* published by Writer, Inc.; most of the periodicals listed pay for articles. Information on payment may not be of much help to you, Abe, in reporting economic research, for economics journals shun economic compensation for their authors.

The best compilations I have found so far are listings in *Scholarly*

Publishing by a librarian, Stanley P. Lyle. Look over his listings in your field of economics, but don't forget to return Lyle's compilations to me. Here is one published in 1979 and a follow-up published in 1984.

Authors' Guides to Scholarly Periodicals–I

Stanley P. Lyle

Communication of studies and research findings through scholarly journals can be a relatively slow process, and delays are lengthened if authors do not intelligently place their work. Scholars owe the academic and professional communities the effort involved in finding an appropriate vehicle for communication, for the sake of advancement of knowledge. From the scholar's point of view, research is in itself sufficiently demanding without the frustration of excessive delays in publication which can result from submitting the manuscript to inappropriate journals. . . .

Help is also available from a number of reference books which serve as authors' or contributors' guides to periodicals publishing unsolicited manuscripts. The subject coverage of these guides varies. A few range across all disciplines or are interdisciplinary, but most concentrate on specific areas such as sociology or literature. The amount of information given for each journal varies from guide to guide.

One of the more comprehensive is *Education/Psychology Journals: A Scholar's Guide,* by Darlene Arnold and Kenneth Doyle, Jr. The entry in this book for the *Journal of Applied Psychology* will illustrate the type and extent of information available in authors' guides. After bibliographic data, paragraphs are devoted to description of the journal ("Devoted primarily to original investigation . . . "), intended audience, and special features. The acceptance/rejection criteria include "significance in contributing new knowledge" and "conciseness and respect for reader time." Additional sections state that blind reviews may be obtained, two to three months are required for the editorial decision and ten to twelve months from acceptance to publication, and 24 percent of submitted manuscripts are accepted. Also included are notes on manuscript disposition, style requirements, payment, and reprints. Not all authors' guides include this much information.

Authors seeking a journal for communication of their work can of course get some of this information from a copy of the journal itself. However, few 'instructions to authors' sections include information on

From Stanley P. Lyle, "Authors' Guides to Scholarly Periodicals," *Scholarly Publishing,* University of Toronto Press, April 1979, pp. 255–261. Reprinted from *Scholarly Publishing: A Journal for Authors and Publishers,* April 1984, by permission of the author and University of Toronto Press.

acceptance/rejection percentages or criteria, or on manuscript disposition. Also, the author's local library or information centre may not subscribe to all the journals which might be interested in a particular manuscript. Author's guides put the necessary information in a handy format and may even lead a scholar to a source not previously considered.

How is the information in these guides compiled? The editors of most state they obtain their information by submitting questionnaires to journal editors and by examining recent issues of the periodical. Most guides state clearly the source of their information as well as their criteria for journal inclusion.

The bibliography which follows is a selected list of authors' guides to periodicals. Particular titles are included if they contain information felt to be of use to scholars beyond that provided in standard sources such as *Magazines for Libraries*. The ISBN and LC numbers as well as price are included for those titles listed in the 1978-9 *Books in Print*. The guides are divided into the broad subject areas of behavioural and social sciences, business and economics, education, humanities, interdisciplinary, multi-subject, and sciences. The few not personally examined are marked with an asterisk. Haworth Press is planning two new titles covering business and nursing.

Behavioural and Social Sciences

MARKLE, ALLAN and ROGER C. RINN, eds. *Author's Guide to Journals in Psychology, Psychiatry & Social Work*. Author's Guide to Journals Series. New York: Haworth Press, 1976. LC 76-50377 ISBN 0-917724-00-3 $14.95
Includes manuscript submission address, subject orientation and scope, preferred topics, manuscript acceptance rate, review period lag time, publication lag time for accepted manuscripts, and early publication options for some 475 journals.

*MERSKY, ROY, ROBERT BERRING, and JAMES McCUE, eds. *Author's Guide to Journals in Law, Criminal Justice & Criminology*. Author's Guide to Journals Series. New York: Haworth Press, 1977. LC 78-18805 ISBN 0-917724-06-2 $16.95
Includes acceptance figures, review period, publication lag time.

MULLINS, CAROLYN J. *A Guide to Writing and Publishing in the Social and Behavioral Sciences*. New York: John Wiley & Sons, 1977. LC 77-1153 Cloth ISBN 0-471-62420-9 $16.95; paper ISBN 0-471-02708-1 $9.95
Covers the entire publishing process from the first draft to selection of journal or publisher to negotiation of contract. On pages 134-58, in tabular form, includes information regarding subject scope, abstract requirements, pre-

ferred article length, style requirements, review period lag time, publication lag time for accepted manuscripts, manuscript acceptance/rejection rates, publishing fees, query letters, and submission fees for some 500 journals.

RHOADES, LAWRENCE J., comp. *The Author's Guide to Selected Journals.* ASA Professional Information Series. Washington, D.C.: American Sociological Assoc., 1974.
Entries typically include preferred manuscript subjects and types, evaluation time, acceptance rate, manuscript length, acceptance to publication time, plus some other data, for more than 220 journals.

*SUSSMAN, MARVIN B., ed. *Author's Guide to Journals in Sociology & Related Fields.* Author's Guide to Journals Series. New York: Haworth Press, 1978. LC 78–1952 ISBN 0–917724–03–8
Includes information on manuscript submission address, manuscript acceptance rate, journal orientation and scope, preferred topics, review period lag time, publication lag time for accepted manuscripts, and early publication options for approximately 450 journals.

TOMPKINS, MARGARET and NORMA SHIRLEY. *Serials in Psychology and Allied Fields.* 2nd. ed. Troy, N.Y.: Whitson Publishing Company, 1976. LC 75–38213 ISBN 0–87875–083–5 $22.50
Includes information on editorial address, preferred article length, payment, copyright, and objectives of more than 800 journals.

Business and Economics

KURTZ, DAVID L. and A. EDWARD SPITZ. *An Academic Writer's Guide to Publishing in Business and Economic Journals.* 2nd ed. Ypsilanti, Michigan: Eastern Michigan University Bureau of Business Services and Research, 1974.
Presents information on manuscript submission address, journal scope and orientation, preferred article length, presentation of quantitative data, and style requirements for more than 200 journals.

TEGA, VASILE G. *Management and Economics Journals: An International Selection.* Management Information Guide, no. 33. Detroit: Gale Research Co., 1977. LC 76–4578 ISBN 0–8103–0833–9 $18.00
Includes editorial address, journal orientation and scope, manuscript acceptance rate, review period lag time, publication lag time for accepted manuscripts, and major reasons for rejection for 161 U.S. and foreign journals.

Education

ARNOLD, DARLENE B. and KENNETH O. DOYLE, JR. *Education/Psychology Journals: A Scholar's Guide.* Metuchen, N.J.: Scarecrow Press, 1975. LC 74–23507 ISBN 0–8108–0779–3 $6.00
Includes information on editorial address, journal scope and orientation, in-

tended audience, acceptance/rejection criteria, manuscript acceptance/rejection rates, manuscript review period lag time, publication lag time, style requirements, and extent of comments on rejected manuscripts for more than 120 journals.

CAMP, WILLIAM L. and BRYAN L. SCHWARK. *Guide to Periodicals in Education and Its Academic Disciplines.* 2nd ed. Metuchen, N.J.: Scarecrow Press, 1975. LC 75-6784 ISBN 0-8108-0814-5 $19.50

Gives editorial address, journal orientation and scope, preferred manuscript length, style requirements, manuscript review period lag time, publication lag time, and disposition of rejected manuscripts for more than 600 journals.

HARTY, HAROLD and TOBY BANWIT. *Submission Guide for Journals in General Teacher Education.* Teacher Education Forum Series, vol. 1. no. 11. Bethesda, Md.: ERIC Document Reproduction Service ED 096 270, 1973.

Includes information on manuscript submission address, typical manuscript topics and types, audience, manuscript length, style requirements, and disposition of both accepted and rejected manuscripts.

HERNON, PETER, MAUREEN PASTINE, and SARAH LOU WILLIAMS. *Library and Library-Related Publications: A Directory of Publishing Opportunities in Journals, Serials, and Annuals.* Littleton, Colo.: Libraries Unlimited, 1973. LC 73-84183 ISBN 0-87287-068-5 $10.00

Includes information on editorial address, journal scope, typical contributors, manuscript evaluation lag time, style requirements, preferred article length, and abstract requirements for 210 journals.

KREPEL, WAYNE J. and CHARLES R. DUVALL. *Education and Education-Related Serials: A Directory.* Littleton, Colo.: Libraries Unlimited, 1977. LC 76-47040 ISBN 0-87287-131-2 $15.00

Lists editorial address, journal scope and orientation, preferred article length, style requirements, manuscript review period lag time, and publication lag time for 501 journals and other serials.

Humanities

GERSTENBERGER, DONNA and GEORGE HENDRICK. *Fourth Directory of Periodicals Publishing Articles in English and American Literature and Language.* Chicago: Swallow Press, 1974. Cloth ISBN 0-8040-0675-x $10.00; paper ISBN 0-8040-0676-8 $3.50

Includes information on editorial address, major fields of interest, preferred manuscript length, style requirements, and manuscript review period lag time for more than 600 journals.

HARMON, GARY L. and SUSANNA M. HARMON. *Scholar's Market: An International Directory of Periodicals Publishing Literary Scholarship.* Columbus, Ohio: Ohio State University Libraries. LC 73-620216 ISBN 0-88215-033-2 $14.50

Lists information on editorial address, journal scope and orientation, preferred manuscript topics, length and style, manuscript review period lag time, publication lag time, and disposition of rejected manuscripts for nearly 850 periodicals.

Interdisciplinary

BIRKOS, ALEXANDER S. and LEWIS A. TAMBS, eds. *African and Black American Studies.* Academic Writer's Guide to Periodicals, no. 3. Littleton, Colo.: Libraries Unlimited, 1975. LC 74-31262 ISBN 0-87287-109-6 $11.50
Entries include information on editorial address, journal subject scope, editorial policies regarding query letters, style requirements, and preferred manuscript length.

———. *Academic Writer's Guide to Periodicals: East European and Slavic Studies*, Vol. 2. Kent, Ohio: Kent State University Press, 1973. LC 70-160685 Cloth ISBN 0-87738-127-0 $10.00; paper ISBN 0-87338-128-9 $7.50
Gives manuscript address, editorial interests, editorial policies regarding style, manuscript length, and query letters for nearly 500 journals.

———. *Academic Writer's Guide to Periodicals*, Vol. 1. *Latin American Studies.* Kent, Ohio: Kent State University Press, 1971. LC 70-160685 Cloth ISBN 0-87338-119-x $10.00; paper ISBN 0-87338-120-3 $7.50
Includes information such as editorial address, special editorial interests, editorial policies with regard to query letters, manuscript length and style, and payment for more than 300 journals.

JOAN, POLLY and ANDREA CHESMAN. *Guide to Women's Publishing.* Paradise, Calif.: Dustbooks, 1978. Cloth ISBN 0-913218-80-4 $9.95; paper ISBN 0-913218-79-0 $4.95
Section 1 of this work includes a listing of feminist journals. Typical entries include address, usual manuscript content, and some remarks to authors. Section 3 lists feminist presses.

MURPHY, DENNIS D., comp. *Directory of Conservative and Libertarian Serials, Publishers and Freelance Markets.* Tucson, Ariz.: D. D. Murphy, 1977. Paper ISBN 0-918788-02-1 $4.95
Entries for journals and publishers typically include subject coverage and viewpoint; some entries also note policies regarding payment, query letters, and manuscript review lag time.

Multi-Subject

Directory of Publishing Opportunities in Journals and Periodicals. 4th ed. Chicago: Marquis Academic Media, 1978. ISBN 0-8379-2302-6 $44.50 + $2.50 for postage and handling.

Nearly 3,500 journals are grouped into subject areas such as biology, philosophy, political science, and chemistry. Journal entries typically include information on editorial address, audience, subject coverage, style requirements, preferred manuscript length, query letters, review period lag time, publication lag time for accepted manuscripts, and disposition of rejected manuscripts.

KOESTER, JANE and BRUCE J. HILLMAN, eds. *Writer's Market.* Cincinnati: Writer's Digest Books, annual. ISBN 0-911654-54-2 $14.95
Aimed more at popular than scholarly audiences, but does include high-quality academic periodicals in many subject areas. Entries include information on addresses, manuscript evaluation lag time, and query letters.

Sciences

*AMERICAN CHEMICAL SOCIETY. *Handbook for Authors.* Washington, D.C.: American Chemical Society, 1978. LC 78-6401 Cloth ISBN 0-8412-0425-x $7.50; paper ISBN 0-8412-0430-6 $3.75
Gives brief descriptions of journals published by the ACS and also presents information on writing the scientific manuscript and the editorial process.

*ARDELL, DONALD, ed. *Author's Guide to Journals in the Health Field.* Author's Guide to Journals Series. New York: Haworth Press, 1978. $16.95
Includes information on manuscript submission address, manuscript acceptance rate, review period lag time, publication lag time for accepted manuscripts, early publication options, journal orientation and scope, and preferred topics for approximately 450 journals.

O'CONNOR, ANDREA B. *Writing for Nursing Publications.* Thorofare, N.J.: Charles B. Slack, 1976. LC 76-14600 ISBN 0-913590-36-3 $6.50
Includes in an appendix information on editorial address, intended audience, and subject content for 57 journals.

Authors' Guides to Scholarly Periodicals-II

Stanley P. Lyle

Five years ago this journal published a list of reference books which serve as authors' or contributors' guides to periodicals publishing un-

From Stanley P. Lyle, "Authors' Guides to Scholarly Periodicals," *Scholarly Publishing*, University of Toronto Press, April 1984, pp. 273-279. Reprinted from *Scholarly Publishing: A Journal for Authors and Publishers*, April 1984, by permission of the author and University of Toronto Press.

solicited manuscripts. The bibliography which follows is a selected list of such guides published since 1979.

Authors' guides are designed to help writers market their manuscripts by providing information about individual journals such as preferred topics, requirements for submission, and details of the review process. Most recently published guides focus on relatively specific subject areas such as social work, religion, and history, but a few, including the *Directory of Publishing Opportunities in Journals and Periodicals*, cover all major disciplines. While other reference sources list periodicals by broad subject areas, authors' guides, through their selection of journals and keyword indexes, provide a means for identifying journals likely to publish manuscripts which discuss very specific or specialized topics.

One of the more comprehensive authors' guides is the *Directory of Publishing Sources: The Researcher's Guide to Journals in Engineering and Technology*, by Sarojini Balachandran. Balachandran's entry for *Computers and Operations Research* illustrates the type of information typically found in such guides. Initial paragraphs cover scope and content (' . . . original papers in the area of ecology, transportation, safety . . . '), type of acceptable contributions (' . . . original papers . . . occasionally tutorial and state-of-the-art papers . . . '), and manuscript submissions procedure (margins, numbers of copies, etc.). Next come several paragraphs which discuss the journal's style regarding title, author's name, abstract, references, illustrations, tables, mathematical equations, computer programs, and abbreviations. A miscellaneous section describes handling of original manuscripts after publication. (Some entries include in this section details on page charges, reprints, and copyright.) Finally, a 'survey results' section indicates number of referees (two or three), review period (eight weeks), availability of referees' comments (yes), publication lag time (five months), acceptance rate (50 per cent), and proportion of invited manuscripts (15 per cent). Not all authors' guides include this much information.

The particular titles in the following list are included because they contain information likely to be of use to scholars beyond that provided in standard sources such as *Magazines for Libraries*. The ISBN and LC numbers as well as price are included for works listed in the 1983–4 *Books in Print*. The guides are arranged by the broad subject categories of behavioural and social sciences, business, education, humanities, multisubject, and sciences. Those books not personally examined are marked with an asterisk.

Behavioural and Social Sciences

MENDELSOHN, HENRY N. *An Author's Guide to Social Work Journals*. Silver Spring, Md.: National Association of Social Workers, 1983. ISBN 0-87101-121-2 $3.95

Entries for 62 journals include editorial focus, submission details such as style requirement, review time, acceptance rate, and publication lag time.

Political and Social Science Journals: a Handbook for Writers and Reviewers. Clio Guides to Publishing Opportunities, no. 2. Santa Barbara, Calif: ABC—CLIO, 1983. LC 82-18455 Library binding ISBN 0-87436-026-9 $24.85; paper ISBN 0-87436-037-4 $12.85

Covers editorial focus, submission details such as letters of enquiry, style, and preferred length, referee process, and review policies; includes review period and acceptance rate for some of more than 440 journal entries. Also includes essays with advice on article writing and publishing, legal aspects of authorship, and book reviewing. A broad subject index helps in the matching process.

Business

CABELL, DAVID W. E., ed. *Directory of Publishing Opportunities in Business, Administration and Economics.* 2nd ed. Beaumont, Texas: Cabell Publishing Company, 1981.

Entries for more than 250 journals include details on review process, acceptance rate, time required for manuscript review, number of reviewers, availability of reviewer comments, charge for review (if any), and proportion of invited articles. Also gives information on readers, editorial address for submissions, and publication guidelines. Many entries include a copy of manuscript guidelines, editorial policy, and objectives. Broad subject index helps in identifying titles of interest.

*FRIEDMAN, JACK P. *Author's Guide to Real Estate Publications.* College Station, Texas: Texas Real Estate Center, Texas A & M University, 1979.

Entries for 40 real estate journals and newsletters include information intended to help the potential contributor decide where to submit a manuscript and to aid contributors and editors by describing desired manuscript formats.

*VARGO, RICHARD J. *The Author's Guide to Accounting and Financial Reporting Publications.* Revised ed. New York: Harper & Row, 1981.

Lists some 120 journals published by academic and professional societies, universities, state CPA societies, and others, with information intended to help authors wanting to submit manuscripts for publication.

Education

*MANERA, ELIZABETH S. and ROBERT E. WRIGHT. *Annotated Writer's Guide to Professional Education Journals.* Scottsdale, Ariz.: Bobets, 1982. ISBN 0-9609782-0-8 $9.95

Information on 162 English-language journals in the fields of education and educational psychology contains descriptions of the readership of each. Entries also include the editorial address, manuscript requirements such as style and number of copies, preferred topics and length, details of the evaluation process such as the time required for acknowledgement and review, and the publication lag time. Also included are several essays which discuss pointers for the prospective author, guidelines for reporting educational research, and article publishing practices of journals.

STEVENS, NORMAN D. and NORA B. STEVENS, eds. *Author's Guide to Journals in Library & Information Science.* Author's Guide to Journals Series. New York: Haworth Press, 1982. LC 80–20964 ISBN 0–917724–13–5 $19.95

Lists standard bibliographic details, audience, preferred topics, manuscript submission information such as style, number of copies, and preferred length, review process and time, availability of reviewer comments, acceptance rate, publication lag time, and more for some 140 journals. Also includes an essay on writing for publication and association-keyword-subject index.

WOODS, WILLIAM F., ed. *A Directory of Publishing Opportunities for Teachers of Writing.* Charlottesville, Va.: Community Collaborators, 1979. LC 79–54036 ISBN 0–930388–04–6 $3.50

Gives submission details, preferred subject matter and treatment, and readership characteristics for roughly 140 journals. Entries do not include information on review period, acceptance rate, or publication lag time. Entries are grouped by broad subject area; geographic and subject indexes provide access.

Humanities

GENTZ, WILLIAM H. and ELAINE WRIGHT COLVIN. *The Religious Writers Marketplace.* Philadelphia: Running Press, 1980. LC 80–20534 Cloth ISBN 0–89471–132–6 $14.95; Library binding ISBN 0–89471–106–7 $19.80

Includes information on target audience, publisher's purpose and theological identification, kinds of materials sought, and submission mechanics such as average article length, desirability of enquiring before submitting a manuscript, review period, publication lag time, payment practice, special instructions, etc. for more than 600 Christian and 60 Jewish periodicals, some scholarly, some popular. Lists similar details for more than 200 religious book publishers in North America. Also discusses several other religious writing opportunities such as diocesan papers, greeting cards, and films.

MACKESY, EILEEN M. and KAREN MATEYAK, comps. MLA *Directory of Periodicals: a Guide to Journals and Series in Languages and Literatures.* New York: Modern Language Association of America, 1981. ISBN 0–87352–423–3 $75.00

Typical entries include bibliographic details, editorial description such as scope and languages accepted, submission requirements regarding style, length, and number of copies, and manuscript processing information such as review period, publication lag time, number of reviewers, and disposition of rejected submissions for more than 3000 journals and series. Includes detailed subject index.

STEINER, DALE R. *Historical Journals: a Handbook for Writers and Reviewers.* Clio Guides to Publishing Opportunities, no. 1. Santa Barbara, Calif.: ABC-CLIO, 1981. LC 80–26215 Cloth ISBN 0–87436–312–8 $28.50; Paper ISBN 0–87436–337–3 $13.85

Entries typically discuss subject focus, manuscript submission details including query policy, referee process, review period, and acceptance rate for more than 350 North American journals. Many entries explain how to become a reviewer for the particular journal. A broad subject index aids matching of manuscript and journal.

Multi-Subject

Directory of Publishing Opportunities in Journals & Periodicals. 5th ed. Chicago: Marquis Academic Media, 1981. LC 81–80807 ISBN 0–8379–2303–4 $52.50

The latest edition of this comprehensive guide gives information such as audience, submission requirements, and review process details for around 3900 journals arranged by broad subject categories.

Sciences

ARDELL, DONALD B. and JOHN Y. JAMES, eds. *Author's Guide to Journals in the Health Field.* Author's Guide to Journals Series. New York: Haworth Press, 1980. LC 80–13403 ISBN 0–917724–09–7 $19.95

Presents for 261 non-clinical journals information such as editorial addresses for submissions, preferred article types and content, submission requirements such as style and number of copies, review period and acceptance rate, page charges, and publication lag time. The introduction includes an essay on getting published, containing several comments from editors to authors. Also includes subject-title-keyword index.

BALACHANDRAN, SAROJINI. *Directory of Publishing Sources: The Researcher's Guide to Journals in Engineering and Technology.* New York: Wiley-Interscience, 1982. LC 82–2758 ISBN 0–471–09200–2 $30.50

Lists publisher, desired scope and content, manuscript submission procedure, style guide (relatively detailed, not just name of guide), number of referees, review period, availability of referees' comments, evaluation time, acceptance rate, and percentage of invited manuscripts for 224 journals. Includes keyword index.

MILLER, RICHARD K. *Directory of Technical Magazines and Directories.* Atlanta: Fairmont Press, 1982. Text ISBN 0–915586–33–9 $45.00

Entries for 149 magazines cover publishers' addresses, audience, subject mat-

ter, and payment policy. Also includes information for marketers such as the cost of a full-page advertisement and availability of the subscriber list.

NATIONAL CANCER INSTITUTE. *A Compilation of Journal Instructions to Authors.* Publication 80-1991. [Bethesda, Md.]: US Department of Health, Education and Welfare, Public Health Service, National Institutes of Health, National Cancer Institute, 1979.
Reprints detailed instructions to authors from 219 health science journals.

WARNER, STEVEN D. and KATHRYN D. SCHWEER. *Author's Guide to Journals in Nursing & Related Fields.* Author's Guide to Journals Series. New York: Haworth Press, 1982. ISBN 0-917724-11-9 $24.95
Gives submission details such as address, preferred topics and manuscript length, and number of copies for more than 350 'journals most pertinent to the nursing profession.' Entries also list style requirements, review period and procedure, acceptance rate, publication lag time, and more. A subject-title-keyword index aids in the matching process.

Information for Contributors

The Editors of Science

Papers published in *Science* often receive far more attention than papers published in specialty journals. As a consequence, the rate of submission of papers is high—about 5000 manuscripts are submitted each year. The rejection rate of about 80 percent contrasts with that of most specialty journals, which is usually about 30 percent. Most of the material submitted to *Science* is of good quality and worthy of publication, and virtually all the scientific papers are eventually published somewhere. In selecting papers for *Science,* the editors consider the needs of a broad audience. Preference is given to items that seem to be of general significance.

General Information

Five types of signed papers are considered: Articles, Research Articles, Reports, Letters, and Technical Comments. The author's membership in the AAAS is not a factor in selection. Material that has been published before is ineligible for publication. Papers are considered with the understanding that they have not been published and are not under consideration elsewhere. Authors will usually be notified of acceptance, rejection, or need for revision in 6 to 8 weeks (Research Articles and Reports) or 8 to 10 weeks (Articles).

Outside reviews. Most articles and reports are sent to two or more outside referees for evaluation. Some papers are returned promptly to the authors without an external review if they are unlikely to be chosen for publication. Referees are selected from *Science* files as well as from lists provided by authors. Papers that depend on statistical inference for their conclusions may be sent to statisticians (in addition to other referees) for review.

Length limits. Papers that exceed the length limits cannot be handled expeditiously and will usually be returned without review.

1) Articles: Up to 5000 words (approximately five printed pages in *Science*), including the references and notes *and* the figure and table legends. The illustrations (figures and tables) when printed in *Science* should together occupy no more than one page.
2) Research Articles: From 2000 to 4000 words (3 to 3½ printed pages in *Science*) including the references and notes *and* the figure and table legends. Illustrations (figures and tables) may together occupy up to one printed page.
3) Reports: Up to 2000 words (approximately 1½ printed pages in *Science*), including the references and notes *and* the figure and table legends. The illustrations (figures and tables) when printed in *Science* should occupy no more than half a page.
4) Letters: Up to 250 words.
5) Technical Comments: Up to 500 words, including references and notes.

Selection of Manuscripts

1) Articles: About half the Articles published in *Science* are solicited by the editor. Both solicited and unsolicited Articles undergo outside and in-house review. Articles are expected to (i) provide a review of new developments in one field that will be of interest to readers in other fields, (ii) describe a current research problem or a technique of interdisciplinary significance, or (iii) present a study of some aspect of the history, logic, philosophy, or administration of science or a discussion of science and public affairs. Readers should be able to learn from a technical Article what has been firmly established and what are significant unresolved questions; speculation should be kept to a minimum. Preference is given to Articles that are well written, well organized, and within the length limit. Balance of subject matter in *Science* is an important consideration when a choice is made between acceptable Articles.

2) Research Articles: These articles, selected for publication on the basis of outside and in-house reviews, are expected to contain new data and to represent substantial contributions in their fields.

3) Reports: Reports are selected on the basis of reviewers' comments and an in-house review. Reports are expected to contain solid research results or reliable theoretical calculations. Preference is given to those that describe departures or discoveries that will be of broad interdisciplinary interest or of unusual interest to the specialist. In making the final selection, the editors take into consideration (i) the reviewers' comments; reports most likely to be accepted are those that receive persuasive outside reviews favoring publication; (ii) clarity of presentation within the prescribed length limit; and (iii) subject matter in relation to that of other papers on hand. An attempt is made to balance the subjects of Reports so that one discipline is not overrepresented to the exclusion of others.

4) Letters: Letters are selected for their pertinence to material published in *Science* or because they discuss significant problems of interest to most scientists. Letters of a highly technical nature are usually transferred to the Technical Comments section. Letters pertaining to material published in *Science* may correct errors, provide support or agreement, offer different points of view, clarify, or add information. Outside reviewers may be consulted on questions of accuracy. Insinuations and conjecture about another author's motives, abilities, or intelligence are considered inappropriate for publication. The selection of letters is intended to reflect the range of opinions received.

5) Technical Comments: Technical Comments may be selected for publication if they express significant criticisms of papers published in *Science* or offer useful additional information. The authors of the original paper are usually asked for an opinion of the comments and are given an opportunity to reply if the comments are accepted for publication. Discussions of minor issues or priority claims are not deemed appropriate, nor are questions that can be resolved by correspondence between the critic and the original authors.

6) Book Reviews: The selection of books to be reviewed and of reviewers is made by the editors.

Submission of Manuscripts

Submit an original and two duplicates of each manuscript, together with a letter of transmittal giving:

1) the name(s) and telephone number(s) of the author(s);
2) the title of the paper and a statement of its main point;
3) the names, addresses, telephone numbers, and the fields of interest of four to six persons in North America but outside your institution who are qualified to referee your paper;

4) the names of colleagues who have reviewed your paper;

5) the total number of words included in your manuscript; and

6) a statement that the material has not been published and is not under consideration for publication elsewhere.

Manuscript Preparation

Typing. Use double-spacing throughout the text, tables, figure legends, and references and notes.

Units of measure. Use metric units. If measurements were made in English units, give metric equivalents.

Symbols and abbreviations. Define all symbols, abbreviations, and acronyms.

References and notes. Number references and notes in the order in which they are cited in the text. Place references cited only in tables or figure legends after the text references. Gather all acknowledgments into a single, brief statement at the end. Use *Bibliographic Guide for Editors & Authors* (American Chemical Society, Washington, D.C.) for abbreviations of journal titles. For journals not listed there provide the full title. Use the following forms:

For a journal paper: H. Smith, *Am. J. Physiol.* **98**, 279 (1931).

For a book: F. Dachille and R. Roy, *Modern Very High Pressure Techniques* (Butterworth, London, 1961), pp. 163–180.

For a paper in a compilation: F. Dachille and R. Roy, in *Reactivity of Solids*, J. H. de Boer, Ed. (Elsevier, Amsterdam, 1960), pp. 502–516.

For unpublished material: A. Giraud, paper presented at the American Nuclear Society Conference, Washington, D.C., November 1976.

Illustrations. For each illustration submit three copies of a quality suitable for reproduction. Label each on the back with the name of the author and the figure number. Plan figures for the smallest printed size consistent with clarity. Color may be used if necessary but authors are expected to pay the full cost of reprints. Cite all illustrations in the text and provide a brief legend for each.

Tables. Type each table on a separate sheet, give it a number and title, and cite it by number in the text. Give each column a heading. Indicate units of measure in parentheses in the heading for each column and do not change the unit of measure within a column.

Equations and formulas. Use quadruple spacing around equations and formulas that are to be set off from the text. Define all symbols.

Special Requirements and Procedures

1) Articles: Provide a title of one or two lines of not more than 26 characters and spaces each; a brief author note giving your position and address; and a summary of 50 to 100 words. The summary should convey to the general reader the main point of the paper and outline the

results or conclusions. The introduction should portray the broad significance of the work, and the whole text should be intelligible to scientists in different disciplines. Explain all technical terms likely to be known in only one field. Insert short subheadings at appropriate places in the text to mark your main ideas. Provide a reference list in accord with *Science* style. Reference lists should not be exhaustive; citation of a single review article can often replace many references. A maximum of 40 references is suggested.

2) Research Articles: Provide a title of one or two lines of not more than 54 characters and spaces each and an abstract of about 100 words. The abstract should portray for the general reader the results described and their significance. The whole text should be intelligible to readers in more than one discipline. Provide a brief outline of the main point of your paper in a short introductory section, then describe your experiments and the results, and conclude with a discussion. Subheadings may be used to indicate the different sections of the paper. Provide a reference list in accordance with *Science* style. A maximum of 30 references is suggested.

3) Reports: Provide a title of one or two lines of not more than 54 characters and spaces each and an abstract of 50 to 75 words. The abstract and the first portion of the report should portray for the general reader the results described and their significance. The body of the report should be intelligible to scientists in other fields of expertise. Complete documentation need not be presented but should be available in cited references.

4) Letters: Letters should be short (up to 250 words) and to the point; they should be carefully phrased, free of technical jargon, and nonrepetitive. When a Letter refers to an article published in *Science* the original author is usually given an opportunity to reply. Letters are frequently shortened and edited. Letters are acknowledged by postcard; authors are notified if their letters are accepted for publication. Letters must be typed with double-spacing.

5) Technical Comments: Technical Comments on Reports or Articles are published at the end of the Reports section. When a Technical Comment is accepted for publication the authors of the original paper are usually given an opportunity to reply.

6) Book Reviews: Instructions accompany review copies when they are sent to reviewers.

Printing and Publication

Editing. Before being sent to the printers, papers are edited to improve accuracy and effectiveness of communication. When changes are needed because the author's meaning is not clear, the editor may consult the author by telephone; when the editing is extensive, the manuscript may be returned to the author for approval or further adjustment before the type is set.

Proofs. One set of galley proofs is provided for each paper. Alterations should be kept to a minimum and marked only on the proofs. Extensive alterations may delay publication.

Scheduling. Papers are not scheduled for publication until *Science* has received corrected galley proofs from the authors. The median delay between acceptance of papers and mailing of galley proofs to authors is 4 to 8 weeks (allowing for editing and typesetting); the median delay between receipt of authors' galley proofs by *Science* and publication is 4 to 6 weeks (allowing for proofreading, layout, and paging). There may be additional delays in publication for papers with tables or figures that present problems in layout and for papers accompanied by cover pictures.

Reprints. An order blank for reprints accompanies proofs.

Cover Photographs

Particularly good photographs that pertain to a paper being submitted will be considered for use on the cover. Submit prints (*not* slides, negatives, or transparencies) together with the manuscript, and indicate in the letter of transmittal that a possible cover picture is enclosed.

6

Book Reviewing

Charlie has thought over Bill's advice on breaking into print. As a new and young assistant professor, he recognizes some possible opportunities for him in book reviewing. He has some further questions about book reviewing. What is a good review? What types of book reviews are published? What cautions does Bill have for the book reviewer?

Charlie. Here I am again. Maybe I will do some book reviews after all.

Bill. That makes good sense, Charlie. Anyone worthy of the ancient and honorable word "scholar" should as a matter of course be reading the best of the newest books published in the field. Why not capitalize on such reading by writing reviews? Even if your reviews are not published, the very act of writing should be helpful to you. Reviewing helps you to remember the content of a book more readily, for people remember best the things to which they react. It forces you to appraise the quality of the book. Your written review becomes a handy reference to which you can turn for teaching purposes. You have nothing to lose by writing down your impressions and much to gain.

Charlie. I'm optimistic, Bill. I'm confident that some of my reviews will be published.

Bill. Then your additional gains include sharing your thoughts about new books with fellow scholars. You have an opportunity to call attention to the best and to steer readers away from the worst. You become better known to the profession and to magazine and journal editors; your published reviews may lead to requests for more reviews or for an article on topics you have discussed in your critique.

Charlie. What makes a book review good?

Bill. There is no formula. The fields of academia are wide, professional publications are numerous, and reviews and reviewers are diverse. One of the reasons we read reviews with anticipation is that we never really know what's coming. I do have some preferences and predilections, though.

Charlie. Such as?

Bill. I want to know what the book is about.

Charlie. Can't we take for granted that the reviewer will tell you?

Bill. Unfortunately, no. Some reviewers write so pretentiously and obscurely that after reading their reviews I can't describe the book. I used to think that the failure was mine; now I ascribe it to bad communication by the reviewer. Some reviewers are so eager to advance their own opinions that they don't bother to tell their readers about the content of the book. However, in the tradition of Hamlet's qualifications in his advice to the players, I must warn you against a pedestrian recital of the content of each chapter, ''In Chapter 1, author Kallikak says . . . in Chapter 15, the author contends . . . ''

Regardless of the length of the review, make sure to summarize as fairly and objectively as possible what you think the author has attempted to say. The task of the reviewer of professional books is to give readers enough useful information about a book so they can decide whether they want to read it, to recommend it to their colleagues, and to assign it to their students, if they teach.

Charlie. You mention length. Like all other types of writing, reviews vary widely in length?

Bill. Yes. Some scholarly journals carry long critical essays on selected books or on several related books. These are judicial reviews, scholarly critiques written by an authority for a limited group of scholars. However, most professional magazines confine a review to a single column or a single page concerning a single book. Such reviews are usually addressed to wider audiences than specialists alone. Study the most recent half-dozen issues of the magazine that will be the target for your book review.

Charlie. Any other things you appreciate in a review?

Bill. I certainly want to know something of the background of the author, what earlier books he or she wrote, or, if that list is too long, at least the kind of writing the author has done. This is part of the information a reviewer owes me.

Charlie. And?

Bill. Personally, I like to encounter the views of reviewers. I want more than bland reportage. To me, review means re-view, viewing the author's views from the reviewer's perspective. I want discussion, opinion, appraisals, comparisons, evaluations. I am willing to hear some applause and some boos. Give me the salt and savor of both the author and the reviewer, their commitments and ways of looking at the subject. I agree with Orville Prescott, a veteran daily reviewer of books for *The New York Times*, who said that all criticisms consist of only two things: information and highly personal opinion.

However, there is another school of thought about reviewing. Some scholars want reviews that are completely reportorial, as objective and neutral and descriptive as humanly possible. State the facts and supply us with the information, they urge, and we as readers will provide our own assessments. We don't need to encounter the prejudices and biases of reviewers.

I must admit that when I read reviews that unduly parade a reviewer's personality before my eyes while withholding from me information about the book and the author, I develop a sneaking sympathy for advocates of dispassionate descriptive reporting. But in general I prefer a review that combines objectivity and subjectivity and that supplies both descriptions and impressions.

Charlie. The decision as to whether to supply information or opinion or both is mine to make as a book reviewer?

Bill. You had better not send a review bursting with opinions to a journal that prides itself on objective impersonal reviews. Such a review might be better received by an editor who runs subjective and impressionistic appraisals. Take comfort, though; most professional periodicals use both types or a combination of each. There may even be editors who have never recognized the differences between reporting and opining.

Charlie. Any approaches I should avoid?

Bill. Some reviews seem to be written to impress readers with the color, brightness, and all-around classiness of the reviewer. Throughout, the reviewer's superiority is demonstrated at the expense of the supposedly dull pedestrian author. Such reviews, often permeated with quips and sallies, are usually negative. They are exhibitions of skillful swordsmanship or of strength in wielding the bludgeon rather than honest opinions of an author's contribution. The reviewer discovers a chink in the armor and skewers the author on some matter on which the reviewer believes himself or herself the world's greatest authority.

Criticism to such reviewers means "give them hell," though the usual literary definition of criticism is "the art, skill, or profession of making discriminating judgments and evaluations, especially of literary or other artistic works; a review or other article expressing such judgment and evaluation." New reviewers especially adopt the colloquial definition "a passing of unfavorable judgment; censure; disapproval."

Charlie. I gather that authors are often not madly in love with reviewers?

Bill. Publishing is full of ancient wars. The struggle between the critics and the authors is one of the oldest. Samuel Johnson had critics in mind when he wrote, "There is a certain race of men that either imagine it their duty, or make it their amusement, to hinder the reception of every work of learning or genius, who stand as sentinels in the avenues of fame, and value themselves upon giving Ignorance and Envy the first notice of a prey."

Charlie. On the other hand, some reviewers repay authors for past favors or friendship or tutelage?

Bill. True. Meanwhile, others carry on vendettas and revenge themselves for past real and fancied slights. In the Bible, Job voiced the credo of the vengeful reviewer: "My desire is . . . that mine adversary had written a book."

Charlie. Do I hear you calling, like the old Greeks, for nothing in excess?

Bill. I suppose so. What I would really like to leave with you, though, is the thought that the greatest vice in reviewing of professional books is not exhibitionism or toadyism or vitriol poured on the hapless author's head. The most prevalent vice in professional writing, including reviews, is blandness and dullness. Shun these like the proverbial plague.

Charlie. Any practical tips for me when I actually write a review?

Bill. Underline passages in the book as you read. Scrawl in the margin. Jot down notes, including related page numbers. As you read along, get involved in what the author says, yet keep some section of your mind detached. Before you write your review, take time to think over the message of the book and the angle from which you intend to approach your commentary.

Charlie. I think I will try my hand at book reviewing.

Bill. A reviewer should bring along head and heart too. When a reviewer undertakes a published review, the individual is assuming a serious responsibility to others. Any book, whether good or bad, brilliant or dull, represents an investment of at least a year of the author's working life, and probably more. It also represents a substantial financial investment by the publisher. It is not too much to ask the reviewer, in turn, to invest sufficient hours in reading the book thoroughly, not just skimming it or trying out speed reading ability. The reviewer for a professional publication is not up against the journalist's daily deadline; such a professional is writing on a relatively flexible schedule.

The reviewer has an obligation to readers, too. Most readers of the review will never get around to reading the book itself. Sometimes the review is the only estimate of that particular book—and of the author— that a reader will ever encounter. Some readers may intend to read the book; the review may determine whether they do. The reviewer has an obligation to call to their attention books that are worth their while and worth their time investment. Sometimes the book reviewer can happily introduce them to an author who deserves recognition, or to ideas whose time has come. Sometimes the critic can warn well-informed readers that they will find little that they do not already know. Meanwhile, the reviewer has the opportunity through reviews to foster ideas that could lead to a better profession. The reviewer has a chance to demonstrate competence and scholarship, sensitivity to truth, and mastery of the language.

All in all, book reviewing is a serious responsibility, not something to be done with the left hand, reserving the right hand for the reviewer's "own work." The reviewer's "own work" may eventually be embodied in a book. When that happens, the reviewer too will yearn to have it reviewed by a fair, well-informed, and responsible reviewer.

Charlie. Any lighter closing note to reduce my anxiety?

Bill. The elegant poet Edna St. Vincent Millay once wrote inelegantly in a letter, "A person who publishes a book willfully appears before the populace with his pants down. . . . If it is a good book nothing can hurt him. If it is a bad book, nothing can help him." If she's right, your review will not make or break a book. But never believe authors who say that they do not read reviews of their books. They read them avidly, though sometimes secretly, and their memories are longer than that of the elephant. Consequently, never write a scathing review of a book written by your dean.

And a final anxiety-reducer—professional periodicals are eager for reviews. The door is open.

LETTER ON BOOK REVIEW PROCEDURES OF MODERN FICTION STUDIES

From an editor to the author of this book, who had inquired about book review procedures.

Dear Professor Van Til:
    A characteristic letter of invitation to review some books for <u>Modern Fiction Studies</u> would run as follows:
    Dear Professor_____:
        Could I persuade you to undertake, omnibus fashion, a review for <u>MFS</u> of five books on Faulkner? We would have space for from 2000 to 2500 words and would not need the manuscript until October 1, for our Winter 1979-1980 issue.
        The books are (author and title).
        We are unable to pay reviewers, but we would of course send you the books, two copies of the journal, and a gathering of offprints.
        If you could undertake this assignment for us, I would be much pleased. Could I please hear from you soon?

                        Cordially,

                              Wm. T. Stafford, Editor
        This is basically what I send out about eighty percent of the time. To be sure when the reviewer is someone I personally know, I am likely to vary it somewhat (ask about his wife and kids, for example, if I happen to know them) or make some other personal comment if it is appropriate for the individual concerned.
        A characteristic response is usually simply a polite yes or no, sometimes with explanation, sometimes not. When we mail the reviewer the books, we enclose the attached two forms, one a copyright release form, the other a book review style sheet. We give no other instructions.
        When a review is received, an editorial assistant usually sends the following acknowledgment: Dear Professor _____:
Just a note to acknowledge receipt of your review for <u>MFS</u>. Everything appears to be in order, but should any questions arise, Professor Stafford (or Church, my co-editor) will get in touch with you. In any case, you should receive galley proofs within the next few weeks. Please, therefore, keep us informed of any change of address.
        Nine times out of ten, no other correspondence follows, except for an instruction form about how to read galley proofs when they are returned to authors.
        In about one case out of ten, I have to return reviews to authors because of excessive length. In that case, I usually return manuscript to the author with a copy of my original letter, simply asking that it be reduced to the originally specified length. Occasionally I cut it myself, then return it to him or her for his or her approval. I almost never make any other kind of revision--other, of course, than stylistic changes, almost always minor.
        Once in a blue, blue moon a potential impropriety pops up. If I happen to catch it, I usually query the author about a possible change. There is almost always an agreement.
        Perhaps the only other correspondence that occurs regarding reviews is from an occasional irate author who thinks his book has been reviewed unfairly or in some way inadequately.

If that happens, our standing policy is to send a copy of the complaining letter to the reviewer, inviting him to respond or not as he likes in our correspondence column, alongside the original letter of complaint. When copy is available, we run that column in all our general issues for correspondence about anything we publish.

That is usually it. You might note that we give no instructions whatever about how to write reviews. We try to be careful about selecting only reviewers knowledgeable about the subject of the books we send them. But once having done so, we think he or she has the freedom, indeed, the right, to react to those books any way he or she pleases, insisting finally only on scholarly decorum and some sense of taste.

William T. Stafford
Editor
Modern Fiction Studies
Purdue University

BOOK REVIEW PROCEDURES OF EDUCATIONAL STUDIES

Dear Publisher:

The editorial staff would like to consider for review the book(s) listed below. Since it began in 1970, Educational Studies has published more reviews of education books than any other educational journal in the same time period.

Because we do not have a specific budget to purchase books, we request complimentary copies. The books we receive are used strictly for review purposes, not for instructional use. In return for complimentary books, you receive a tearsheet of the review as it appeared in our journal.

Educational Studies now goes to more than 1500 individuals and institutions in thirty-five countries. More than one hundred books and films are reviewed each year by highly qualified professionals.

Advertising rate sheet and specifications are available on request.

Thank you for your prompt attention to this request.

Sincerely,

Editorial Assistant

Author: _____
Title: _____
ISBN No.: _____
Publisher: _____

Dear _____:
    Thank you for expressing an interest in writing reviews/
notices for Educational Studies. If you have not already
sent a vita or résumé, please do so. This helps us assign
books more appropriately.
    We apologize for the impersonal nature of this communica-
tion, but the large volume of correspondence forces us to
use time and laborsaving expedients.
    If you have special talents (e.g., languages or area
study skills), please call these to our attention.

                                        Cordially,

Dear _____:
        Thank you for expressing an interest in reviewing
for Educational Studies.
        We will send you something in our next mail out,
which will occur within the next six weeks.

                                        Sincerely,

                                    Editorial Assistant

Dear <u>Ed Studies</u> People:

☐ Yes, I will write a _____ review/notice of the book(s) you sent by ____.

☐ I will do the requested review/notice, but I need the deadline extended to _____.

☐ My schedule will not permit me to accept this assignment. I am returning the book(s).

☐ The subject matter of this work is outside my area of specialization. I am returning it for someone else to do.

☐ Note that my return address on the other side of this card is different from the address you used.

_____
(signed)

Dear <u>Ed Studies</u> Friend:

    Your review/notice of the book(s) and/or film(s) listed in the lower right-hand corner of this card has arrived. It is scheduled to appear in the Spring/Summer/Fall/Winter issue. You should receive galley proofs about two months before the issue is due. Your prompt checking and return of these will help us.

    Thank you for your assistance in keeping <u>Educational Studies</u> up-to-date in its coverage of current literature.

Cordially,

Editorial Assistant
<u>Educational Studies</u>

Titles:

7

Writing Columns

After talking of book reviewing, Charlie thinks of a type of writing that Bill had not discussed with him or with Mary. What about writing columns? Bill's eagerness to talk about the preparation of columns is apparent.

Charlie. Mary told me about her conversations with you on writing for professional magazines and scholarly journals. But there's one kind of contribution that I occasionally see in periodicals that you didn't mention, Bill.

Bill. What's that, Charlie?

Charlie. Columns.

Bill. Ah, yes!

Charlie. Why do you get that glint in your eye and that obvious relish in your voice?

Bill. Because, Charlie, writing columns for a magazine that speaks to members of one's own profession is the nearest thing to pure pleasure that authors like us can experience. Imagine being able to write whatever you please. Imagine being allowed to choose your genre, whether satiric, pleading, angry, humorous, commendatory, condemnatory, descriptive, analytical, emotional, or whatever. Yet you are guaranteed that what you write will appear in print with regularity. Columnists are free to say what they want to say in the style or manner they prefer to use. They are limited only by their own abilities and the space restrictions. A happy situation! Columnists are the freest of all the writers for professional publications. Of course, like all responsible authors, they should use good taste and observe the laws on copyrights and libel.

Charlie. Sounds good. What do they do with this freedom?

Bill. Columnists can campaign for a neglected idea. They can explore an unexamined concept. They can rejoice or despair about developments. They are free to examine the foibles of their fields. Or they can practice the fifth freedom—freedom to laugh at ourselves.

They can deal with the big topics about which everyone in their profession is concerned. They can also opt for consideration of the small but mighty matters about which no one else has yet written.

Charlie. I wish I didn't always look for serpents in Eden. Bring on the snakes.

Bill. The snakes may be inherent in the form. Brevity, for instance. A column is often literally just that—one column of space in a periodical. Sometimes it is a page, sometimes two, but seldom more. Else the column becomes an article, and that's a different cup of tea. So columnists avoid biting off more than they can chew. They delimit the content of a column.

Yet brevity is a challenge to the literary-oriented people who write columns for their fellow professionals. Brevity necessitates the use of exact words, precise language, and clear communication. The columnist puts together a series of small swift touches to build one central mood or impression or idea. If the column is really effective, it makes an impact on the reader.

Charlie. How does a person break into column writing?

Bill. One way is to write a column for a local newspaper, then send the published columns to the editor of a professional periodical with a persuasive letter. Don't be surprised by rejection; columns are usually prepared by experienced people whose names are well known in the profession.

Sometimes an established columnist uses guest columns. When that happens, sticky problems of coordination may arise because the guest column involves the contributor, the conductor of the column, and the editor. Yet it provides a way of breaking in.

Charlie. What is hardest about column writing?

Bill. Some say the selection of a topic. Of all the possible topics to write about, what should you choose? Though selection of a topic is difficult, I think the hardest thing about column writing is determining your impact, your approach, your angle, and your protagonists.

Charlie. You've lost me.

Bill. Deciding what you are going to write about is only the opening gun in the battle. Now you move into a network of interconnected factors.

What do you really want to say about the topic? What impact do you hope to make on your reader? What do you want the reader to carry away from a reading of the column?

What approach? How can you best make your impact on readers

and convey what you want to communicate? Humor? Or indignation? Or satire? Or rhetoric?

Once you have made a tentative commitment to an approach, you are still not out of the woods. What angle do you select? Autobiographical? The world of the future? An actual incident? An imagined institution? Someone's personal experience? A patently absurd situation? A mass of empirical data?

Then there is the matter of protagonists. Yourself? Some people you have observed? Some characters made of whole cloth? Animals?

Charlie.   Animals?

Bill.   Yes, animals. For a period of years Harold Benjamin, author of the marvelous fable called *The Saber-Tooth Curriculum*, wrote a column, "The Importance of People," for *Educational Leadership*. He used animals so often that editor Robert R. Leeper once jestingly threatened to change the name of the column to "The Importance of Animals."

Writers like to tell the apocryphal story of the budding author who was told by his instructor that three topics were surefire: a great historical character, the medical field, and animals. The young writer promptly titled his first effort *Lincoln's Doctor's Dog*.

Charlie.   This must be the same instructor who told his short story class that action, aristocracy, and sex were an unbeatable combination. So a student began a story with " 'Take your hand off my leg,' snapped the duchess."

Bill.   After choosing your topic, combine four elements: the nature of the impact you want to make, your approach, your angle, and your protagonists. Mix well in the pot called creativity, and you have your columnar dish. Then check and recheck for consistency. Is the impact unmistakable? Have you been faithful throughout to the selected approach or genre? Have you maintained your angle and not been led astray? Do your protagonists conform throughout to whatever principles or courses of action they are assigned by you?

Charlie.   Writing a column is a highly personalized venture, isn't it?

Bill.   It is and it has to be. A column has to carry your distinctive brand. Your editor has to be a mightly tolerant person.

Charlie.   An editor makes no suggestions?

Bill.   Suggestions yes; changes without permission no. I have been lucky in my own column editors: Robert R. Leeper during the years I wrote "The Importance of People" for *Educational Leadership*; Dale Baughman, "One Way of Looking at It" for *Contemporary Education*; Stanley Elam, "One Way of Looking at It" for *Phi Delta Kappan*. Each made suggestions but scrupulously changed lines only with my approval. Each had the right to reject a column if he thought it libelous, slanderous, obscene, or offensive, which, fortunately, none of them ever did. They even allowed me an occasional scoop.

Charlie. Such as?

Bill. Column writers and editors set their deadlines as late as possible to provide maximum timeliness. Elam, of *Kappan,* printed "What to Expect If Your Legislature Orders Literacy Testing" the month before he ran a theme issue on minimum competency testing. He went along with me on my gamble that Jimmy Carter would be elected president in 1976 and set in print "Education and Jimmy Carter" for the November 1976 issue before the election returns were in.

Charlie. You both would have had egg on your faces had Gerald Ford won.

Bill. My face especially. I would have heard from the readers. When I wrote "Alternative Reagans," on what educators might expect from a Reagan administration, Editor Robert W. Cole, Jr., was more cautious; *Kappan* carried my projection after the election of 1980 had been held.

Charlie. Columns do draw responses?

Bill. In my experience, comments made in person to columnists are usually positive. Letters are usually negative. People only bother to write letters when they get mad. Anything related to religion, for instance, brings forth negative letters. But even that is better than the deafening silence that usually follows a professional publication. In my less optimistic moments I think that writing for professional publications is like dropping a rose leaf in the Grand Canyon and waiting for an echo.

Charlie. But some columns bring forth more person-to-person responses and more mail than others? Which of your columns has drawn the greatest volume of responses?

Bill. "The Raccoon Died."

Charlie. An animal story?

Bill. Yes, it was an animal story. But it was more than just that. At least, my readers tell me so.

Charlie. I'm listening.

A COLUMN

The Raccoon Died

My wife and I now live in the country. Events in nature which people have long learned to take for granted are new to us and sometimes troubling. The ways of small animals, for instance.

By William Van Til, from *Contemporary Education,* April 1970, Volume XL, Number 4, pp. 244–45.

One day in December, Smoky came upon something new under a big white pine and barked loudly to tell me. The newcomer was a small gray and black animal which sat immovably on its haunches and stared fixedly at my collie and me despite Smoky's lunges and my own nearness. Both Smoky and I were puzzled that whatever it was didn't dash for the nearby brier-covered slope where it obviously belonged.

I remember now that I immediately suspected that the animal might be injured or sick; I am not sure what Smoky thought but she clearly decided to dance round the newcomer but not harm it. I noticed that nature had supplied the intruder with a small black mask under the eyes similar to that worn by highwaymen in romantic novels. While Smoky danced and grew distantly acquainted, I went into my house to tell Bee about the visitor and to consult my favorite family encyclopedia, *The American Educator*. We made a few poor guesses as to the animal and then hit pay dirt under "raccoon." *The American Educator Encyclopedia* carried a fine full-page picture and said in the text, "On its white, fox-like face are black markings that make the raccoon look like a masked bandit." The animal was a raccoon all right.

We went back to look. The raccoon still sat immovably and stared at us, no matter how close we came. It almost seemed that it needed help of some sort from us. I returned home, got my camera, and took several excellent pictures of Smoky and the raccoon with their noses only inches apart. The sun was going down and it was getting chilly that December afternoon, so we left the raccoon and went home to dinner.

The next day the raccoon had moved. It now sat halfway between the big white pine tree and our house. The visitor walked about a bit but did not disappear down the slope. From my chair in my living room I saw, through my binoculars, Smoky rubbing noses with the raccoon in a friendly way. The weather was getting colder so I didn't venture out save to throw the little animal some scraps.

On the third day, the raccoon came and sat outside the floor-to-ceiling windows which enclose our living room. The animal hardly moved. It just looked at us. That night the raccoon slept with its nose next to the glass sliding door; I guess some heat seeped out from the house into the cold outdoors. We again left a few scraps within the raccoon's reach.

The fourth day the raccoon gave us up and retreated halfway down the sharp slope that ends with the lake. It huddled tightly and it hardly moved. We watched the animal with growing concern.

On the morning of the fifth day it was apparent that the raccoon hadn't moved all night. I scrambled down the hill and looked quite closely. Then I said to Bee, "The raccoon is dead."

I can't get out of my mind the feeling that the raccoon was asking me for help—and in vain. I can't get out of my mind a parallel between the way I behaved and the way we as a nation act when confronted by a social problem, whether it be deteriorating education or the inner city slums or race relations or pollution or whatever. I think I behaved as a nation does.

I looked at the animal, concluded it was in trouble, but expected it to go away. We as a nation look at a social problem, conclude that trouble is involved, but expect the problem to go away.

I looked up the animal in *The American Educator Encyclopedia* and gave the animal a name. The nation makes a massive survey of the problem and gives the matter a name, such as the disadvantaged child or whatever.

I took pictures of the raccoon, and from my warm house I watched it through binoculars. We as a nation take pictures of the social problem and in our warm houses we watch the problem through television.

I threw the racoon some scraps. We as a nation throw the problem some scraps.

I talked a lot about the raccoon. But I didn't do anything really decisive about what might have been its plea for help. We as a nation talk a lot about the social problem. But we don't do anything really decisive about what might be the pleas for help from people involved in the problem.

And, after all, was there really anything which I actually could have done for that raccoon? And, after all, is there really anything we as a nation actually could do about the social problem?

But the raccoon died. All I really know for sure is that the raccoon died.

8

Editing and Writing Yearbooks

Writing chapters for yearbooks of professional organizations
The work of the organization's publications committee
The choice of an editor
The selection of authors
Committee meetings
Distinguishing between planners and authors
The case of the inadequate chapter
When people receive invitations to write

Charlie talks with others on campus about writing, among them Roberta, an associate professor on her way to a full professorship. He learns that Roberta, though well along in writing for professional publication, is troubled by not being sought out by editors with invitations to submit contributions. Roberta is particularly puzzled by her national organization, which as yet has not asked her to write for or edit one of the yearbooks of the organization. Charlie brings the case of Roberta to Bill and particularly inquires about the preparation of yearbooks.

Charlie. Bill, I've been wondering about something. When does a writer for professional publication reach the stage of being invited by editors to write? To contribute to a yearbook, for instance?

Bill. I'm not sure I know what you mean. Expand on that, Charlie.

Charlie. I don't mean a yearbook published by the senior class or a yearbook published by an encyclopedia or medical society containing information about the past year. I was referring to a yearbook that is made up of separate chapters on a current topic and is published annually by a professional organization as a service to its members.

Bill. Now I'm tuned in.

Charlie. Take our friend Roberta as an example. She's an associate professor and has published some creditable articles. For instance, her writing has appeared several times in the major journal in her specialized academic field and she also has published in general magazines in the broad area. Recently, she did an excellent scholarly summary of major studies in her field for a research journal.

She holds a state office in her national professional organization, NAAX. But Roberta still queries editors; they don't turn to her with requests for contributions. As yet, NAAX hasn't invited her to do a chapter for the yearbook. Will she ever be invited? Or is writing for yearbooks a closed shop, the exclusive preserve of an in-group made up of the organization's influentials?

Bill.   Put yourself in the shoes of the leaders of NAAX, Charlie. The organization is committed to publishing annually a magazine, some pamphlets, and a yearbook. A publications committee meets with the organization's director of publications during the annual conference and suggests themes for nine magazine issues to be published next year, five pamphlets to be released in a year or two, and a yearbook to be published three or four years from now.

Charlie.   They plan that far ahead for yearbooks?

Bill.   They have to. The organization has promised its dues-paying membership that a major book on a significant topic will be mailed to members each year. In publishing, there are many slips between cup and lip. Consequently, they start early.

The publications committee, after much discussion and some argumentation, establishes a theme for the future yearbook. Committee members take into account proposals they may have received from committees or individuals within the organization. Then the committee discusses who should be invited to serve in the pivotal role of yearbook editor. Whom do you think the committee members invite?

Charlie.   Not me, obviously. And apparently not Roberta either.

Bill.   They invite whomever they regard as an outstanding scholar on the selected theme. In determining their choice, committee members rely on their own reading and on hearsay. They try to assess the individual's national reputation. They take into account personal characteristics, such as dependability, objectivity, and ability to work with others. Unfortunately, they also sometimes listen to gossip and scuttlebutt about the candidate.

Sometimes the publications committee (or editorial board) names additional yearbook committee members; sometimes they merely suggest possible members; sometimes they leave selection of the yearbook committee completely up to the new editor. They may suggest a few possible authors and a tentative structure. Then, their duty discharged, publications committee members sit back and hope that they will have a book that the membership will appreciate and that outsiders will buy. As the committee's representative, the director of publications of the organization will follow through on schedule, deadlines, and correspondence with the editor.

The person the publications committee has named as editor is invited and usually, despite other commitments, accepts—unless scheduled for a sabbatical in Outer Mongolia. Editing a yearbook of one's professional organization is no small honor. Sometimes the committee must turn to a second choice, very rarely a third. The newly named editor then writes individuals inviting them to serve as the yearbook committee. If individuals have been specified by the publications committee, the editor invites them. If individuals have been simply suggested as possibilities by the publications committee, the editor takes these suggestions into account, but does not necessarily follow them. Incidentally, if the choice has been left up to the editor, whom do you think he or she selects?

Charlie. Colleagues in the university where the editor teaches?

Bill. Not unless the editor is a provincial. The wise editor turns to the best people available on the national scene. Admittedly, an editor may think that "the best" includes some of the editor's former students and those scholars sensible enough to understand and appreciate the editor's earlier writings and contributions.

Charlie. Aha!

Bill. Yearbook editors are mortal men and women, Charlie. Don't fear, though, that the editor will load the committee with minor leaguers; the editor, with reputation on the line, wants to produce the best possible book. As a matter of fact, out of caution, an editor is more likely to select veterans than untried authors.

So the newly appointed yearbook committee meets for a long weekend of planning at organization headquarters or some central location relatively convenient to yearbook committee personnel. The members hammer out agreements on an outline of chapters, the nature of the possible content, and writers to be invited. Some of the writing will be done by yearbook committee members; other chapters will be assigned to authorities who are not members of the committee. Again, choices are made on the basis of a judgment of the individual's past performance—including ability to meet deadlines.

Charlie. Can we always assume that the best yearbook planners will also turn out to be the best writers?

Bill. A perceptive question, Charlie. One eminent yearbook editor who refused to make that very assumption was William Heard Kilpatrick, a great teacher of philosophy of education. In my salad days, I served as his right-hand man as he developed *Intercultural Attitudes in the Making,* a yearbook of the John Dewey Society for the Study of Education and Culture. Kilpatrick brought together people whom he regarded as the best thinkers in the nation on building racial, religious, and ethnic group understandings and combating prejudice. He made it clear that this planning committee was temporary. Its responsibility was to build an outline, suggest possible authors (including some already on the committee), and then go out of existence. The planning committee was succeeded by a permanent committee, a group made up of specialists in the field of intercultural education who also were skilled writers. These authors were to write within the framework established by the planning committee.

The dual approach worked. *Intercultural Attitudes in the Making* was both a critical success and one of the best-selling yearbooks in the John Dewey Society series published by Harper.

More professional organizations should use a dual approach similar to this one. Most organizations, however, keep the initial planning committee in existence throughout the entire period of preparation of the yearbook. Most lean heavily on the planning committee for written contributions to the yearbook. They haven't learned what Kilpatrick knew, that our best planners are not always our best writers.

Charlie.   Do the yearbook writers meet while the manuscript is in preparation?

Bill.   Usually not. Organizations often allocate funds sufficient for only one or two meetings of the planning committee. However, the planning committee may meet with writers of the yearbook at the national convention of the organization.

Charlie.   This puts a great deal of responsibility for shaping and editing the yearbook into the hands of the yearbook editor, doesn't it? What happens if a yearbook writer submits an inadequate chapter, to put the matter delicately?

Bill.   That's embarrassing, particularly for the yearbook editor and committee members who have asked the writer to do the chapter in question. After all, this isn't an unsolicited manuscript that an editor can reject with impersonal regrets. Remember also that no one involved in the preparation of a yearbook receives any financial remuneration. Consequently, the editor (and sometimes the director of publications who supervises production of the yearbook) works with the author. The editor may suggest major changes, edit, and sometimes rewrite. Once in a long while, a chapter must be rejected and a new author assigned to the material.

Charlie.   That's one reason yearbooks I have read sometimes seem to me spotty, some chapters excellent, others weaker.

Bill.   Right you are. It takes a forceful editor to shape a cohesive and well-integrated yearbook. The best contributors are often mavericks. One definition of a professor is "a person who thinks differently."

One problem bedeviling organizations that produce yearbooks is the swift pace of change in society and in the field that the organization represents. This is the age of the knowledge explosion. The time lapse from selection of theme and writers to the appearance of the yearbook may result in an irrelevant or obsolete publication. Desperate yearbook editors have been known to try to rewrite some of the contents in the galley or even page proof stages.

Charlie. I assume that the contributors read galleys and page proofs to check accuracy and make sure that their ideas and phrasings aren't overedited by the yearbook editor or the copyeditors who work with the director of publications?

Bill. Contributors almost always read galleys and sometimes page proofs too.

Charlie. Let's return to our friend Roberta. When might we expect that she will be invited by NAAX to contribute to the organization's yearbook?

Bill. From your description of her work, possibly quite soon. Meanwhile, Roberta will have to keep on doing significant work and keep on writing about it and keep on submitting manuscripts. She might also prepare a yearbook proposal for the consideration of the publications committee of NAAX. It might be good strategy for her to add the influentials in the organization to the list of people to whom she sends reprints of her articles. The people who develop yearbooks should eventually think of her as a possible contributor.

I realize this doesn't seem fair to you—or to Roberta. However, the people who plan yearbooks can only act on what they know and whom they know. As I have indicated, they are likely to turn to the experienced and proven pros for a yearbook. Yet they are acutely conscious that there is gold in them thar hills which hasn't yet been discovered.

Charlie. One additional factor. Some of the prospectors may be sexist in orientation.

Bill. It's possible. Yet I have observed that the decision-makers rarely operate as a closed conspiratorial cabal, though I can understand that you and Roberta suspect that they do. When the decision-makers come to know Roberta, primarily from her writing, and when her specialty happens to be chosen as a yearbook subject, they may invite her to write for a yearbook. Later they may ask her to edit one.

If Roberta does edit a yearbook, she should be aware of the time investment involved. It may be the book of year X to its readers, but for its editor the development of a yearbook stretches over several years.

Figure 8-1 *Chronology of the Development of a Yearbook of a Professional Organization*

Year One	February	Exploratory letter from a member of the Board of Directors of the National Society for the Study of Education and representing the Board, to 23 secondary education specialists requesting reactions to two possible approaches to preparation of a yearbook on secondary education and asking about willingness to serve on a planning committee and/or to be considered as potential contributors if invited.
	March	Progress report on the proposed secondary education yearbook to the Board of Directors.
	Spring	Selection by Board of six persons to prepare preliminary outline and discuss possible authors.
	July	Letter from Board, inviting six potential committee members to meet in Washington, D.C., travel expenses paid.
	August	Preliminary discussion of possible yearbook by six invited specialists and a representative of the Board of Directors in Washington, D.C.
	Late Summer	Appointment by Board of chairman, and two committee members. Additional appointment of committee members by chairman. Chairman prepares drafts outlining structure and suggesting possible authors.
	Late Fall	Meeting of yearbook committee members, expenses paid. Consideration and revision of third draft by chairman on possible issues and yearbook structure. Suggestion of possible authors.
Year Two	Spring	Letters of invitation to authors of yearbook chapters.
	May	Achievement of full complement of contributors to yearbook. Five-page letter to yearbook writers reminding them of deadline, length of contribution, and sharing suggestions from individual writers and responses to individual writers by the chairman. The letter was intended to contribute toward the integration of the individual chapters.
	Late Fall	Receipt of chapters from yearbook writers.
Year Three	January–May	Editing of chapters by chairman, revision by authors, substantial correspondence with authors.
	Spring	Copyediting by National Society for the Study of Education editorial staff.
	Fall	Galleys to chairman, to authors, and to NSSE editorial staff. Correspondence concerning galleys.
	Late Fall	Page proofs handled by NSSE staff.
Year Four	Winter	Xeroxed copies available to chairman, yearbook committee, and authors for presentations at National Association of Secondary School Principals, February; American Association of School Administrators, February; and Association for Supervision and Curriculum Development, March.
	March	Copies of yearbook available to contributors.
	April	Yearbook distributed to members of NSSE.

9

Developing Anthologies

Is anthology editing easy?
Changes in demand
The importance of ideas and structure
Getting permissions for anthology inclusions
Costs of permissions
Who holds the copyrights
Compensation to anthology authors
Who pays the permission fees

Charlie has talked with a colleague who told him of an easy road to fame and fortune as a writer for professional publication. Writing an anthology is a cinch, his colleague assures him. Bill thinks otherwise. Among other aspects of preparing a book of readings, the complexities of obtaining permissions complicate the anthologist's life.

Charlie.   I have a colleague who used to have scruples; however, he lost them somewhere. My unscrupulous friend says that editing an anthology is the easiest way into print. All a person needs, he says, is a photocopy machine and a pocket full of dimes. Then the royalties roll in.

Bill.   Nickels, not dimes. Advances in technology have reduced the price of reproducing a page to a nickel. Come to think of it, that's about the only thing the nickel can buy. I remember when a nickel could get you—

Charlie.   Don't change the subject. How about the contention of my disreputable colleague concerning putting together a book of readings? Isn't there some truth in my cynical friend's view of the making of an anthology?

Bill.   Very little. Opportunists have sometimes sent publishing houses a sheaf of miscellaneous articles and book excerpts topped by a tricky title and a page modestly bearing the anthology editor's name. The sheaf testifies to diligent reproduction but has no structure or organization, no background on contributors, no introductions or commentary by the supposed anthology editor. Few such shoddy assemblages find their way into print. Developing an anthology just isn't that easy.

Another dodge is inexpensively assembling minor publications by little-known staff members from the immediate locality, gracing the miscellany with two or three pieces by celebrated professors with nationally recognized names, and selling the whole to an editor on the basis of inclusion of the celebrities. Editors and publishing houses are wary of that approach too.

Charlie. Are commercial houses eager to publish anthologies?

Bill. The aspiring anthologist had better recognize the existence of fashions in ideas in publishing as in the production of TV programs and movies. In the turbulent 1960s, the market for books of readings flourished. Professors and students wanted variety, immediacy, timeliness. Relevance was a key concept. In the more conservative social climate of the 1970s, some publishers were burned by a declining demand for anthologies. Stuck with remainders, publishers grew cautious. Hardback textbooks for the course made a comeback; paperback anthologies experienced a decline. How about the 1980s? Ask me in 1990.

Some of the market for anthologies has been taken over by do-it-yourself collections. Through them, professors who teach large classes, or who control the selection of the required book in several sections of a large-enrollment course, assemble books of readings primarily for use in the professor's own university. A publisher prints the book; the local bookstore stocks it; the students enrolled are required to buy the collection. Critics term this a captive audience approach. Defenders prefer to describe such selections as tailor-made and say the students are no more captive than they are in other courses that require purchase of a textbook.

Charlie. What's the first requisite in developing a good book of readings?

Bill. That the anthologist have a significant central idea (or ideas). Through wide reading, the potential anthologist must be fully conversant with a specialized field. He or she must then develop a significant, provocative, and innovative way of grouping relevant writing in this field. One anthologist may identify the major controversies in the area and decide to present pro and con entries on each controversy. Another anthology editor may take positions on carefully selected issues and choose contributors who successfully document and defend the positions. In each case, the important thing is to arrive at a readable, teachable, and creative way of looking at the field. Chronological? Topical? A good deal of the anthologist's battle is won when a good structure or organization is established.

Decisions must be made as to the anthology editor's own contribution to the volume. Introductory essays opening each section? If so, largely about the field or the controversial issues or the contributors?

Short biographies of each contributor as headnotes prefacing each selection or footnoting each entry? Inclusion of already published writing
by the anthologist?

Following arousal of a publisher's interest through the customary
query and prospectus come long hours of reading in the library. Reproduction by a copying machine of the proposed entries for the book is
actually anticlimactic, not central.

Tell your unscrupulous friend that it takes a formidable amount of
editorial time to organize material to be included in a book of readings.
It also takes substantial time to reconcile methods of documentation used
by the varied authors. The reader anticipates variety of styles in an anthology yet usually appreciates consistency as to footnotes, placement
of bibliographies, and the like. And during the necessary drudgery of
copyediting for accuracy, clarity, and consistency, what does the anthologist do about errors not caught by the original editor? Readying an
anthology for publication is no cinch for the compiler.

Charlie. Then off goes the manuscript to the publisher, who handles details from then on.

Bill. Details?

Charlie. Such as getting permission from the authors to use their
writings in the anthology.

Bill. Doubly wrong.

Charlie. One wrong is enough. How doubly wrong?

Bill. In the first place, it's the anthologist, not the editor in the
publishing house, who obtains the permissions. In the second place,
the anthologist obtains permission from the copyright holder, and authors frequently cede their rights to periodicals and publishers. Publishing houses usually ask assemblers of books of readings to complete
all permissions correspondence before submitting the final manuscript.
Begin early, they always warn.

Charlie. Let's take these one at a time. You mean that as an anthology editor, I must obtain the permissions unaided. I do this through
corresponding with somebody?

Bill. As the anthology editor, you send the copyright holder a
permission form specifying the exact material you want to use in your
book of readings. Your publisher will send you copies of the form to be
used. One form is to be used in obtaining permission to use already
published material. Another form is for permission to use unpublished
material written expressly for your proposed anthology. Authors hold
copyright on their unpublished work as soon as it is ''set down in tangible form,'' such as a typed page. The copyright holder usually grants
permission, subject to certain specific conditions.

Charlie. Such as?

Bill. The copyright holder will stipulate that you acknowledge
the source of whatever writing you use. Sometimes a particular form of

acknowledgment will be specified. Frequently the owner of the copyright will also require monetary compensation.

Charlie. How much?

Bill. Here's where we get into a Wonderland that pales Alice's. The representatives of one periodical may give you permission to reproduce articles gratis. Representatives of another may specify widely varied sums, as little as twenty-five or as much as several hundred dollars. It all depends on the policies of the particular magazine or journal.

The permissions editor of a publishing company will name an amount that must be paid if you wish to use an excerpt from one of the company's publications. Suppose, for instance, you request from three different companies eight pages from a book each has published. The permissions editor of one company may request one sum, while another asks for a different amount, and a third requires yet a different sum.

Charlie. How do they determine such amounts?

Bill. Each company has its own formula—which ordinary mortals like you and me will never fathom.

There's an additional Wonderland aspect of permissions for a book of readings. Some journals that hold the copyright will require you also to obtain permission from the authors. Some will specify a sum to be paid to authors or allow the authors to name their own sums. Yet some will grant permission without requiring any correspondence with authors.

Publishing houses usually will refer you to authors only if the authors hold the copyright. Otherwise, the publishing house simply grants the permission without referring the matter to the author. Incidentally, the publisher collects whatever fee is involved; the book author usually receives half.

When the author has published the material you request as a magazine article prior to its appearance in book form, the permission process grows even more complex. On one occasion, not having noticed that the author held the copyright, I wrote to the editor of a magazine for permission to reproduce an article. The editor referred me to the author. The author referred me to his agent. Since the article had been incorporated in a book by the author, the agent referred me to the permissions editor of the book company that had copyrighted the book. The permissions editor was uncertain as to whether she could legitimately grant me permission to reproduce the content of the article since it differed in phrasing and emphasis from the inclusion in the book. However, the article seemed to me more readable than the inclusion in the book. So I gave up. The author did not appear in my anthology.

Charlie. An anthologist apparently writes many letters.

Bill. You find yourself writing for permissions to the copyright holders, who, to get to the second part of your doubly wrong comment, are frequently the magazines and the publishing companies. You also sometimes find yourself writing to authors, either because they own the rights or because the periodical or publisher holding the copyright requires you to write the authors. Fortunately, you don't have to correspond with the governmental bureaucrats, for government publications are in the public domain unless partly underwritten by nongovernmental groups.

Charlie. Can authors who have transferred to others the copyright on their published writings ask for some compensation for use of the materials they wrote?

Bill. They do, some through innocence of copyright regulations and some through weariness at constantly granting permission to profit-making projects for reproduction of articles originally written without compensation to the author. Legally they may not have a clear case. But your hypothetical unscrupulous colleague would have to be mighty brash to use their material without their permission and without paying the requested compensation in a volume on which he anticipates royalties. People do talk.

Most authors, however, will be happy to appear in your anthology without financial compensation. Remember that many have a message that they are eager to get across. They want to be heard. Their tangible financial rewards come primarily by way of recognition, rank, promotion, and tenure. New authors are especially eager to be represented in anthologies. Even the well-established writers are usually happy to appear. They too want to communicate widely. Also, if they didn't appear, what might people think? That their work was no longer significant? That they were over the hill?

By the way, it is good manners to inform all authors with whom you haven't already corresponded that their work is scheduled to appear in your anthology and that you deeply appreciate their contributions. Once in a long while an author may possibly respond to your courtesy letter with an anguished protest, perhaps because of a change of view on a theory or contention. The author may not want to be represented in the anthology by the selection you have chosen. One more problem for you.

Charlie. Then after all permissions are granted, the publisher of the anthology compensates the copyright holder. . . .

Bill. It is true that about the publication date your publisher sends out checks for all permissions granted. But the publishing house is mailing out *your* money.

Charlie. My money? Not the publisher's?

Bill. Usually you pay for the permissions, not the publisher. In the contract for a book of readings, the publisher usually agrees to advance a sum toward payment of permissions costs, which may be $2,500, or whatever you agree to in your negotiations. The actual amount advanced is deducted from your first royalty check or, when necessary, checks. The word "advance" is a polite term for money you owe, money that is to be subtracted from your royalities.

Charlie. If any.

Bill. Better tell your disreputable colleague that developing an anthology is not really as easy as it seems. I know of only one universal law: "Things are more complicated than most people think."

Take the permission forms, for instance. They are not particularly complex. But as any anthologist or house editor can tell you, the process of completing all permissions through these innocent-looking forms is beset by snarls, delays, and anxiety before the anthology is published.

PERMISSION FORM FOR PUBLISHED MATERIAL

Leading Educational Publishers since 1868

Allyn and Bacon, Inc.
7 Wells Avenue, Newton, MA 02159
617/964-5530

Dear Sir or Madam:

In my book on _____ designed for use
as a hardcover (paperback) textbook priced at approximately $_____, and
scheduled for publication by Allyn and Bacon, Inc., in _____, I would
like to include the following material:

May I have your permission to include this material in my forthcoming book and
in all future editions and revisions thereof, covering nonexclusive world rights
in all languages? These rights will in no way restrict republication of your
material in any other form by you or by others authorized by you. Should you not
control these rights in their entirety, would you tell me who does?

A release form is provided below and a copy of this letter is enclosed for your
files. Your prompt consideration of this request will be appreciated.

Sincerely,

****

CREDIT LINE TO BE USED:

I grant the permission requested on the terms stated in this letter.

DATE _____   BY _____

                                      _____

                                      _____

PERMISSION FORM FOR UNPUBLISHED MATERIAL

Grantor has written original material consisting of approximately _____ words, on the subject of _____.

   Grantor hereby assigns and transfers said material to
grantee, without limitation or restriction, as the sole and
exclusive property of grantee and with the exclusive right
to copyright it in the grantee's name or any other name in
all countries and in all languages.

   Grantor guarantees that he (she) is the sole owner of
said material and that he (she) has full power and authority
to copyright and to make this agreement; that said material
does not infringe any copyright, violate any property rights,
or contain any libelous or unlawful matter; and that he (she)
will defend, indemnify and hold harmless the grantee against
all claims in connection with said material.

_____   _____
Grantor (and title of post)   Date

_____   _____
Grantee   Date

10

Writing Textbooks

Getting acquainted with your editor
Decision-making by the publishing company
Deliberating on a contract
Suggestions by editors and outside reviewers
The time textbook writing takes
Differences between a completed draft and a final manuscript
Hypothetical schedule of writing and publishing
Desirable dates of publication
Participation of authors in the editorial process

Several weeks later Charlie appears with Jane, an associate professor who is being considered for a full professorship. Her many published articles on psychology have been well received. She has decided that the time has come to explore the possibility of writing a textbook. Her initial overtures to a new company expanding its lists have been well received. Now she wants to know what is involved in the development of a textbook. Bill traces the steps and acquaints her with the long road ahead.

Charlie. I figured that if Mary could bring Abe with her, you wouldn't mind if I brought Jane to our conference. Jane's field is psychology, as you are well aware.

Bill. Welcome to both of you. What's the topic this time, Charlie?

Charlie. Writing textbooks.

Jane. Charlie told me about your suggestions on approaches to book publishers—the query and the prospectus. I tried them, Bill, and they seem to be working. The prospectus for my proposed textbook is now out to readers, and an editor wants to talk to me about my textbook proposal during the coming APA convention. So I want to know more about what I might be getting into.

Bill. You're moving into the pleasantest step in the development of a textbook. At the convention, the College Department editor will invite you to one of the best restaurants in town, along with any other company representatives in attendance at APA. Since your hosts are on expense account, you need pay no attention to the prices on the menu. I suggest the filet mignon or the lobster.

Jane. That would be a nice change. What's the function of this meeting? What are we supposed to talk about?

Bill. Small talk. Everybody is charming. However, on the company side of the table an attempt is being made to appraise you as a potential co-worker in what usually becomes a long and difficult struggle, the writing and production of a textbook. I suggest that, on your side of the table, you too try to find out what kind of co-workers the company representatives will be. Consequently, a mutual sizing up of personalities will probably occur.

Ask the kinds of questions that give you insights into the editor's ways of working. If he or she proves to be highly formal or rigid and your lifestyle happens to be highly informal and open—or vice versa—this doesn't augur well for a long-time working relationship. Test through your questions. In the process, acquire general information about the company, such as its experiences with recent publications, the size of its sales staff, anticipated sales of its textbooks in several fields, frequency and likelihood of revisions, promotional and advertising approaches, and similar shop information. Talk about other psychology textbooks, what's good and bad about them, who reads them, what is the nature and scope of the market, and so on. At this early stage, you can't get hard and fast commitments as to your own proposed textbook, so don't try.

It's quite possible that at the postprandial stage of this lovely evening—do you prefer brandy or cordials?—the editor will show his or her hand. If the reviews of your prospectus are in and are favorable, and if an editorial meeting has given the green light to the project, there may be mention of a contract and even some superficial discussion of its nature. Or the editor may tell you that you will be getting a follow-up letter soon.

Jane. What happens in this latter case?

Bill. For some days or weeks, nothing will seem to you to be happening. What is actually happening is that, in intervals between work on other books, the editor may be looking over readers' reports on your prospectus, talking to colleagues, reviewing the market situation, considering possible agreements to reach with you, and discussing your manuscript in editorial meetings. The company is contemplating its collective navel.

Charlie. This I'd like to see.

Bill. Meanwhile, if you are so fortunate as to have more than one company considering the possibility of publishing your textbook, you are free to follow up on any interest shown by other publishers. It will do you no harm at all to tell the original company that you are talking to other publishers. An alternative offer may develop that you might prefer.

If not, some day the editor with whom you dined will send you a contract accompanied by complimentary optimistic remarks, a "consensus" of reviewers' suggestions, and the editor's specifications as to major revisions in the overall plan and the sample chapters. Or, on the other hand, the editor will explain that unanticipated changes and circumstances have caused the company to regretfully decline the proposal.

Charlie. Take the contract and run, Jane.

Bill. Don't. Proceed instead with deliberation and caution. Unfortunately, the inexperienced textbook writer often does scan the contract hastily, sign it, and joyfully send it back to the publisher in the next mail. Then repentance takes place at leisure.

Read the contract carefully. Seek the advice of colleagues who have written textbooks. If relations are good and opportunities available, some potential textbook writers talk to their former advisers in the doctoral program or to their present department chairpersons. Some authors even consult a lawyer.

Then write the editor about questions raised in your mind by the contract or the editor's letter accompanying the contract or left over from the conference. Don't be overly impressed by the legal form and florid verbiage of the contract. Codicils may be added and provisions deleted if both parties agree. Ask for any needed information or clarification and straighten out any potential misunderstandings. Editors and authors have an interdependent relationship.

Jane. Assume that I'm offered a contract and, after thinking about it, decide to sign. What then?

Bill. The honeymoon stage continues for a while.

Jane. When do the author and the editor settle down to married life?

Bill. When you receive your first post-contract letter from the editor. A characteristic letter may enclose copies of the outside reviewers' reports to the editor, with "suggestions" and the editor's "endorsement" of the "suggestions." You may learn of "suggestions" from in-house readers and some things that the editor classifies as "important." You may learn of specific timetables and deadlines (which always seem earlier than you had anticipated). The editor may have questions on which the company needs immediate answers. You may legitimately wonder why these matters were not discussed before the contract was signed—some companies do discuss "agreements" prior to issuing contracts, and some include reviewers' and editor's comments in the letter that accompanies the contract.

If you get a post-contract letter containing unanticipated suggestions and criticisms, you may feel somewhat the way doctoral candidates do when, after months of cooperative work on the thesis with advisers, they encounter their advisers' vigorous and probing questions during oral examinations; you may be surprised by a role change. On the other hand, you may not hear from your editor, save for an occasional cordial note, while you are writing a substantial segment of your manuscript—in which case, Jane, you may feel somewhat neglected.

Jane. What if some of the suggestions are contrary to my assumptions and some of the deadlines unrealistic?

Bill. Better bite the bullet right away and negotiate on these matters. If you don't, they will persist and will reappear. Conflicting views have the nasty habit of not going away.

Jane. What's an illustration of possible problems?

Bill. In section 1, you may have proposed to discuss three schools of psychological thought. One of your reviewers suggests that there are four schools. Or your editor proposes to send the first half of your manuscript to outside readers by a specific date, though you prefer to defer outside reading until your entire manuscript is completed.

Think it over before you respond. Maybe there *are* four schools. Maybe you *would* write a stronger second half if outside readers criticized the first half. If, after reconsideration, you still hold to three psychological schools or having outside reviewers react to the manuscript as a whole, inform the editor of your views. Then be ready to negotiate. Meanwhile, begin to devote as much time as you can to the actual writing of the manuscript.

Jane. How long?

Bill. Who really knows? Perhaps a year. Seldom less, unless you have a remarkably light teaching load. Perhaps two years, including trying out first drafts on your students. Seldom more, because publishers regard more than three years of preparation of a college textbook manuscript as comparable to infinity. Comfort yourself that a textbook manuscript for elementary or secondary school students usually takes even more time to prepare because the editorial staff often participates in the actual writing and because drafts are sometimes field tested.

If your textbook is soundly based on detailed lecture notes you have already used in your teaching, you will be off to a fast start. You will find that those carefully prepared five-by-eight-inch cards are a blessing. Anyway, late some summer or early some fall, you'll find yourself proofreading the last typed chapters—

Jane. Why late summer or early fall? Why not some other season?

Bill. Because of two schedules, your own and the publisher's. For most academicians, summer is a time when they are free of teaching classes and thus have the opportunity to complete manuscripts. For the publishing house, receipt in September of the best complete preliminary draft an author can do ties into a publication date fifteen months later.

Jane. Fifteen months! Incredible! What happened to that generalization I've heard that the publication cycle of a book is comparable to the birth cycle of a baby, a period of nine months from manuscript to publication date?

Bill. The gestation analogy doesn't take into account that the best complete preliminary draft by an author differs from a final manuscript that is fully acceptable to the publisher. Let's trace your own hypothetical textbook. Assume you mail your manuscript to the publisher in September. The editor presumably reads it; and so do some subordinates in the office. The editor invites outside readers to appraise it; they accept; a photocopy is sent to each; they read, appraise, write reviews, and mail the manuscript back to the editor. The editor sends you the anonymous reviews, along with suggestions for change that the editor thinks are particularly important. By this time it's at least November.

You finish your revision during Christmas vacation (though you hoped to get to it earlier); and let's say you mail it off on New Year's Day. Again the editor may send it to outside readers. Reading of your final manuscript again takes time. Let's hope the reviewers and the in-house staff find it acceptable. Unlike a trade book, a college textbook must appeal to students and teachers, satisfy the expectations of the author and publisher, and take into account the possibility of some reaction from the public. By now it's February.

If it is acceptable, this is the point of no return for the textbook publisher. On every transoceanic flight, the pilot reaches somewhere along the route the point of no return; now the pilot can go only forward—or down. This also applies to publishing. Up to the time the manuscript reaches delegation to the copyeditor and the beginning of the production process, the company investment has been largely confined to salaries of the editor's office and modest fees to reviewers, plus overhead. Now there will come a substantial investment through varied publishing personnel such as the copyediting staff, the art department, the design editor, the production staff, the manufacturing buyer, the compositors, and, eventually, the printer and allied cohorts.

In a large company, by February/March your accepted manuscript is turned over to a supervisor of copyediting or book production editor, who becomes your regular correspondent in place of the original acquisitions editor. In turn, the supervisor or production editor assigns your manuscript to a copyeditor, who may be regularly employed in the company's offices or who may be a freelancer. Before you receive any proofs, the copyeditor will raise many questions with you. If all goes well, almost one year after your frantic Christmas season revision, your book is in print. It bears as its copyright date the coming new year. From February/March to November/December approximates nine months, the birth cycle of the baby.

The schedule I have described assumes that all will go well. Actually trouble will break out somewhere. A commonly accepted definition of deadline in the publishing industry is "the date from which postponements begin." For instance, your godfatherly editor might be promoted into inaccessibility in the publishing house or might find a better-paid post with another company. *Publishers Weekly,* sampling publishing employees in 1980, found that they averaged 3.2 years with a publishing house. Sometimes a publishing company may merge or come under new ownership with attendant unanticipated delays in editing or production of an author's book.

Jane. Why November/December publication?

Bill. From the point of view of the textbook company, publication late in one year gives book salespeople the winter and spring to persuade professors to adopt your book for their coming summer and fall classes. Fliers can be prepared and distributed; endorsements can be obtained; advertisements, if any, can appear. Winter is the season when professors make their estimates as to the number of copies needed for the summer term. Spring is the season for their estimates for the higher-enrollment fall term. The college bookstores place their orders, and the books are shipped to the stores during the spring and summer.

Jane. Meanwhile?

Bill. Your participation during this year of production depends upon your prior agreements. Some publishing agreements provide the author with an opportunity to read the edited manuscript before it is sent to composition. Authors often read the galleys; sometimes the provision is written into the contract. Some read page proofs too. A conscientious author tries to take part in the act at all stages.

Jane. Let me see if I follow these time sequences. Call this the Year One. I'm soon be holding my conference at APA with the editor. If all goes well, I will write my psychology textbook during the rest of Year One and most of Year Two. Well along in Year Two, I'll submit my best completed draft. At the end of Year Two, I'll complete the presumably final manuscript. The book is edited and produced and published during Year Three. It is promoted and adopted and distributed in Year Four and used in classes during the summer and autumn of Year Four. Let's see, since today's date is—

Charlie. In Year Five, you will receive your first royalty check.

Bill. And, if your book is successful, about Year Seven or Eight your revision of the textbook will be published.

Jane. That sounds like from here to eternity.

Bill. And to think that it began with some kind of query and a carefully developed prospectus! Bear in mind that my time estimates may be optimistic.

Jane. Optimistic?

Bill. Listen to this comment from *Books: The Culture and Commerce of Publishing:*

. . . . We should remind ourselves how the traditional textbook is written. Typically, an acquisitions editor reviews current market figures, consults with college travelers, draws on personal experience, and comes to the conclusion that the firm can successfully market a new introductory book in, say, psychology. The editor already has a potential author in mind, a professor at a midwestern school with large introductory classes, someone who writes well, is known to be a good teacher, and who, for a variety of reasons, needs some money. But that professor, it often turns out, does not want to write the book and recommends someone else instead. Finally, after a year's search, the editor signs a contract with a professor who more or less matches the description of the original candidate. The academic gets an advance of perhaps twenty thousand dollars, half paid immediately, half on delivery of the manuscript. That manuscript, however, is slow in coming. Although the professor has hired a secretary and a graduate assistant or two, various other academic obligations delay completion of the book, which is delivered to the publisher only after five years. The original editor has meanwhile moved on to another company, the new editor wants a somewhat different slant, and the academic reviewers to whom the manuscript is sent put in their criticisms, all adding up to more delay. Eventually the book is published, but by this time the market for psychology texts may have changed dramatically. The process is slow, tortuous, and uncertain.[1]

[1]Lewis W. Coser, Charles Kadushin, Walter W. Powell, *Books: The Culture and Commerce of Publishing* (New York: Basic Books, 1982), p. 271.

GUIDELINES FOR DEVELOPING A PROSPECTUS AND TABLE OF CONTENTS

 Allyn and Bacon, Inc.

Guidelines for Developing a Prospectus and Table of Contents

A prospectus is an invaluable tool that has a two-fold purpose. It gives you a chance to "sell" your book to us, and it clarifies the book for reviewers. A prospectus is of equal importance if the book is at the idea stage, or if sample chapters are being submitted.

I. PROJECT

   A. Brief Description
      In one or two paragraphs, describe the project, your rationale for writing it, approach, and biases (if any) towards the topic.

   B. Outstanding Features
      List briefly what you consider to be the outstanding, distinctive, or innovative features of the book.

   C. Apparatus
      Will the book include examples, cases, activities, strategies, teaching suggestions, glossaries, bibliographies, appendices, chapter summaries, questions, answer books, problem sets, student guide, instructor's manual, etc.?

II. MARKET CONSIDERATIONS

   A. Primary Markets
     1. COLLEGE: In which college courses will this book be applicable? Are these introductory, undergraduate, or graduate courses? Would it be used as a basic text and/or a supplement?

     2. PROFESSIONAL REFERENCE: Is the book suitable for purchase or personal reference? Who would purchase it — teachers, administrators, nurses, engineers, etc.? Where are they likely to be located — schools, businesses, hospitals, etc.?

   B. Secondary Markets
      Library, trade, foreign, etc.

III. COMPETITION

   A. Consider any existing books in this field and discuss their strengths and weaknesses. (If possible, supply title, author, publisher, date of publication, and number of pages.) How will your book be similar to, as well as different from, competing texts?

B. Please discuss each competing book in a separate paragraph so that we will have some basis on which to compare your material. If no competitive book exists, try to cite a book which comes closest to your own.

IV. STATUS OF THE WORK

A. What is your timetable for completing the book? What portion has been completed? When will sample chapters be available for review?

B. What do you estimate to be the size of the completed book? (Double-spaced, typewritten pages normally reduce by approximately one-third when set in type. For example, 450 typewritten pages equal approximately 300 printed pages.)

C. Will the book contain any photographs, line drawings, charts, graphs, diagrams, etc.? If so, approximately how many of each?

D. Has your material been previously class tested, either in your own course or in other sections, courses, schools, etc.?

V. VITA

Include a copy of your most recent vita or resume, listing degrees and previous publications (if any).

VI. TABLE OF CONTENTS

Include a detailed table of contents in outline form, incorporating headings and sub-headings. If possible, include a brief annotation or description of each chapter.

EXAMPLE: CHAPTER I: LOCATION SKILLS
    A. Library Skills
        1. Card Catalogues
        2. Reference Books
        3. Resource Materials

VII. SAMPLE MATERIAL

If you have begun writing, send two or three (or more) chapters for review. The chapters should be representative of the book but not necessarily sequential.

VIII. COVER LETTER

Include where it is most convenient to reach you by both telephone and mail.

IX. MAIL TO:

_____, Editor
Allyn and Bacon, Inc.
7 Wells Avenue
Newton, MA 02159
(617) 964-5530

11

Writing Trade Books

Nonfiction trade books on professional subjects
Writers of trade books on professional topics
Scholars as popularizers
What the general reader purchases
What trade editors prefer
The influence of scholars who write trade books

Charlie, alone this time, drops in on Bill toward the end of the semester. Charlie is feeling good. Two of his book reviews have been accepted, an article is being read by referees, and another article is on the drawing board. Feeling his oats, he wonders about writing books other than textbooks for members of the professions. Though he suspects he might be going beyond his depth, he inquires cautiously about writing trade books on professional subjects.

Charlie. Maybe I should throw my hat into the doorway before I come in.

Bill. Why?

Charlie. Because I'm not professionally ready to do the kind of writing I want to know more about.

Bill. I'm forewarned. Go ahead, Charlie.

Charlie. I look at books with handsome jackets in a bookstore downtown or in a shopping center, or I read advertisements in newspapers by publishers or by book clubs, or I read the book reviews in newsweeklies or journals of opinion or the Sunday edition of *The New York Times.* Suddenly I encounter—and soon I find myself reading—an important brand-new book on a professional subject. It's obviously not a textbook; there are no bibliographies or suggested activities or questions for students attached like a bustle to the rump of the chapters. The style is more informal and readable than typical academese.

Bill. That's a trade book, Charlie, a book published for distribution to the general public primarily through bookstores or clubs, as distinguished from a textbook or a specialized book or a reference work.

Charlie. I know that. But these trade books are professional publications that deal with professional topics.

Bill. Many nonfiction trade books are on professional subjects. Trade books are often of great interest and importance to professionals, whether in medical science, biology, business, chemistry, English, engineering, music, psychology, history, mathematics, or whatever. Books for the general public are often used in classes along with or sometimes in place of textbooks. They are distributed through booksellers in the customary retail outlets. Sometimes they are also sold through college bookstores, where they are stocked as required books for a course or displayed on racks of paperbacks.

Charlie. Who writes these trade books on professional subjects?

Bill. A great variety of authors. Some are freelance writers who earn their living through books and articles. Some authors of trade books of importance to a profession are editors, journalists, media specialists, or people in other occupations who combine their regular employment with writing.

Many authors of trade books are practicing professionals who write in their own professional fields or in related fields for both general readers and specialists. I once jotted down this list and I regularly add to it after reading reviews of new trade books. A sampling of well-known professionals who have written widely read trade books might well include: in anthropology, Margaret Mead and Loren Eiseley; in astronomy, Carl Sagan; in architecture, Lewis Mumford and R. Buckminster Fuller; in art, Kenneth Clark; in biology, Barry Commoner; in communications, Marshall McLuhan; in education, John Holt and Jonathan Kozol; in bacteriology, Paul de Kruif and Hans Zinsser; in history, Arthur Meier Schlesinger, Jr., and Henry Steele Commager; in literary criticism, Edmund Wilson; in medicine, Hans Selye and Howard Rusk; in music, Deems Taylor; in philosophy, Will Durant; in religion, Pierre Teilhard de Chardin and Jacques Maritain; in psychology, B. F. Skinner and Jerome Bruner; in sociology, James M. Coleman, Daniel Bell, and Herbert J. Gans; in economics, Robert L. Heilbroner and John Kenneth Galbraith; in population biology and ecology, Paul and Anne Ehrlich; in food resources, Lester R. Brown; in human sexuality, William Masters and Virginia E. Johnson; in English literature, Paul Fussell; in psychiatry, Elisabeth Kübler-Ross.

Charlie. I recognize many of the names. Would I be right in thinking that, while most of these people are well regarded by their fellow professionals, the list contains some who are not particularly beloved by their colleagues in the discipline? Possibly even a few who are not respected?

Bill. Right you are. As an instrument salesman said in *The Music Man*, "It comes with the territory." If the territory one maps out is wide rather than a small corner of the terrain, if the author takes positions on controversial issues that are disputed within the territory, if the author dares to address the general public, and if the writer commits the venal academic sin of writing books that sell—then the scholar is suspect in the eyes of many colleagues within the discipline. Such a scholar is called a popularizer—always pronounced by academicians with a snarl.

Charlie. Specialists also get edgy about popularizers who write in fields that aren't their native habitat.

Bill. Many of those I mentioned have done just that: anthropologist Loren Eiseley on the universe and universals; astronomer Carl Sagan on evolution of intelligence; psychologist Jerome Bruner on school curriculum; biologist Barry Commoner on power as well as the environment; and R. Buckminster Fuller and Lewis Mumford in their roles as social philosophers on an unclassifiable range of subjects. Probing minds often reach beyond the narrow boundaries of disciplines. This makes some specialists uneasy; still others regard it as unforgivable.

So far we have talked only about luminaries, however controversial. A great many professionals who write trade books aren't as well known as the academic celebrities we've been mentioning. Think of the number of English professors who have published biographies and critical appraisals of major authors—so many that some are now reduced to writing about minor literary figures, living or dead. Or think of the number of historical works being published. Think of the volume of self-help books dealing with health or psychology. Or the various social problems that sociologists, political scientists, economists, and other social scientists explore. In some subject fields, the trade books far outnumber the textbooks.

Charlie. And the public, as well as the specialists, purchases them. How can anyone tell whether a trade book on a topic important to a profession will be bought by the general reader?

Bill. That's the great imponderable. In the case of the textbook, the modern publisher, with the help of the computer, can estimate the market for a textbook designed for a particular course, even though the publisher can't predict the segment of the pie that will go to a specific textbook. To some degree the publisher can predict the proportion of professionals who will buy a trade book or scholarly book or monograph that deals with their discipline or occupation. But what John Q. Public will purchase lies on the lap of the gods—or on John Q.'s lap.

Charlie. No clues particularly as to trade books on professional subjects?

Bill. A broad one—the situation prevailing in the culture at a particular time. Victor Hugo recognized this when he said, "Greater than the tread of mighty armies is an idea whose time has come." A specialist on solar energy would be unread in the 1960s, yet could be a celebrity in the 1980s.

Charlie. Any other illustration?

Bill. In your own field, Charlie, a spate of trade books critical of traditional education and advocating an education geared to the needs of the learner appeared in the troubled 1960s and 1970s. Their authors— John Holt, Jonathan Kozol, George Dennison, James Herndon, Nat Hentoff, Neil Postman, Charles Weingartner, and others—wrote trade books with such titles as *How Children Fail, The Underachieving School, Death at an Early Age, The Lives of Children, The Way It Spozed to Be, How to Survive in Your Native Land, Our Children Are Dying, Teaching As a Subversive Activity.* The climate of the times was congenial to their ideas. But in the 1980s, in the educational atmosphere of back-to-basics and minimum competency examinations, trade books similar to those of these compassionate critics of our recent stormy past were usually flatly rejected.

Charlie. Any other clues?

Bill. Trade editors prefer books that are characterized by good writing style and by appeal to the general reader. In general, the more scholarly and technical the trade book, the less it is supposed to sell to the general public. But, like many other rules, there are notable exceptions, so many in fact that the generalization can't be trusted. Professionals have many books in their personal libraries that are indispensable for their high scholarship and technical detail, yet that are read by the general reader.

Charlie. At least purchased, if not read.

Bill. If there is an aristocracy among writers on professional subjects, writers of trade books read by both the public and fellow professionals belong to it. I don't mean that their views are aristocratic; in fact, most of those I have mentioned are thoroughgoing democrats. I mean instead that they have a special status among writers on professional topics. They are the professionals whose books are reviewed by leading newsweeklies and newspapers, by *New York Review of Books, Commentary, Harper's,* and *The New Yorker.* Celebrities among them appear on TV talk shows. They write articles, before and after book publication, for general magazines read by the well informed. They are often trend setters and pacemakers in their profession because, paradoxically, they readily address a wider audience than the profession alone. They are comprehended by the literate public. A member of a profession who snobbishly neglects reading them because they write for a broader audience does so at considerable risk of falling behind in knowledge of the professional field and in understanding of where the profession is headed.

Once in a while one of them will discuss writing, as John Kenneth Galbraith did in a delightful and perceptive article in *Atlantic Monthly,* "Writing, Typing and Economics." Galbraith, a distinguished economist and frequent author of trade books, tells of the advice on writing he would have given students had he accepted a chair in teaching rhetoric offered him by the University of California:

The first lesson would have to do with the all-important issue of inspiration. All writers know that on some golden mornings they are touched by the wand—are on intimate terms with poetry and cosmic truth. I have experienced those moments myself. Their lesson is simple: It's a total illusion . . .

The question of revision is closely allied with that of inspiration. There may be inspired writers for whom the first draft is just right. But anyone who is not certifiably a Milton had better assume that the first draft is a very primitive thing . . .

After several other nuggets of good advice, he suggests, with tongue in cheek:

The person who undertakes to make difficult matters clear is infringing on the sovereign right of numerous economists, sociologists, and political scientists to make bad writing the disguise for sloppy, imprecise, or incomplete thought. . . . If any of my California students should come to me from the learned professions, I would counsel them in all their writings to keep the confidence of their colleagues. This they should do by being always complex, always obscure, invariably a trifle vague . . .[1]

[1]John Kenneth Galbraith, "Writing, Typing and Economics," *Atlantic Monthly*, March 1978, pp. 103–5.

The Publishing House

About 66,000 people work for book publishers. Of these 15 percent are editorial workers, 25 percent work in marketing and publicity, and 10 percent work in production. The remaining half of publishing employees are engaged in administration and operations, such as personnel and accounting, which are discussed in other sections.

Compensation in the publishing industry works in eccentric ways. First, job turnover is high. A 1980 survey by *Publishers Weekly* (December 19, 1980) found that a sample of 109 publishing employees stayed an average of 3.2 years with each company they worked for. Of 27 people who had been in the field between 6 and 10 years, only a third had been with the same company all that time; about 45 percent had had three or more employers. Of the people who had been in the field 11 to 15 years, 76 percent had changed employers at least twice. People also tend to leave the industry altogether in large numbers, with the result that the average publishing career is quite short; 77 percent of the *PW* sample had not more than 10 years experience in the field, and the average was about 6.

Second, the raises offered to people who change companies tend to be far greater than those who stay with the same company. Fifty-eight percent of the *PW* sample reported raises of 15 percent or less in 1980, and only 14 percent reported raises of 20 percent or more. "By contrast," *PW* reported, "increases that accompanied a move were frequently substantial and sometimes even spectacular."

Which condition is the cause and which the effect is unclear; but one result is that when inflation is figured in, the salary levels at which people are hired are frequently the levels they remain at for as long as they stay with the same company. Even raises accompanied by promotions are often only marginally better than the inflation rate. The primary way for a publishing employee to advance his salary is to move to another company. . . .

Editorial Department

> *Acquisitions Editors*—Frequently called Senior Editors, their primary responsibilities are deciding what books the company will publish, negotiating with writers and their agents to decide how much they will be paid, and working with writers to ensure that manuscripts are turned in on schedule and in reasonably good condition. Once the manuscript comes in and is accepted, the editor shepherds the book through the various stages of production; he or she also attends sales and publicity meetings to explain why the book deserves more advertising and why the company's salesmen should push it harder to bookstore owners. Responsibility for actual editing—i.e., marking manuscripts with a pencil—varies considerably from editor to editor.
>
> *Assistant and Associate Editors*—Work is similar to that of Senior Editors, except that they usually handle fewer books and less prominent authors, and have less autonomy in deciding what books they will acquire and in negotiating fees. The last two functions are often reviewed closely and sometimes taken over by Senior Editors. In many houses the Assistant or Associate Editor only reads and edits manuscripts that are under contract.
>
> *Editorial Assistants*—Often they are treated as glorified secretaries, and the main evidence of their glorification is that they are paid less than secretaries. However, many times this position does serve the function of an apprenticeship, which was its original intention. In addition to typing letters and contracts, filing, and related tasks, Editorial Assistants are sometimes permitted to

read unsolicited manuscripts and give their recommendation for rejection or acceptance.

Developmental Editor—Often the impetus to produce a book comes not from an individual author but from the publisher, as in the case of many textbooks and reference books. In this case the so-called Developmental Editor takes a much more active role in the writing of the book: He or she will find the writers, explain to them in detail what is required, edit the work closely, and often write some of the material.

Production Editor—Sometimes called a Managing Editor, coordinates activity between editors, designers, copy editors, typesetters, and other people necessary to prepare a manuscript for printing. He or she establishes a production schedule, makes sure it is followed, and often sets and supervises the editorial budget.

Copy Editor—Reads manuscripts for grammatical accuracy, consistency of style, phrasing, word use, and logical consistency. Also usually proofreads galleys, repro, and mechanicals (the final boards from which printing plates are made) to see that the typesetters and paste-up artists have followed the editor's instructions.

Advertising, Sales, and Publicity

Publicity Director—It is the Publicity Director's job to make sure the company's book receives attention in the media. Toward this end he or she sends out copies of newly published books to publications likely to review them, tries to get authors on TV and radio shows, and arranges other engagements for authors, such as autographing sessions in bookstores and lecture tours of colleges.

Publicist—Under the supervision of the Publicity Director, performs essentially the same job, except that he or she may deal with less important authors and books, or may be restricted to a specific aspect of publicity.

Copywriter—Writes material intended to sell books. This includes advertising copy, press releases, and the laudatory plot synopses found on the inside flaps of book jackets and called "flap copy."

Marketing Director—Is in charge of the overall effort to sell published books. On the basis of projected sales, he or she decides how many copies of a book will be printed and how and where they will be distributed, oversees the sales staff, and decides how and where books will be advertised.

Advertising Director—Places advertisements in selected publications, such as book review supplements of newspapers and journals aimed at the book's intended audience, and in the case of best-sellers and other mass-market books, TV and other media. A few publishers still prepare their own advertising rather than rely on agencies, so here the Advertising Director also supervises the writing and design of ads and helps set the advertising budget for each book.

Sales Manager—Supervises the sales staff, makes sure they receive all the necessary materials such as press releases and news of new publications, receives their reports and orders for new books, and generally coordinates their activities with those of the rest of the company.

Salespersons—Spend most of their time on the road, visiting bookstore owners and gently persuading them to buy as many books as possible and to display them as prominently as possible. Then they make follow-up visits to make sure the books and other materials (such as those large cardboard display stands, called "dump bins") have arrived satisfactorily. Salespeople also report back to the main office their customers' comments on the quality of service, what kinds of books they are asking for, and other information. Because of the knowledge they thus acquire of the book market, salesmen are sometimes promoted to editors.

Subsidiary Rights Director—A book's circulation seldom ends with its hardcover sales. It may be sold to a book club, a movie company, or a paperback publisher, parts of it may be reprinted in magazines, or all of the above may happen. The Subsidiary Rights Director, usually in concert with the author's agent, promotes and manages these sales. Over the past decade, as subsidiary rights contracts for top books have climbed into the millions of dollars, "sub-rights" directors have become increasingly important at major publishing houses. They now exercise a strong influence over the acquisition of new books and the advances paid to writers based on the chances of subsequent sub-rights sales.

Subsidiary Rights Assistant—Usually handles a specific area of sub-rights sales, such as magazines, foreign rights, or book clubs.

Production Department

Art Director—Determines what the book will look like. Along with the Acquisitions Editor and Production Director, he or she selects the typeface, book size, paper, jacket design, display type, and other elements of the book's design. The Art Director also procures the necessary illustrations and photographs (sometimes these are supplied by the author) and determines how they will be placed in the book. Finally, he or she supervises illustrators, freelancers, and paste-up artists.

Managing Editor—See Production Editor under "Editorial Department."

Traffic Manager—Large publishing houses with complex production schedules often require a traffic manager to keep track of everything. The Traffic Manager oversees the flow of work between the editorial and art departments, the typesetter, and the printer; sets schedules; and keeps records of what stage of development each project is in. The Traffic Manager's job is similar to the Production Editor's, and indeed the two often work closely together; but the Production Editor's concern is primarily with the needs of the editorial department, while the Traffic Manager coordinates work among all departments.

Production Director—Supervises the work of the production department, sets a budget for the preparation and printing of each book, and negotiates contracts with typesetters, printers, paper manufacturers, and other suppliers.

12

Writing Specialized Books

Undaunted, Charlie inquires about scholarly books, and Bill responds with reflections on the variety of specialized books that professionals write. Learning of the variety of outlets for specialized books, Charlie takes heart. His next major publishing effort may prove to be the writing of a book. Charlie even looks forward to the day when he will no longer be a beginner. He will have arrived. Knowing Charlie, Bill will not at all be surprised.

Charlie. Bill, how about scholarly books—

Bill. I'm willing to use the term "scholarly books" and discuss the category if you'll recognize that trade books, and textbooks, and other professional publications can also be scholarly. No publishing category holds a monopoly on scholarship.

Charlie. Understood. Maybe a better term for the category I'm asking about is "specialized." Some books are neither trade nor text. They are books that are important to professionals but have little or no appeal to the general reader. Yet they are not designed to be used as textbooks in school or college classes.

Bill. All of the descriptive terms are awkward and overlap other categories, including "specialized." For instance, a textbook or a trade book can also be "specialized." Let's use the word, however, and assume that it includes what are variously called "scholarly," "technical," "reference," "monographs," and, sweepingly, "professional" books.

Charlie. Those are the classifications I'd like to hear about. I want to know about the publication of scholarly or technical or professional books that my colleagues and I have on our shelves and/or borrow from the university library. How about monographs that report research? They are of interest to scholars who are working on similar problems, not to the general public. Or reference books we consult for facts or information but don't read in bed?

Bill. Whenever there is a community of specialized readers large enough and book-hungry enough to support possible publications, commercial firms publish books expressly for this community. Among the largest markets are the medical, engineering, business, psychological, scientific, and legal communities. The larger commercial publishers have special divisions to develop scholarly, technical, professional, and reference books. Some companies become noted for their major specializations; for instance, McGraw-Hill for technical and business books and John Wiley for biomedical and health publications. On the other hand, some companies limit the scope of their publishing to the particular profession. Still other companies develop subsidiaries or "spin-offs" that specialize in scholarly, technical, professional, or reference books. In addition, monograph houses specialize in learned treatises that describe scientific advances and serve as research tools for scholars. Since more than 15 percent of employed persons are classified as professional and technical, the market for scholarly and technical books and for monographs and reference books is substantial.

Even relatively small professional communities afford a market for publishers of specialized books. For instance, there aren't nearly as many architects or astronomers or anthropologists as there are practitioners in the medical fields, the law, and psychology—to say nothing of more than two million teachers. Yet architecture, astronomy, and anthropology too have their specialized publications for professionals, as well as the handsomely illustrated trade books that find their ways to the coffee tables of the more affluent members of the general public.

Charlie. University presses provide additional outlets for scholarly books and monographs.

Bill. One of the most open and inviting publication outlets for the specializing scholar is the university press. Blessings on those universities that subsidize scholarly books by professionals for professionals! Good university presses publish books of lasting value and keep these books in stock and available for scholars. University press books are frequently characterized by excellent design, typography, paper stock, and so forth. They are usually well edited for accuracy, consistency, clarity, and English usage. University presses frequently take on works of serious scholarship for the advancement of knowledge, books that a commercial publisher concerned for profit couldn't publish.

Charlie. These widely varied ways of handling specialized works confuse me. Suppose I have written a manuscript on the French Revolution—which I haven't. Where do I send my query or prospectus? To which of the types of publishers?

Bill. That depends on your judgment as to your potential readership. If your book on the French Revolution is for the general reader, you send it to the Trade Books Department or Division of a commercial publisher, large or small. If the Trade Books Department of the publishing house employs a social science or history editor, send it to that individual. But remember that most trade book publishers have to sell between 10,000 and 50,000 copies to break even.

If your book on the French Revolution will be read primarily by college students, send it to the College Department or Division. If the College Department includes a history or social science editor, address that person.

Charlie. If my hypothetical book on the French Revolution stands a good chance of being read by the general public as well as by scholars, would a university press possibly publish it?

Bill. These days that's a real possibility. University presses are taking on more books that are of general interest to readers, in addition to continuing their publication of specialized scholarly works.

Charlie. Suppose my hypothetical book on the French Revolution is intended especially for professors who must read my book in order to be thoroughly knowledgeable historians?

Bill. Try the scholarly publishers in the social sciences. They sometimes publish books that sell 2,000 to 6,000 copies. Try university presses also.

Charlie. Suppose my book on the French Revolution is so specialized that it would be read only by scholars of the French Revolution, not by historians in general?

Bill. Monograph publishers sometimes publish as few as 1,000 copies.

Charlie. Where do I go to find the titles of the various divisions in publishing houses and the names of editors?

Bill. Check with *Literary Market Place,* familiarly referred to as *LMP* and published annually by Bowker, the great reference publisher. Your library undoubtedly has it. *LMP* lists publishers, along with company divisions and names of editors. You may even find a specific listing for history or for the social sciences. Scholars who can't find a specific listing for their disciplines usually send the manuscript to the director of the particular division that seems most relevant to their manuscripts. The director will bump a query or prospectus along to the proper editor.

Charlie. Suppose my book on the French Revolution does get published. How would it be distributed and marketed?

Bill. Trade books are sold in retail bookstores in communities, through advertisements in national media such as book supplements of newspapers, and through calls made on trade bookstores by company salespeople. Textbooks are sold through letters and brochures mailed to professors, displays at conventions, personal calls on professors made by college travelers, and judicious distribution of free copies. Scholarly books, technical publications, and monographs are largely sold by mail, through fliers, convention displays, and journal advertisements directed to specialists and librarians. Reference works are purchased primarily by libraries and also by individuals who need them as tools of their trades.

Charlie. I am selfish enough to be concerned about prestige.

Bill. If the book is good, any of the types of publication we have been talking about can bring prestige to the author. Many academics regard the trade book and the scholarly book and the monograph as more reputable than the textbook. Note the grudging acceptance of textbook writing in *The Publication of Academic Writing*, published by the Modern Language Association: "The textbook maker is unjustly belittled in some quarters, for the creator of a genuinely scholarly textbook or any other good aid to teaching deserves honor in the academic world. An exclusive preoccupation with textbook making, however, does not strengthen a scholarly reputation. The young teacher is well advised to put his first efforts into scholarly writing."[1]

Textbook writing is generally assumed to be more financially profitable. But this is not always the case, for some trade and technical books sell well. Authors of trade books may achieve national reputations; authors of scholarly books, technical books, and monographs are often especially recognized in their profession. Authors of reference works occasionally become as famous as Webster or Bartlett but, I fear, are usually unsung. Remember too that commitment of several years to a major book reduces the likelihood of smaller writing projects.

Charlie. I've been thinking about a possible sequence for my future writing. I plan to begin with book reviews and to write articles for both professional magazines and scholarly journals. Then anthologies? Yearbooks? Columns? Textbooks? Trade books? Scholarly books, technical treatments, monographs, entries for encyclopedias? Which?

Bill. That's one of the best things about being a young professional who wants to write for professional publication within a free country.

Charlie. What?

Bill. Freedom of choice.

---

[1]Oscar Cargill, William Charvat, and Donald D. Walsh, *The Publication of Academic Writing* (New York: Modern Language Association of America, 1966), p. 6.

Charlie. I'm no longer as apprehensive as when I considered throwing my hat in the door. If others can write books and have them published, why not me? How many books are published each year anyway?

Bill. Roughly 47,000 new books and new editions (paperbound and hardbound) each year. An even more important statistic for you, Charlie, is that in these United States of America more than 15,200 publishers named books to be included in a recent *Books in Print*.[2] Unless you propose to write the Great American Novel, your major book publication possibilities as an academician are the textbook, the trade book, the scholarly book, the technical book, and the monograph. Admittedly, writing any book is a gamble. Yet there may be more opportunities for you, Charlie, than you originally thought.

Charlie. So I'll study the directories of book publishers and persistently query?

Bill. Let's hope that you reach the stage in which you no longer need to query.

Charlie. What do you mean?

Bill. Eventually you should be so well established as a professional that instead of your seeking out the publishing house, the representatives of the publishing house will come seeking you. For instance, you have published several books with a company and the editor asks urgently about when to expect your next book. Or the editor goes on the road to hunt talent or attend a convention or do both, and seeks you out as the right person to write a needed book.

Charlie. Any stage between my unsolicited contact with a publishing house and the editor's tracking me down to persuade me to write?

Bill. Here are some examples of the intermediate stage. A well-established professional with a good record with a publishing house suggests you to an editor as a promising possibility. An advisory editor for a publisher suggests that an editor scout your work. An editor comes to respect your potential through your thoughtful and incisive reviews of manuscripts. Over lunch, an editor for one house expresses regrets at being unable to publish your manuscript; the ears of an editor for another house register this information and you receive a letter from the second editor.

Charlie. So eventually there may come the day when I can safely ignore Van Til's First Law, "Query, always query."

Bill. When that day comes, Van Til's Second Law will prevail, "Feel free to pay no attention to Van Til's First Law."

---

[2]*Books in Print 1983–84* (New York: R. R. Bowker, 1983).

Publishers' Decision-Making: What Criteria Do They Use in Deciding Which Books to Publish?

For nineteen months I conducted field observations in two commercial publishing houses, one a fairly small, prestigious scholarly firm which publishes less than 100 books a year almost exclusively in the social sciences, the other a large, prosperous monograph house that publishes over 400 books a year, of which approximately one-eighth are in the social sciences. . . .

My observations are limited to scholarly and monograph publishing in the social sciences. Scholarly publishers direct the majority of their publications to academics and practicing professionals. Their books appeal to a broad spectrum of the scholars in a particular discipline, not to a narrow subfield of specialists. . . .

Monograph publishing is even more specialized in its appeal. Monographs generally report research advances and are of interest primarily to scholars working on similar problems. . . .

I ended up with three general types [ways projects came to be considered]:

(1) The author initiates the contact with the publishing house (this includes projects that come in over the transom, or an author approaches a representative of the house at a convention or a meeting—in any case the author has not had any prior contact with the house).

(2) The author has some previous association with the house, or with a person who has had such an association who acts as a broker for the author or the house (this includes referrals from other publishers, informal advisers to the house, or situations where the house has an informal arrangement with particular institutions to publish their materials).

(3) The project is acquired as a result of the editor's efforts or contacts (such as personal friends of the editor, or situations where the editor went hunting for material either on a trip, at a convention, or over the phone). . . .

To summarize, the argument is as follows: An editor devotes a greater or lesser amount of attention to manuscripts according to the manner in which they were acquired. The materials that arrive in the house via category one, that is, unsolicited, are the most frequently received and receive the least attention. The materials that come in as a result of cat-

From Walter W. Powell, "Publishers' Decision-Making: What Criteria Do They Use in Deciding Which Books to Publish?" *Social Research*, Volume 45, Summer 1978, pp. 227–52.

egory three, that is, through the direct efforts of an editor, which is the least frequent means of acquisition, are precisely the materials that receive the most attention. The more attention a manuscript receives, the more likely it is to be published. Materials submitted by an author who has had no prior contact with the house, of which there are over 1,800 in a year, have less than one in a hundred chances of getting published. In contrast, projects that come in as a result of an editor's efforts or connections, which average about fifty a year, have a chance of about one in three of being published.

University Presses Under Pressure

. . . University presses are now under pressure to become self-supporting. New sources of funding and new markets are being sought. Increased export sales, increased subsidiary rights income, alumni book clubs, and co-operative promotion and distribution are but a few of the possibilities that university presses are pursuing. There is also the challenge of new technologies—microform publication, video-discs, electronic journals, and computer data bases for on-demand publishing— which may or may not offer new, more efficient, and less costly means of publication.

In addition, changes in the structure of trade publishing have created new opportunities. University presses and commercial scholarly houses are moving into the territory the larger trade houses have vacated in their quest for blockbusters. As trade publishers have increased their expectations of the number of copies a book needs to sell in order to be deemed successful, they have become less willing to take on books that are eminently worthwhile but have modest sales potential. The crush of big books has given impetus to scholarly presses. As a consequence, there has been a change in the mix of titles published by some university presses. Their lists now include novels, a few basic textbooks, and even how-to-do it books. In general, there are more trade-oriented titles and fewer specialized scholarly books. These changes have not gone unnoticed by university faculty or by commercial publishers. Questions are raised as to whether university presses can compete with commercial publishers as well as whether this competition is even appropriate. Should university presses vigorously compete with commercial houses?

From Walter W. Powell, "Adapting to Tight Money and New Opportunities," *Scholarly Publishing,* October 1982, pp. 9–10. Reprinted from *Scholarly Publishing: A Journal for Authors and Publishers,* October 1982, by permission of the author and the University of Toronto Press.

PART II

THE WRITER AT WORK

13

Finding Time

The problem of finding time
Scheduling your life
Allocating time for writing
Writing during the academic year and vacation periods
Locales for writing
Writers' patterns
Motivation, priorities, family relationships, self-discipline

During the semester in which Bill was advising Charlie and his friends on the problems of beginners in writing for professional publication, Bill moved into a new house. His next-door neighbor is a professor of English, a well-established academic. Bill had long admired Andy's publications and his general reputation in university circles. Though the men had only a nodding acquaintance on campus, an invitation to dinner was inevitable. Andy and Bill grow acquainted through discussing that perennial problem of authors, finding time to write.

Andy.   Bill, have another?

Bill.   No thanks, Andy. I've reached my self-imposed limit.

Andy.   Good to have a chance to talk as neighbors. A problem in life at this university is that we have too many opportunities to talk with colleagues in our own fields and too few chances to talk with those in other areas. Travel broadens; universities narrow.

Bill.   There's also the split between professors in the liberal arts and the staff of vocationally oriented colleges. Since you happen to be in the English Department, Andy, and I happen to be in the School of Education, we're supposed to curse at each other, not converse.

Andy.   Personally, I leave that struggle to the local influentials we elect to Faculty Council and to my committee-happy colleagues. If I engaged in much faculty politicking, I wouldn't have time to write.

Bill.   I also choose my wars with care. Writing takes time. What are you writing these days?

Andy.   The working title of my next book is *The Lost Generation in the Depression Era.* It's about what happened to the leading fiction writers of the 1920s when depression and fascism emerged in the 1930s.

I also plan to follow up on my Thomas Wolfe monograph with a biography. But finding time is my problem. How do you manage?

Bill. A long while ago I realized that everybody has 168 hours of life each week. A major chunk of a professor's time goes to earning a living: teaching classes, conferring with students, working with national professional organizations, and some consultation.

Andy. You probably don't include gossiping in the faculty lounge.

Bill. Another segment of people's lives goes to the necessities and amenities of life—sleeping, eating, shaving or putting on makeup, traveling back and forth to work, housework, shopping, cooking, lawn mowing, and so on. Despite the women's liberation movement, women writers often have sole or major responsibility for rearing children, going shopping, preparing food, and maintaining the home. They may have to work at night while other family members are sleeping.

Andy. This is beginning to sound like Puritan advice.

Bill. Not really. Another block of time is spent with family and friends; a writer is a human being who should not feel guilty about spending abundant time with his/her spouse—

Andy. I understand that the proper phrase these days is "significant other."

Bill. —and friends and children. However, *both* parents don't have to spend every waking hour with the children. Just as household work can be divided between husband and wife, so can time for child care. Kahlil Gibran said it well, "Let there be spaces in your togetherness."

Still another chunk of time should be given to recreation or plain doing nothing. This should be a substantial portion of life. Hobbies, sports, and other diversions, alone or with others, are important for mind and body. Take breaks. Walk the dog. Relate to people.

Andy. A person doesn't have to be a hermit in order to be a writer. Though it helped Thoreau, most of us need more than life at Walden Pond if we are to write anything significant.

Bill. When I subtracted the four segments from the 168 hours a week each of us has, I found that a considerable amount of time was left. Much of that remainder could be spent in writing.

Andy. A person would have to give up some drugs, though.

Bill. What do you mean?

Andy. Like the game on TV between two teams about which you couldn't care less.

Bill. Or the grade D late-night movie on the tube.

Andy. And the vapid entertaining in which everything has already been said long in advance of the occasion.

Bill. Or the repetitious bridge game at the faculty club.

Andy. I notice you even refused my invitation to have a third martini.

Bill. As you just said, a person has to give up some drugs.

Andy. How many hours a week for writing do you think a professor might come up with?

Bill. During the regular academic year fifteen to eighteen or so. Not as much when teaching during the summer session. During vacation periods much much more. All in all, a professor might spend more than a thousand hours a year on writing, which is less than the average American spends watching television annually.

Andy. I never calculated the hours. The freshman composition section takes a formidable amount of my time. When I do write, I like to surround myself with books in my study or immerse myself in the library. The library carrel is a blessing. However, summer has been my best time for writing. I need large uninterrupted blocks of time.

Bill. I need blocks of time too. I envy the people who don't. Some of my friends can write in the hour before a class, or on a plane or in the airport. One hearty colleague of mine can even write in the dentist's or doctor's waiting room.

Andy. Not me. The summer I wrote the novel that practically nobody read, I needed long periods of solitude. I have to be in the mood to do creative writing. I need the right atmosphere. We have a vacation cabin in the woods.

Bill. I'm a great believer in the old adage that the secret of writing is applying the seat of the pants to the seat of the chair. Edison said that genius is 1 percent inspiration and 99 percent perspiration.

Andy. I agree writing is hard work. Yet I suspect the old adages oversimplify the process.

How did you arrange for blocks of time for writing during the regular academic year?

Bill. Some years ago I taught undergraduates every weekday in nine, ten, and one o'clock classes, a fifteen-hour teaching load. I established my office hours at eight-thirty to nine and eleven till twelve. Whenever students didn't drop in, I worked on class preparation. From Mondays through Thursdays at two I moved to the library and worked as long as the spirit moved me. At home, Saturday morning was a good time for writing. Total, about fifteen hours.

Later I taught three graduate classes, each a three-hour block, a nine-hour assignment. One full day plus one morning each week, I wrote in my study at home. Add one weekend evening plus Saturday mornings and writing time amounted to about eighteen hours.

Andy. What did your colleagues think of your absence from your office?

Bill. I never inquired and they never indicated. The more productive of them followed somewhat similar patterns. The difference between teaching at Podunk College and at a college or university that values writing and research as well as teaching and guidance is that

Podunk College assumes some connection between office chair-warming from nine to five and academic virtue. An institution that values scholarship recognizes that work can be done in varied vineyards, not exclusively in the holy of holies, the office.

Some people say that there are day writers and night writers. Do you believe that?

Andy. To a degree, yes. I'm a night man myself. I do my best work when the rest of the family are in bed and the house is quiet. But morning comes too early.

Bill. Sleep late.

Andy. With a nine o'clock freshman composition section? No way. I think I will try to use some late-afternoon blocks of time for writing. Night writing might be just a habit. Amateur writers constantly inquire about writers' ways of working. Surely there must be some magic time or place or even quill! They never learn that there are no "secrets."

Bill. From what you have said, I assume you believe a person can work more effectively in a pleasant locale. Your summer place for instance.

Andy. I tell myself that, but I suspect it's a rationalization. The history of literature testifies that major writers have written in homes, offices, libraries, and on park benches.

Bill. Even prisons.

Andy. I wouldn't recommend that. I still prefer my cabin.

Bill. Similarly writers may use pencil, pen, typewriter, dictating machine, or word processor. Some warm up to the day's writing by rereading and correcting whatever they wrote last time; others go right on, never looking back.

Andy. Most write sitting down, but some write standing up. Thomas Wolfe stood and wrote in large ledgers.

Bill. My only specifications as to place are that it be quiet and that my tools be available.

Andy. So you think place is less important than finding the time?

Bill. I say make the time. Everyone's time is already found—those predetermined 168 hours that make up each week of living. I think it comes down to the question of whether a person will make the choices that provide the time for writing. It's a matter of motivation and setting priorities and achieving mutual understanding and support among family members.

Andy. And of self-discipline.

Advice from a Major Novelist

John Steinbeck

1. Abandon the idea that you are ever going to finish. Lose track of the 400 pages and write just one page for each day, it helps. Then when it gets finished, you are always surprised.
2. Write freely and as rapidly as possible and throw the whole thing on paper. Never correct or rewrite until the whole thing is down. Rewrite in process is usually found to be an excuse for not going on. It also interferes with flow and rhythm which can only come from a kind of unconscious association with the material.
3. Forget your generalized audience. In the first place, the nameless, faceless audience will scare you to death and in the second place, unlike the theatre, it doesn't exist. In writing, your audience is one single reader. I have found that sometimes it helps to pick out one person—a real person you know, or an imagined person—and write to that one.
4. If a scene or a section gets the better of you and you still think you want it—bypass it and go on. When you have finished the whole you can come back to it and then you may find that the reason it gave trouble is because it didn't belong there.
5. Beware of a scene that becomes too dear to you, dearer than the rest. It will usually be found that it is out of drawing.
6. If you are using dialogue—say it aloud as you write it. Only then will it have the sound of speech.

From George Plimpton, ed., *Writers at Work: The Paris Review Interviews*, 4th Series (New York: The Viking Press, 1976). Taken from chapter on John Steinbeck, ''On Getting Started,'' pp. 181–200.

Advice from a Freelance Writer

Jerome E. Kelley

"Write? I can't write regularly! I'm too busy."

Take a closer look at this excuse and you'll see that's exactly what it is—an excuse. The majority of today's employers require from an employee 37½ hours each week, 50 weeks each year, with about eight paid holidays annually. So, even if you're employed by a relatively unenlightened company, you're actually working only 49 weeks, or 1,837½ hours. Subtract this from the number of hours in each year and you have 6,922½ hours. Now, for each day subtract seven hours for sleeping, two hours for eating, and three hours for watching the tube. This leaves 2,542 hours of net unoccupied time. Out of this we'll be generous and give you 1,542 hours for social activities.

You're now left with a measly 1,000 hours. For our purposes, we'll assume you are a plodding researcher, so we'll give you 500 hours to perform this important function. This leaves you with only 500 hours for actual writing.

What can you do with 500 hours when you're an excruciatingly slow writer who can wring only a single, double-spaced typescript page out of your Model 12 Underwood in an hour?

The answer is: You can multiply. Roughly 250 words fit on a typed page, so if you multiply 250 × 500 you arrive at the final figure of 125,000 words per year, which equals fifty 2,500-word magazine articles or two thin books.

Now what was that you said about not having the time to write?

From Jerome E. Kelley, *Magazine Writing Today* (Cincinnati, Ohio: Writer's Digest Books, 1978), p. 6.

Advice to Every Young Writer

Thomas Wolfe

. . . Now I was faced with another fundamental problem which every young writer must meet squarely if he is to continue. How is a man to get his writing done? How long should he work at writing, and how often? What kind of method, if any, must he find in following his work? I suddenly found myself face to face with the grim necessity of constant, daily work. And as simple as this discovery may seem to every one, I was not prepared for it. A young writer without a public does not feel the sense of necessity, the pressure of time, as does a writer who has been published and who must now begin to think of time schedules, publishing seasons, the completion of his next book. I realized suddenly with a sense of definite shock that I had let six months go by since the publication of my first book and that, save for a great many notes and fragments, I had done nothing. Meanwhile, the book [*Look Homeward, Angel*] continued to sell slowly but steadily, and in February 1930, about five months after its publication, I found it possible to resign from the faculty of New York University and devote my full time to the preparation of a second book. That spring I was also fortunate enough to be awarded the Guggenheim Fellowship which would enable me to live and work abroad for a year. And accordingly at the beginning of May, I went abroad again.

From Thomas Wolfe, *The Story of a Novel* (New York: Charles Scribner's Sons, 1936), pp. 26–27.

A Recipe for Writers

Sinclair Lewis

And as the recipe for writing, all writing, I remember no high-flown counsel but always and only Mary Heaton Vorse's jibe, delivered to a bunch of young and mostly incompetent hopefuls back in 1911: "The art of writing is the art of applying the seat of the pants to the seat of the chair."

From Elmer Adler, ed., *Breaking into Print* (New York: Simon & Schuster, 1937). Taken from chapter by Sinclair Lewis, pp. 117–23.

14

Getting Ideas

Individual background as a source
Advice on finding appropriate subjects
Journals as sources
Clues from daily life
Indexes and abstracts as sources
Whether intellectual pump priming is needed
Choices among possibilities by authors

After dinner, Andy and Bill talk about how writers get ideas. By now they feel they know each other well enough to feel comfortable in disagreeing. As to decisions on what to write, Andy doesn't find pump priming necessary, Bill thinks there is a case for it. The disagreement is amicable, and each learns from the other.

Bill. Andy, in the workshops and clinics I conduct on writing for professional publications, I'm often asked how a writer decides on topics and subjects. What would you say to the question "Where do you get your ideas?"

Andy. The major source has to be one's own individual background. In my case, I discovered the public library when I was very young. The librarians kindly allowed me to withdraw what they termed "grown-up books" after I had read what interested me in the children's section. I read omnivorously, mostly fiction. English became my favorite subject. Naturally, I majored in literature in college. During my graduate study, the focus became American literature and, eventually, twentieth-century American literature. Along the way, I aspired, like many English professors, to write the Great American Novel. So the die was cast. Necessarily, I wrote out of my background.

Bill. Still, twentieth-century American literature is a broad area. How do you account for your specific choices or emphasis?

Andy. As an undergraduate, I came on the novelist Thomas Wolfe and his hunger for life. His torrents of words and his cascades of images made a deep impression on me. As a young man, I read everything he ever published, then began reading critical appraisals and biographies.

With maturity, I became more aware of his weaknesses as well as strengths. So I contributed my own critical studies and began my own biography of Wolfe and his family and friends.

Bill. Any connection between Wolfe and your *Lost Generation* book?

Andy. Oblique. Through reading in my field I soon recognized the difficulties the postwar writers experienced in communicating to depression-generation readers. Wolfe, of course, was too young for World War I and can't be classified as a lost generation man along with Hemingway, Fitzgerald, et al. Yet Wolfe's own problems in adapting his romantic individualism to the climate of the New Deal supported my general thesis.

Bill. I would conclude, Andy, that you are a specialized scholar whose future subjects will probably grow out of your past work. The parameters you have already established will largely determine what you will write. You seldom need to ask yourself, "What shall I write about now?" Right?

Andy. That's a fair assessment. I will write on my specializations; I doubt that anyone will ever refer to me as a Renaissance man.

But back to your question—what do you advise when people ask about finding appropriate subjects?

Bill. I respond with questions about their own backgrounds, including the nature of their doctoral dissertations, the content of the courses they teach, what they study in preparation for classes, and the ideas that excite them or stir their students. This often leads them into suggesting for themselves some possible topics.

I also ask them about the professional magazines and scholarly journals in their fields. What are their titles? Which do they regularly read? Which do they like best? In which would they like to publish? What kinds of articles do their editors favor? What are the trends? Are themes used? Are the articles a miscellany? Do any subjects regularly recur?

If potential authors are somewhat vague as to specifics, I suggest that they check the table of contents or thumb through the last two years of the periodicals. Many ideas occur to people after they look anew at the journals and magazines to analyze the content.

Similarly, I ask them about books they have been reading. Can they identify subjects for writing from their reading patterns? I inquire about their reading of books and magazines and newspapers other than those related to their profession. How about *The New York Times*, the news magazines, the journals of opinion, and fiction and nonfiction books?

Andy. The point I hear you making is that only writers themselves can decide on what to write. You can't tell them. Nobody can. No one could suggest to me the theme of my next novel—if any. I have to mine my theme out of my own life and experiences—indeed, my own psyche.

Bill. The best anyone can do is to suggest sources that might generate ideas in the writer's mind. Depending on the person's background and inclinations, I may recommend informal content analysis of magazines read by the general public, or newspapers and newsweeklies, or TV specials and talk shows. I may recommend listening with a sharp ear to conversations during delimited time in the coffee room or faculty club. I may suggest seeking out knowledgeable people for discussion on campus, in the local community, or at conventions. I try to open up a range of possible sources.

Some time spent with R. R. Bowker's Company's *Forthcoming Books* and *Subject Guide to Forthcoming Books* will inform authors of new books in their fields that are scheduled for publication. *Subject Guide to Books in Print* will tell them what has already appeared.

Indexes and abstracts can also provide authors many leads as to publication outlets. Many a time I have used *Education Index*— an old-timer that lists periodical publications, relevant books of all kinds, and yearbooks of professional organizations—not only for research but also in planning toward my next publication. A relative newcomer, *Current Index to Journals in Education,* is even more useful; it provides main entries including abstracts of articles, along with indexes to subjects, authors, and journal contents. A few minutes with *CIJE* will inform an education author of what articles specific professional magazines and journals have carried in recent months. *Resources in Education* provides a key to the Educational Resources Information Center, familiarly known as ERIC, a world of publishing in itself.

Andy. Similar indexes and abstracts exist in every imaginable discipline. For instance, psychologists can turn to *Psychological Abstracts* and related sources. Scholars in social science disciplines can consult *Social Sciences Index* and *Sociological Abstracts,* among others. Engineers have the *Engineering Index.* I use *Humanities Index* for language and literature. Indexes exist for many subdivisions within disciplines.

However, I grow impatient with people who require such intellectual pump priming on what to write. A person should know. People who have to ask, "What should I write about?" probably have little that is significant to say. They may simply be driven by the publish-or perish requirement.

Bill. And some are. On the other hand, not everybody is a self-impelled creator who is going to write about what he or she knows or feels regardless of market. Some writers are journalists who write on assignment by editors. Still others need to take into account what editors are likely to use. For instance, a freelancer who writes many articles may keep a systematic card file of ideas for articles.

Like journalists and freelancers, people who write for wide-ranging magazines in a particular profession may develop a list of possible topics for future articles. It makes good sense for them to keep informed on the themes scheduled for magazines in which they want their work to appear. The scheduled theme may precipitate an idea for a contribution. Of course, this may also lead to a stampede toward "hot topics" through articles marked by painfully poor scholarship.

Andy. Perhaps the category—whether books, articles, reviews, or so on—makes a difference. I suspect that most authors of books have thought about their next publication or publications while they were writing their present manuscript. Good books grow out of what you already know or are learning. I will admit that the suggestions of a perceptive editor or, more rarely, a critic sometimes prove useful. In general, however, you can't learn from others what your next book should be. Nor can I, as a specialist, depend on abstracts or indexes to suggest the topics of my articles.

Bill. A good book reviewer, however, is constantly alert for cues to new books for possible appraisal. The generalist who writes articles frequently gets leads from others. A columnist employs sensitive antennas to receive ideas for possible columns. For most professional publications, wide reading helps. Awareness of what colleagues are concerned about is also rewarding.

Andy. But after all ideas are heard, the choice of a subject must be made by the individual author. Otherwise the writer becomes a hack journalist who is assigned to a story rather than an independent author who writes for professional publication.

Bill. Harold Taylor, who frequently writes on education, also strongly emphasizes the importance of choosing significant subjects that matter to the individual writer. He wrote me: "When I write for professional publications it is simply because I want the others among my friends and colleagues to know what I am thinking and what I am working on. I also want to change their minds if their minds seem to me to need changing."

I agree that professionals should write on subjects that are highly important to them and that are highly important in themselves. However, an author's choices must be made within a framework of editorial needs. If the subject that is selected does not find its way into print through some publication outlet, whether book, pamphlet, or periodical, the writer is left with a manuscript, not a publication. Not all writers become published authors.

So my advice to those who write for professional publication is to combine creativity with receptivity. Combine reliance on background experiences with alertness to ideas from many sources. Then getting ideas won't be a formidable problem for the aspiring or established writer.

Andy. Possibly. I think though that you may underrate the importance of creativity.

A SAMPLING OF INDEXES

Current Index to Journals in Education. Phoenix: Oryx Press, monthly with a semiannual cumulation.
A guide by author, subject, and journal content to current periodical literature published in major educational and education-related journals.

Education Index. New York: H. W. Wilson Company, monthly and annual.
A cumulative author and subject index to a selected list of educational periodicals, proceedings, and yearbooks.

Engineering Index. New York: Engineering Index, Inc., annual with a monthly bulletin.
A guide to current international engineering literature; to abstracts from professional and trade journals; to publications of engineering, scientific and technical associations, universities, laboratories, government departments and agencies, and industrial organizations.

Humanities Index. New York: H. W. Wilson Company, quarterly with an annual cumulation.
This volume covers author and subject entries in archaeology, folklore, history, language and literature, literary and political criticism, the performing arts, philosophy, religion, theology, theatre, and film.

Readers' Guide to Periodical Literature. New York: H. W. Wilson Company, twice monthly with annual cumulation.
An index to periodicals of general interest.

Social Sciences Index. New York: H. W. Wilson Company, quarterly with annual cumulative issue.
Author and subject entries to periodicals in the fields of anthropology, economics, environmental studies, geography, law, criminology, area studies, political science, psychology, public administration, and sociology.

A SAMPLING OF ABSTRACTS

Computing Reviews. New York: Association for Computing Machinery, monthly.
Critical reviews in the computer sciences.

Psychological Abstracts: Nonevaluative Summaries of the World's Literature in Psychology and Related Disciplines. Washington, D.C.: American Psychological Association, Inc., monthly.
Summaries covering 850 journals, 1,500 books, monographs, and technical reports. Contains a subject index as well as author index.

Resources in Education. Washington, D.C.: U.S. Government Printing Office monthly, with an annual cumulation.

Reports literature related to the field of education, permitting the early iden-tification and acquisition of reports of interest to the educational community.

Sociological Abstracts. San Diego: Sociological Abstracts, Inc., five issues per year.
Short summaries of articles broken down by subject area.

Women Studies Abstracts. Rush, N.Y.: Rush Publishing Company, quar-terly.
Indexing and abstracting source for research in the study of women.

15

Using Tools of the Trade

Dictionaries
Thesauruses
Books of quotations
Almanacs
Atlases
Biographical sources
Specialized volumes in disciplines
Guides to references
Books in the individual's own scholarly discipline

Naturally, a return invitation to dinner is inevitable. Writers are understandably curious about each other's workshops. So the two men spend some time in Bill's study looking over and swapping experiences with tools of the trade.

Andy. This is a pleasant study. Do you do most of your writing here at home?

Bill. Yes. When I need library resources, I work in library carrels. However, I keep many of my tools right here at home.

Andy. I do too. An unabridged dictionary, *Webster's Third New International Dictionary of the English Language,* is my pride and joy.

Bill. I would like to own the unabridged edition of *The Random House Dictionary of the English Language.* But unabridged dictionaries are expensive tools.

Andy. Not necessarily. I saw an advertisement by Barnes and Noble Bookstores for *Webster's New Universal Unabridged Dictionary;* 2,300 pages; 320,000 words; $14.95 plus $3 postage and handling.

Bill. Temporarily I have settled for two excellent desk dictionaries, *The American Heritage Dictionary of the English Language,* and *The Random House College Dictionary.* There is a paperback version of *Random House Dictionary* in my office. My other staple is this copy of *The New Columbia Encyclopedia.* In the library I often use the multiple-volume *Encyclopedia Americana.*

Andy. I'm tempted to buy the new *Britannica.* Another category—a book of synonyms and antonyms, such as *Roget's International Thesaurus*. I particularly like a thesaurus in dictionary form, whether *Webster's New Dictionary of Synonyms* or *Roget's Thesaurus in Dictionary Form*.

Bill. Or J. I. Rodale's useful simplification, *The Synonym Finder*.

Andy. Another resource that is essential in my work is a book of quotations, such as *Bartlett's Familiar Quotations*, the *Oxford Dictionary of Quotations*, or *Home Book of Quotations*.

Bill. Bartlett is essential for me. I supplement it with Bergen Evans's *Dictionary of Quotations* and *Peter's Quotations*, compiled by Laurence J. Peter. I also like a wonderful paperback collection, *The Great Quotations*, compiled by George Seldes, which is light on poetry and nature and heavy on great ideas. To help offset sexism, I also use *The Quotable Woman, 1800–1981*.

Andy. I'm glad to know about that one. Women have been shortchanged in reference volumes, even in as fine a source as *Who's Who in America*.

Bill. There's still another category, the latest almanac such as that hardy perennial, *The World Almanac and Book of Facts*. The statistician can supplement almanacs by trips to the library to use the *Statistical Abstract of the U.S.* and other governmental statistical data.

Andy. Minimum essentials for any writer for professional publication are an up-to-date dictionary, encyclopedia, dictionary of synonyms, book of quotations, and almanac. Beyond these, specialization sets in.

Bill. There may be a halfway house prior to specialization. Atlases are used by others besides geographers. Every writer's study should include a good recent world atlas.

Biographical source books are not only for reference scholars within libraries or for my use in my study. My *Who's Who in America* and *Who's Who in the World* supplement my viewing of the evening news, documentaries, talk shows, and drama on TV. I learn from them many things about individual backgrounds that TV never tells me.

Andy. *Webster's Biographical Dictionary* supplies me with the notable names and biographical data I need.

Sometimes volumes prepared for specialists in one discipline are useful to workers in another field. For instance, American literature has a social context, so I keep handy a historian's tool, *The Almanac of American History* edited by Arthur M. Schlesinger, Jr.

Bill. A less well-known reference, *The Timetables of History* by Bernard Grun, a ''horizontal linkage of people and events,'' is also useful. Choose any period from 5,000 B.C. to A.D. 50 or any single year from A.D. 51 to date. Before your eyes, there parade digests of history and politics; literature and the theatre; religion, philosophy, and learning; visual arts; music; science; technology and growth; and daily life of that period or specific year. What a tool for writers who want to enliven their references to prosaic dates!

Andy. Add to these the hundreds of reference books for specialists—

Bill. Like my *Encyclopedia of Educational Research* or *Biographical Dictionary of American Educators.*

Andy. Or my *Contemporary Authors* or *The Oxford Companion to American Literature.* My acquisition of reference books is limited only by my purse. Fortunately, we have libraries that provide a treasure of specialized resources and references.

Bill. Those writers who heavily use reference sources will save themselves considerable time if they look over books such as Rivers's brief *Finding Facts.* Any writer for professional publications should supplement dictionary, encyclopedia, book of quotations, synonym listing, almanac, atlas, and general biographical references with substantial reference volumes in the individual's own discipline. The guides to references suggest many sources, the more voluminous to be used in the library, the more compact to be added to the shelf nearest to the writer's desk.

Andy. Yet the writer will always remain a lonely creator. As John Berryman said, "Writing is just a man alone in the room with the English language, trying to make it come out right." I will admit that a carefully selected collection of reference books at the writer's elbow does help.

DICTIONARIES

The American Heritage Dictionary of the English Language - New College Edition. Boston: Houghton Mifflin Company, 1981.

The Random House College Dictionary. New York: Random House, 1982.

The Random House Dictionary of the English Language. Unabridged ed. New York: Random House, 1981.

The Random House Dictionary. New York: Ballantine Books, 1980. Paperback.

Webster's Instant Word Guide. Springfield, Mass.: Merriam-Webster Company, 1980.

Webster's New Twentieth Century Dictionary. 2nd ed. New York: Simon and Schuster, 1983.

Webster's New Universal Unabridged Dictionary. New York: Dorset and Baber, Simon and Schuster, 1983.

Webster's New World Dictionary of the American Language. 2nd college ed. New York: Warner, 1983.

Webster's Ninth New Collegiate Dictionary. Springfield, Mass.: Merriam-Webster Company, 1983.

Webster's Third New International Dictionary of the English Language. Springfield, Mass.: Merriam-Webster Company, 1981.

ENCYCLOPEDIAS

Collier's Encyclopedia. Edited by William D. Halsey. New York: Macmillan Educational Corp., 1984.

The Concise Columbia Encyclopedia. Edited by Judith S. Levey and Agnes Greenhall. New York: Avon Books, 1983.

Encyclopedia Americana. Edited by Alan H. Smith. Danbury, Conn: Americana Corp., a division of Grolier, Inc., 1983.

Encyclopedia of Computer Science and Technology. Edited by Jack Belzer. New York: Dekker, 1980.

The New Columbia Encyclopedia. 4th ed. Edited by William H. Harris and Judith S. Levey. New York: Columbia University Press, 1975.

The New Encyclopaedia Britannica. 15th ed. Edited by Warren Preece. Chicago: Encyclopaedia Britannica, 1983.

The Random House Encyclopedia. Edited by James Mitchell and Jess Stein. New York: Random House, 1983.

THESAURUSES

Roget's International Thesaurus. Revised and edited by Robert L. Chapman. New York: Thomas Y. Crowell, 1977.

Roget's Thesaurus in Dictionary Form. Edited by Norman Lewis. New York: Berkeley Publishing, 1984.

The Synonym Finder. Edited by J. I. Rodale. Emmaus, Pa.: Rodale Books, 1978.

Webster's New Dictionary of Synonyms. Springfield, Mass.: Merriam-Webster Company, 1984.

Webster's New World Thesaurus. New York: Warner, 1983.

BOOKS OF QUOTATIONS

Dictionary of Quotations. Edited by Bergen Evans. New York: Delacorte Press, 1968.

Familar Quotations (by John Bartlett). 15th ed. Edited by Emily Morison Beck. Boston: Little, Brown and Company, 1980.

The Great Quotations. Edited by George Seldes. New York: Lyle Stuart, 1983.

Home Book of Quotations. Edited by Burton E. Stevenson. New York: Dodd Mead & Company, 1967.

The International Thesaurus of Quotations. Edited by Rhoda Thomas Tripp. New York: Thomas Y. Crowell, 1970.

Oxford Dictionary of Quotations. 3rd ed. Oxford: Oxford University Press, 1979.

Peter's Quotations. Edited by Laurence J. Peter. New York: William Morrow and Company, 1977.

The Quotable Woman, 1800–1981. Edited by Elaine Partnow. New York: Facts on File, 1983.

ATLASES

The New Rand McNally College World Atlas. Chicago: Rand McNally and Company, 1983.

The New York Times Atlas of the World. New York: Times Books, 1983.

World Atlas. Maplewood, N. J.: Hammond, 1982.

GENERAL BIOGRAPHICAL REFERENCES

Webster's Biographical Dictionary: A Dictionary of Names of Noteworthy Persons with Pronunciations and Concise Biographies. Edited by William Allan Neilson. Springfield, Mass.: G. & C. Merriam Company, 1972.

Who's Who in America. Chicago: Marquis Who's Who, Inc., every two years.

Who's Who in the World. Chicago: Marquis Who's Who, Inc., every two years.

HISTORICAL AND SPECIALIZED BIOGRAPHICAL REFERENCES

The Almanac of American History. Edited by Arthur M. Schlesinger, Jr. New York: Putnam Publishing Group, 1984.

Biographical Dictionary of American Educators. Edited by John F. Ohles. Westport, Conn.: Greenwood Press, 1978.

Contemporary Authors. Edited by Carolyn Riley. Detroit: Gale Research Company. Annual.

GRUN, BERNARD. *The Timetables of History: A Horizontal Linkage of People and Events, Based on Werner Stein's Kulturfahrplan.* New York: Simon & Schuster, 1975.

The Oxford Companion to American Literature. 5th ed. Edited by James David Hart. New York: Oxford University Press, 1984.

Webster's Guide to American History. Edited by Charles Van Doren and Robert McHenry. Springfield, Mass.: G. & C. Merriam Company, 1971.

GUIDES TO REFERENCE BOOKS

Best Reference Books: Titles of Lasting Value Selected from American Reference Books Annual 1970–1980. Edited by Susan Holte and Bohdan S. Wynar. Littleton, Colo.: Libraries Unlimited, 1981.

CHANDLER, GEORGE. *How to Find Out.* Oxford, N.Y.: Pergamon Press, 1982.

JOHNSON, ELEANOR and JANET HOROWITZ. *1983–84 Directory of Editorial Resources.* Alexandria, Va.: Editorial Experts, Inc., 1983.

RIVERS, WILLIAM L. *Finding Facts: Interviewing, Observing, Using Reference Sources.* Englewood Cliffs, N.J.: Prentice-Hall, 1975.

SHEEHY, EUGENE P. *Guide to Reference Books.* 9th ed. Chicago: American Library Association, 1975 (1980, 1982 supplements).

STEVENS, ROLLAND ELWELL and D. DAVIS. *Reference Books in the Social Sciences.* Champaign, Ill.: Stipes Publishing Company, 1977.

16

Word Processing

How writers write, revise, rewrite, ad infinitum
Word processing to the rescue
Checking spelling through dictionary software
Help with writers' chores
Keyboards and cursors
Screens and scrolls
Central processing and random access memories
Magnetic media and floppy disks
Printers—paper at last
Essential software, the word processing program
Telling the computer what to do
Advice to purchasers

Bill's son pays his family a visit. Jon, a sociologist, has recently bought a computer with word processing capabilities and has become an enthusiastic convert to writing with a word processor. Andy and Bill, loyal Gutenberg men, are both curious and dubious about the electronic developments that are revolutionizing writing.

Jon. Think of it as just another tool for the writer. A good micro-computer with word processing capacity is a user–friendly machine that can do many things for writers and editors.

Bill. It's hard for me to think of a computer as friendly, Jon. Throughout my life, machines have baffled me. I don't even understand what makes automobiles, air conditioners, and dishwashers work.

Jon. You don't have to be an auto mechanic to drive a car or a refrigeration expert to turn on the air conditioning or a repairman to run a dishwasher. You don't have to be a physicist or an electrical engineer to write with a word processor. Tell me how you write your articles and books and I'll tell you what word processing can do for you.

Bill. I stare at a page and begin putting down words, sentences, and paragraphs with some help from scribbled notes and a dictionary. I cross things out and insert new material, and when I'm through I can hardly read the damned thing. Then I copy it over again and give it to your mother or a secretary who tries to read my handwriting and types me a first draft. Then I attack the typed draft with my pencil or, if overconfident, with a pen. I cut and paste. The revision is typed again. This goes on forever, it seems. Eventually I produce something I'm willing to send to an editor who marks it up with corrections and supposed improvements and sometimes sends back the manuscript, which I butcher some more. Then come the galleys; I make changes in them. If I'm writing a book, I also read page proofs and hunt for typos.

Andy. I type my own drafts accompanied by much throwing away of paper and utterance of fierce oaths. Otherwise it's the same process. Write, revise, rewrite, revise again and sometimes again, proofread the manuscript, galleys, and page proofs.

Jon. How would you like to have a supertypewriter that at the press of a finger deletes the words and sentences and paragraphs you no longer want, inserts what you want to add, moves your paragraphs or even pages anywhere you wish, tells you which words you have misspelled, numbers your pages, prints for you a beautiful clean copy, reproduces as many as you want, and does everything but mail your manuscript to your editor? It reduces sharply your typing and retyping of drafts. No more waiting for the typist to provide you with a clean copy.

Andy. I have to admit I'd like that. Tell us more.

Jon. Almost immediately after writers put down a few words or sentences they begin crossing out or inserting. With a word processor you can swiftly delete offending words or sentences and insert the words and sentences you now prefer. Soon you may discover that a paragraph belongs elsewhere. So with a few touches you move it. All of a sudden you realize that some pages you have written fit in better earlier or later. No problem; the word processor will shift them wherever you wish.

You don't have to constantly throw away old drafts because you can immediately change, revise, and rewrite on your word processor. Think of the time you can save by not having to retype! Any typing errors you commit while making changes on your word processor can be swiftly corrected. You'll not introduce new errors as you might if you retyped. So you save time for the more creative aspects of your writing.

Andy. I like what I'm hearing. Can the machine also help me in the later stages of my writing and editing? For instance, suppose I discover very late that I've persistently misspelled an author's name. Tell me about this dictionary magic that points out the words I have misspelled.

Jon. That's one of the supplemental features you can buy. Spelling checkers have been available for some time. As of 1984 a person could check a document against a dictionary of 80,000 plus words to identify mistakes. You yourself can add additional words to the dictionary, such as proper nouns and names and words that are specific to a discipline. Then, Andy, if you unfortunately had misspelled Thomas Wolfe through forgetting the final *e*, you could give the word processor its instruction. It would then change Wolf to Wolfe in one single fell swoop even if you had used the misspelling some 211 times!

Recent supplements include thesaurus efforts to identify alternative words, tests for excessive use of the passive voice, and word counts to identify sentences of excessive length. Grammar checks are also among the newer developments.

Bill. Alchemy! Are there similar programs to help with a writer's chores?

Jon. Definitely. There is software on the market to generate tables of contents, indexes, and bibliographies. There are programs that will insert footnotes in the proper places and automatically readjust them when the document is edited. New software is constantly making word processing more and more useful and saving writers from the tedious aspects of writing.

The hardware of a complete word processing system includes a printer that can produce your clean copy, using your preferred type font and putting in the underlinings, boldface, and italics you want to use. The printer can reproduce additional copies for you and do it even while you're working on another publication.

Bill. Hardware and software. Maybe you had better explain these categories. And remember that we are ignorant. We do not speak computerese.

Jon. I'll try to avoid the jargon. Let's look at the major components of a word processing system—the essential hardware. First there's a keyboard that looks like the conventional typewriter keyboard. Of course, the user has to get familiar with several additional gadgets. For instance, on machines like the IBM there are four keys controlling the cursor. Apple's Macintosh keeps its cursor control separate from the keyboard. . . .

Andy. You've already lost me in your language. What's a cursor?

Jon. A cursor is an indicator of the spot where any instruction given the machine by the writer will be performed. The cursor tells you where you are in your document. Basically it's a marker, a movable square of light on the screen that identifies where in the document a given change (insertion, deletion, addition, and so on) can be made. You can move your words, sentences, and paragraphs around or you can correct or wipe out what you have typed. Any action that takes place with respect to a document is not done by the cursor. It is done, rather, by the word processing program that is resident in the computer's memory. The cursor merely marks the place at which the action will take place. IBM's cursor on its personal computer is located on the keyboard.

Apple's Macintosh uses a "mouse," a box the size of a cigarette pack, that moves the cursor and enters your commands. The "mouse" is separate from the keyboard.

Andy. Where do I see the words I want to delete or move around?

Jon. What you have typed is displayed on a screen. The second component of the word processor is a screen that resembles a television screen. In computerese it's called a monitor. This is where your writing appears.

Andy. How much of my writing do I see on the video screen?

Jon. What you see on the screen is a function of the word processing program and the hardware. Some monitors will carry about the equivalent of half a double-spaced page, some less, some more.

Bill. Suppose I want to see something I've already written, say a page or so of a book?

Jon. The machine will roll your writing back and forth—it's called scrolling—and allow you not only to look at your pages but also to substantially change them. For instance, you can move a paragraph or page forward or backward in your document, as the computer people like to call whatever you are writing.

Bill. Isn't squinting at the screen hard on the eyes? All those dancing green letters on a small screen . . .

Jon. There's some possibility of eyestrain since you're looking at light surrounded by blackness. But it isn't necessary to stare at the screen constantly. Technicians are experimenting with colors and backgrounds to improve the visual image. Larger video viewers are replacing the early small ones.

Andy. How about neck and back strain?

Jon. A detachable keyboard will let you place the keyboard where it's best for your typing comfort.

Andy. Where do my words go after I've typed and edited them?

Jon. Into the computer's memory in the central processing unit.

Bill. Not onto paper? Writers love paper, Jon.

Jon. Sorry. Your words are written in light, not on paper.

The central processing unit, the third component, is the most mysterious to writers. This box is the heart and brains of the operation. Here the words you have typed and moved around are stored temporarily. If you turn off the computer, your words are gone just as the numerals on your hand calculator disappear when you turn off the battery. But you want to keep what you have temporarily stored in the computer's random access memory. So to keep your edited words, the word processor can record them on disks. So the fourth component involves slots for magnetic media.

Bill. Any illustration of the use of magnetic media in the world Andy and I inhabit?

Jon. Yes. For instance, the cassette tapes you use to record music or speeches. Though some computers still use cassette tapes, the better personal computers now use disks, sometimes called diskettes, mini-disks, or floppy disks.

Andy. Why floppy?

Jon. Because they are soft or flexible. But for heaven's sake don't fold them. Hard disks of solid aluminum, which are speedier and can hold much more writing, are sometimes used in place of soft disks. However, most word processors use floppy disks.

Andy. I like that adjective—it makes the machine sound more human.

Jon. There's another way in which disks resemble humans—they are sensitive. They don't like anything spilled on them. They don't like dust or magnets such as your magnetized paper-clip holder. They suffer whenever anything heavy is placed on them or if you park them on top of your TV set. So a word processor user treats floppy disks gently and stores them carefully.

Bill. What do they look like?

Jon. Floppy disks are three and one-half or five and one-quarter or eight inches in diameter. They live in cardboard envelopes; don't try to take them out. They can be erased and reused.

Your computer contains one or two slots called disk drives into which the disks can be inserted. Two slots are preferable because the contents of one disk can be transferred to another disk. The memory of the computer holds only a limited amount of material. After let's say 1,000 words are reached, the computer automatically transfers your words from your program disk to your work disk.

Bill. Now you're getting into an area I've been worrying about. When I write on paper I have something tangible, even if only partially legible and not worth the paper it's written on. To put it bluntly, might some mechanical failure cause my immortal words to disappear?

Jon. It's possible. One writer on word processors even made a formidable list of circumstances under which your immortal words could perish. For instance, the processor might chew up your floppy disk.

Andy. What a horrid thought! Cannibalism!

Jon. Or there might be a power failure. Or there might be some malfunction by the machine. Or, by mistake, the word processor might be turned off before you finished your typing. Or you might cancel what you have written through hitting the wrong keys.

Bill. Then what happens to what we have written?

Jon. It simply disappears. As William Zinsser puts it in *Writing with a Word Processor*, your words could "vanish into the electricity."

But be of good cheer. There are safeguards. The most dependable is to have the computer transcribe the equivalent of each page you write to a second disk, your work disk, for storage. Then the most you can lose is one page, not a whole article or a large chunk of a book. At the end of your workday transcribe what you have done to a backup disk so that you have a duplicate. Store your backup disk safely.

Bill. I'm still hungering to see my words on paper.

Jon. This brings us to component five, that bulky and expensive part of a complete word processing operation, the printer. The characters that have been stored on the disk are loaded into the computer's memory and then sent to the printer. The printer may remind you of a teletype machine as it types back and forth, left to right and right to left at incredible speed. In a few minutes you have your precious words.

Bill. I've seen some of those printed products since you have taken to writing your letters home by word processor. They strike me as light impressions when compared with a conventional solidly printed book.

Jon. That's because I use a dot matrix printer that produces dots to form letters. I use the dot matrix because it is faster and less expensive than the letter quality printer that produces copy resembling the work of an electric typewriter. After all, I'm an author, not a printer. My book or article is going to be edited and then printed by a publisher. I hear that some publishers are insisting on letter quality only and not accepting dot matrix. If I encounter such publishers, I will have to conform.

Andy. Suppose I want another copy of my—document. Notice that I'm learning your language, Jon.

Jon. Set the printer to work again. Send a copy off to your editor and preserve the disk. When the editor has copyedited your manuscript, put the disk back into the machine and make the needed changes. Make your backup disk. Set the printer to work again, this time producing the revised copy. If at the last moment you discover that you've made an unforgivable factual error or omitted an essential idea, make your changes and reprint the page or chapter. By then your manuscript should be so clean that your editor could go directly to production of page proofs, saving the many weeks formerly given to galleys. Note that changes in the manuscript have been made without retyping the entire document. As I mentioned, new errors often creep into retyping. That's why writers become gray prematurely.

Tuck away the backup disk and pull it out years later when you revise the book for a second edition. Update the statistics, sandwich in new paragraphs, and drop the obsolete. Print. Selah, your revision!

Andy. Wouldn't it be possible for writers to omit the printing stage and turn their disks over to editors?

Jon. Spoken like a potential devotee of word processing, Andy! It's happening. The writer sends or brings his edited disks that serve as his "final copy" to the editor. The publisher's designer provides specifications as to type, spacing, handling of tables, and so on. Then the disks go to a photo-setting company, which typographically codes them for a master computer. This versatile computer follows specifications and picks out the desired typefaces from its memory bank. The photo images created are fed to a camera that makes negatives. The printing company makes offset photos from the negatives. Page proofs are ready for the editor and the author in a remarkably short time, perhaps a week, rather than the customary several months.

Bill. Knowing many authors, editors, and publishers as I do, I'll believe this when I see it.

Andy. List for us again the usual components of the personal computer.

Jon. Keyboard, video screen, central processing unit, disk drives for magnetic media, printer. Some computer buffs prefer to phrase the components as computer (keyboard and central processing unit), monitor (video screen), disk drives, and printer. These, along with optional additional equipment, constitute your hardware. But there's one more essential to make your computer a word processor. You need a program.

Just as a record player needs a record, a computer needs a program. In computer language, programs are described as software. The computer requires a budget program to enable you to prepare your budget or a game program to enable you to play a video game. The computer also needs a word processing program if you intend to write via word processor. So you run a word processing program that tells your computer what to do. It is the software, the word processing program, that enables the computer to perform the unique instructions that are a part of word processing. The program tells you what to do to get the computer to do what you want it to do.

Andy. How do we instruct this computer to do what we want it to do?

Jon. Without the software the computer can do nothing. The program gives you choices and asks you questions. You respond through your keys and your cursor.

You type and your letters and words appear on the screen. Maybe you decide to delete a sentence. You tap "delete" and the machine asks you "delete what?" You move the cursor—that's the marker I mentioned—to what you want to delete. By following the instructions in your manual, you tell the machine through your cursor and keys how much you want to take out. What you want to eliminate disappears and the rest of the paragraph moves back to fill the empty space.

Andy. So our imperfection is washed away.

Jon. Through similar taps you can insert, move blocks of content around, change page numbers, and so on. Consequently, you always see on your screen clean copy rather than a dirty draft. For a writer that's psychologically healthy.

Andy. So I respond to questions by striking certain keys on the keyboard?

Jon. I'd better not go into details because each brand of word processor has its own procedures and gimmicks. Each computer's manual for users explains the steps in a strange new language that at first may turn you off. Unfortunately, you'll have to learn the jargon if you are going to write by word processor.

For instance, would you like me to tell you about automatic pagination or justification? Want me to define bytes or files or initialize or default? Want me to give a lecture on how you can store research on your disks and use it when you need it? Want me to tell you how you can tie in from data banks that gather, store, and distribute data?

Andy. No thanks, not at the moment. I have only one pitiful objection. All these marvels must be expensive.

Jon. The savings in time and energy and retyping costs are so substantial that people who steadily use their word processors will eventually save money on their original investments in equipment. Happily, computers with word processing capacities are one of these products that steadily shrink in price as they grow newer and better. I wouldn't dare estimate the cost for fear that the figures would quickly become obsolete. Speaking of obsolescence, I'm even fearful that some of the information about word processing that I've just shared with you will be obsolete before I draw my next breath. The computer revolution is on and change is accelerating.

Bill. It's a new ball game, Andy.

Andy. As the New Yorker cartoon character put it, "Whither goeth literature, there also must I go." You have a convert in me, Jon.

Bill. I suspect I'll plod along in my old-fashioned way. But I'll accompany Andy on his visits to our local user-friendly computer salesperson.

Jon. A word of warning. There's nothing lonelier than an unused computer. You can add that to the possible disadvantages you implied in your questions.

So buy with care. Compare brands. Buy software selectively. Consult the latest buying guides.

You might also orient yourselves through school or university courses. Get familiar with computer-related facilities in the community. Maybe some equipment is available to you at little or no cost.

Bill. Jon, sum up the advantages to us of using word processors in our writing. Tempt me further.

Jon. I like Peter A. McWilliams's summary of advantages for writers. He says here in *The Word Processing Book:*

1. Change is effortless.
2. Retyping is unnecessary.
3. Spelling is perfect.
4. Word processors are quiet.

5. You are not chained to a typewriter table. The detachable keyboard, available on many personal computers, is wonderful.
6. No more carriage returns.
7. Correspondence is easy. How often have you wanted to write essentially the same thing to five friends?
8. Research is easier.
9. Other programs are available.
10. They're fun.[1]

WHY I WRITE WITH A WORD PROCESSOR

Using a word processor results in my personally doing more typing and my secretary doing less. The payoff, though, is immediate access to the material, in either hard copy (paper) or soft copy (television screen) so that the process of revision may start at once. The result has been more courageous revisions since I no longer feel guilty about having a secretary spend hours preparing a manuscript just for me to take a red pen to the text. Now I know I can revise and change at my pleasure without worrying about the secretary. The product will be ready immediately.

I could never compose on an electric typewriter. The whir of the motor seemed to be ordering me to keep moving, to work faster. My word processor uses less energy than my electric typewriter and is much quieter. Overall, I have found a very patient machine which tolerates my stopping to think as I write. This has led to much more composing of material on the word processor and less time being spent with paper and pencil.

The real satisfaction from a word processor comes from the immediate feedback which is available. With the printer attached there can be a polished copy of a manuscript within minutes and the pleasure of reviewing a finished product is very rewarding.

Arthur M. Horne
Professor of Counseling Psychology
Indiana State University
Terre Haute, Indiana

The time to create my initial draft on a word processor is about equal to the time needed on a typewriter. The advantages become apparent when revision is needed. Spelling, punctuation and grammatical errors can be quickly corrected on the screen, without having to resort to correcting fluid. Major rearrangments of the text, whether sentences, paragraphs, or pages, can be accomplished, in only a few seconds, and the modifications examined immediately.

I am a fast but erratic typist, and my eclectic approach to spelling is quickly brought under control through the use of a spelling checker. When

[1]Peter A. McWilliams, *The Word Processing Book* (Los Angeles: Prelude Press, 1983), pp. 108–11.

I feel the need to hold my work, a copy can be printed at high speed, and then read through at my leisure. Errors that slip by the spelling checker (such as substituting "their" for "there") can be noted and changed when I return to the word processor. Admittedly one is at the mercy of several gadgets, but proper precautions will safeguard the unlucky from lost documents, stray electronic surges, disk storage errors, and the host of other ills that word processors are prone to.

Chris Bell
Computer Science Department
Quincy College
Quincy, Illinois

VIEWS ON WORD PROCESSING

CHRISTENSEN, JANE. *Word Processing Simplified and Self-taught*. New York: Arco, 1983.
A guide for the beginner.

FLUEGELMAN, ANDREW AND JEREMY JOAN HUGHES. *Writing in the Computer Age: Word Processing Skills and Style for Every Writer*. Garden City, N.Y.: Anchor Books, 1983.
A book on word processing specifically for the use of writers.

FOSTER, TIMOTHY R. V. AND ALFRED K. GLOSSBRENNER. *Word Processing for Executives and Professionals*. New York: Van Nostrand Reinhold, 1983.
Broad in appeal to employers of word processors, including writers among other users.

MCCUNN, DONALD H. *Write, Edit, and Print: Word Processing with Personal Computers*. San Francisco: Design Enterprises of San Francisco, 1982.
A guide to the varied uses of word processing.

MCWILLIAMS, PETER A. *The McWilliams II Word Processor Instruction Manual*. Los Angeles: Prelude Press, 1984.
An enjoyable spoof on computerese as used in manuals.

MCWILLIAMS, PETER A. *The Personal Computer Book*. Los Angeles: Prelude Press, 1982.
All about personal computers and their uses.

MCWILLAMS, PETER A. *Questions and Answers on Word Processing*. Los Angeles: Prelude Press. 1984
A companion volume to The Word Processing Book *for those who still have questions.*

MCWILLIAMS, PETER A. *The Word Processing Book*. Los Angeles: Prelude Press, 1983.

A short course in computer literacy by a highly readable writer. Includes a brand-name buying guide.

POYNTER, DAN. *Word Processors and Information Processing.* Santa Barbara: Para Publishing, 1982.
A manual on the varied uses of word processors containing technical details and a consumer's guide for the potential purchaser.

PRESS, LAURENCE. *Low-cost Word Processing.* Reading, Mass.: Addison-Wesley Publishing Company, 1983.
What word processors can do.

ROCHESTER, JACK B. AND JOHN GANTZ. *The Naked Computer.* New York: William Morrow and Company, 1983.
A compilation of humorous and fascinating facts about computers.

STULTS, RUSSELL ALLEN. *The Illustrated Word Processing Dictionary.* Englewood Cliffs, N.J.: Prentice-Hall, 1983.
Help for the writer.

TENNANT, RICH AND JOHN BARRY. *Unofficial I Hate Computers Book.* Hasbrouck Heights, N.J.: Hayden Book Company, 1984.
A delightful book of cartoons for those who dislike computers.

WILL, MIMI AND DONETTE DAKE. *Concepts in Word Processing: The Challenge of Change.* Boston: Allyn and Bacon, 1982.
A textbook for beginners in word processing.

WILLIS, JERRY AND MERL MILLER. *Computers for Everybody, 1984 Buyer's Guide.* Beaverton, Oreg.: Dilithium Press, 1983.
Consumer information on 144 current computers with advice to buyers.

ZINSSER, WILLIAM. *Writing With a Word Processor.* New York: Harper & Row, 1983.
A highly readable manual for beginners in the form of a personal account of an author's first experiences in using a word processor.

17

Developing Style
and Using Manuals

The need for readable writing by professionals
Trade books on writing
Principles of composition by Strunk from *The Elements of Style*
Approaches to style by E. B. White
Weaknesses in academic writing
Using initials and fancy words
The importance of clarity
Differences among style manuals
Avoiding sexism

During another conversation Bill solicits advice on how to help mature professionals improve their style. Andy suggests some books; Bill recommends "the little book" in particular. Their comments on style manuals lead into differing views on how writers can avoid sexism.

Bill.   I need your advice, Andy. I can help enrollees in my writing workshops to develop queries, identify promising publication opportunities, plan their time, and assemble tools of the trade. However, these are largely mechanical matters. In your opinion, is there anything I can do to help people develop more readable styles? Some educators write pedaguese; some academics communicate in academese; some graduate students have been taught to write graduatese.

Andy.   Still worse, some are proud of their gobbledygook. They think that obscurity indicates their profundity, vagueness demonstrates their scholarly caution, and confusion shows the complexity of their mental processes. Dullness is mistaken for wisdom, and incomprehensibility is regarded as evidence of high standards.

Bill.   In all fairness, we have to acknowledge that there are also many professors and other professionals who write well. They understand what John Goodlad, of the Graduate School of Education at UCLA, an able writer on education, meant when he told me that he wrote primarily for two reasons: "First, writing clears my mind and makes errant thoughts more precise. Second, writing is in itself a creative process through which thoughts hitherto not formulated begin to take shape.''

However, I worry about those who don't clarify their thinking and develop new ideas through the process of writing.

Andy. Good style grows out of clear thinking, extensive reading, good vocabulary, abundant prior writing, plus additional elements that are indefinable. You can't remedy lifelong weaknesses in such areas through a brief workshop on writing. Let's not be utopian, Bill. These are mature people with set habits; as Montaigne said, ''Habit is second nature.''

However, you might suggest potentially helpful reading experiences. Don't prescribe formal grammar textbooks; they would only repel your workshop participants. Instead, recommend lively and entertaining trade books that sensitize readers to words and their uses.

For instance, Edwin Newman, noted news commentator, has written the amusing *Strictly Speaking* and *A Civil Tongue* about abuses of the English language by contemporary media communicators. Newman can help our colleagues to identify their own clichés, stereotypes, jargon, and plain errors. Theodore M. Bernstein, a *New York Times* editor, wrote *Watch Your Language; The Careful Writer; Miss Thistlebottom's Hobgoblins; Do's, Don'ts, and Maybes of English Usage.* Bernstein can help a reader identify obsolete rules and wrongly defined words. H. L. Mencken's *The American Language* is a classic exploration of the development of English in the United States. Mencken delights in the origins of American departures from standard English. Rudolf Flesch, in *The Art of Plain Talk* and *The Art of Readable Writing,* suggests techniques of simple communication and provides a readability formula. Flesch advocates getting rid of empty words and syllables. He calls for simple sentences, concreteness, and the human touch. More recently, Flesch in *Lite English* has compiled 250 words once taboo and now often used. William Zinsser has published a readable informal guide for writers of nonfiction. The subtitle of John Simon's *Paradigms Lost* is a cue to his views, ''reflections on literacy and its decline.'' William Safire, who often discusses uses of words in his newspaper column, has written *On Language* and *What's the Good Word?*

Bill. Despite your warning against recommending to mature readers the study of formal grammar, could I suggest one source for the writer who wants to review the basic grammatical rules? Couldn't I beg a dispensation for *The Elements of Style,* created by William Strunk, Jr., a Cornell University professor, and revised and expanded by the distinguished essayist E. B. White?

Andy. Dispensation readily granted. *The Elements of Style* is priceless. I see on your shelves ''the little book,'' as Strunk's students called it. Strunk's elementary principles of composition are memorable. Here they are, listed in the table of contents:

Choose a suitable design and hold to it
Make the paragraph the unit of composition
Use the active voice
Put statements in positive form
Use definite, specific, concrete language
Omit needless words
Avoid a succession of loose sentences
Express co-ordinate ideas in similar form
Keep related words together
In summaries, keep to one tense
Place the emphatic words of a sentence at the end[1]

Bill.   Pass the book, please. I also like White's addition to the book. Here are his approaches to style:

Place yourself in the background
Write in a way that comes naturally
Work from a suitable design
Write with nouns and verbs
Revise and rewrite
Do not overwrite
Do not overstate
Avoid the use of qualifiers
Do not affect a breezy manner
Use orthodox spelling
Do not explain too much
Do not construct awkward adverbs
Make sure the reader knows who is speaking
Avoid fancy words
Do not use dialect unless your ear is good
Be clear
Do not inject opinion
Use figures of speech sparingly
Do not take shortcuts at the cost of clarity
Avoid foreign languages
Prefer the standard to the offbeat.[2]

Andy.   Strunk puts his finger on several weaknesses of our academic brethren. For instance, writers for professional publication often

---

[1]William Strunk, Jr., and E. B. White, *The Elements of Style*, 3rd ed. (New York: Macmillan, 1979), p. viii.

[2]Ibid. pp. viii–ix.

use the passive voice: "There were several factors that entered into the situation." Strunk advocates more use of the active voice: "Several factors entered into the situation." Then, Strunk would have the writer insert a colon and name the factors, using "definite, specific, concrete language." Some academics adore the abstract and abhor the concrete.

Bill. "Omit needless words" is another principle many academicians violate. I yearn for my editorial blue pencil when an educator writes, "Owing to the fact that there are not many alternative schools . . . " instead of "Since few alternative schools exist . . . "

Andy. Or adds to needless words an unnecessary negative, "The question as to whether alternative schools are not effective . . . " instead of "Whether alternative schools are effective . . . "

Bill. Some professors never recover from graduate student caution. Despite their acknowledged expert status, they write timidly, "It is sometimes urged by some students of the matter that . . . " They won't risk a definite assertion.

Andy. One of E. B. White's points is often ignored: "Do not take shortcuts at the cost of clarity." The use of initials that are incomprehensible often ruins communication.

Bill. My ASCD and NSSE colleagues agree that use of initials is NG.

Andy. My colleagues in MLA and CEA also warn against using pretentious fancy words. They advise writers to avoid peppering their prose with foreign words and phrases.

Bill. You mean that *lingua* characterized by rodomontade and fustian is *de trop*?

Andy. *Touché!* Eschew obfuscation!

You mentioned clarity; I like White's advice, "Clarity, clarity, clarity. When you become hopelessly mired in a sentence, it is best to start fresh; do not try to fight your way through against the terrible odds of syntax. Usually what is wrong is that the construction has become too involved at some point; the sentence needs to be broken apart and replaced by two or more shorter sentences."[3]

Are you familiar with van Leunen's *A Handbook for Scholars*? She too calls for clarity and the avoidance of obscure pedantic prose. Your writers could learn much about usage as well as the mechanics of scholarship from this book.

Bill. And if I can't get writers to cherish such books?

Andy. At least you might persuade them to use one of the manuals of editorial style. Almost certainly, their manuscripts will be edited in accordance with the style manuals of the American Psychological Association (APA), University of Chicago Press (UCP), or the Modern Language Association (MLA). Writers can avoid many corrections if they

---

[3]Ibid., p. 65.

know which of the style guides their editors use and so prepare their manuscripts accordingly. Young professionals had better put aside the manuals from their student days, such as Turabian's *A Manual for Writers of Term Papers, Theses and Dissertations* and Campbell and Ballou's *Form and Style: Theses, Reports, Term Papers.* Their days of apprenticeship are over; self-preservation dictates the use of authors' manuals.

Bill. The *Publication Manual of the American Psychological Association* is frequently used by research journals in education and the social sciences, as well as psychology. All instructions are neat, tidy, and highly organized, ideal for reporting research in scholarly journals. Some young writers don't realize that articles in the more general professional magazines frequently depart markedly from APA rigidities.

Andy. I'm more familiar with the manuals of the University of Chicago Press and the Modern Language Association. The Chicago manual takes up the preliminary matter at the front of a book, the text of a book, and the use of references. Aspiring authors will encounter abundant details on rules of grammar, and how to index and to prepare tabulations. The Modern Language Association's style resembles Chicago's more than APA's, yet differs in details as to citations and references. All of which demonstrates that, unless writers enjoy the process of erasure, they had better know which style manuals will guide the editing of their manuscripts.

Bill. Specialized fields and organizations sometimes have their own guides. For instance, the American Mathematical Society has published *A Manual for Authors of Mathematical Papers.* Despite the prevalence of manuals, the wary writer should note the instructions on preparation of articles that many periodicals carry in each issue or furnish on request. Book publishers also have their stylistic idiosyncrasies; consequently, major publishing houses issue comprehensive guides for their authors. Obtaining the house's guide early can reduce editorial toil.

Andy. Preparing and revising manuals and guides has become a publishing industry in itself.

Bill. Better not advocate standardization; too many people in publishing would be thrown out of work.

Andy. Some guides have become obsolete because of their sexism. By now, many publishing houses have issued guides on avoidance of sexism. I applaud.

Bill. Use of nonsexist and nonracist language makes good sense. Some new words constantly remind us that a struggle for equality has not yet been won. I can't say "chairperson" without being reminded that sex discrimination has existed and still exists in university departments.

Andy. However, I refuse to accept such language distortion as referring to a chairperson as a "chair." Chairs are to be sat upon; they were never intended to administer departments. Nor will I ever become reconciled to the abolition of "he" as a generic word.

Bill. Use plural forms. Or "he and she." Or "he/she."

Andy. I know the current recommendations. But the result is often tortured prose. There is no substitute in sight for "he" used generically for both sexes. One of the dictionary definitions of "man" is "any human being, regardless of sex or age; a member of the human race; a person."

Bill. But not everybody understands your generic "he"; some will link "he" and "man" to the male gender. I can manage the new pluralization, and I regard "humankind" as an improvement over "mankind." I guess you and I will have to agree to disagree on what language usages should be regarded as sexist, and thus avoided. In any case, content matters at least as much as form and usage. The *way* women are represented in a publication is of greatest importance.

Andy. No disagreement with that.

BOOKS ON WRITING STYLE

APPELBAUM, JUDITH and NANCY EVANS. *How to Get Happily Published.* Rev. ed. New York: Harper & Row, 1982.
Deals with learning to write, getting started, working with editors, promoting your book, self-publishing, and financial considerations.

BERNSTEIN, THEODORE M. *The Careful Writer: A Modern Guide to English Usage.* New York: Atheneum, 1977.
A concise yet thorough handbook.

BERNSTEIN, THEODORE M. *Do's, Don'ts and Maybes of English Usage.* New York: Times Books, 1977.
Help on usage from a distinguished editor of The New York Times.

BERNSTEIN, THEODORE M. *Miss Thistlebottom's Hobgoblins.* New York: Farrar, Straus and Giroux, 1973.
An alphabetical guide to difficult traps in words, syntax, idioms, and style, well described in the subtitle, "The Careful Writer's Guide to the Taboos, Bugbears, and Outmoded Rules of English Usage."

BERNSTEIN, THEODORE M. *Watch Your Language.* New York: Atheneum, 1965.
A lively informal guide to better writing based on experiences at The New York Times.

FLESCH, RUDOLF. *The Art of Plain Talk.* New York: Harper & Row, 1946.
A book on writing readable simplified English, based on his studies of readability.

FLESCH, RUDOLF. *The Art of Readable Writing*. New York: Harper & Row, 1949.
A highly readable book which contains sound advice on writing and which applies the Flesch readability formula, revised after publication of The Art of Plain Talk.

FLESCH, RUDOLF. *Lite English*. New York: Harper & Row, 1984.
The jacket says, "Popular words that are OK to use no matter what William Safire, John Simon, Edwin Newman and the other purists say."

FOWLER, H. W. *A Dictionary of Modern English Usage*. 2nd ed. Revised by Sir Ernest Gowers. New York: Oxford University Press, 1983.
The classic guide to English usage, which provides authoritative help to writers.

HODGES, JOHN C. and MARY E. WHITTEN *Harbrace College Handbook*. 9th ed. New York: Harcourt Brace Jovanovich, 1982.
Grammar, mechanics, punctuation, spelling, effective sentences, and elements of composition.

McCARTNEY, EUGENE S. *Recurrent Maladies in Scholarly Writing*. New York: Gordian, 1969.
A short and humorous style guide for scholars that explains the advantages of simple, logical, correctly spelled writing.

MENCKEN, H. L. *The American Language*. New York: Alfred A. Knopf, 1963.
A classic on the development of English in the United States by a vigorous, irreverent journalist.

The New York Times Everyday Reader's Dictionary of Misunderstood, Misused, Mispronounced Words. Edited by Laurence Urdang. New York: Quadrangle Books, 1975.
A dictionary for those who are having trouble with especially abused words.

NEWMAN, EDWIN. *A Civil Tongue*. New York: Warner 1983.
A readable account of sociolinguistics.

NEWMAN, EDWIN. *Strictly Speaking: Will America Be the Death of English?* New York: Warner 1983.
A delightful examination of the state of the English language as often used by speakers and writers.

SAFIRE, WILLIAM. *On Language*. New York: Avon, 1981.
A provocative look at uses and misuses of language.

SAFIRE, WILLIAM. *What's the Good Word?* New York: Times Books, 1982.
Readable commentary helpful to writers searching for precision in the use of words.

SIMON, JOHN. *Paradigms Lost*. New York: C. N. Potter, 1980.
A vigorous criticism of contemporary use of language.

STRUNK, WILLIAM, JR., and E. B. WHITE. *The Elements of Style*. 3rd ed. New York: Macmillan, 1979.
The original work by Strunk, plus introductory material and a chapter on writing by E. B. White.

VAN LEUNEN, MARY-CLAIRE. *A Handbook for Scholars*. New York: Alfred A. Knopf, 1978.
Considers many of the problems scholars encounter in writing, including the mechanics of citations, quotations, footnoting, and many stylistic matters.

Writers' Handbook. Edited by S. K. Burack. Boston: The Writer Inc. 1985 Annual.
A compendium of articles on how to write, writer's markets, and the editorial process. Especially useful for fiction and popular writers and of particular use to members of the professions contemplating writing for general magazines or publishing trade books.

ZINSSER, WILLIAM. *On Writing Well: An Informal Guide to Writing Nonfiction*. New York: Harper and Row, 1980.
A book for the person who wants to communicate effectively through nonfiction.

STYLE MANUALS

The Chicago Manual of Style. 13th ed. Chicago: University of Chicago Press, 1982
(See preceding dialogue for annotation.)

DAY, R. A. *How to Write and Publish a Scientific Paper*. Philadelphia: iSi Press, 1983.
A helpful guide for authors of scientific papers.

The McGraw-Hill Style Manual. Edited by Marie M. Longyear. New York: McGraw-Hill Book Company, 1982.
General standards for writing, technical standards for mathematical and scientific publishing, as well as grammar and usage.

A Manual for Authors of Mathematical Papers. Providence, R.I.: American Mathematical Society, 1979.
Specific information for writers in the field of mathematics.

M.L.A. Style Sheet. New York: Modern Language Association, 1970.
(See preceding dialogue for annotation.)

The New York Times Manual of Style and Usage. New York: Times Books, 1982.
A desk book for writers and editors.

Publication Manual of the American Psychological Association, 3rd ed. Washington, D.C.: American Psychological Association, 1983.
(See preceding dialogue for annotation.)

SKILLIN, MARJORIE E. and ROBERT M. GAY. *Words into Type*. 3rd ed. Englewood Cliffs, N.J.: Prentice-Hall, 1974.
Great detail on how to prepare a manuscript, work on copy and page proofs, maintain consistent copyediting style, understand typographical style, improve grammar and choice of words, and plan illustrations.

U.S. Government Printing Office Style Manual. Washington, D.C.: 1983.
Especially useful to professionals working on publications of the U.S. government. The address is G. P. O., Supt. of Documents, Washington, D.C. 20402

18

Finding
a Publisher

When publishers seek out authors
Authors in search of publishers
Approaching major commercial publishers
Regional presses
Small presses
Publication programs of professional associations
University presses
Self-publishing
Subsidy presses
Problems of the vanity press or do-it-yourself routes
The many opportunities for book publication

By now, Andy and Bill have decided that they enjoy discussions marked by both agreements and disagreements. So they come together again at Andy's home to talk about how writers of professional books find publishers. They agree that more opportunities for book publication exist than most authors recognize.

Bill. Andy, if only there were a foolproof way for authors to find a publisher, instead of the scramble that now prevails! Accident, fluke, and chance usually determine the so-called selection of a publisher.

Andy. From an author's point of view, I suppose that the ideal way would be the publisher's finding the author, not vice versa. Author has something to communicate. Publisher, learning of this, entreats author to write book. Author graciously consents. Writes fine book. Magnificent reviews. Best seller. Author flooded with invitations to speak here and there.

Bill. And, as in the other childhood fables, author and publisher live together harmoniously for the rest of their days.

Yet, even this variation on "finding a publisher" actually exists. Sometimes a person in a profession writes knowledgeable articles, yearbook chapters, monographs, or whatever on a particular topic. The topic suddenly ignites. An editor for a commercial publishing house decides that a book is needed. Editorial research turns up our author, who is right and ready. Result: an invitation from the company and, in time, a book.

This sometimes does happen in both trade and college textbook publishing. As to textbooks for elementary and secondary school students, the standard practice is for their authors to be invited; editors usually ferret out el-hi writers.

Andy. Even as in the sports or entertainment world, celebrities are recognized in the professions. They don't have to bother about finding a publisher; perceptive editors seek them out. If the topic is already hot, so much the better for the author and the editor. If not, the name of the celebrity, coupled with capable treatment of material, may heat up the topic—at least, so the editor hopes.

Bill. Even so, any invitation handed a person in a profession by an editor involves a high element of chance. No editor can foresee with certainty which topics the profession and the public will welcome a year or two from now. Even history textbooks change in emphasis and content with the times, as Frances FitzGerald demonstrated in *America Revised*.

Andy. An editor can make some shrewd guesses, though. In literature, for instance, interest revives in particular authors. Suddenly, after a period of relative neglect, a spate of books on Henry James or William Faulkner appears.

Bill. Fashions in ideas influence educational publishing too. For instance, American school systems began developing middle schools in the 1960s and 1970s. At once, every self-respecting education editor wanted the firm's new catalog of publications to include a book on middle schools. Because so many publishers and authors got into the act, few middle school books for the college market sold well.

During the late 1970s the requirement of minimum competencies for promotion from grade to grade and eventual graduation from high school became an educational vogue in our state legislatures. So editors sought out experts in competency-based education to write books on the subject. They went to their files for the names of authors suggested by sales representatives in the field; they called on knowledge of possible writers acquired at conventions; they flipped over their lists of reliable and productive outside readers; some even checked their files of rejected proposals.

In 1984 the presidential candidates argued over competing political prescriptions for ailing education. Battles over educational policies were fought through books, articles, and the mass media. National reports on education were widely distributed. The report of the National Commission on Excellence in Education, *A Nation at Risk*, called on schools for more science and mathematics, the introduction of required computer courses, a longer school day and year, and more homework to meet the international technological challenge to America. Study groups such as those headed by Ernest L. Boyer (*High School*), John Goodlad (*A Place Called School*), Theodore Sizer (*Horace's Compromise: The Dilemma of the American High School*), and Gordon Cawelti (*Redefining General Education in the High School*) contributed differing perceptions and alternative programs for the improvement of secondary education. These latter publications often called for a wider range of educational purposes than did *A Nation at Risk*. They questioned whether more of the same was necessarily better.

Andy. Understandably, an editor likes to strike when the iron is hot, not wait several years for a possible cooling-off. Authors lucky enough to have already written a manuscript on currently timely topics will get an enthusiastic response from publishing houses.

But the usual situation is that the publisher doesn't find the author; the author finds the publisher. The author asks, "Where do I turn?"

Bill. Consumers recognize and respond to national brands—Zenith and Panasonic, Exxon and Texaco, Kodak and Polaroid. Authors of professional publications have similar kneejerk responses—McGraw-Hill and Macmillan—

Andy. Harper & Row; Harcourt Brace Jovanovich; Scott Foresman; Houghton Mifflin.

Bill. Prentice-Hall; Jossey-Bass; John Wiley and Sons; Holt, Rinehart and Winston—and so on through one or two or, at the most, three dozen publishers.

Andy. Plus houses with prestige in special fields. Alfred A. Knopf, Charles Scribner's Sons, and Random House, for instance, are well respected in the literary world. Academic Press, a subsidiary of Harcourt Brace Jovanovich, is known for its medical, scientific, and technical books.

Bill. A behavioral or social scientist is likely to think of Basic Books as a desirable publisher. So off go the queries to the leaders with the recognized names.

Andy. Nothing wrong with that, is there, Bill? After all, authors want to be read. The big companies have large sales staffs, the capacity to advertise, and the ability to attract reviewers for the better journals. The prestige of the respected companies rubs off on their authors.

Bill. The problem is that everybody else is also sending queries and prospectuses and unsolicited manuscripts to the publishing industry leaders. Even though the larger of the companies we mentioned publish more than 350 books annually, the rejection rate is horrendous. Solid and firm figures on rejections are hard to come by because many publishing houses see no point in keeping track of the volume of rejections. After a half-dozen turndowns, the author, already busy with other professional work, despairs, and the manuscript is shelved.

Yet other commercial publishers exist. Companies that annually publish fewer books than the giants, yet are familiar names to people in particular professions, include—let's look at *Literary Market Place*—Allyn and Bacon, educational publisher; American Book Company, publisher of el-hi titles; Appleton-Century-Crofts in medicine, nursing, and allied health fields—and that, Andy, is only a sample from the A's in *LMP*. Hundreds of additional publishers have names that are not household words to the average member of a profession.

Andy. Sometimes the smaller commercial companies are willing to take a flier with an unconventional manuscript that the giants would reject. The commercial giants are often cautious.

Bill. Maybe that's how they became giants. For instance, college departments of the larger companies favor hardbacked textbooks designed for courses with an assured market that provide a comfortable profit margin. The profit margins are thinner for paperback anthologies. Consequently, the large commercial publishers may shy away from anthologies.

If an author describes a book as "supplementary" or, indeed, can't describe an assured market, the major publishers often say "no thanks"—if they bother to respond at all. The educator who wants to write on alternative schools, or values, or drug abuse by students, or a hundred other specialized matters dealt with in courses but not scheduled for a semester of study, may encounter more receptive ears in the offices of smaller commercial publishers. They sell fewer books than the giants, yet manage to return sufficient profit to stay in business.

Some authors report that the larger the potential market, the more the editors want to participate in shaping the content of the book. The smaller the market, the fewer are the editorial pressures to shape the book to ensure widespread adoption in courses. Thus, it is argued, authors of books on education and other professional subjects are freer to express themselves when they publish with smaller houses that are not constantly eyeing textbook adoptions. However, this may be another rule to which there are too many exceptions.

Editing is especially heavy on textbooks for elementary and high school students. A Stanford University research institute study reports that about 75 percent of classroom time is textbook-centered and 16 percent of the total sales of publishers are el-hi textbooks. Since pressure groups and vested interests are especially sensitive to inclusions and omissions in elementary and high school textbooks, editors and authors tread softly. Each state defines for itself how textbooks are selected; the processes range from local selection through various state adoption plans. Almost half the states follow state adoption procedures for elementary and high school textbooks. Textbook publishers contend fiercely for adoptions by large states like Texas, where centralized state adoption procedures prevail.[1]

Andy. When local school systems choose from among possible textbooks or select fiction for study or decide on supplementary readings, who makes these decisions?

Bill. A 1981 survey of school administrators indicates that nearly 56 percent of schools or school systems have their own instructional materials selection committees. Everybody and his cousin may be represented, including teachers, school board members, parents, department heads, teacher union representatives, students, principals, civic leaders, and an array of specialists within the school system such as librarians. Whether a school system has a materials selection committee or not, responsibility for final selection of learning materials is lodged with the school board, which usually depends on evaluations and recommendations brought to them by the superintendent and principals who, in turn, depend on materials committees or teachers. So community groups that are critical of sex education or the teaching of evolution, or that object to profanity or what they regard as irreligion in books, often monitor material according to their own criteria and then usually address any complaints to local school boards or state education boards.

Andy. Compromises—to use a polite term—are sometimes used by authors and editors in the production of textbooks. Prior to the civil rights movement, publishing companies had been known to produce Northern and Southern editions of school history textbooks. The Northern edition described what the author called the Civil War; the Southern edition called it the War Between the States. Guess in which edition the blacks were always happy on the plantation with their masters.

Today, pressures concerning treatment of minorities may come from ethnic and black and civil rights organizations; minority groups are understandably sensitive to racial and ethnic slights and omissions. Unfortunately, classics like *The Merchant of Venice* or *Huckleberry Finn* are sometimes assailed.

Bill. Pressures are also applied by conservative forces. For instance, *Man: A Course of Study,* a National Science Foundation program; various textbooks used in Kanawha County, West Virginia; and programs of values clarification have been targets of criticism by conservative forces. Fundamentalists who challenge the customary teaching of evolution in science classes recently have persuaded some state legis-

[1]Sherry Keith, *Politics of Textbook Selection* (Stanford University, California, Institute for Research on Educational Finance and Governance, 1981).

latures to mandate the teaching of creationism. Though courts have ruled against such laws, science textbook publishers, in their effort to survive and compete, sometimes are influenced by creationist criticisms.

Andy.   Spokesmen for groups claiming to represent the morality of Americans have protested strong language in contemporary literature on reading lists of English classes and have objected to ideas and language of passages within literature anthologies. Their libertarian-minded opponents condemn such objections as censorship. Holden Caulfield of J.D. Salinger's *Catcher in the Rye* has many stout defenders. Among the books frequently attacked are *Forever* by Judy Blume, *Of Mice and Men* and *Grapes of Wrath* by John Steinbeck, and *Slaughterhouse-Five* by Kurt Vonnegut, Jr. Critics have also attacked Dante's *The Divine Comedy*, Homer's *Odyssey*, and Thomas Paine's *The Age of Reason*, as well as the *American Heritage Dictionary*, *Mary Poppins*, and children's books by E.B. White.

Bill.   Economics is another field in which textbook publishers and authors experience pressures.

Andy.   Is there really any way of guarding against frustrating experiences in writing textbooks?

Bill.   I don't know of any, save acquiring hearsay on the company's reputation and attempting to find a compatible editor. If you're inclined to write as you please, better avoid an editor who secretly wants to write a book, namely yours. On the other hand, if you welcome many suggestions as to content and as to modifications of your style, avoid an editor who rarely blue pencils or adds to your copy.

Andy.   Yet when you do find compatibility, the editor may be promoted or fired or may leave for another job. The turnover among editors may be worse than among football coaches or college presidents.

So far we've talked primarily of commercial publishers. Though they do publish the majority of America's books, the writer of professional books does have other options. For instance, the regional publisher is highly important to writers on literature, the social sciences, folklore, and the arts. A scholar may write about California novelists for a Far Western regional publisher or about regional history for a Southern press. The market and sales may be limited. Yet such publications are highly respected by one's colleagues and nonmonetary rewards may be considerable. Regional presses also publish specialized books on local crafts and customs, whether cookery or quilting or trout fishing or whatever. Some achieve surprisingly wide distribution.

Bill.   Not only do the regional presses publish specialized books; a number of other small presses publish books on a wide variety of interests. Name a specialization, and these days there are likely to be publishing opportunities: environment and ecology, health, sports, aviation, international relations, ethnic groups, and many others. *Avant-garde* and counterculture publications are among the writer's many alternatives.

The mind boggles at the number of specialized topics and the number of available books.

Andy. Many small presses are listed, along with descriptions of their interests, in *Literary Market Place;* but *LMP* lists only publishers of more than three books each year. Many books published by small presses are mentioned in the *Small Press Record of Books in Print,* which lists over 4,000 titles and authors published by 900 small presses. An author can also use the *International Directory of Little Magazines and Small Presses.* Richard Balkin, in his very good book *A Writer's Guide to Book Publishing,* differentiates between small commercial companies and the "small press," which he describes as unintentionally a nonprofit-making institution. He says there may be anywhere from 1,000 to 2,000 such presses, including regional and alternative presses. Hard facts about the number of publishers are difficult to come by.

Authors often overlook another outlet for their books. Though academics are highly aware of the journals of their professional associations in which they often publish, they sometimes forget that their professional organizations may also be book publishers. One of my book-oriented colleagues developed, from the *Literary Market Place* roster of association presses, a list of organizations that rival many commercial houses in number of books published.

Bill. In addition, organizations often publish pamphlets in education; for instance, Phi Delta Kappa both publishes books and issues many "fastbacks" (highly current pamphlets). The National Education Association has a massive publication program. There are also associations that publish less than 1,000 copies of a pamphlet.

Scholars have another publishing opportunity that is uniquely theirs—the university press. Since the university provides a subsidy, a university press does not have to make a profit. Books can be judged on their scholarly merit. But lately sales of the average university press book have suffered. The decline has resulted from shortsighted federal agencies, which reduced available federal funds, and from equally shortsighted university administrations, which cut library budgets during times of financial stringency. Continuing inflation has also gnawed away at university press budgets. Faced by hard decisions, libraries have often chosen to continue buying journals at the expense of acquiring new university press books.

Andy. Some of the powers-that-be in university press publication have tried to cut their losses through greater emphasis on sales. I don't mean that they have forgotten their original mission of publishing scholarly works. Their books are still solid. Yet greater consciousness of the desirability of wide distribution enters into decision-making.

Bill. Our colleagues often tend to submit to the largest university presses and to neglect the smaller, repeating the error they make in submitting proposals to commercial publishers. College professors tend to think of the university presses that publish more than 125 titles annually: Chicago, California, Harvard, Columbia, and a few others. They would benefit by inquiring into specializations of the university presses, such as the University of Oklahoma's publications on Indians, or Southern Illinois University's publications of John Dewey's work, or the Ohio State University's works on educational philosophers, or the University of Arizona's studies of the Southwest, or the University of Washington's studies of Alaska and Eskimos. They might find that the usual university press which publishes twenty or thirty titles annually might be more hospitable to their efforts than the large presses located at the major centers of scholarship. The Association of American University Presses publishes a directory, and, as usual, *LMP* and *Writer's Market* also provide listings. If a writer's drive is toward the enhancement of knowledge rather than the acquisition of a yacht, the university press should not be a last resort.

Andy. Speaking of last resorts in finding publishers, what do you think of two possibilities, self-publishing and the subsidy press?

Bill. In both cases the author pays to have the book published. If members of the profession so urgently want to publish that they are willing to finance their publications from their own pockets, they should carefully compare the two possible routes. In self-publishing the book is financed, owned, and distributed by its author. In subsidy press publication, the book is financed by the author but is owned and distributed by the publisher (though actually a great deal of the responsibility for distribution still devolves upon the author). A self-publisher usually contracts with a printer for printing and binding and individually handles all matters of design, editing, proofreading, promotion, advertising, sales, etc. A subsidy press usually assumes all of these functions in exchange for a fee.

Andy. As to sales, few people buy the average subsidy press book; it's not unusual for a subsidy press book to sell only a few copies. Just a small fraction of subsidy press authors get their money back; a popular current estimate is 10 percent. Yet the investment can be substantial. Bookstores seldom carry subsidy press books, and few reviews appear. Editing is usually minimal.

Bill. In self-publishing, the author also bears the costs of publication for a book that may be carried only in the local bookstores and noted only in the local newspaper. The author often spends a formidable amount of time in his new roles as businessperson, including the unpleasant chore of attempting to collect from deadbeats who order by mail and are shipped books yet don't pay for them. When we take into account the author's time investment as editor, designer, salesperson, promoter, and Lord knows what all, few self-published books repay the author in monetary terms.

Andy. Yet the self-published author is often repaid in other ways.

Colleagues recognize that many distinguished authors have self-published some of their work. The self-publisher is often admired as a person of integrity who stubbornly believes in the importance of the written word. For a literary craftsman, what a treat it is to shape and design one's own book, to do all but print it oneself—and some even do their own printing!

Bill. People who disagree might say that these are distinctions without a clear difference. Subsidy publishers claim that had subsidy presses been in existence, writers such as crusading Tom Paine and iconoclastic Sam Clemens would have used their services, and maybe they would have. Certainly a good many people do today, for the subsidy presses publish approximately 2,000 titles a year. The number of supposedly "scholarly books" published by the subsidy presses is increasing as budgets grow tighter at university presses and as trade publishers grow more profit-minded.

Andy. Who says the books are "scholarly"? Only the authors, who serve as judge and jury.

Bill. The subsidy presses do leave decisions as to quality up to the author, who is understandably biased. That's why the subsidy press is often called the "vanity press," a label the subsidy publishers dislike. But authors of self-published books also serve as both judge and jury.

Andy. There's a difference. The colleagues of authors who publish through a subsidy press often take a dim view of what they regard as vanity press publications. Members of the professions who pay presses to publish their works may lose face. In the eyes of some colleagues, the vanity press imprint carries with it a stigma. Even a good book can suffer if the professional for whom the book is intended judges it to keep bad company. A writer for professional publication should think long and hard before deciding to finance and publish a vanity press book.

Before writers for professional publication decide to finance their own publications through publishers who advertise that they are seeking authors and who send representatives to communities to talk with potential authors, they might well read "Does It Pay to Pay to Have It Published?" a *Writer's Digest* reprint available from the magazine. They might also read articles on vanity publishing as well as the literature they can readily obtain from subsidy publishers. They might get a view from an insider through reading Edward Uhlan's *The Rogue of Publishers' Row*.

Bill. Like you, I prefer self-publication to the vanity press if a person has written a good manuscript for the profession that isn't marketable through the customary channels. I recognize the dangers to the academician in vanity publishing. Yet I don't totally condemn this form of publishing. If a person who hasn't scholarly pretensions wants to leave an autobiography for the grandchildren, or to publish poems that no one seems to want to buy, or to urge an unfashionable cause, and if the person regards the product as worth the investment and is willing to accept financial losses—why not?

I do think any claim to higher rank or salary based on vanity press publication should be carefully scrutinized by university decision-makers. But I think the same caution should prevail as to self-published work.

Once in a while a self-published book is picked up and taken over by a well-established publishing house. But the more likely destiny of a self-published book is the remainder counter of a discount bookshop.

As to cost, I am convinced that the do-it-yourself way costs the author less than the vanity press route, and that the volume of sales is at least equal. Some self-published books eventually return out-of-pocket expenses to their authors. When you deal in person with a printer, you avoid the vanity publishers' profit-taking. And in either case, you prove to be the salesperson or, more likely, the gift-giver. So, if it's a case of any port in the storm, an author who has sufficient funds might put in at the harbor of self-publishing. Without funds, the writer can only keep on bailing the sinking ship through mailing query letters or the unsolicited manuscript.

Andy. The writer who contemplates self-publishing might study *The Publish-It-Yourself Handbook*, published by Pushcart Books Press for experiences of some who tried it or some of the manuals on self-publishing that have recently been developed, such as *The Self-Publishing Manual* by Dan Poynter, published by Para Publications. Before going the self-publishing route, authors would benefit by hours spent in homework in the library with *LMP, Writer's Market*, the directories published by the Association of American University Presses, and other such listings.

Bill. I doubt that anyone will ever claim that professors and other writers can easily find publishers for their books. But book publishing is a wide-ranging, diversified field. Opportunities for publication do exist, as we have indicated. If authors spent as much time studying how to find a publisher as they did in writing their Chapter 7, still more books would be published.

Andy. Let's not commit ourselves on whether or not that would be a good thing.

DIRECTORIES OF BOOK PUBLISHERS

Publishers Directory. Detroit: Gale Research Company. 1984.
  Comprehensive guide for librarians, booksellers, and readers to many specialized publishing operations.

Books in Print. (By authors—3 vols. By title—3 vols. By subject—4 vols.) New York: R. R. Bowker.
> *Authoritative volumes listing books in print and including publishers' addresses. The 1983–84 edition is derived from 15,200 publishers.*

Directory, Association of American University Presses. New York: Association of American University Presses, 1982-83.
> *Guide to the various university presses in America.*

International Directory of Scholarly Publishers. Toronto: United Nations Educational Scientific and Cultural Organization, 1977.
> *Basic information about any press or organization in the world which is the publishing division of an institution of higher learning.*

International Literary Market Place. New York: R. R. Bowker. Annual.
> *The international version of* Literary Market Place.

KURIAN, GEORGE THOMAS. *The Directory of American Book Publishing.* New York: Simon and Schuster, 1975.
> *A history and brief description of major publishers.*

Literary Market Place. New York: R. R. Bowker. Annual.
> *A valuable directory of American book publishing, including names and addresses of publishing companies publishing more than three books annually.*

Publishers, Distributors and Wholesalers of the United States. New York: R. R. Bowker, 1983.
> *List of 37,500 editorial and ordering addresses.*

Small Press Record of Books in Print. 7th ed. Paradise, Calif.: Dustbooks (P.O. Box 1056), 1978.
> *Listing of titles and authors published by small presses.*

U.S. Book Publishing Yearbook and Directory. White Plains, N.Y.: Knowledge Industry Publications, Inc. 1982.
> *Industry statistics, company financial information, plus original analysis of the economic condition of the industry.*

Writer's Market. Edited by Bruce Joel Hillman. Cincinnati, Ohio: Writer's Digest Books. Annual.
> *"4,000 places to sell your short stories, articles, books, poetry, novels, plays, fiction, scripts, fillers, gags, photos."*

19

Contracting
for a Book

Why an author should carefully study a contract
Royalty rates
Negotiating a higher royalty
Advances on books
Delivery date
Deleting and adding contract provisions
Overediting
Author's alterations
Special provisions—ancillary materials, revisions, foreign sales
Other provisions—future works, permissions, cost of artwork, subsidiary
    rights, libel, escape clauses
Negotiations prior to contract signing

*Both Andy and Bill have had experiences with book contracts. Each has
advice for writers for professional publication. Inevitably, royalties enter into
the conversation, and a calculator is passed from hand to hand. They differ
on the desirability of advances. Their suggestions as to modifications and
understandings concerning contracts are varied and numerous.*

Andy. Eventually a publisher is found.

Bill. We hope so.

Andy. I'm glad you didn't say "hopefully," an abominable usage
dear to the hearts of TV weather forecasters. Now comes the matter of
a contract. I'm referring to book publication, of course; in the case of
the journal article, the author simply receives a letter indicating editorial
interest, specifying desired deadline dates, possibly suggesting em-
phases, and containing some phrases giving the editor the option of
using the manuscript or not. Contracts are rarely used in relations between authors and editors of professional periodicals, though they are
on the increase.

Bill. Yearbooks are one type of book authorized by a letter from
the organization, not a contract.

Andy. For other books—whether trade, text, or specialized (scholarly, technical, professional)—the publisher has on hand stacks of contract forms, formidable and legal in appearance.

Bill. Not only legal in appearance, also in substance. That's why I advise authors to read contracts carefully, solicit advice, and raise necessary questions with editors rather than promptly sign and send the contracts back in the next mail. A contract is a legal agreement, enforceable under the law.

Andy. And the contract is prepared by the publisher, not the author. Naturally, the lawyers who develop contracts carefully protect the interests of the publishers. A cynic might even say that the typical contract is loaded in favor of the publisher.

Bill. Loaded like dice?

Andy. Not in the sense that the dice are loaded to rig the game and cheat the author. In my experience, the contract dice are honest, even in the case of vanity publishers. However, the dice happen to be *owned* by the publisher. So let the buyer beware—in this case, the author is cast in the buyer's role.

Bill. I suspect the author looks most closely at the typed-in section of the contract that specifies royalty arrangements, rather than the printed legalese. Royalty language is sometimes baffling. Anybody can understand the meaning of the royalty percentages, whether 10 or 12½ or 15 percent (or that rarely used number 18), but phrases like "list price" and "net receipts" send authors who are not business majors to the dictionary.

Andy. Which doesn't always help. List price simply means the price on the cover of the book, the retail price. On trade books, the list price is used in calculating royalties. Usually, the trade book author receives 10 percent on the first 5,000 copies sold, 12½ percent on the next 5,000, and 15 percent beyond the first 10,000. Let's suppose a book is priced at $15 for bookstore sales—

Bill. In the great American supermarket tradition, probably $14.95. Today, though, many books cost considerably more than that.

Andy. Call it $15 to avoid complexity. If the book sells 5,000 copies, the author receives $7,500. If 10,000 copies, $16,875. If 15,000, $28,125. Or forget all the mathematics and call the royalty $1.50 per copy on the first 5,000 copies printed.

Bill. Textbook royalties are calculated on a different basis—the net receipts. Translated, net receipts or price means the amount the publisher receives from the college bookstore, usually 80 percent of list price. As in the case of trade books, royalties on textbooks often begin at 10 percent for 5,000 copies, jump to 12½ percent for the next 5,000, and culminate at 15 percent for more than 10,000. So, on a $15 book, the textbook author receives $6,000 for the first 5,000 copies; $13,500 for

10,000; and $22,500 for 15,000 copies. That's $1.20 for each of the first 5,000 copies of the textbook sold. Right?

Andy. Except that we are grossly oversimplifying. These days discounts to college bookstores may be as high as 33 percent, making the base for net receipts of textbooks as low as 67 percent. Result: less royalties for the author and a bit more gained for the college bookstore. College bookstores complain that they make little money on textbooks. That's why you walk through the section selling T-shirts, insignia, beer mugs, etc., before reaching the textbook section. The major profit is in merchandise other than textbooks.

Bill. Conversely, sometimes royalties are higher than the 10, 12½, and 15 percent sliding scale. Suppose a textbook author's contract specified a flat 15 percent on all copies sold. Result: more royalties per book than the author would have received via the sliding scale.

Returning to our simplified illustration, a $15 book at 15 percent royalty on net receipts (80 percent) on all copies sold pays an author $9,000 for the first 5,000 copies; $18,000 for 10,000 copies; and $27,000 for 15,000 copies. This comes to $1.80 royalties to the author per book sold, whether one copy or 15,000 copies.

Andy. Pass the calculator. Contrast a sliding scale (10, 12½, 15 percent) royalty that would pay, as you said, $1.20 per copy on the first 5,000 books, with a flat 15 percent arrangement. Since the scale increases, the author's royalty would be $1.35 per copy on the first 10,000 books, and $1.50 a copy on the first 15,000 books. The total royalties on 15,000 textbooks would be $22,500 on the sliding scale, or $4,500 less than on the flat 15 percent arrangement. Quite a difference!

Bill. The royalty difference is particularly sharp on the first 5,000 copies—50 percent. More professional books sell fewer than 5,000 copies than reach the 15,000 copies mark. Yet permissions fees must be paid out of royalties on books with low sales as well as those with high sales.

The price of the book also makes quite a difference. Nonfiction is often priced higher than fiction. When the volume of sales is equal, a hardback textbook at a higher price understandably brings an author more royalties than a paperback anthology at a lower price. The 1984 Bowker *Annual of Library and Book Trade Information* reported that, excluding the highly expensive volumes costing $81 or more, hardcover books in 1983 cost about $23 and trade paperbacks about $12.

Of course, an author has no say in the pricing of a book; that matter is strictly between the publisher, the computer, and whatever gods publishers worship.

Andy. Authors have no say on pricing. But the setting of book prices may not be as simple as you imply. Pricing of a book occurs early and must be determined by a variety of factors. They include cost of composition and such manufacturing costs as paper, printing, and binding. Publishers have to take into account editorial expenses, including honoraria to outside readers; the cost of any ancillary materials such as instructors' guides; cost of covers and jackets; art and design expenses; and advertising and marketing costs. Prices have to include a profit margin for the publisher, and they have to reflect the inflation rate. Royalties paid to authors also enter into the pricing decision.

Bill. How a book is marketed also makes a difference in authors' royalties. Since selling books by mail is expensive, authors receive half of the usual royalties or less on mail sales of their books—5 percent is a figure sometimes used. Selling specialized books by mail is on the increase. Writers of scholarly, technical, reference, and other professional books should carefully check on the probable proportion of books to be sold through the mail as contrasted to higher-royalty bookstore sales. As Holiday Inns advertise, "The best surprise is no surprise."

Andy. In your experience, can an author negotiate a higher royalty?

Bill. That depends on how urgently the publisher wants the book—and how badly the author wants to be published. As you reminded me earlier, the publisher owns the dice in the publishing game. Publishers dislike making exceptions to their established royalty rates; other authors might scream. Authors of professional books in their specialized fields are often in no position to negotiate successfully. Not only do they urgently want to publish; sometimes they are not greatly concerned about royalties, for the rewards lie elsewhere—in rank and salary and consultation. An author's agent is in a better position to negotiate a higher royalty rate and a better total contract than is a writer for professional publications. However—Catch 22—an agent usually will not agree to represent an unpublished writer. Few writers for professional publication ever engage an agent. Authors are often deterred by the standard agent's commission, 10 percent of royalties, and realistic agents are not eager to represent authors of professional books with prospects of limited sales—Catch 22 again.

Andy. In contracting for a book, an author also should take advances into account. I asked for and was granted a $3,500 advance on my *Lost Generation* book; half was paid on signing the contract, and half is payable after I deliver the manuscript.

Bill. I've never asked for an advance on my books.

Andy. Why not?

Bill. An advance, by definition, is eventually deducted from one's royalties. So an advance is simply borrowing from yourself. If a contract is canceled for some reason or if the author can't deliver the manuscript, the publisher can insist on the return of the advance. Also a book may not sell enough copies to cover the advance to the author. So I wait for the royalties.

Andy. I think you're making a mistake. You could negotiate for a contract in which the advance is guaranteed and nonreturnable. For instance, suppose my new trade book is priced at $15, with a 10 percent royalty on the first 5,000 copies. However—and this is a consummation devoutly *not* to be wished—suppose my book is a commercial failure—

Bill. Though a critical success—

Andy. —and sells only 2,000 copies. My royalties would come to $3,000; or $500 less than my advance. As author, I am not obligated to return the original advance, since it was guaranteed and is nonreturnable.

More importantly, an advance has a psychological effect on a publisher whose money has been invested in an author. Publishers like to get back money they have paid out. They are less likely to reject a manuscript. They're more likely to take an interest in getting out a book early and in promoting it vigorously. Speaking of interest, authors who receive advances can spend or invest their advances early.

Bill. I must admit that these are good arguments for advances. However, a good agent may be more skillful in negotiating a guaranteed advance than a humble author. Once, though, this particular humble unagented author did get a flat grant to cover secretarial and research help on a book that promised to sell well. That happened in the late 1960s, a good time for textbook publishers. A flat grant, of course, is not deducted from royalties; today flat grants are rare.

Andy. Many of the troublesome aspects of a contract have nothing to do with royalties, advances, or financial matters in general. Date of delivery of the final manuscript, for instance. Authors are an optimistic breed. With editors, they set a date that gets written into the contract. Yet most authors are several months or even a year late in the delivery of their manuscript. Sometimes they are so late that the publisher exercises the contract option of cancellation for late delivery. More often editors are resigned to lateness; they allow a reasonable margin of up to three months before talking cancellation. Life would be better for all involved if authors and editors set realistic dates for delivery of manuscripts.

Bill. Both the royalty rate and the date of delivery are typed onto the contract, not printed, and give the impression of possible flexibility. Authors, however, are sometimes awed by standard provisions printed in the contract. They wrongly think that sections and phrases can't be modified or deleted. One section of contracts that I personally dislike is the option that grants the publisher the right to accept or reject the author's next book. Thus the author is obligated to submit any new manuscript to the publisher of the previous book. Suppose the author is dissatisfied with the original publisher's editing or promotion or whatever? Our author is nevertheless committed. Fortunately, the option clauses are disappearing from contracts for books on professional subjects; when they persist, I say strike them out.

Andy.   I'm more interested in putting in some provisions than striking others out. As I pointed out, authors commit themselves to delivery dates and should respect their deadlines. Since authors must commit themselves, publishers should also commit themselves to publication within a reasonable time after receipt of an acceptable manuscript. If a contract does not contain such a built-in provision, an author should negotiate for its inclusion. A supernegotiator might even attain a clause specifying a financial penalty for late publication by the house.

Also, sometimes an advertisement in a particular journal is crucial to a book's acceptance in the marketplace. Professionals should attempt to get agreement on this and include it in the contract; if an author simply suggests ads on the Author's Questionnaire, the request may be ignored.

Bill.   Another provision an author might attempt to modify concerns editing. I want my writing to be well edited, but I resist over-editing. As a professional, I ought to know what I want to say and how I want to say it. Sometimes I intend to qualify a statement, or emphasize a point, or lighten my material with humor, or step up the fact-load, or consciously repeat a concept. Modifications of such matters may change my meaning. Yet one of my recent standard contracts stipulated, "The Publisher shall have the right to make editorial changes in the manuscript as it deems desirable and necessary, but the Author, if he requests it, shall be given the opportunity to review such changes." Only if requested? Only "review"? No right to reject overediting that distorts meaning? I much prefer substitution of this provision: "The work shall be subject to editing and alteration by the Publisher at the original printing and at any reprinting; provided, however, that such editing and alteration shall not materially change the meaning or otherwise materially alter the meaning of the work."

Andy.   Artistic control should remain with the artist. In the authors' ideal world, the writer would be empowered by contract to select the editor who is to shepherd the manuscript through production. In reality, only your supernegotiator with great clout could get such a provision in a contract with a publisher.

Bill.   In the section that deals with proofs, I say strike out a qualifier. Retain "The Author agrees to read the proofs." Now strike the rest—"if requested to do so by the Publisher." An author should *always* read the first proofs, which are the galleys, or the final proofs, which are the page proofs. A conscientious author will attempt to persuade the editor to sanction the reading of both galleys and page proofs by the author.

Andy.   However, advances in technology and problems of schedule now have to be taken into account. Many publishers are now skipping galley readings by authors because of new composition methods. Some new composition techniques do not even offer the option of galleys. Besides, reading of edited manuscripts, galleys, and page proofs by authors could add a month or more to the usual production schedule of books.

Bill. I'll settle for a contract providing for two out of three possible readings, though I prefer the author's participation at all three stages.

Andy. Our author, however conscientious, had also better recognize that a contract contains a limitation of 10 or 15 percent on alterations of proofs by the author. This means that the cost of changes by the author on galleys or page proofs may not exceed 10 or 15 percent of the cost of the original typesetting. The costs of excessive author's alterations (a.a.'s to the editor) can become substantial and are deductible from royalties.

Bill. Some provisions of contracts are of special importance to authors of certain types of books. For instance, a textbook author should look closely at the section on ancillary materials and become aware that the author bears the cost of indexing and that the author supplies, without royalty, an instructor's manual or "other teaching aids."

Textbook authors should inquire about the probability and frequency of revised editions, though no guarantee can be written into the contract. Textbook authors should be well informed on past precedents as to revision, along with being fully knowledgeable about number of salespersons and employees, customary promotional techniques, extent of sales by mail, and so on.

If foreign sales are likely, the author should recognize that the contract probably will specify royalties at less than the regular rate. An author who is also a frequent consultant might be particularly interested in obtaining a substantial discount, such as 25 to 40 percent, on books the author buys.

Andy. An author who plans to write related works in the future should recognize that contracts often specify that an author may not write, participate in, or be connected with a later book that might interfere with or injure sales of the present book.

An author-editor preparing an anthology should look hard at the section (or write-in) on permissions, noting the author's responsibility for obtaining and paying for permissions, and noting how much the company agrees to pay toward permissions on publication while debiting the cost against the author's forthcoming royalties. A contract for a book of readings should allow the anthologist to submit printed material as well as typewritten; thus the substantial cost of retyping (double-spaced and in triplicate) articles and book excerpts can be avoided.

Sometimes a contract will specify that the author is to bear part or all of the cost of preparation of the artwork, particularly if the book is to have a great deal of art.

Subsidiary rights are seldom of importance to authors writing for their professional colleagues. Yet lightning might strike. So should there be a possibility of film, drama, TV, radio, record, bookclub, or paperback rights, the author should be aware of contract arrangements for a share of income. Excerpts or abridgments or adaptations for magazines and journals, whether before or after publication, can constitute a problem for some who write for professional publications.

Bill. Similarly, books for professional readers seldom deal with content that could be termed scandalous, libelous, or unlawful. However, if any risk exists, the author should know that the standard contract places full responsibility on the author. When in doubt about possible libel, alert the editors early and have the manuscript read by the firm's lawyers to detect any potentially libelous materials.

One of the least noticed clauses in a book contract gives publishers an easy way of canceling the agreement, despite the surrounding legalese commitments. "Acceptable to the publisher" is the handy escape clause. Sometimes it is spelled out sonorously: "If prior to publication the author shall not deliver the manuscript and ancillary materials as herein contemplated, *or if any part thereof is not satisfactory to the Publisher in its judgment* [italics mine], the Publisher may terminate this Agreement by written notice to the Author by registered or certified mail. . . ." However phrased, the standard contract contains an escape hatch for the publisher.

Andy. We've dealt only with the tip of the iceberg. But the moral is clear. An author should study a contract with care. Rather than regard the proffered contract as a tablet graven in stone, the sensible author, alone or with help, will identify passages that currently or potentially may present problems. Negotiation with the editor through correspondence should follow. The sensible author also avoids asking for too many deletions from or additions to a contract. A few changes might be incorporated into the contract; others can be handled through letters to the author. Clarification letters from editors should be filed by the author with the contract.

Bill. For instance, contracting for my textbook in secondary education, I asked whether an anthology on secondary education with another publisher would be regarded as interfering with or injuring sales of my textbook. My editor assured me in writing that it would not.

Andy. For their protection, authors should read about contracts. Tad Crawford's *The Writer's Legal Guide* is comprehensive and helpful. The Authors Guild publishes a pamphlet, *Your Book Contract*, unfortunately available only to members of the Guild. The Society of Authors' Representatives has a long and somewhat idealistic model contract.

Bill. If still in doubt, the wary author might consult a lawyer rather than depend on what people like you and me say or write about contracts. I recognize that most editors and many writers regard legal advice for authors as quite unnecessary and stress instead the importance of mutual trust.

Andy. Let's face it—the publisher has more power than the author of a professional publication. Though some amount of mutual trust must be involved in relationships of authors and publishers, some old adages about caution also apply to authors and their book contracts.

Bill. What adages?

Andy. "Look before you leap." "Fools rush in where angels fear to tread."

A CONTRACT

Agreement made ...., 19............, between
ALLYN and BACON, INC. ("Publisher"), and..
...., ("Author").

The Parties Agree As Follows:

1. The Author is commissioned and will write for publication a work on the subject of:

....

Grant of
Rights

which shall be considered a work made for hire; and without limiting the foregoing, he grants
this work to the Publisher with the exclusive right to print, publish and sell the work, under its
own name and under various imprints and trade names, during the full term of copyright and
all renewals thereof, and to copyright said work in the Publisher's name or any other name in
all countries; also the exclusive rights in said work set forth in paragraph I below; with the
exclusive authority to dispose of said rights in all countries and in all languages.

Delivery of
Manuscript

2. The manuscript, containing about .... words or their equivalent,

shall be delivered on or before .... 19...........

Book
Royalties

3. When the manuscript has been accepted and approved for publication by the Publisher, it will be published at the Publisher's own expense. The Publisher will pay the Author
a royalty, based on the actual cash received by the Publisher, of

Payments

4. The Publisher will render semi-annual reports of the sale of the work during Jan-
uary and July each year, covering the period ending the prior October 31 and April 30, and
with each report will make settlement for any balance shown to be due.

5. Paragraphs A-N inclusive, on pages 2 and 3 following, are parts of this agreement
as though placed before the signatures.

Author Signature   Social Security Number or
                                                    Taxpayer Identification

....

ALLYN and BACON, INC.

By ....

[1]

**Author's
Changes**

A. The manuscript delivered by the Author to the Publisher shall be in typewriting, or in typewriting and printed matter in anthologies and revisions, in triplicate (a fourth copy to be retained by the Author) in proper form for use as copy for the printer, and shall be in such form and content as the Author and Publisher are willing to have it appear in print. The Author will read the successive proofs, correct the proofs in duplicate and promptly return one set of proofs to the Publisher. The Author will be responsible for the completeness and accuracy of such corrections. All costs of corrections and alterations made by the author in the proof sheets (other than those resulting from printer's errors) exceeding ten per cent of the cost of typesetting shall be borne by the Author and shall be deducted from the first royalty payment due the Author. If such charge exceeds the first payment due the Author, he shall pay the Publisher the balance upon receipt of the account setting forth such charge.

**Matter
Supplied
By Author**

B. The Author will supply with the manuscript a title page; preface or foreword (if any); table of contents; complete and final copy for all illustrations, charts, diagrams, and forms (if any) properly prepared for reproduction; and, when requested by the Publisher, an index, a bibliography or list of sources of his materials. The Author will also supply the Publisher by .... with a complete, final camera-copy manuscript, properly prepared for reproduction for a Solutions Manual and Instructor's Guide to accompany the work. The Publisher will use the same care in protecting the manuscript and other material supplied to it hereunder as is its customary practice in protecting similar material in its possession, but it shall not be liable for damages, if any, resulting from the loss or destruction of such material, or any part thereof.

**Author's
Guarantee**

C. The Author guarantees that he is the sole owner of the work and has full power and authority to copyright it and to make this agreement; that the work does not infringe any copyright; violate any property rights, or contain any scandalous, libelous, or unlawful matter. The Author will defend, indemnify, and hold harmless the Publisher against all claims, suits, costs, damages, and expenses that the Publisher may sustain or incur by reason of any scandalous, libelous, or unlawful matter contained or alleged to be contained in said work, or any infringement or violation by said work of any copyright or property right; and until such claim or suit has been settled or withdrawn, the Publisher may withhold any sums due to the Author hereunder.

**Copyrighted
Material**

D. The work shall contain no material from other works without the Publisher's consent and the written permission of the owner of such material. Such written permission shall be obtained by the Author and filed with the Publisher. The Author shall pay any fee required for permission to use such material, and, if said fee is paid by the Publisher, the Publisher shall deduct that amount from the first royalty payments due the Author under this Agreement.

**Editing by
Publisher**

E. The work shall be subject to editing and alteration by the Publisher at the original printing and at any reprinting; provided, however, that such editing or alteration shall not materially change the meaning or otherwise materially alter the text of the work.

**Publisher's
Determi-
nations**

F. The Publisher shall have the right: (1) to publish the work in one or several volumes, and in such style as it deems best suited to the sale of the work; (2) to fix or alter the title and price; (3) to use all customary means to market the work:

**Free
Copies**

G. The Publisher will furnish six copies of the published work to the Author without charge. Additional copies for the Author's use shall be supplied at a 20% discount from the lowest list price.

Revision

H. The Author agrees to revise the work, to permit the Publisher to publish a revised edition every four years from the year of publication of the original or succeeding edition, if the Publisher considers it necessary in the best interests of the work. The provisions of this agreement shall apply to each revision of the work by the Author as though that revision were the work being published for the first time under this agreement. Should the Author be unable or unwilling to provide the manuscript of the revised work within a reasonable time, or should the Author be deceased, the Publisher may have the revision done and charge the cost against royalties due or that may become due the Author, and may display in the revised work, and in advertising, the name of the person or persons, who revise said work.

[2]

Promotion

I. The Publisher may permit others to publish, broadcast over the radio, make transparencies, recordings or mechanical renditions, publish book club and micro-film editions, make translations and other versions, show or produce in theatres and motion pictures and by television, serialize, syndicate, quote and otherwise utilize the said work, and material based on the said work. The net amount of any compensation received by the Publisher from such use by others shall be divided equally between the Publisher and the Author. The Publisher may authorize such use by others without compensation to the Author or the Publisher, if, in the Publisher's judgment, such use may benefit the sale of the work. If any of the foregoing rights (other than publishing the regular edition) shall be exercised by the Publisher itself, the Author shall be paid a royalty of 5% of the cash received by the Publisher.

Other Rights

J. On copies of the work or sheets sold outside continental United States and Canada, or copies of any special edition in any language produced by the Publisher for foreign sales, the Publisher shall pay to the Author a royalty of 10% of the cash received by the Publisher. On copies of the work or sheets sold by radio, television, mail order or coupon advertising direct to the consumer, the Publisher shall pay to the Author a royalty of 5% of the cash received by the Publisher. Should the Publisher deem it advisable to sell any copies of the work at a reduced price, the Author shall be paid the regular royalty rate on such sales except that, on sales made below the manufacturing costs of the book plus royalties, no royalties shall be paid. On any materials sold, collateral to the text, such as practice sets, workbooks, problem books and student manuals, the Publisher shall pay the Author a royalty of 5% of the cash from such sales. All copies of the work sold and all compensation from sales of the work under this and the preceding paragraph shall be excluded in computing the royalties payable pursuant to paragraph 3 hereof, and shall be computed and shown separately in reports to the Author.

Discontinuance of Manufacture

K. If the balance due the Author for the period ending October 31 or April 30 of any year shall be less than ten dollars, no accounting or payment shall be required of the Publisher until the next settlement period when the balance has reached ten dollars. When in the judgment of the Publisher the public demand for said work is no longer sufficient to warrant its continued manufacture, the Publisher may discontinue further manufacture and destroy any or all plates, books and sheets without liability to the Author.

Competing Work

L. The Author agrees that, during the term of this agreement, he will not contract to publish or furnish to any other publisher any work upon the same subject that shall conflict with the sale of the work herein specified.

Changes

M. This agreement shall not be subject to change, modification or discharge, in whole or in part, except by written instrument signed by the Author and an officer of the Publisher. The Author hereby consents to the assignment by the Publisher of this agreement, together with the assignment of copyright in the work, to any person, firm or corporation designated by the Publisher. This consent is given by the Author with the understanding that the rights and obligations of the original parties to this agreement will continue in full force as between the Author and the Assignee.

Construction, Heirs

N. This agreement shall be construed and interpreted according to the laws of the State of New York and shall be binding upon the parties hereto, their heirs, successors, assigns, and personal representatives; and references to the Author and the Publisher shall include their heirs, successors, assigns, and personal representatives.

LETTER ACCOMPANYING A CONTRACT

Leading Educational Publishers since 1868

Allyn and Bacon, Inc.
7 Wells Avenue, Newton, MA 02159
617/964-5530

Dr. Ernest Author
Anyplace, U.S.A.

Dear Professor Author:

I certainly enjoyed talking with you on the phone today. I am looking forward to working with you in publishing this potential "best seller." We feel confident we can do an excellent job in both producing and selling your book, <u>Juvenile Delinquency</u>, to the in-service education market and to the pre-service market.

(Discussion of reviewers' comments here.)

When you return the signed contracts, I hope you will include your reactions to the reviewers' and my comments.

I would like to take this opportunity to again describe our publishing program.

Our basic policy has always been to produce a limited number of select titles. This means we are able to offer personalized and helpful editorial assistance in the development and completion of your manuscript. I will be providing you with the reviews, assistance, and market research your book deserves. You can be assured that Allyn and Bacon will provide you with many unique services. A series editor as well as a book production editor are assigned to each title and work thoroughly and carefully from the contract signing to the book's publication.

In addition to editorial assistance and careful production, an author needs a strong promotional effort to establish his or her book as a best seller. In this regard, Allyn and Bacon has established itself as one of the leading publishers in the country. We invest a great amount of money in promoting each of our titles. For example, the Longwood Division will send out 8 million pieces of promotional material this year. In addition to direct mail advertising to in-service personnel and college professors, we also advertise in magazines, journals, and at conventions.

(Discussion of specifics of the contract here.)

I would like to draw your attention to Paragraphs I and J of our enclosed publishing agreement. Although the royalty rate is 15 percent of cash received for all quantity sales of the book (i.e. bookstore sales), sales solicited through mail order (i.e. single copy sales to high schools, etc.) have the lower royalty rate of 5 percent. It is anticipated that we will have a substantial portion of the sales on this title as the result of mail order promotion due to the particular nature of the book and its market. Bookstore sales (i.e. class adoption orders) are sold at 80 percent of the list price. Most single copy mail order sales are made at the full list price.

On each of the contracts, I have placed red checkmarks. You should place your initials next to these marks in all places on all <u>three</u> of the contracts to indicate your acceptance of the various additions. After you have initialled and signed all <u>three</u> copies of the contract, you should return them to me.

After our Vice-President signs the contracts, I will return one copy to you. With publication assistance, long-range sales potential in many markets in association with a limited number of quality titles, I truly believe that Allyn and Bacon can offer you a publishing program that is the best in the industry.

In conclusion, Professor Author, at the risk of sounding redundant, I would like to reaffirm strong interest in your work. I feel that there is not another publisher in the country that can do a better job for you in helping you develop the manuscript, research the markets, and produce the product in a format most suitable for market needs. Our company has spent over 116 years establishing a reputation for quality in the education area, selling across a broad spectrum of pre-service and in-service markets and college markets. We would like the opportunity to prove to you that our reputation is a well-deserved one.

I look forward to receiving the signed contracts from you in the near future. If I can answer any questions, please feel free to contact me.

Cordially,

Sig Illegible
Acquisitions Editor

Enclosures

20

Developing a Manuscript

Reducing correspondence between author and editor
Following instructions
Corresponding on permissions
Author's files
Artwork
Apprehensions of theft

Some weeks go by. Back again in Bill's study, Andy and Bill talk about the process of developing a manuscript. They recognize the volume of correspondence that goes into the making of a book by a member of a profession. They open the question of protection of unpublished manuscripts. Bill intends to follow this up through a forthcoming conversation with his editor on the new copyright law.

Andy. Since we last talked, I looked over some current books of advice to writers. Their authors often make a quick jump. In one chapter the writer is told how to query popular magazines and develop a prospectus for a book. In the next chapter the writer is told how to prepare the final manuscript—double-space, type on one side only, leave an inch-and-a-half margin, pack the manuscript carefully, and similar rudimentary instructions. The struggles that take place during the months of developing the article or the years preceding book publication are often ignored.

Bill. Would that it were so easy! The writer gets an idea. An editor indicates interest. The writer sends in final manuscript. Nothing important in between.

Actually, the all-important business of developing a manuscript takes place. The volume of work that goes into producing that manuscript can be enormous. Reading, researching, talking to associates, trying out ideas with students or other potential readers. Writing a first draft, seeking the reactions of others, throwing pages away, rewriting, rewriting. Or making changes via a word processor.

During the process, some degree of correspondence between the author and editor usually takes place. One way of reducing excess letters or phone calls is through acquaintance with the writer's outlet and its ground rules. An author should have on hand copies of the journal or magazine that is the intended outlet, along with whatever instructions or style sheet the periodical uses. If the outlet is a book, the writer should have on hand books published by the company that is the writer's target, along with the general style guide used by the publisher, whether Chicago, MLA, APA, or whatever, and the specific author's guide, if there is one, prepared by the company especially for its authors.

Andy. You're assuming that the prospective author has queried the journal editor and has received an invitation or at least encouragement to submit an article or has submitted a prospectus to a book publisher and has been given the green light. How about the unfortunate author who hasn't gotten a go-ahead signal from a specific periodical or publisher?

Bill. My tough-minded advice is "Don't write a manuscript until an editor has made a commitment to you based on your query or prospectus, or has at least expressed interest." However, out of eagerness to begin writing the immortal work, or out of a burning desire to find out what, if anything, they really have to say, many authors will disregard this pearl of wisdom. So my tender-minded advice is to select an outlet, whether journal or book publisher, and write as though you had a commitment from its editor. Never address a manuscript to the universe in general. The universe is notoriously uncaring and indifferent.

Andy. By having a target, the author also saves time through avoiding unnecessary editorial changes. If the author's target is a journal that uses a particular approach to footnotes or headings or tables, why complicate everybody's life by using techniques that are unacceptable? If a book company's standard way of handling extracts, those extended quotations from other sources, is through indentation while retaining double spacing, why not prepare the manuscript accordingly? If illustrations are not used by the target periodical, why submit them? Editor-author correspondence on such matters would not be necessary if authors did their homework.

Bill. A writer who neglects details in the instructions concerning proper footnoting will probably be in no great trouble, though in for some needless later corrections of manuscript or galleys. But a writer who ignores editorial specifications on deadlines or content emphasis or manuscript refereeing and reviewing procedures is courting rejection. For instance, an editor may spell out the date by which the article must be received if it is to be included in a special issue. If the date is missed, the author may have to wait until the next time such a special issue is scheduled, possibly a delay of several years. Or a journal editor might describe a particular emphasis especially appropriate for that journal's readers. A writer who doesn't take the hint might acquire one more rejection slip as a reward for obtuseness.

Andy. Letters from journal editors are usually blessedly brief and infrequent. Nor are letters from trade book editors especially long or frequent—unless the manuscript is overdue. Of all authors, the writers of textbooks and specialized scholarly, technical, professional, and reference books are the most likely to receive voluminous correspondence from editors. So let's talk of such books.

After contract correspondence is completed, the editor may have a few surprises for the author. Now the editor may suggest dates for the delivery of segments of the first and second drafts of the manuscript and dates for revision of segments after reviewing by outside readers, along with dates of delivery of the total manuscript for final review. The editor may specify the extent of artwork, including the limited number of halftones (translated as pictures) admissible in the finished product. Or the editor may have second thoughts on the appropriate length of the book manuscript, along with complicated advice on word-counting techniques. Above all, a post-contract letter from a College Department editor may contain suggestions from in-house and outside readers as to content and style.

Bill. Speaking of correspondence during manuscript development, if the work is an anthology the author becomes involved in considerable correspondence. Along with a stack of permissions forms for copyright holders, the editor will probably send advice to the anthologist on setting up permissions procedures and files. The gist will be to begin requesting permissions early, follow up promptly on ambiguous responses or referrals to other copyright holders, keep a dossier for each entry in an anthology, stay within the agreed budget for permissions, and keep a photocopy of everything the anthologist mails to the editor.

Andy. Correspondence on permissions is not restricted to anthologists. Authors of trade books, textbooks, and specialized books frequently find it necessary to request permission to quote. The volume of correspondence depends on the extent of quoted materials an author decides to use in the body of the book and in appendixes or supplements.

Bill. Most publishing houses sanction 250 words quoted from a book as fair use. Letters of permission from the author to the copyright holder are usually required for use of more than a total of 250 words from a book. Fair use of quotations from articles is often interpreted as either 250 words or up to 5 percent of the total article; beyond that, permission is required. For briefer writings, particularly poetry, even a line or two requires permission from the copyright holder. Authors like me, who like to quote, accumulate a substantial file of correspondence, along with permissions costs deducted from royalties. Even generous souls who levy no tolls on their precious works are apt to request in an offhand way a complimentary copy of the published book.

Andy. For many writers, the most important file during manuscript preparation is their own assemblage of notes. Yet a writer's notes are often a disorganized chaos of references, quotations, facts, and ideas jotted on scraps of paper and tossed into a folder. The day comes when the writer can't find the right piece of paper, though he's certain that it was put somewhere, possibly in an old brown envelope. Or if run to earth, the material is incomplete. What was the source? What was the page? Where did I find that quotation? Did I check that fact or assume it was accurate? Down the drain goes some of the author's time and energy!

Bill. Systematic people use file cards and key the cards to chapters or topics. I don't think it matters whether the writer uses cards or sheets of paper or folders or a word processor file, so long as the system works for the user. However, when translating notes into artwork or tables, an author should follow editorial instructions with care.

Andy. In writing about literature, I use few photographs and fewer tables. What else is included in artwork beside pictures?

Bill. Artwork is the publisher's term for anything that is illustrative; it may be a photo, or a drawing, or a painting, or a transparency, or a reproduction of a page, or it may be a map, chart, or graph. Book editors want the artwork numbered according to placement in a chapter. For instance, throughout a fourth chapter artwork should be numbered Figure 4.1, Figure 4.2, etc.

A table is typeset and is not classified as artwork. The author pastes tables onto manuscript-sized paper, gives them brief titles, and carefully lists the source below. Tables become Table 4.1, Table 4.2, and so on, if they appear in the fourth chapter.

The author is responsible for indicating in the manuscript approximately where figures (or potential pieces of artwork) and tables should appear. Dumping a miscellany of notes as to illustrations and tables upon an editor is strictly forbidden. Most editors specify that separate packets of artwork, clearly labeled as to placement, should accompany the manuscript in the final mailing.

Andy. When that happy day comes, apprehension often strikes the author. Is the precious manuscript protected from theft?

Bill. Registering or insuring the package, plus keeping a verbatim carbon copy or photocopy, provides sufficient protection. Requesting a return receipt guarantees that the author won't be told months later, "We never got it!"

Andy. True, but that's not what I had in mind. I've found that a number of neophyte authors fear that some sinister force in the periodical or publishing office will make off with the manuscript. Unsophisticated: "Would an editor steal my manuscript and publish it as the editor's own work?" More sophisticated: "Might an editor reject my manuscript and turn over my materials to a staff writer or favorite son author?" More sophisticated still: "Might an editor assign my basic idea to someone else? Plagiarism!"

Bill. That's somewhat paranoid. I have a colleague who says that the nearest he comes to prejudice is against the whole breed of editors. But even he doesn't attribute thievery to the editorial race.

Andy. But is the unpublished author sufficiently protected?

Bill. Like most authors, I don't know as much about copyright protection as I should. I plan to learn more about the new copyright law in a conference soon with my editor. I understand though that, under the new law, unpublished writing by an author is protected as soon as it is "set down in tangible form," such as a typed page. That should be consolation for authors who are fearful of theft of their words.

Andy. Yet it doesn't protect them against a referee or a reviewer who might occasionally "borrow" an idea from an unpublished manuscript—unconsciously, we hope. Nor would it protect them from an unscrupulous colleague who might hear about the author's idea and scoop the writer through a "quickie" publication.

Bill. Unscrupulous colleagues are rare.

Andy. You must live above the nether world of scramblers where anything goes in looking out for Number One.

So as not to be mistaken for an unprincipled professor, writers of professional publications should take pains with permissions correspondence, including getting permission from their students to quote their unpublished writing.

Bill. It seems that we have agreed that correspondence may characterize the development of a manuscript.

Andy. To say nothing of the hardest part of all.

Bill. What's that?

Andy. Actually writing something publishable.

Pam. □ Shall I tell you about our present practices or about the processes we'll use in the future?

Bill. □ What do you mean?

Pam. □ Our company still publishes books in the standard manner. But the new computer technology could revolutionize the book publishing industry.

Bill. □ For instance?

Pam. □ Here are several possible scenarios. Authors may write their books on their word processors, then send them on floppy disks to publishers. The publishers would then put the disks into company computers and produce proofs for editing by the company and the authors. The company would then print the book.

¶ However, a publisher could bypass printing the author's words by editing the disks and then feeding the result into the memories of computers owned personally *and so on* by individuals or collectively by libraries, businesses, etc. People could then read the resultant videotex on their computer screens or could store the material on disks or could print it out. Another possibility is that after editing, publishers could sell floppy disks directly to the consumers, the owners of computers.

Jack. □ Who might then possibly reproduce the disks and sell them to their friends and neighbors $\frac{1}{M}$ or even possibly market them to strangers?

Pam. □ Piracy of software is at present among the unsolved problems of the sponsors of the new technology. Financial *matter* problems including the highly important of profitability, still persist. So for a time at least our company will continue to produce books in the customary way. Yet we'll stay alert to the new technology as it develops. Some publishing companies already have staff members assigned to exploring electronic possibilities.

Jack. □ While we await the arrival of a new era in book publishing, what should today's authors expect as to the publication process after submission and acceptance of their manuscripts?

Figure 20–1 *Edited Manuscript*

LETTER FROM EDITOR ABOUT MANUSCRIPT

Dr. William Van Til
Indiana State University
Terre Haute, Indiana

Dear Bill:

I want to comment on your Chapter 8, and get your help on a few matters.

First, as in your other chapter we are going to footnote each published item you mention in the text, in accordance with our regular style. We've had no difficulty in getting the necessary bibliographic information on the items. (There are no problems on which I need help.)

Second, because you give greater detail on the Seven Cardinal Principles than Beck did in Chapter 1, I am going to include a reference in the footnote in that chapter to your discussion. I think that will help to give greater unity to the yearbook as a whole, since it will acknowledge that important items are properly discussed in more than one of the chapters. I want to keep an eye out for that sort of thing as I work through the remaining chapters.

Third, and in a similar vein, I think we should avoid repetitions of metaphors and the like that have already appeared earlier. For example, in this chapter (8) you refer to the "quagmire" of Vietnam and to the concept of the "spaceship earth," both of which you used effectively in your introductory chapter. I do not think it is necessary to repeat them in this chapter. I hope you will agree.

Fourth, I wonder if you haven't overworked a bit the idiom you use on pages 2 and 3 (On the side of the watershed called past, lay . . . etc.). I think it is quite effective expression at the outset, and I realize that it represents a striving for parallelism throughout the section. I shan't object further if you want to keep it throughout, but I thought I at least should let you know my reaction after several careful readings. I think occasional substitutions for the verb "lay" would fix things to my satisfaction.

Now for a few quite specific points.

Page 2 and elsewhere. You occasionally use the term "interdisciplines" as a noun. I do not find such usage in any dictionary I've consulted. I think we could easily substitute "interdisciplinary study."

Page 3. You have left blank some spaces in which you must have intended to supply some percents-- lines 10, 14, 15. Can we have those, please?

Page 8. You refer to the Commission on the Reorganization of Secondary Education here, but I am sure you must mean the Commission on Secondary School Curriculum. Likewise on page 9.

Page 10. In the quote from Kozol, do the initials E.D.C. refer to the Educational Development Corporation-- or something like that? I don't think we should use just initials, even though Kozol may have done so.

Page 21. Last line. Can you figure out what the referent is for "it" in this line? I've gone to the original article to try to figure that out, and it is not clear to me what the referent is. Does he mean

dealing with the moratorium or the de-emphasis to
which he refers in the same sentence? Or does it
refer to something in the preceding sentences, which
you did not quote? Maybe we'll just have to let it
stand as is, but the referent is certainly not clear
to me.

Page 33. Paragraph beginning "Secondary education
provides . . ." In the things you list as opportunities
for the study of "world views" everything seems to fit
very well except for "the search for truth through the
sciences." I understand that you are wanting to cite
ways in which one can come to understand alternate
world views, but the "search for truth through science"
hardly seems to me to lead to alternate world views
unless one assumes something like "alternate truths,"
and that appears to be a difficult assumption to make.

On that same page the first sentence under "Recreation and Leisure" is not clear to me. Could it be revised to make it clearer? In my judgment it could be
deleted easily, for the point is well made in the sentences that follow.

As in your Chapter 2, I am wondering again about the
matter of permissions for quotations in this chapter. I have
in mind the fairly long quotes on pages 8-9; 9-9a-10; 11;
13a-14; 16-17; 20-21.

Apart from the points I have raised here, I have no
problems with this Chapter. I think it will make a very
useful part of the book. If we can settle the points I have
mentioned I see no need to return the edited version to you.
If other questions occur to me you may be sure I'll get in
touch with you.

Over this holiday weekend I hope to get at much of the
rest of the manuscript we have in hand, and I'll write you
or the authors directly (copy to you) if there are matters
on which I shall need help.

An additional query. On page 3 you mention the "titles"
of the post-1893 reports. I am not sure that those are the
actual titles, although they do suggest the subjects with
which the committee reports dealt. At first I thought these
were all NEA-initiated committees. Apparently the first
three were so initiated, for we find references to them under NEA. But the fourth has us stumped. Could it be that
you are referring here to the PEA Commission on Relation between School and College--the Commission that generated the
Eight-Year Study? I can find no reference to a Committee of
Nine on Articulation of High School and College. Yet I have
a feeling there was a committee by that name.

It would be very helpful if you could give us the documentation (that is, publication information) for the reports, including the name of the committee responsible, the
title(s) of the respective reports, the date and place of
publication of those reports.

Cordially,

Kenneth J. Rehage

LETTER FROM WRITER ABOUT MANUSCRIPT

Dr. Kenneth J. Rehage
National Society for the Study of Education
5835 Kimbark Avenue
Chicago, IL 60637

Dear Ken,

This letter will deal with Chapter Eight. I will take up your suggestions in order.

You indicate first that there are no problems on which you need help with respect to footnoting each published item.

Second, it is a good idea to footnote to Beck on the Seven Cardinal Principles.

Third, I do hope you will catch these repetitions and call them to my attention. By all means eliminate the "Quagmire" reference. Also eliminate the "Spaceship Earth" if you feel that it does duplicate, even though in the present context it is a good reference and integral to the paragraph.

Fourth, I have revised the parallelism to avoid repetition of the verb "lay."

Page two, substitution of interdisciplinary study is good.

Page three, I have supplied percentages for a revised version along with a footnote.

Page eight, you are quite right that I was in error in the name of the commission which is the Commission on Secondary School Curriculum.

Page ten, I have eliminated the sentence rather than expand the initials. It is not a necessary sentence.

Page twenty-one, Bruner is grammatically wrong in having no referent for the word "it." Since it is an important sentence which appears in the original in italics (incidentally, should we use?), I believe we simply must let it stand.

Page thirty-three, I have modified the sentence to read "the knowledge accumulated through the sciences."

Page thirty-three, I have clarified the reference further. I would, however, like to keep it, for it is the kind of allusion that I would like to make. We could of course footnote to the Bible but, somehow, this seems silly to me. I do have the specific Bible references if this is absolutely necessary.

As to the permissions, I have dealt with this in my letter on Chapter One. You will find that none of the quotations are beyond 250 words. If, however, we have a policy of requesting permissions for shorter quotations this will then become necessary and you can tell me whether I do this or you.

If time permits, I would like to see the edited version following your changes in connection with this letter. As we found with respect to Chapter One, I usually go along with editorial changes but occasionally want to retain a word. If we don't have time, I will correct minor items in galleys.

Thanks again for the scrupulous and careful editing.

Cordially yours,

William Van Til

WVT/rr

P.S. I am attaching data from which footnotes to the four reports could be developed. To give you full information since reports are tricky, I am enclosing basic data to construct as you judge best.

21

Reading Edited Manuscripts, Galleys, and Page Proofs

Bill strongly urges writers to continue their relationships to editing after submission of their manuscripts. He thinks that professional publications would be improved by more reading by authors of edited manuscripts/galleys/page proofs. Andy contends that some reality factors in publishing may block this. Bill cites some of the errors that inevitably creep into books. However, Andy attempts to provide some comfort for authors.

Andy. There is a breed of writer whom I grudgingly admire. This type sends off a final manuscript, then turns full-time attention to the next opus. With mailing of the copy to the editor, work on the book by the author is terminated.

Bill. Temper your admiration. I suspect such authors of contempt for the quality of the final product.

Andy. What do you mean?

Bill. A great deal can happen to a manuscript between submission of a final draft and publication date. If the writer assumes a neutral role, the final product may not be all its author intended. The conscientious author attempts to develop a continuing relationship to editing.

Andy. Many editors will disagree with you. They'll contend that the personnel of the journal or the publishing house have all the production expertise that is necessary. Authors, like Victorian little children, should be seen but not heard.

Bill. Let's recognize, however, what actually happens to a manuscript euphemistically termed ''final'' by an author. If the manuscript is to become a textbook or a specialized book, a final reading by one or more readers always takes place. Trade manuscripts also may receive final readings by outside reviewers. Back to the author come suggestions for changes to be incorporated into final copy before typesetting. Or the suggestions may be passed on to the copyeditor. As you know, new members of the cast come on stage after receipt of a supposedly final book manuscript—the copyeditor who sees the book through into print and, in some large organizations, the supervisor of copyeditors who takes over correspondence with authors for the company. If the manuscript is to be published in a journal, the familiar editor-author relationship may continue; however, if the journal is large, a copyeditor usually takes over.

Andy. The appearance of new parents for the fledgling book or article is sometimes startling to the author. By now, the author has to some degree gotten used to the ways of the original editor with whom the author has been corresponding. Now enter Mr. X or Ms. X, the copyeditor or supervisor or production editor, possibly old to the journal or publishing house, but new to the author and the manuscript. The copyeditor does what comes naturally in the role; copyeditors edit copy.

Bill. But sometimes overediting takes place. Changes may be made that trouble writers. These changes should be approved or disapproved by the author during the process of editing, not belatedly discovered by the writer when the project has reached the stage of cold, irrevocable print. Writers have their own distinctive ways of expressing themselves. Unless demonstrably ungrammatical or unclear or just plain wrong, these characteristics of individual authors should be retained.

Andy. What do you recommend?

Bill. Active involvement of the author at the crucial stages of editing. For instance, before the manuscript is set in print in galley form, a copyeditor usually works directly on the manuscript, making modifications and changes. Many woes can be avoided if the author looks over the edited manuscript prior to production of galleys. Some publishing houses, I am glad to say, routinely have their authors read the copyedited manuscript before the composition stage.

Andy. You're going to have a hard time persuading all editors to accept that recommendation. Editors are aware of the ego involvement of authors in their phrasings. Changes made directly on manuscripts may be perceived by authors as direct challenges to their grammatical abilities or communication skills. The likelihood of hassles between journal/house and author is increased. On the other hand, fresh new galleys, clean of all proofreader's marks, often read well to writers. Authors may even be pleasantly surprised at the subtle improvement they dimly sense in their copy. Authors are less likely to insist on restoration of a favorite sentence in place of an editorially doctored one.

Bill. I'm afraid that I can illustrate your point on authors' egos. Once when I was reading galleys on a book I was doing on consumer education, I came upon a paragraph I particularly enjoyed rereading. In a self-congratulatory mood, I said to my editor, "Good writing in that paragraph, Fred." Fred glanced at the copy and said, "Certainly is. Most of the paragraph I wrote myself." I checked back to the original manuscript. He had. His editing was so much in the spirit of my writing that I couldn't tell where Fred left off and I began.

But not all editors have his touch. So I'll still request a look at the edited manuscript before the copy begins to freeze into galleys. If author-editor struggles have to occur, let them take place before type is set.

Andy. Though all editors may not agree that authors should see edited copy before typesetting, they often will agree with you that authors should read galleys. The long sheets with the big margins provide ample opportunities to eliminate bugs that various gremlins have inserted. The margins supply ample space for insertion of proofreading marks. For the neophyte author, the time has come to learn a new language, that of the proofreaders and printers. If an author masters and uses the new language, communication with a copyeditor is easy. If the author refuses or invents a private proofreading language, communication is blocked.

Bill. When I read my galleys, I try to avoid the temptation to say, "I'll catch that problem on page proofs." Better look for the errors now. Better by far to settle the matter by a trip to the library to recheck a minuscule detail rather than wait for the heavy-breathing page proof stage. The ingenuity of the gremlins that introduce typographical errors into copy can never be underestimated. They have a gift for the totally unexpected. If you read proofs yourself and also manage to talk a literate loved one or a graduate assistant or a generous colleague into proofreading, you'll reduce the gremlin's triumphs.

Andy. Many authors don't want to spend their precious time in reading edited manuscripts or even galleys or page proofs. Furthermore, some are quite weak at checking their own writing; F. Scott Fitzgerald, for instance, was a notoriously poor speller. Some seem unable to check their bibliographies, tables, or quotations, so they rely heavily on editors to make corrections. Some books of advice to authors encourage them to believe that proofreading by the printer and by the house or journal copyeditor will suffice for catching typos.

Bill. Don't believe it for a minute. Not only do editors and printers miss typographical errors—I have caught typos *inserted* into my copy through printer's errors and editorial changes.

I also insist on reading page proofs. The author's last battle against the bugs takes place at the page proof stage.

Andy. Even so, you will never completely eliminate all bugs. A favorite place for the gremlins to strike is the first sentence of an otherwise well-edited book! Or even on the title page or the jacket or the spine.

Does your search for errors result in substantial alterations?

Bill. If an author reads the edited manuscript before typesetting, there is no reason for extensive changes by the author in galleys. If the edited manuscript is not made available to the author, the place for changes has to be the galleys. Authors should think of galleys as their last real chance for changes. "Now or never" should be their slogan. If an author is to be assailed by the horrid thought, "What will Authority So-and-so think—or, even worse, say—when he reads this page?" let the reconsideration come at the galley stage, not in page proofs. Page proofs are no place for second thoughts, no place to remedy overediting. At the stage of page proofs, authors and editors can merely tinker, replacing a word of seven spaces with another word of seven spaces. Substantial rewriting is not feasible. Too much resetting of type would be required.

These days more and more books are going directly from manuscript to pages. This makes it particularly important that the author very carefully review the entire edited manuscript instead of relying on bland assurances by the editor that the writer will be able to take care of any problems in page proofs.

Andy. I sympathize. Yet I find that authors don't fully understand the costs of changes made at either the galley or page proof stage. They are considerable.

Printer's errors are supposed to be caught by the typesetter's proofreader. If the compositor has misspelled a word that is spelled correctly in the manuscript or leaves out a phrase, the typesetting company bears the cost of resetting that line or those lines. But even a good proofreader for a compositor may not mark all the printer's errors that appear on the galleys that reach the author. Incidentally, "printer's errors" is a misnomer; they should be attributed to the compositor.

Such errors as a word misspelled by an author should be caught by the copyeditor in the editing process, before the typesetting stage. If errors missed on the manuscript are caught on galleys or page proofs, the journal or the publishing house is expected to accept responsibility.

But there is a category in addition to printer's errors (often marked on the master copy of the galleys as p.e.'s) or editorial errors (often marked as e.e.'s). This is the category marked a.a.'s, author's alterations. If the costs exceed the amount allowed by the book contract, usually 10 percent of the typesetter's first bill, the author pays for the alterations through deductions from royalties.

Bill. Even though an author looks over the copyedited manuscript, author alterations on galleys and page proofs are bound to occur. Sometimes new developments since the writing of the manuscript force authors to change their minds. If a manuscript is timely, the temptation to revise a statistic or to add a name or a new development is almost irresistible. If such changes are clearly the author's choice, they should be regarded as author alterations. If they become excessive, the author should pay the price. But I would hate to see an author billed for author alterations that were in actuality correction of overediting through too zealous copyediting.

Andy. There's one consolation for the conscientious author who, despite Herculean efforts, finds that the gremlins have inserted some bugs into the published book or article.

Bill. What's that?

Andy. The consolation is that only that author is conscious of the bugs. No one else notices these flaws and blemishes.

Bill. I'd like to believe that, but I don't think it is so.

Andy. It's true. When did you ever have a reader point out to you a typographical error in one of your books or articles?

Bill. Very seldom, though typos have appeared despite my best efforts to catch all.

Andy. How often have you been called on a misstatement of fact?

Bill. I've rarely been taken to task, though I've made mistakes. But I thought I was a lucky exception whom the hawk-eyed book reviewers and periodical readers had overlooked.

Andy. I don't think you are an exception. Reviewers usually don't read books that carefully. Readers of a book or article seldom write the author about typographical errors. If the typo, or even the factual misstatement, comes to their attention, they attribute it—and often rightly— to the anonymous editorial process, not the author.

Bill. You're better for me than a psychiatrist. Though I recognize that perfectionism is pernicious, I am jolted when a typo or a bald error creeps into my publications. So I'll continue to proofread closely.

Andy. By all means. But try to avoid the sense of panic that besets the overly conscientious author who, soon after the book is published, receives a correspondence-concluding letter from the editor requesting a list of all errors to be corrected in a prospective second printing. The editor gives the list the horrid names errata or corrigenda. What a way to destroy an author's euphoria! Post-publication depression sometimes follows. On rereading the book the author will find some errors. And only the author will ever be conscious of them. Criticism is more usually directed to matters of substance. As for me, I am happy as a lark when one of my efforts appears in print. My worries, if any, take place in the pre-publication stage.

Bill. I hope criticism of scholarship is healthier and stronger than you say. At any rate, since I will always have to live with me, I'll keep on battling the gremlins, whether in manuscripts, galleys, or page proofs.

Andy. Good. Yet shrug rather than suffer when a gremlim triumphs.

Gremlins at Work

Letter to the Editor

Dear edotir,

I was upsat to sea that the Essay Revue articul on the Rom in you rWinter edison had been soo badli profred that eevn I a good speeler an drittre was nunplacedat sevril poonts: Since this is de riguer inane academik journel—I truss you wil talk steeps to sea that it dose nart hopen agone?

Yours leteratly

John Harrison
Concordia University
Montreal

ES Replies

Proofing oversights are constant menaces and a source of editorial nightmares. Until recently, we were perplexed to understand how errors could crop up after five proofings by four different people: by the typesetter, author, and someone in the ES office in galley stage, and by a different ES staff member in paged-proof stage and in blue line. On April 12 of this year, however, Charles Scribner, Jr.—a man with many years of publishing experience—explained this phenomenon to the Circumnavigators Club (as reported by *Publishers Weekly*, 6 June 1977, p. 47):

> Many years ago, in the time of Johannes Gutenberg, the Devil was alarmed by the sudden proliferation of Holy Bibles. So he assigned an army of gremlins to watch over printing plants. It was their mission to make sure that from then on a great many things would go wrong. That army was superbly trained and, believe me, it is still on the job.

This explanation may not satisfy Mr. Harrison, but it seems thoroughly sensible to us.

"Letters to the Editor," *Educational Studies*, Vol. 8, No. 3 (Fall 1977), p. vi. Reprinted by permission of *Educational Studies*.

Abe. Mary told me about your query approach. Should research scientists use it in publishing the kind of scientific paper you have described?

Bill. Only to a limited degree and then mostly to determine whether the manuscript is suited for the journal. Editors of scientific journals usually encourage contributors simply to submit their manuscripts. Consequently, the author must take special care in deciding upon the most likely journal. Authors should read with special care any general information carried by the journal, descriptions as to the scope of the journal in instructions to the authors, and the characteristic content of recent issues. Since it may be a long time until a manuscript is accepted or returned, authors should take into careful account the factors of selection that are most important to them. Some may value prestige; others may opt for wide circulation; still others may be interested in how often the journal is published, since they wish to avoid lag in publication time. Still others are concerned about some combination of factors.

Mary. Bill, why does publishing in scholarly journals take so long? The article based on my dissertation took a full year from completion to acceptance, and a research article Abe wrote took seventeen months to appear in print. I hear horror stories of even longer delays.

Bill. Several factors, Mary. For one thing, the competition is intense. Take the category of professors alone. It seems that all of them are being urged, whether gently or harshly, to publish, and especially to publish in scholarly journals. Tenure committees often play the numbers game, and countless assistant professors are forced to play along, cranking out articles.

The large majority of American professors have written doctoral dissertations and would like to share their findings. An unknown proportion are actually carrying on research beyond their original doctoral studies. So even though the number of journals increases steadily, the opportunities for publication can't keep pace with the volume of potential contributors. To cite one of the oldest truisms of Abe's profession, factors of supply and demand must be taken into account.

To increase the opportunities to appear in print, service publishing has developed, essentially the printing of small editions of largely unedited camera-ready manuscripts by authors. New journals edited as a labor of love for a few subscribers often spring up when editors have available a typewriter and about $500. Reproductions of typed manuscripts are also made available on demand through microfilming and photocopying. Yet for numerous would-be contributors the road to publication is long and rough. Competition for space is keen.

Another reason for time lag is that the people who conduct the scholarly journals are often part-time editors. Some of them proceed in the leisurely way attributed to academics. Few of them resemble the stereotype of the hyperactive city editor of a newspaper or the harried staffer of a newsweekly. And—don't tell anybody—not all of them are highly competent editors. All this contributes to delay.

Even if the editor is a workaholic or a competent full-time professional, the scholarly journal is almost always refereed.

Mary. When I hear the word "referee," I think of boxing or football.

Bill. But, as you well know, in professional publication refereeing indicates that an article competing for space in the journal is read by outside readers. The referees may be members of the journal's editorial board. They may be chosen from a panel of names accumulated by the editor and advisers. They may be individuals to whom the editor turns occasionally for help on a specialized topic. Their role is to advise the editor whether the article advances and contributes to knowledge, is based on good scholarship, is free from errors in its facts, and arrives at legitimate and logical conclusions. A good referee can contribute to maintaining high editorial standards.

Referees for journals are usually highly experienced professionals. This means that they are busy with their own teaching, counseling, research, consultation, conferences, and writing. Naturally, your article isn't their highest priority. Result—delay. Perhaps two readers get their reports in on time. But everything may be suspended while awaiting a third reader's report. Even when that is received, all may not be smooth sailing. The referees may disagree; the editor may turn to other readers or may temporize. Sometimes a new editor takes over, and when that happens the journal may change policies.

[1]Philadelphia: ISI Press, 1983.
[2]Philadelphia: ISI Press, 1984.

Figure 21–1 *After Editing, a Galley*

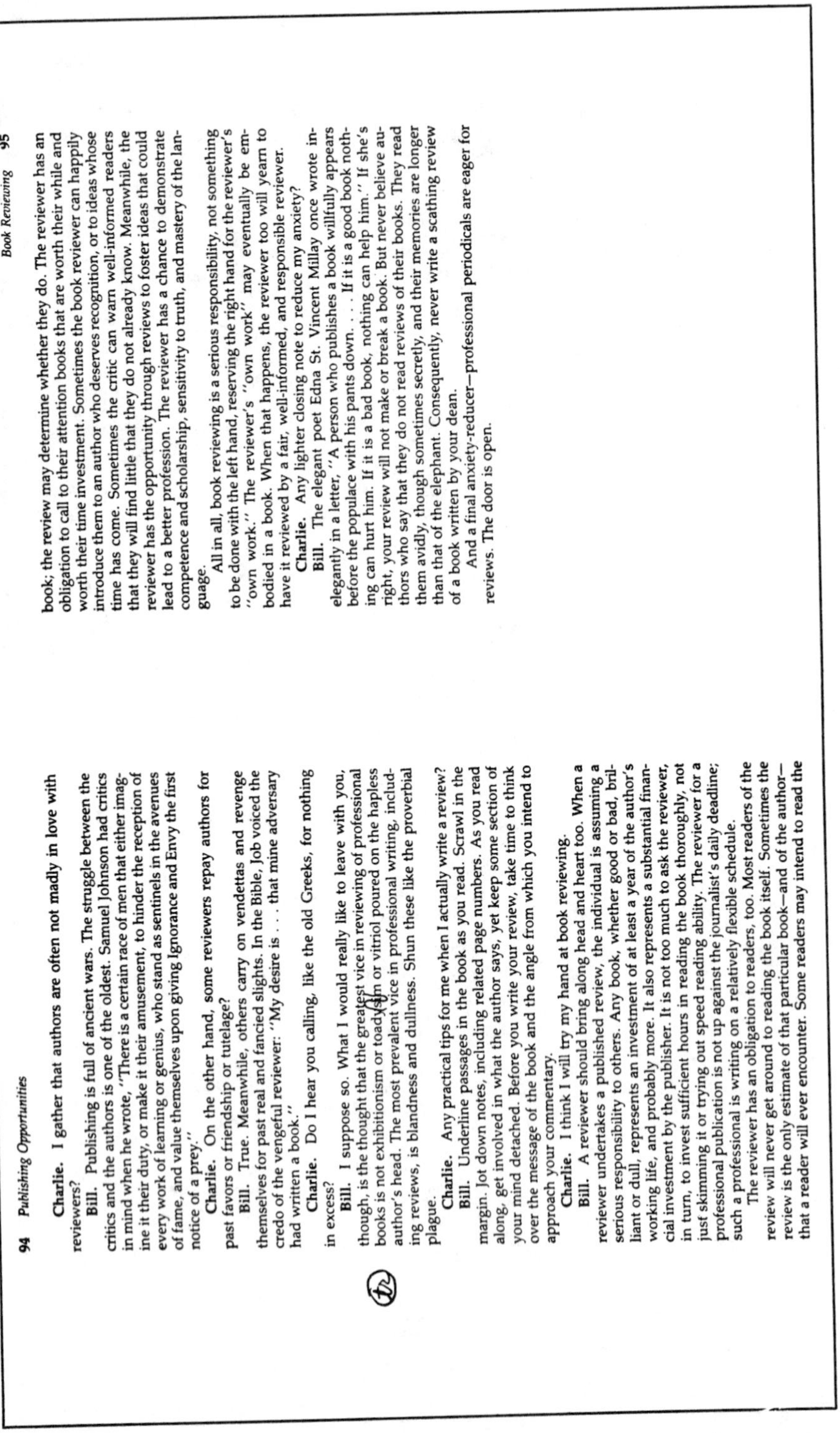

Charlie. I gather that authors are often not madly in love with reviewers?

Bill. Publishing is full of ancient wars. The struggle between the critics and the authors is one of the oldest. Samuel Johnson had critics in mind when he wrote, "There is a certain race of men that either imagine it their duty, or make it their amusement, to hinder the reception of every work of learning or genius, who stand as sentinels in the avenues of fame, and value themselves upon giving Ignorance and Envy the first notice of a prey."

Charlie. On the other hand, some reviewers repay authors for past favors or friendship or tutelage?

Bill. True. Meanwhile, others carry on vendettas and revenge themselves for past real and fancied slights. In the Bible, Job voiced the credo of the vengeful reviewer: "My desire is . . . that mine adversary had written a book."

Charlie. Do I hear you calling, like the old Greeks, for nothing in excess?

Bill. I suppose so. What I would really like to leave with you, though, is the thought that the greatest vice in reviewing of professional books is not exhibitionism or toadyism or vitriol poured on the hapless author's head. The most prevalent vice in professional writing, including reviews, is blandness and dullness. Shun these like the proverbial plague.

Charlie. Any practical tips for me when I actually write a review?

Bill. Underline passages in the book as you read. Scrawl in the margin. Jot down notes, including related page numbers. As you read along, get involved in what the author says, yet keep some section of your mind detached. Before you write your review, take time to think over the message of the book and the angle from which you intend to approach your commentary.

Charlie. I think I will try my hand at book reviewing.

Bill. A reviewer should bring along head and heart too. When a reviewer undertakes a published review, the individual is assuming a serious responsibility to others. Any book, whether good or bad, brilliant or dull, represents an investment of at least a year of the author's working life, and probably more. It also represents a substantial financial investment by the publisher. It is not too much to ask the reviewer, in turn, to invest sufficient hours in reading the book thoroughly, not just skimming it or trying out speed reading ability. The reviewer for a professional publication is not up against the journalist's daily deadline; such a professional is writing on a relatively flexible schedule.

The reviewer has an obligation to readers, too. Most readers of the review will never get around to reading the book itself. Sometimes the review is the only estimate of that particular book—and of the author—that a reader will ever encounter. Some readers may intend to read the

book; the review may determine whether they do. The reviewer has an obligation to call to their attention books that are worth their while and worth their time investment. Sometimes the book reviewer can happily introduce them to an author who deserves recognition, or to ideas whose time has come. Sometimes the critic can warn well-informed readers that they will find little that they do not already know. Meanwhile, the reviewer has the opportunity through reviews to foster ideas that could lead to a better profession. The reviewer has a chance to demonstrate competence and scholarship, sensitivity to truth, and mastery of the language.

All in all, book reviewing is a serious responsibility, not something to be done with the left hand, reserving the right hand for the reviewer's "own work." The reviewer's "own work" may eventually be embodied in a book. When that happens, the reviewer too will yearn to have it reviewed by a fair, well-informed, and responsible reviewer.

Charlie. Any lighter closing note to reduce my anxiety?

Bill. The elegant poet Edna St. Vincent Millay once wrote inelegantly in a letter, "A person who publishes a book willfully appears before the populace with his pants down. . . . If it is a good book nothing can hurt him. If it is a bad book, nothing can help him." If she's right, your review will not make or break a book. But never believe authors who say that they do not read reviews of their books. They read them avidly, though sometimes secretly, and their memories are longer than that of the elephant. Consequently, never write a scathing review of a book written by your dean.

And a final anxiety-reducer—professional periodicals are eager for reviews. The door is open.

Figure 21–2 *After Galleys, the Page Proofs*

22

Indexing
a Book

Andy and Bill conclude their conversations by, appropriately enough, talking of the last pages of books by members of the professions—the index. Bill leans toward employing a professional indexer; Andy recommends indexing by the author. Andy suggests some guidelines to indexing by authors of the do-it-yourself persuasion.

Andy.   Even after preparing a manuscript and reading galleys and proofs, the writer of a book on a professional topic has a chore.

Bill.   What's that?

Andy.   Indexing the book.

Bill.   I've always delegated that responsibility to a professional, someone engaged by my supervisor of copyediting. Usually the professional indexer employed has been a freelancer, not an employee of the publisher.

Andy.   Have you been satisfied with the indexing of your books?

Bill.   Yes and no. It depends on the abilities and the insights of the indexer and the controls and checks maintained by the editorial staff. Some indexes have been excellent; they have been accurate, comprehensive, and highly usable.

However, once I read the page proofs of an index for one of my books and protested vigorously to the supervisor of copyediting. Major headings had been left out. The selection of names of individuals to be included seemed capricious to me; some names I regarded as of major significance to the reader were omitted. As you know, potential users of a textbook often scan an index for names—professors who are authors may even look for their own!

The editing staff agreed that the index was inadequate and allowed me to insert headings and appropriate names. I ended up doing as much of the work as if I had developed the index myself. I learned that authors should seriously consider employing indexers of their own choosing.

Andy. Why don't you prepare the indexes yourself?

Bill. Because I respect professional specialization and I don't regard myself as a professional indexer. Also, indexing is time-consuming.

Andy. I prepare my own indexes. No one knows my books or my intentions as well as I do. Besides, preparing my own indexes saves money. What are the customary charges these days?

Bill. During the 1980s the cost of indexing, which of course was deducted from my royalties, ranged from $1,000 for a long book to $100 for a brief one. For the mid 1980s, an author might calculate the round figure to come to $2 for each page of the book. By the way, you may have overlooked another argument for the author preferring to do his or her own index.

Andy. What's that?

Bill. An index brutally reveals flaws. On one page, the author uses the full name of an authority, while another page carries only the initials of the first and middle names of the same person. The same word may be spelled differently on pages 77 and 142. Even worse, a statistic on one page is different from a supposedly identical statistic on another. Authors who prepare the index before returning page proofs—or at least check the index—can catch errors they would otherwise never detect.

Andy. That's a logical argument, but unfortunately not always applicable. The editor, bedeviled by deadlines and delays, may want page proofs returned immediately and may assure the writer that the index can wait until all page proofs have been returned. So an author will probably develop or check the index only after the body of the book has been put to bed.

Bill. Can an author who is an amateur in the field of indexing do an adequate job?

Andy. Indexing is not as difficult as most authors think.

Bill. How does one proceed?

Andy. First of all, an author should ask, "What is the purpose of my book?" "How will it be used?" "Who will really read it?"

Bill. The questions come a bit late. They should have been asked before the writer first hit the typewriter keys. However, they are certainly sensible.

Andy. Honest answers to these questions may help the author to decide whether one general index, the dictionary type as in most books, is needed, or more than one, such as separate author and subject indexes as in a bibliographic index. Next, the author tries to walk in the readers' shoes. What will readers want to look up? How can the index help them find what they need?

Bill. I assume that if a book is organized by headings and subheadings, the author has a good start on indexing. How broad should the index entries be?

Andy. If the book is on psychology, the author shouldn't list psychology as a topic in the index. Since the book is presumably all about psychology, an entry "Psychology, 1–555" won't help anyone. Chapter headings, however, might well be indexed.

Bill. Specifically, what should I do in preparing my index? I'm willing to learn.

Andy. Look hard for your major topics. Thumb through your page proofs, finding headings, subheadings, and other important categories in your copy. If you have a duplicate set of page proofs, underline key words in your copy.

Your goal is to record each topic as a major entry on an individual three-by-five-inch card. Use separate cards for each entry; don't try to shortcut by placing several entries on one card. Find the key word in each of your topics; it will probably prove to be a noun, not an adjective or a verb. If necessary, add selected modifiers to the key words. You will find that you have to invert the qualifying words, for everything must read back to the selected key word or words. Record the pages devoted to the topic. Develop frequent cross-references to synonymous words, instructing the reader to "see" another entry. Help the reader by suggesting "see also." You may find more than one way of phrasing and arranging your key words.

Now you have your major entries on cards. The basic structure of your index is established when you determine the major headings.

Bill. But readers want more than a broad referral to pages 119–142, or referral to a long string of page numbers. How about subheadings under the major entries?

Andy. Enter each subheading, pithily phrased, on a separate card. Be sure each card also carries the main heading. This is to remind you that this particular card represents a subheading that will eventually appear under a major heading. If you use a second order of subhead—a sub-subhead in effect—carry both the overall heading and the first subheading on the card. Indent the first subheading and further indent the second-order subheading. Please—no more than two orders of subheadings if you plan to keep your sanity.

Bill. As an indexer, I will also prepare cards for significant persons, places, things, publications, charts, etc., included in my page proofs?

Andy. Right. However, you will find that you are forced to make choices. Should you include all names, places, publications, etc., mentioned in your book? All in the textual content? All mentioned in foot-notes? In bibliographies? If you do, your index will be formidable. Better include only whatever you think your reader will really look up.

Bill. I assume that I then arrange the cards into twenty-six stacks representing the letters of the alphabet and then alphabetize the stacks. That sounds easy.

Andy. It is if you remember to alphabetize according to the order of the letters before your first comma. Subheadings and second-order subheadings also must be well ordered. When all seems to be in order, strike out the major headings on cards that carry subheads and strike out both major headings and subheadings on cards carrying second-order subheads. They have served their purpose as guides to where your various subheadings belong.

Before finally numbering the cards in order and then having them typed, give the cards a last editing. Are the first words of each entry capitalized? Is each entry separated from its modifiers and page numbers by commas? Have you eliminated all adjectives standing alone? Can some entries be dropped? Should more cross-references be added? Should "see also" be used more frequently? Should any critical key words be rephrased? Should additional phrasing of key words be added to the index for the convenience of the reader?

Then number your cards consecutively and turn the batch over to your typist. The index should be double-spaced or even triple-spaced to allow you to insert a heading or a subheading you may have neglected. Make your final check of the typed copy against your page proofs. Check for accuracy and inclusiveness. Even at this late stage you'll occasionally pencil out an entry or find an error as to page numbers. I've found this check list from my copy of Skillin and Gay's *Words into Type* helpful:

> Has a wise choice of headings been made?
>
> Is the information given under the headings the searcher would be most likely to look for first, and have cross-references been made from other possible headings?
>
> Are the headings nouns or substantive phrases, not adjectives or descriptive phrases?
>
> Are phrase headings indexed logically, inverted if necessary to bring the significant word to the key position?
>
> Have headings been sufficiently divided by subheadings to enable the searcher to find quickly the material for which he is looking?
>
> Are the subheadings correct subdivisions of the key word?
>
> Do the subheadings read back properly to the key word?
>
> Are the subheadings arranged logically—alphabetically or chronologically—and consistently?
>
> Have all citations on a given subject been given under a single heading, not divided between singular and plural forms of the key word?

Are the entries concise, containing no such phrases as *concerning, relating to,* and no unnecessary articles and prepositions?

Have the rules for alphabetical order been accurately and consistently followed?[1]

Bill. Any technicalities I should have in mind?

Andy. Some. If you list a book in an index, better follow it with the author's name in parentheses. Too many people have written books titled *An Autobiography.*

You also have to decide how to handle some Scottish and Irish authors, such as Scotch MacLean and Irish McCarthy. Should Mc and Mac precede your letter M category? Should Mc and Mac be strictly alphabetized under M? Should Mc and Mac be mixed as though all were spelled Mac? Better refer to your publisher's chosen style guide or author's guide.

Bill. If I need more help on specific problems of indexing, where do I turn?

Andy. Try *Words into Type,* an excellent compendium on moving from a manuscript to the printed words, or *Indexes and Indexing* by Robert L. Collison, or *Into Print* by Mary Hill and Wendell Cochran, or *The Chicago Manual of Style.*

Bill. Maybe I'll turn back to individuals engaged by the publisher or by me. You've convinced me that professional indexers earn their money.

Andy. Yet I know a professor who indexed his book while watching his favorite television programs.

Bill. I hope his book is more reliable than his index.

[1]Marjorie E. Skillin, Robert M. Gay, and other authorities, *Words into Type,* 3rd ed. (Englewood Cliffs, N.J.: Prentice-Hall, Inc., 1974), p. 96.

An Index

Cross reference used instead of page numbers

Volcanic dome. *See* Dome, volcanic
Volcanic dust, 101–102
Volcanic features, table of, 121–123

From *Into Print: A Practical Guide to Writing, Illustrating and Publishing.* By Mary Hill and Wendell Cochran. Copyright © 1977 by William Kaufmann, Inc., Los Altos, CA 94022. All rights reserved. Page 144, Figure 32.

*Additional references
listed at end*

hanging valleys in, 159–160;
photos of, cover, center section.
See also Domes, granite; Yosemite
Falls; Yosemite Valley; various
Mts.

PART III

IN THE EDITORIAL OFFICES

23

The Role of Editors

Roles of an acquisitions editor and a journal editor
Contributions by editors to manuscripts
Factors in acceptance or rejection of an article
Roles of referees in acceptance or rejection
Process of acceptance and rejection in publishing houses
Time lapses in decision-making
Good and poor editorial relationships with authors
Editorial problems

While participating in a conference of his national organization held out of town, Bill visits the offices of the acquisitions editor of the company that will publish his next book. Pam is an experienced editor; on her way to the editorship, she has learned a good deal about the process of publishing. Also attending the conference is Jack, an editor of a journal and an author for another company, who has come along to learn more of what happens within a book editor's office. Pam has scheduled a block of time to talk with them. Pam and Jack compare and contrast the work of journal editors and book editors in response to Bill's questions.

Bill. It's not often that a writer has the opportunity to sit down with both a College Department editor in a publishing house and an editor of a journal. I'm particularly appreciative of the opportunity to learn about the similarities and differences in your editorial work as you two see it.

Jack. Bill, one of the differences between Pam's establishment and my shop struck me immediately on my way in. I had to look hard for her room number on that long list of officials, departments, and functions of the publishing house in the building directory on the lobby wall. The size of the book publishing organization is in sharp contrast to that of my own operation at the journal, consisting of my office, the managing editor's office, the copyeditor's room, and the space for our two secretaries, all housed in one of the university's older buildings.

Pam. A large organization has its advantages. But don't forget, Jack, the disadvantages of what Supreme Court Justice Louis Brandeis once called "the curse of bigness." With size and specialization come substantial sharing and joint decision-making. Sometimes I think we have too many vice-presidents.

Bill. That's a thought you have in common with most university professors. How do you see your role, Pam, as acquisitions editor?

Pam. Recognize first that it is acquisitions editor within a specific territory, the College Department, developing textbooks and supplementary materials for use in college courses. The School Department, which develops materials for elementary and high school students, is a separate entity. So is our largest department, Trade, sometimes called General.

Jack. Do you work together?

Pam. To a limited degree. Major departments in publishing houses are often distinct empires.

Bill. That's the way it is in universities too. I know best the people in my own department, am acquainted with the rest of our college staff, and encounter people in the other colleges only through occasional committee assignments or out-of-university committee and social contacts.

Pam. Like other publishers, we are trying to build closer interrelationships. But manuscripts that their authors intend for both text and trade markets are handled either by the College Department or Trade, not both. Authors often don't recognize the necessary distinctions in marketing between the two types of publishing. A book termed scholarly or professional or technical by its author goes one or the other route—either Trade or College—or the author is told to try another house.

College Department authors—and their spouses—sometimes complain that their books are not carried in our company's booth at a convention they have attended. Upon checking, we find that the booth was underwritten by the School Department to display el-hi books. That booth is not our baby.

Jack. Our journal is a separate entity and is relatively independent. Of course, we are responsible to the total university structure and its bureaucracy, and we work with the university's printing shop. My role is to plan, develop, carry through, and distribute the quarterly issues of a ninety-six-page journal. However, my major work is teaching graduate classes.

Pam. Our staff is, of course, larger. The College Department includes acquisitions editors (in some houses called series or directing editors) in the social sciences, language arts, foreign languages, science and mathematics, business education, health and physical education, and education. Acquisitions editors study possible markets, plan series in their fields, acquire appropriate books, and follow through from manuscript to published book. In some houses acquisitions editors do a preliminary editing for basic content and style. The number of books an editor handles is dependent on the type and complexity of the books, market factors, and other considerations.

The production department handles such tasks as checking of permissions, final editing of copy, scheduling, production coordination, design, layout, preparation of art, and checking of proofs for the interior, cover, and jacket. In many cases a production editor will be responsible for performing all of these functions or seeing that they are carried out by various specialists, such as copyeditors and designers. In other houses a supervisor of copyediting will handle the general production tasks, in addition to overseeing the work of individual copyeditors.

Above all of us in the editorial hierarchy is the managing editor (sometimes called executive editor) who coordinates the work of acquisitions editors; and an editor-in-chief for the department, to whom the managing editor, in turn, is responsible. An acquisitions editor, if lucky, may have an editorial assistant to whom legwork is delegated.

Bill. How can a journal or publishing house contribute improvements to a book or article by a writer who works in a profession?

Jack. Through helpful feedback. The opinions and reactions of readers of the refereed journal. The editor's suggestions. However, editors of professional journals are often so busy that they haven't time to reshape articles to make them publishable.

Pam. The ideas of outside readers and in-house staff. A summary of readers' suggestions that seem valid to us.

Bill. My friend Andy told me that Maxwell Perkins, a great trade editor, once wrote to an author, "The book belongs to the author." Do you accept that?

Pam. Not completely. I like to think of the author and editor as partners. Each should respect the other's expertise. Each should strive for the best possible product, the finished book. Editors are more than comma-catchers for authors. A good editor makes a contribution to content. The editor-author relationship should be a collaborative arrangement and a healthy partnership.

Jack. I agree. Editors should supply rigorous proofreading, should cut freely and tighten up manuscripts, and should help authors to put across their ideas. I frequently find that articles are too long and benefit by pruning.

Bill. I agree too. But suppose the author rejects suggested content changes? Who then decides?

Pam. The author, if the meaning is changed by the editing. But I argue loud and long for the changes I recommend. If the changes are necessary for the readers' acceptance of the book and if the author still rejects such changes, I won't publish the book. But such hassles are rare.

Bill. That's a considerable distance from Maxwell Perkins's "The book belongs to the author."

Pam. My obligation to the readers is at least as great as my obligation to the author. My obligation to the company is paramount.

Jack. In my experience in journal editing, the question of editorial changes seldom comes up. Frankly, this may be in part because many of our contributors hunger for publication. They are delighted with acceptance, and they don't quibble. We seldom do more than copyedit their contributions, out of respect for our scholars' expertise. My decision whether to run the article or not is made after the article is submitted and I have received readers' reports. If I ask for rewrite as a condition of acceptance, I assume that suggested changes—or at least most of them—will be made if the writer wants to appear in our journal or that the writer will convince me that the changes need not be made.

Bill. What factors, Jack, do you take into account in accepting or rejecting an article?

Jack. My own judgment, admittedly subjective and aided by that of the referees. I ask myself whether the article is appropriate for my readership. I consider the length of the article in the context of available space. I ask whether the material is a significant contribution. Is it timely? If the subject is old, is it handled freshly and competently? Is it scholarly?

The quality of the writing is important to me. Manuscripts characterized by good scholarship, written well, and reported with clarity will get published—if not by me by some other editor.

We carry a brief description of requirements for submission of manuscripts in each issue, and I have a supplementary sheet I send to potential authors. This has helped us to avoid inappropriate submissions and to receive the type of manuscripts we want to consider.

Bill. How about the article writer's experience, affiliation, reputation, status? Writers tell me that they believe journals use an "old boy" network—use articles by the same established scholars too frequently.

Jack. That's a half-truth. Many journals invite authors to contribute to themed issues. Naturally, an editor of an issue with a theme will invite those who have already demonstrated that they have something to say on the questions being discussed. This means that the authors who are invited to contribute probably do have well-established credentials. However, in the case of unsolicited articles, the attempt is to judge on the basis of the quality and appropriateness of the article, not on the basis of affiliations, reputation, and the like. Consequently, unknowns get published. If journals don't publish ideas from future leaders, they don't stay current.

Bill. Would you run an article by a graduate student?

Jack. An outstanding article, yes. I admit it would have to be very good.

Bill. How about acceptances and rejections in the field of book publishing, Pam?

Pam. In short, quality and marketability. I don't have to remind you that sales are a major consideration. We hope that an introductory course textbook will sell 20,000–50,000 copies. Advanced texts are expected to sell considerably less.

As to names, we understandably prefer experienced writers with reputations. Yes, we lean to writers with doctorates from top-level institutions and affiliations with major colleges or universities. However, we have published and will continue to publish good manuscripts regardless of the affiliations or prestige of the authors. Authors from prestigious institutions sometimes can't write for students enrolled in run-of-the-mill colleges. And in today's tough academic marketplace, many gifted professionals are employed in relatively obscure institutions.

The more scholarly the book, the more important the author's reputation and affiliation become. Names are important to scholars and librarians who purchase scholarly books by professionals.

Bill. The three sociologists who wrote *Books: The Culture and Commerce of Publishing* say that, to get a book published, recommendation through an informal circle or network is close to being an absolute necessity.[1] Members of "invisible colleges" who share the same heritage and ideas can influence acceptance of articles or books.

Pam. The writers who suspect the existence of an "old boy" network are partly right and partly wrong. Even the "old boys"—and should we now add "old girls"?—had to break into print somehow and somewhere. Tell the Young Turks not to give up too readily. They'll be labeled Old Guard all too soon.

Bill. I imagine there are some major differences between journals and books as to who makes the decision to accept or reject.

Jack. The process is simple for the usual journal. Sometimes the editor makes a swift independent decision. If the journal is refereed, the editor sends the article to several reviewers, who, in time, respond. The editor then decides.

Bill. Not the advisory board?

Jack. At some journals the advisory board serves as the journal's referees. At other journals, an advisory board or committee, possibly eight or ten people, meets only once or possibly twice a year in order to set broad policies, determine themes, and supervise the publication. Between times, individual editorial board members may serve as referees. Other referees may also be used by the editor.

---

[1] Lewis A. Coser, Charles Kadushin, Walter W. Powell, *Books: The Culture and Commerce of Publishing* (New York: Basic Books, 1982), p. 231.

In both types, the editor usually has autonomy on specific articles. Sometimes the editor cooperates with a guest editor on an issue. Some editors also write editorials for their journals.

Bill. Do you always follow the advice of referees?

Jack. Usually but not always. For instance, I can't when referees divide somewhat evenly—though the presumption in that case is against acceptance. Once in a long while I'll run an article most or all of the referees have rejected or I won't carry an article most or all have recommended. This happens very seldom.

Pam. Decision-making is more complex in book publishing. After the prospectus is read by me—

Bill. Do textbook editors read proposals or manuscripts themselves, or do these go to a "slush pile" for first reading by a subordinate?

Pam. I can't speak for everybody. Trade receives so many unsolicited manuscripts that first readers on the in-house staff are needed. However, as a textbook editor, I read all proposals and at least look over all unsolicited manuscripts. Whatever survives is read by outside readers along with in-house staff. Then, favorable recommendations in hand, I send a summarizing memorandum to the staff members who will be involved in decision-making. Sometimes the prospectus and reader reactions go along to them too. The memorandum is accompanied by a form I have filled in concerning production costs, the market, the contract, my editorial opinion, and a suggested price. Then an editorial conference is held involving, among others, representatives of sales, research, art and design; other series editors; and the managing editor. In some houses, the series editor simply obtains the approval of the managing editor in a person-to-person conference.

Jack. What kinds of ideas are traded in the editorial conference?

Pam. If I've carried the manuscript this far as sponsoring editor, I am usually supportive. The sales manager may report on sales of comparable books we have published. Research may provide data on the size of the possible market. An editor may retail some gossip on the author's previous relationships with another publisher. An editor just returned from a convention may mention comments on the author that were picked up at the conference. The art department may talk about some problem with design or call attention to some needed expensive artwork. Anybody may comment on possible competing books, in print or planned. The opinions of people above my level in the editorial hierarchy are especially important. Eventually a decision is made, usually by consensus, to proceed or not.

Remember, though, that publishing is a highly individualistic business and that there are many deviations from this pattern. Much depends on the process of decision-making that the house influentials prefer. In some companies, board members actually make the decisions. Editors have little authority.

Bill. How do you inform the writer of your decision?

Pam. Acceptances are often conveyed by phone and followed up by mail. By now, some kind of personal relationship with the author has been established. We usually also discuss possible contract provisions in that notification call. Rejections are most often handled by mail.

Jack. Journal editors usually inform the potential contributor of acceptance or rejection by mail. Some editors send form letters; I still try to write brief personal letters. If the rejected writer responds by asking for more information on why he or she was rejected, I'll write again. I may send an author the referees' comments after I've masked the referees' identities.

Bill. A common grievance of authors against editorial processes is that decision-making usually takes a long time.

Pam. Admittedly, good decision-making takes time. In book publishing, the time span between receiving a prospectus and reaching a decision on it may vary from one to six months.

Jack. In the case of journals, the time from manuscript receipt to editorial decision ranges from a week to a year.

Bill. A year?

Jack. Thumbing over the *Directory of Publishing Opportunities in Journals and Periodicals*, I found that some remarkably speedy journals decide within a week. Others may take as long as a year. I even found one journal that described its decision time as one week to one year! The large majority, however, decided within three months. Most of these specified about six to ten weeks. On the average, a journal will publish an article about seven months after acceptance. But it may publish earlier or take longer. Journals differ and so do the paces in the various scholarly fields.

Bill. Writers often ask me when they should inquire about their manuscripts if they have had no word from the editor aside from a routine acknowledgment. What would you advise?

Pam. In the case of an unsolicited manuscript, I'd advise authors to follow up with a letter, preferably polite, to the editor after about a month. In the case of a proposal, tardy reviewers may account for delays. Give the editor about two months and then find out what's going on.

Jack. I'd advise them to check the *Directory* I mentioned or a similar source to determine the time needed for decision by the specific journal to which the manuscript has been submitted. If the journal claims to decide within one to two months—and I say "claims" because I suspect the estimates of decision time to be optimistic—write the editor after two months. There's little point in writing a plaintive monthly letter urging a decision on a journal that has plainly stated its decision might take nine months to a year. Writers who can't wait shouldn't submit manuscripts to such laggard journals.

Bill. I hate to inquire about rejection rates because I dislike bearers of bad news.

Pam. Frankly, we don't keep records of the volume of manuscripts rejected. For my company, I would estimate that 96 to 99 percent of manuscripts that come over the transom are rejected. No one knows for sure. You recognize that more manuscripts come over the transom in Trade, less in the College Department, and much less in the El-Hi Department.

Jack. One study in the 1980s reported that the large majority of the education periodicals responding accepted less than one-third of the articles submitted. Some rejected almost all the unsolicited manuscripts they received. Sometimes editors reject good publishable articles simply because they don't have space.

Bill. Let's get back to a more cheerful topic, acceptances. After acceptance of an article, who continues the relationship with the author?

Jack. I do, until the manuscript reaches galley stage. At the galley stage the copyeditor usually handles further correspondence. If there's a major problem, I step in.

Pam. I do until we move into the stage of production, including copyediting. That's after the final manuscript is received and reviewed and all signs are "go." I move out as the project moves into the copyediting stage.

Bill. But you still maintain some relationship with the project?

Pam. Definitely. If authors have problems that can't be resolved in correspondence with the supervisor of copyediting or the production editor, they write their acquisitions editor.

Bill. From the editors' point of view, what's a good relationship with an author? Or a poor relationship?

Pam. The best relationships are with authors whose on-time manuscripts are readable, well checked for accuracy, carefully proofread by the writer, and consistent with our style guide. We appreciate authors who obtain all their permissions and who prepare their art packages carefully. We have good relationships with authors who take into account outside reviewers' suggestions and who are willing to change their manuscripts in accordance with perceptive suggestions and to discuss with us the suggestions they reject. Our relationships are good with authors who make only minor changes on galleys and practically none on page proofs.

Our poor relationships are with authors who can't meet deadlines, who write clumsily, are shaky on facts and careless about typos, and who ignore our style sheets. We don't like late permissions and confused directions on art packages. We have a hard time with authors who argue continually with reviewers' judgments, with our suggestions, and with copyeditors' changes. Some authors take affront at any suggested changes; others fall in love with their phrasing and stubbornly resist modifications. Worst of all are the authors who rewrite their books at the galley stage or come up with impossible demands for changes on page proofs.

Bill. I assume that most authors think that publishers insufficiently publicize and advertise their books.

Pam. That's been my experience; however, I let the advertising director and sales manager worry about that.

Jack. I seem to have fewer problems with authors than Pam does. Our major problems are with procrastination in delivery of manuscript and return of galleys. From the writers' point of view, their major grievances are the time lapses between acceptance and publication. In response, I can only apologize and point the finger of blame at the composition and printing establishment—or at the referees who give a low priority in their time schedules to judging my manuscripts.

Bill. After coffee let's talk further about reviewers of articles and books.

SUGGESTIONS FROM AN EDITOR
OF A PERIODICAL

[Adapted from "Manuscript Memo," distributed by the Michigan Association of Secondary School Principals, publisher of *The Journal* and *The Bulletin*, and used until recently by *Contemporary Education*.]

```
                    Contemporary Education
                      School of Education
                    Indiana State University
                      Terre Haute, Indiana

Manuscript Memo
To:  Contributors to Contemporary Education
From:  Dr. M. Dale Baughman, Editor

     Good writing is rewarding for the writer, editor, and
reader; but as you know it is hard work.  To aid prospective
writers for our publication we have gathered familiar tips
on approach, organization, and mechanics from many sources
and adapted them to our specific needs.  We hope they will
make the task easier and the results more satisfying.

Decide:  What outcomes you desire, what you want to say.
     Is the topic timely?  Interesting to the reader?  Is
the approach right?  Will you describe a technique, a study,
or a piece of research in relation to trends, principles,
theories, or philosophies rather than let it stand alone?
If you describe trend, principle, theory, or philosophy, will
you relate it to the reader's interests and experiences?  Our
readers include professors, students, in-service professionals,
and non-educators.

Organize:  Ideas and facts in the best order to further your
objectives.
     Is the order logical?  Is all relevant material included
and all irrelevant material omitted?  Is the scope right for
the length?  Have you written a head and subheads which indi-
cate content, implement your objectives, and invite and
assist the reader?

Write:  Simply and clearly.
     Are you saying exactly what you mean?  Do you weigh words
for accuracy?  Do you avoid jargon--"educationese"--when plain
English will do?  When technical phrases are used, are they
necessary and correct?  Is the length appropriate to the
topic?  Are you skimping on major issues and belaboring the
insignificant?  Are you writing with simplicity and economy
of words, regardless of the complexity of the subject?  Are
the facts and figures correct and complete?  Is there contin-
uity from one idea, paragraph, or section to the next?

Document and illustrate:  When necessary, simply, accurately,
completely.
     Are references necessary?  Are they complete?  Are quo-
tations significant?  Is the author given credit?  Are they
quoted and footnoted accurately?  Are tables and charts used
only where essential?  Are they simple and accurate in design?

Read, correct, improve, and rewrite:  Preferably after a
cooling-off period.
     Have you said what you intended, in the way you intended?
```

Have you organized relevant ideas and facts in logical order?
Have your subheads both aided and revealed good organization?
Have you expressed yourself clearly? Simply? Smoothly?
Accurately? Can you delete words, paragraphs, or sections
without loss?

Prepare final manuscript: Legibly, accurately, and in a
form to meet the mechanical requirements of the editorial
staff.
   Check the following with your typist: Is the manuscript
typed double-spaced, preferably 72 characters wide, six inches,
elite type? Are footnotes inserted in the text directly
after the references? Have you included a footnote giving
your name as you wish it to appear in print; title, position,
location and any other information basic to the preparation
of the article? Have you told the editor what to do if your
manuscript is not to be used? Have you enclosed a stamped,
self-addressed envelope if you wish it returned?
   Have you followed a recognized authority such as Webster's
New Collegiate Dictionary for spelling, capitalization, and
abbreviation? The editor and his proofreaders use A Manual of
Style, The University of Chicago Press, as a basic reference
and for bibliographic style.

And what does the editor do?
   Decides: How content, format, and layout can further the
objectives of the publication, within the framework of University policies and costs. Whom to approach for articles
on specific subjects. Whether articles are appropriate as
to quality and subject.
   Organizes: Subjects and specific articles for each issue.
Solicits specific articles from appropriate authors.
   Edits: Reads manuscripts and suggests major improvements.
Smooths copy for easy reading. Corrects for accuracy, consistency, grammar, and style. Adjusts heads, subheads, and
length of copy to suit requirements of appearance and space,
for each page and for the entire journal. Has copy retyped.
Marks copy with instructions for the printer--measurements,
type faces. Works with the printer's representative on printing details. Corrects galley proofs, makes up page dummy,
and corrects page proofs. Readjusts copy for exact fit,
deleting words and lines when necessary. Sends complimentary
copies to the authors and hopes for the best.

   Manuscript should be no more than 12 double-spaced, typed
pages accompanied by a self-addressed, stamped envelope.
Send at least 2 copies of the article. References preferred
at the end.

AUTHOR'S CHECK LIST

Leading Educational Publishers since 1868

Allyn and Bacon, Inc.
7 Wells Avenue, Newton, MA 02159
617/964-5530

Author: Please indicate the items you have included with the final manuscript, or give the approximate date on which you plan to send them.

		INCLUDED (Yes/No)	WILL BE SENT (Date)
I.	SUGGESTED TITLE		
II.	COMPLETE TEXT, including all chapters		
III.	PERMISSIONS		
	1. Quoted Material		
	2. Illustrations		
	3. Tables		

IV. FRONT MATTER
   1. Title page, giving title and subtitle, if any, and your name with affiliation, as it should appear in the book
   2. Complete table of contents, showing all items planned for the book, in intended sequence
   3. Preface
   4. Acknowledgments (if any, may be included in Preface)
   5. Dedication (if any, not necessary)

V. END MATTER
   1. Appendix (if one is intended)
   2. Bibliography (if any)
   3. Answers to problems (if any)
   4. Do you plan to make your own Index (done after page proofs are complete) Yes ___ or have it prepared by Allyn and Bacon and charged to your royalty account ___

VI. ILLUSTRATIONS
   1. Photographs (if any) How many?_____
   2. Any other illustrative material (finished artwork, rough sketches for figures, etc.)?
   3. Captions and credits

VII. AUTHOR'S SUGGESTION FORM (Complete)

VIII. OTHER MATERIAL (Please describe in detail any other material not noted above):

Signed _____ Date _____

24

The Reviewers
of Manuscripts

Author John Doe, Editor Richard Roe, and the anonymous outside readers
Criticism of Richard Roe's editorial procedures
Consideration of editorial suggestions
Criticism of manuscript-reviewing procedures
Defense of manuscript-reviewing procedures
Backgrounds of referees and outside readers
Questions of anonymity and objectivity

Bill has brought one of his columns to the conference with Jack and Pam at the publishing house. The column is skeptical of current practices by journals and book publishers in the areas of reading and refereeing of manuscripts. As he expects, the column elicits strong reactions from the two editors.

Bill.   I'd like to tap your ideas on the role of reviewers of manuscripts. Book editors such as Pam call them outside readers, and journal editors call them referees, but the responsibilities of each are similar. By reviewers of manuscripts, I mean anybody who reads unpublished works, appraises them, and advises editors accordingly.

From my worm's eye point of view, that of the writer for professional publications, I have some reservations about the customary process of reviewing manuscripts. I once wrote a column on the subject. Take a few moments to read it. Then I'd like to get your editorial viewpoints. Here's the column, which I called "Editorial Roulette":

When Professor John Doe was very young, he became an assistant professor of education. Naturally, he lusted for tenure. He knew that published writing contributes to a young professor's arrival at this honorable estate. So, encouraged by the publication of two of his articles in professional journals, he made some minor revisions in his doctoral dissertation and sent it, unsolicited, to an eminent book publisher. His manuscript was rejected by publishing house after publishing house, with intervening and excruciating delays. Eventually young John Doe grew tired of this experience. His dissertation revision now yellows in a closet used only by passing spiders.

Nowhere in his doctoral ordeal by fire had John Doe learned that the chances of publication of a lightly revised doctoral thesis are only slightly better than those of the proverbial snowball in hell. No one had bothered to suggest that the chances of the snowball may even be better than those of the unsolicited education manuscript coming in over the transom to a textbook publisher's office.

John Doe grew older and wiser. He wrote many more articles, achieved tenure, rose through the ranks, and was recognized as an able educator. People recognized that he had some important things to say about education. He decided to write a textbook that could be used in his favorite education course.

This time he sought the counsel of his more experienced colleagues. They advised him to develop the holy trinity revered by textbook publishers—a query letter, a detailed outline, and a sample chapter. He sent this trio simultaneously to half a dozen publishers, and, happily, one deemed it a distinct possibility. Might editor Richard Roe and the author (a lovely word) meet at a convention or, if the author happened to be visiting Big City, at the editor's office? Meanwhile, editor Roe would send the prospectus off to "outside readers" for "review."

After Richard Roe's cordial hosting of John Doe over an expensive lunch (tax deductible), weeks became months while John Doe waited. "Hurry up and wait" is the rule in publishing, as in the armed forces. Eventually the great day came. An Agreement to publish your Work.

After hastily scanning the legal form, John Doe joyfully signed. At last, a contract allowing him to communicate his ideas to his profession! His query letter had carefully pointed out how his education book would differ from what the publishers like to call his competitors, how it would be more creative and original, more scholarly yet more readable. And his proposal had been accepted! Now he had an iron-clad contract committing a company to publish his book. Professor John Doe settled down for a year or so of combining teaching with writing the Work.

But John Doe was in for some surprises. Editor Richard Roe sent him the "suggestions" of the anonymous readers of his proposal and strongly urged that he incorporate their recommendations. Many of the suggestions were helpful but others seemed to John inappropriate. So he used his own best judgment—after all, it was his book, wasn't it? Editor Richard Roe modestly indicated his own lack of background in Professor John Doe's field and explained that still other outside readers, as well as the in-house staff, would review his first draft. Then Professor Doe would revise and submit a second draft, which in turn would be reviewed by some outside readers. After another revision by the author, John Doe would send in his final draft, which would be reviewed by a reader or two for the last time. Then the manuscript would be copyedited.

So John Doe found himself engaged, along with Richard Roe, in the game of editorial roulette that contemporary textbook publishers play. The underlying theory is impeccable. The assumption is made that some high priests of the educational temple exist and that they can tell the editor and, via the editor, the author, what should and should not appear in the manuscript. In the name of fostering scientific objectivity, the operation is shrouded in anonymity. The manuscript reviewers are not to know who the author is. The author is not to know who the reviewers are. Only the editor knows who all the parties are.

But education is neither revelation nor science. Potential reviewers vary widely in their philosophies, values, and ideologies. They are often turned on by some educational concepts and turned off by other ideas. They subscribe to varied schools of thought. They are mortal humans who are fallible, and they have their differing enthusiasms, preferences, antipathies, and even prejudices. They have varying standards, theories, and commitments. Inescapably, their variant perceptions and backgrounds influence their appraisals of a manuscript and their suggestions to the editor.

Moreover, high priests of the educational temple seem to be in short supply, or at least often busy with other rites. More available are prospective authors whom a company wants to scout, practitioners recommended by book salespeople, acquaintances made by editors or sales representatives at conventions, educators who somehow come to the attention of publishers (sometimes through reactions to an earlier book), and so forth. The selection of readers is influenced by the prudence and great modesty of publishers in payment of honoraria to readers. So the possible readers of John Doe's manuscript, earnest educators all, had a varied assortment of backgrounds and views and standards.

From his pool of possible outside readers, editor Richard Roe selected seven and wrote to them. Four of these agreed to read and react. It took a long time to get back all the reviews. Editor Richard Roe fretted some at the delay, but not as much as author John Doe. Eventually, all reactions were received.

Not too surprisingly, the reviews of the outside readers varied. One pronounced John Doe's manuscript highly publishable and compared his style with that of eminent literary figures. A second reader thought the treatment adequate though not outstanding, and recommended publication. A third declared the manuscript a clinker and described eloquently how it differed from the desirable philosophy and orientation held by the reader. A fourth condemned the manuscript as worthless and the style as miserable, and strongly implied that had a perceptive company invited him/her to write such a book it would be fundamentally different and infinitely superior. Editor Richard Roe was understandably uncertain.

The reviews, carefully masked to assure the outside readers' anonymity, were sent to John Doe so that he might revise the Work. John struggled with the inconsistent perceptions and produced his second draft. Again his manuscript went to some readers. A long period of nothing happening followed. Editor Richard Roe occasionally explained that the reviews were slow in coming in. Then a flurry of correspondence between editor Roe and author Doe.

Finally there came a sad day for John Doe. Gently, with tact and with many expressions of regret, editor Roe called to John's attention a standard provision in the Agreement author John Doe had eagerly signed. The provision read, "If prior to publication the Author shall not deliver the manuscript and ancillary materials as herein contemplated, or *if any part thereof is not satisfactory to the Publisher in its judgment* [emphasis added], the Publisher may terminate this Agreement by written notice to the Author by registered or certified mail, whereupon the only obligation of the Publisher shall be to return to the Author any manuscript or property received from the Author." The contract was not bound in iron, as John had assumed. The publisher's agreement contained a built-in bailout.

But happy endings are preferable to sad endings. John Doe persisted and again queried more textbook publishers concerning the same manuscript. Another publishing house indicated some interest. This time one of the four faceless readers implied that Tolstoy was turning over in his grave in envy of this remarkable Work. A second thought it quite competent. A third deemed it adequate, though he/she personally regretted certain omissions and inclusions. A fourth pronounced it hopeless. John Doe's book was published by this second publisher.

So, in the second round, John won the game of editorial roulette that publishers play. He and his new publisher lived happily ever after—at least until author John Doe wrote still another manuscript.[1]

Pam.   Since the column is about outside reviewers of book manuscripts, I'll be the first to rise to the defense of current editorial practices. I think you're attacking a straw man when you mention the cancellation of John Doe's contract. I admit that publishers have contract clauses allowing cancellation. But the clause is seldom invoked. Editor Richard Roe would be a knucklehead to cancel at so late a date.

Bill.   Why?

Pam.   Because editor Richard Roe is in business to publish books and, in doing so, to return a reasonable profit to his firm. If he waited to say "no" until he received criticisms of the second draft of the manuscript, he would lose the substantial amount of time that he and his associates had already put into the project. He would lose the fees he paid to first draft and second draft reviewers.

The time for Richard Roe to say "no" was immediately after the prospectus was read by outside reviewers. If John Doe couldn't respond to their suggestions in a satisfactory manner, Richard Roe should never have issued John Doe a contract. At the very latest, John Doe should have been cut off at the pass when his first draft was judged favorably by one reviewer, termed only adequate by a second, and reviewed negatively by the third and fourth reviewers.

I wouldn't publish writer John Doe, and I wouldn't hire editor Richard Roe. For one thing, Roe should have been more competent in his selection of reviewers. It sounds as though Roe selected his reviewers at random or chose polar opposites in the profession.

---

[1]William Van Til, "Editorial Roulette," One Way of Looking at It, *Phi Delta Kappan*, February 1978.

Bill. But contracts are often issued before an author has responded to suggestions sent by the editorial staff.

Pam. If Richard Roe had doubts about the manuscript stemming from reviewers of the prospectus, he should have insisted that John Doe respond to suggestions made by outside readers before he issued a contract. Roe should also have supplied Doe with his own editorial suggestions. Instead, he remained silent until the contract was signed.

Bill. The word "suggestions" is a tricky one. Some suggestions may come from the editor and the in-house staff. Many may represent criticisms of the prospectus or first draft by outside readers, often professors who teach courses similar to those for which the book is intended. Sometimes an editor paraphrases the criticisms; sometimes the editor sends the author the full reviews with outside readers' names deleted. So the author, who has already signed a contract, receives an assemblage of suggestions. How seriously should the author take the assorted "suggestions"? How free is the author to accept some and reject others? Understandably, questions like these occur to the author, particularly when suggestions are mutually contradictory or contrary to the author's perception or intentions.

Pam. A helpful editor indicates which of the suggestions the publishing house regards as of major importance. An unhelpful editor simply presents the author with an indigestible smorgasbord of ideas from many sources. In the first case, the author would be well advised to listen closely and try to accept the suggestions (preferably graciously). He or she should reject ideas only after cautious deliberation. In the second case, the author should consider the variety of suggestions as objectively as possible, then share reactions with the editor. The merit of some suggestions should be acknowledged; the value of others disputed; and the relevance of still others debated.

At any rate, an author should respond to suggestions rather than hope they will be forgotten. They won't be—editors have a way of referring back to earlier correspondence. Better debate the matter now, rather than after completion of the manuscript. An author is assumed to have expertise; the reasonable editor will give the author the benefit of the doubt. If the editor is unreasonable, the author might as well learn that unfortunate fact of life right away.

Bill. Even so, the author may not be out of the woods. When a segment, or the manuscript as a whole, is received, the editor may request an appraisal by an outside reader who originally criticized the prospectus. The outside reader discovers that an especially beloved suggestion has been ignored or, at least, not incorporated in the manuscript. The outside reader may point this out, sometimes sharply. Pam, this whole matter of outside readers of textbooks and professional books troubles me. Jack, I'm even somewhat doubtful of the ark of the convenant of the scholar—the refereeing of journal articles.

Jack. Heresy! Honor thy referees! I'll admit that refereeing takes up a good deal of staff and clerical time and costs a great deal, even though the referees themselves are unpaid by the journal.

Nevertheless, refereeing gives the scholarly community assurance that peers have reviewed the article and judged it to be worth publication. Referees often point out errors or suggest additional sources or call for better documentation. They help editors make sound decisions. After all, journal editors can't be familiar with all aspects of a broad field or its many specializations.

Bill. I'm quite aware that somebody has to judge a manuscript and determine whether it's publishable—that's inevitable. I know that manuscripts benefit from criticism and suggested improvements, in addition to copyediting. I know the arguments against the editor or editorial staff having sole responsibility for criticism and judgment—too much concentration of power and authority, fallibility and even prejudices of the individual or staff, the difficulty of appraising and improving highly specialized manuscripts. I accept the potential superiority of multiple evaluations by specialists over a single judgment by a generalist.

However, referees often differ in philosophy and ideology. Political factors may affect their judgments. The result may be disagreement on a manuscript. For instance, some conservative referees may reject innovating manuscripts, and some radical referees may insist on no deviation from radical orthodoxy. Thus the range of a journal may be narrowed. Some reviews by referees are prepared hastily and submitted late.

I even suspect that some journals that aren't top level may be trying to obtain greater respectability by using referees. Some journal editors may use referees only occasionally. Should their journals be regarded as refereed?

Consequently, those who decide on tenure and promotion should take into account the national scope and the overall reputation and scholarly orientation of the journal. Publish-or-perish policies too often focus only on whether or not the journal happens to be refereed.

Pam. Add to arguments favoring reader reviewing the factor of publisher insistence on use of outside readers. An Association of American Publishers' pamphlet tells textbook authors, ''This stage of review and revision is critical in textbook publishing—it ensures high standards of educational excellence and marketability.''[2] Trade book publishers are also increasingly using outside readers to ensure authenticity and protect themselves from publishing phony works. I wonder whether all

[2]College Division, Association of American Publishers, *An Author's Guide to Academic Publishing,* Association of American Publishers, New York, undated, unpaged.

McGraw-Hill editors are required to have signs over their desks reading "Remember Clifford Irving and his Howard Hughes autobiography!"

Bill. My objection to the outside reader system is that it doesn't always work well. The basic assumption made is that the scholar's manuscript will be read by leaders in the specialized field. Usually, though not always, outside readers for refereed journals are leaders in their fields. Editorial Boards or invited referees for journals feel a responsibility and obligation to the national organization that sponsors the periodical, and to the editor who will print the referees' own future scholarly articles.

But outstanding leaders also have other commitments. So reading manuscripts of prospective textbooks often ranks low among the priorities of established scholars. Consequently, as my "Editorial Roulette" column said, outside readers for textbook publishers often are a mixed bag made up of recognized leaders, young scholars on their way up, new authors whose potentiality a company wants to explore, and people the editor happens to have met at conventions. The honoraria publishers pay outside readers are inadequate, to put it gently. Indeed, some letters inviting outside reviewers do not even mention such crass and vulgar matters as money. Yet decisions as to publishability are made and "suggestions" are sent to authors on the basis of judgments of book manuscripts by outside readers.

Anonymity complicates the process. The reviewers are not told who the author is, and the author is not told who the reviewers are. Only the omniscient editor knows.

Pam. Anonymity is in the interest of objectivity. A reviewer might be influenced by an author's reputation or lack of one. An author might develop an undying hatred of a virulent critic. A reviewer might pull punches unless guaranteed that the reviewer's identity will be withheld from the author. Relationships of "you rub my back and I'll rub yours" might prevail. Anonymity also reduces possible editorial discrimination against women or blacks or newcomers.

Bill. Objectivity sounds good and your anti-discrimination point is a good one. But among the many disciplines, exact sciences are few. Most disciplines are rife with conflicting contentions, theories, ideologies, and schools of thought. Though a fellow specialist, a reviewer may be of a different persuasion than an author. Can an author appraise the value of a reviewer's critique without some knowledge of the reviewer's identity and frame of reference? This is a game of the blind leading the blind.

Jack. It's the only game in town for academics. Editors should select referees who are not only experts but also without known biases against a field or a methodology.

As to anonymity, I admit it's seldom foolproof. An author who is well read can make an educated guess as to a referee's identity despite "blind" refereeing procedures, particularly if the referee's comments are quoted to the author. Similarly, a knowledgeable referee can often guess an author's identity despite precautions. How? Through style or methodology or the way a topic is treated. And especially through self-citations, since authors and referees are prone to cite their own works. Yet, despite flaws, the system of refereed journals and outside readers of manuscripts is still preferable to unilateral acceptance or rejection by an editor or staff coterie.

Pam. After you read a number of reviews, you become competent to deduce the grounds on which negative reviews are based. You take into account the reviewer's vested interest or bias. If other reviewers are favorable and if your gut reaction is positive, you may conclude that the reviewer is simply riding a hobby horse.

In general, if the reviews are good, there is a strong likelihood that I will accept the manuscript. If the reviews are strongly negative, I won't. If the reviews are mixed, I'll rely on my own judgment. If I continue to be in doubt, I'm more likely to reject than accept.

Jack. We have been talking as though judgments by reviewers and editors concerning the quality of manuscripts were the only factors in acceptance or rejection of a proposed publication. Often it is not the quality of a manuscript that is in question; reviewers may judge many manuscripts to be highly publishable. But frequently the publishing house or the journal is already committed. The fall list of books to be published is full, or the next twelve issues of the journal are already crowded. Reviewers are not to blame for factors of high supply and limited publication outlets.

Bill. So, according to you two editors, we must continue to expect that Reviewer A will proclaim a manuscript to be comparable to Tolstoy at his best, while Reviewer B terms the manuscript passing fair, Reviewer C blasts it as a turkey, and Reviewer D subtly implies that a book or article on the same topic by Reviewer D would be infinitely preferable?

Pam. I expect so. Though, in fairness, you must admit that many juries readily arrive at consensus. In any event, an author who receives controversial suggestions from an editor based on reports by referees or outside readers had better give priority to communication with the editor until an agreement is reached.

CRITERIA FOR THE SELECTION OF UNSOLICITED MANUSCRIPTS FOR SOCIAL EDUCATION

The reviewer will rate the article using the following criteria:
(1 = no; 2 = perhaps; 3 = yes)

I. Content

1   2   3   A. Does the article fit one of the areas desired by *Social Education?*

1   2   3   B. Does the article contribute new research knowledge, new approaches for the classroom, or new approaches for the social studies?

1   2   3   C. Does the article speak to current, important issues in the social studies?

1   2   3   D. Does the article make the reader think or inspire the reader to apply or use the information?

II. Style

1   2   3   A. Is the article ready for publication without major revision?
1   2   3   B. Is the article of appropriate length?
1   2   3   C. Is the article readable and clear in its presentation?
1   2   3   D. Is the article a unified piece with a coherent introduction and conclusion?
1   2   3   E. Are charts, diagrams, and other illustrative materials significant and integral parts of the article?

III. Scholarship

1   2   3   A. Is the article original as opposed to a restatement of previously published ideas?

1   2   3   B. Are assertions and conclusions substantiated by relevant, reliable sources and by logical reasoning (not just footnotes with concurring opinions of others)?

1   2   3   C. If it is a research article, is the collection and analysis of data defensible?

IV. General Recommendations (Please use the back of this sheet.)

1   2   3   A. To which of the target groups within NCSS does the article address itself?

1   2   3   B. Do you recommend that this article be accepted for publication?

                  C. Other comments.

SUGGESTIONS FOR REVIEWERS
OF TEXTBOOKS

Leading Educational Publishers since 1868

Allyn and Bacon, Inc.
7 Wells Avenue, Newton, MA 02159
617/964-5530

I am most interested in your general evaluation of the manuscript itself, its potential success in the market place, and its competition.

A. GENERAL
  1) Is the material well-organized, up-to-date, and accurate? If not, please include a sampling of specific criticisms.
  2) Has the author placed too much emphasis upon certain topics? Should any be excluded? Added? Transposed? Please feel free to suggest changes.
  3) Are the vocabulary and interest appeal suited to the educational level for which the manuscript is intended (Undergraduate, Graduate, etc.)?

B. MARKET
  4) What are the current trends in this area? Does this manuscript reflect them? In your opinion, will it be up-to-date three years from now?
  5) Do you feel there is a national market for material of this nature? Can you specify sources to support your opinion?
  6) If this text were now available in published form, would you use it or recommend its use?

C. COMPETITION
  7) Are you aware of any comparable texts in the field that might compete in whole or in part with this project? Which ones (Author, Title, Publisher)?
  8) How are they similar or different?

D. PUBLISH
  9) Should we publish this book?
  10) We would appreciate general suggestions for improving the manuscript.

Editor
Allyn and Bacon

REVIEWER TO EDITOR ON MANUSCRIPT

Mr. P. C. Williams, Editor
College Division
Allyn and Bacon, Inc.
7 Wells Avenue
Newton, MA 02159

Dear Mr. Williams:
    Thank you for giving me an opportunity to comment on
the (titled deleted) manuscript. I shall pose my response
as answers to the questions you proposed in your letter of
February 4.

1. The stated aim of the manuscript is for sophomore engineering students and/or technology students. I believe that
the book should be suitable for either group. Although
the level of mathematics of many technology programs is
behind that of the regular engineering programs, the
present manuscript does an effective job with only a
requirement for minimal calculus. Whether this "unsophisticated" approach would turn off potential users
in regular engineering programs, I can't say. My own
personal view is that contemporary thermo books have
turned into monographs with everything in them but the
kitchen sink. Whether these same feelings are broadly
shared, I don't know.

2. I think that the emphasis on various topics is quite even,
by and large. I think that the range of topics is quite
suited for the intended market. There is ample material
for a first course.

3. In addition, one could use much of the material in Chapters
8 and 10 for a followup course on applications. One could
cite topics which <u>MIGHT</u> have been covered, but then we
would have the weighty monographs cited above. The topics
chosen are essentially standard, except for the heavier
emphasis on applications in 8 and 10, which I think is
all to the good. I do not believe that any of the proposed chapters should be deleted or replaced by alternate
topics.

4. The prose is lucid and well-written. The proposal to
include pictures or sketches of "real" equipment is a
much-wished-for feature among many teachers who are sorry
Faires went out of print. I like the intermixture of
conventional SI units. Some may argue that the mixture
produces confusion . . . however, that is the way things
are going to be for the next decade or so. There are
ample problems at the ends of the chapters, each group
testing a variety of concepts. The text is well forti-
fied with illustrative examples given in both sets of
units. The lavish use of worked sample problems is
both a strength and weakness, depending on the point of
view. Some profs feel that students should be challenged
by having to work everything out for themselves with
only minimal examples. They also may want to "save"
some of the concepts to use on tests or homework problems. My own personal teaching philosophy is to "let it
all hang out." Students make enough mistakes through the
learning process or carelessness that I do not believe
it is necessary to hold out or hold back material to
use for tests and homework. The examples are not redundant and do illustrate useful points. One has to
put many such examples on the board in a thermo course,
so the students might as well have them correctly in
their book rather than scrawled in their class notes.

Incidentally, the analysis and problem setup in a thermo
course is often one of the first exposures students get
to situations where they have to assume this or that
about a general case in order to particularize the general case to their particular needs. This is why there
is, or should be, a heavy emphasis on problem analysis
in a thermo text. The text prose introduces and supplements various problems, so it is not just a matter
of an outline type of thing "do this, do this, etc."

I cannot cite any specific weakness in the text. If
there is a snobbery implying that a book suitable for
tech students should not be used for regular engineering
students, one might run into a kind of psychological
barrier. I might point out that this book would be particularly good for Community College transfer programs
or dual degree programs at liberal arts schools. With
the emphasis on applications and illustrations, the book
would be very helpful in such courses, which are often
taught by physics or science teachers who are unfamiliar
with the actual equipment.

The material coverage is less in total content than many
current books. I consider this a plus, since students
are paying for paper poundage they will not use. The
book is written at a kind of "bare bones" mathematical
level. It is quite rigorous and contains all that is
needed in a first course, but I don't know whether the
absence of page after page of integrals and partial der-
ivatives will be looked on as "too elementary" or not.
The treatment of entropy is quite good for the intended
audience and should get that concept across. The treatment of "open systems" is much better portrayed than in
(name deleted), where it is given short shrift. Actually,
the "open system" concept is one of the keystones for
all of the applications.

5. I would most certainly recommend adoption for our tech
course. I would also recommend adoption for the regular
thermo course, although I might be overridden by the
pseudo-scientists who object that the same book should
not be used for both types of students. The text would
also fit in well for the service course in thermo for
other majors, such as civil engineers (although I would
propose a higher level of mathematical content for a
service course for electrical engineering students). The
heavy emphasis on conventional applications in Chapter 8
and contemporary applications in Chapter 10 tends to
make the book unique in terms of what is currently available. Also, I do agree with the remarks in the preface
or introduction that there is a swing toward this type of
emphasis . . . and that many programs are including more
design/applications-oriented material.

6. The above comments indicate that I DO think that there
is a need for this type of book at this time. I think
that the applications orientation, together with the
mixed units approach and the contemporary material in
Chapter 10, make it a good bet for success at this time.

As already noted, the writing is clear and the explanations are complete. They have also inserted appropriate comments or explanations relating the
material to the "real world."

Sincerely yours,

Clifford L. Sayre, Jr.

EDITOR TO AUTHOR ENCLOSING REVIEWS

Leading Educational Publishers since 1868

Allyn and Bacon, Inc.
7 Wells Avenue, Newton, MA 02159
617/964-5530

Dr. Thomas Teacher
Someplace, U.S.A.

Dear Thomas:
   Enclosed are two reviews for your book, <u>INTRODUCTION TO
ACTING</u>. As you will notice immediately, both reviewers had
rather negative things to say about the manuscript material
they have seen.
   Both reviewers have a good deal to say, but there is
only one major objection to the manuscript material raised
by both. They cannot determine to what audience you are
writing. Is the intended audience high school or college
students or amateur theater groups? Is it a book for the
actor or the set designer? My suggestion is that the audience
be defined, and it should be done before you do any more of
your writing. I believe that once this is done, any future
reviews will be more positive.
   As I see this book, it should be written for use by the
actor on the college or amateur level. These actors will
have little or no background, so any technical information
should be kept to a minimum. When technical language is
used, it should be thoroughly explained. Of course, the
high school drama teacher can use this book's information with
the students, but this will not be a high school students' book.
I would suggest that a preface be written in which you
describe the audience in detail.
   I look forward to hearing your reactions to both the
reviewers' reactions and mine.

                              Best regards,

                              Mary Penpusher
                              Acquisitions Editor

25

The Work
of Copyeditors

Influences exercised by journal editors and book editors
The importance of the copyeditor to authors
The work of the copyeditor
The copyeditor's relationship to avoiding sexism and racism
The copyeditor's marks
Insertion of changes by authors on copy
The responsibilities of authors at galley and page proof stages
The contribution of copyediting to publications

At lunch, the conversation shifts to copyediting. Bill pushes Pam for a close description of the responsibilities of the copyeditor. He develops an enhanced respect for the necessary contributions of the anonymous copyeditor.

Bill. Pam, would you say one of the distinctions between the work of copyeditors and your own work is that you edit content while the copyeditor prepares copy for the typesetter and corrects the proofs?

Pam. That's an oversimplification. Developmental editors and/or acquisitions editors and associate editors who sponsor books do edit the content of manuscripts and help shape their organization. However, developmental and acquisitions editors also pick up factual errors and modify style. Preparing copy for the typesetter and correcting proofs for the final printing are the major responsibilities of copyeditors. Yet, in the process, copyeditors can't avoid some content editing. In dealing with content, both sponsoring editors and copyeditors attempt to avoid changing the author's meaning without the author's approval.

Bill. How do editors like you and Jack influence and presumably improve the content of professional publications before the copyeditor goes to work on a manuscript?

Pam. That depends on the individual book editor and the individual writing project. An editor who is expert in the author's field may make many useful suggestions as to content. An editor who is a layperson in the professional field—and that's frequently the case with book editors—may simply convey to the author whatever reviewers' suggestions on content the editor judges to be significant. Independent suggestions as to content by such an editor will largely be common-sense advice based on the editor's knowledge of the market. In general, the more the prospective volume of sales, the more the editor will suggest appropriate content based on reviews and editorial judgment. An el-hi editor will probably make more content suggestions to an author than the editor of a highly specialized volume for professionals in a field.

Jack.   Similarly, a journal editor who teaches in the journal's field may edit an accepted manuscript for content, or may suggest content that should be considered in rewriting. A magazine editor who is a generalist may edit primarily for style improvement and better communication to the potential readership.

However, because of time pressures, most periodical editors accept or reject an article rather than invest much of their time in content editing. Periodical editors do not have to worry about consistency of content within an issue, since periodicals are forums for free trade in ideas. The content of one article may rouse another scholar who will dispute the findings and contribute a dissenting view as an article for a later issue.

Bill.   Soon after acceptance of a manuscript, the copyeditor enters the picture. In the process of publication, how important is a copyeditor to the author?

Pam.   Crucially important. Yet the author seldom meets the copyeditor and may encounter the copyeditor's work only through an intermediary, such as the chief copyeditor, or the supervisor of copyeditors, or a production editor. Yet the copyeditor is the one person, besides the author, who knows the emerging book intimately. The copyeditor works with it from manuscript acceptance until the publication is sent to bed at the printers. In some publishing houses, copyeditors work directly with the author rather than through an intermediary.

Jack.   The journal editor also follows a manuscript through, and the copyeditor of a journal is even less visible to the author than the copyeditor of a book. The resultant work is usually communicated to the author at only one stage before publication, and that is through galleys. A good copyeditor should have a light hand in editing specialized scholarly articles.

Pam.   I like still another metaphor. There is a saying among editors that a good copyeditor does not leave footprints in a manuscript.

Bill.   Elaborate, please, on why the forgotten copyeditor is important to the author.

Pam.   The final manuscript is received and given the green light. The copyeditor, either an in-house worker or a freelancer, then takes the manuscript. Publishers today do less in-house editing than they formerly did; they often send manuscripts outside for copyediting. Freelancers are now frequently called on to do what permanent editorial employees used to do.

The copyeditor's job is to check the manuscript thoroughly for punctuation, spelling, capitalization, dates, quotations, paragraphing, abbreviations, clichés—all the minute details of diction, grammar, and rhetoric lumped together as stylistic matters. Footnotes and bibliographies are labored over by the copyeditor to achieve consistency. Inaccuracies, errors, organizational problems, and conflicting statements are turned up. The copyeditor looks for potentially libelous statements or infringements of copyright. The copyeditor makes many changes to bring the manuscript into accordance with the style books or sheets used by the company. Other proposed modifications can often be resolved through a conversation with the chief copyeditor, or supervisor, or production editor.

Yet, some questions will inevitably come up that can be completely answered only by the author. Sometimes a notation to the author (usually au? or auth?) written in the margin of the pages is sufficient. Or the copyeditor may list questions for the author, citing specific pages and lines. If the questions prove numerous, the copyeditor attaches sheets of paper called flags or fliers to the pages affected.

Copyeditors for our company generally pencil in suggested changes on the appropriate pages, attach questions, and then send the entire manuscript to the author for review. Bear in mind that I am describing our operation, not that of every publisher. Copyediting and proofreading procedures vary from publisher to publisher, and I assume, Jack, that is true for professional magazines and journals too.

Bill. One of the most frequent complaints I hear, especially from writers of textbooks, is that some publishing houses support copyeditors in unilaterally overruling authors.

Pam. A copyeditor sometimes has difficulty in deciding what the author really wanted to say in a sentence or paragraph. In such cases, the copyeditor rewrites the sentence or paragraph and sends it to the author for approval. The author is free to accept the changes or to request that the material be put back into its original form. However, if the copyeditor misunderstands the meaning, the material is probably not entirely clear. Rather than put it back verbatim, the author should rewrite the sentence or paragraph.

If a difference of opinion arises between the copyeditor and the author, the author's viewpoint should prevail. Authors should be overruled only on points of grammar on which they are demonstrably wrong.

Jack. Speaking of rewriting, it can become a technical problem if the manuscript is too tightly typed. Most copyeditors urge that all manuscript material be double-spaced, including footnotes, bibliographies, references, and extracts from other authors, which students customarily single-space. Typed or handwritten corrections by the author are legitimate, but they should be written between lines. Copyeditors deplore the practice of writing sentences sideways in the margins.

Manuscripts are not edited by our copyeditors with the same marks that are used on galleys or page proofs. Copyeditors often write in changes between lines rather than in the margins, which are left relatively clean except for inquiries by the copyeditor to the author.

Copyeditors bless authors whose organization is clearly indicated through headings and subheadings that are internally consistent. Careful proofreading by authors and their observance of style guides saves time for copyeditors and helps speed up production.

Pam. Two of the greatest problems that contemporary copyeditors face are racism and sexism in manuscripts. Through force of habit, many authors use WASP names and references throughout their manuscripts without sufficient inclusion of blacks, Hispanic-Americans, American Indians, and other minorities. Manuscripts abound with "he" and "him." On the other hand, authors who are sensitive to sexism sometimes load their manuscripts with the awkward "he and she" and "him and her." Our copyeditors frequently substitute plurals or, if an author is reporting incidents, alternation of the sexes.

Jack. To reduce sexism, copyeditors sometimes use the passive rather than the active voice. Yet this approach presents some problems, since the active voice is preferable to the passive in vigorous writing, as Strunk and others have pointed out. "He threw the ball" is stronger than "The ball was thrown." But girls throw balls too. "The pupil threw the ball" is nonsexist and in the active voice.

Pam. Don't give up the active voice too readily, Jack.

Jack. Unfortunately, however, a person may have difficulty visualizing who threw the ball.

Pam. An able copyeditor tries to avoid sexism while contributing to the creation of a readable manuscript characterized by graceful style. Copyeditors have to be sensitive to sexism without being oversensitive. They also have to be sensitive to the author's perceptions.

Bill. Once again I must invoke my belief in the virtues of author review of the copyedited manuscript. However, when I commented in an earlier conversation with my friend Andy that there would be fewer author's alterations on galleys and page proofs if all writers were sent complete copyedited manuscripts, Andy thought it wouldn't work.

Jack. He's right. The tender egos of some authors would be crushed. And the changes they would propose would outnumber the stars. Professional magazines and journals seldom return edited manuscript to an author.

Pam. Let's go back to the work of the copyeditor. On receipt of responses to questions and approval of design, the copyeditor marks the manuscript for the typesetter—not the printer, as authors ignorantly assume. That marking accounts for the mysterious symbols in the margin of galleys, such as 9/11 opt x 26.

Bill. I'm not even going to ask what that means.

Pam. It means 9-point Optima on an 11-point slug, 26 picas.

Bill. Thanks a lot.

Jack. It's not as complicated as its sounds, Bill. Optima is the name of a particular style of type. "9-point Optima" defines the size of the type, and "11-point slug" specifies the amount of space from the top of one line to the top of the next. "26 picas" is a measurement of the width of the lines of type.

Bill. Does the copyeditor come up with all that information?

Pam. Not usually. The design of the book has usually been developed by a specialist in the production department—the interior designer. The interior designer chooses typefaces and type sizes, determines the general format of the pages, and then writes up a set of specifications for the typesetter. In many cases a few sample pages will be set according to the specifications so that everyone can see how the design will look. It is only after all concerned have approved the sample pages that the copyeditor puts the final markings on the manuscript, following the designer's specifications.

At that time the copyeditor may also verify that sections, chapters, headings, and subheadings are in proper order. The placement of titles and alterations is checked. Finally, the copy is turned over to the typesetter. Often more than one compositor works on a manuscript; the experienced eye can often detect when an old pro left off and a comparative newcomer took up the typesetting.

Jack. At our journal, the copyeditor remedies errors and makes manuscripts consistent with our style sheet. I can usually resolve most questions that come up without writing or calling the author. If an author disagrees with my interpretation, he or she can catch the matter at the galley stage.

Pam. When the galleys are returned, the copyeditor shifts roles and even symbols. In our pattern, the copyeditor now often becomes a proofreader. The copyeditor turned proofreader looks hard at the galleys to make sure that the work of the compositor has been well checked by the compositor's proofreader in search of printer's errors. Has poor spacing or alignment been detected? Have imperfect letters, crooked lines, and irregular indentations been noted? Has the compositor misspelled words? Is a line omitted or out of place?

The copyeditor then adds corrections. After all, the copy supplied the compositor may have included errors introduced by the author or the copyeditor. The compositor may have misunderstood the copyeditor's penciled corrections. Or the copyeditor may see flaws on the galleys that weren't recognized on the rougher manuscript.

To communicate clearly with the typesetter, the copyeditor adopts proofreading symbols that are placed in the margin, thus calling them to the attention of the printer. A caret ($\wedge$) in the galley proof points to the place in a line where a correction is needed.

Some questions for the author still remain to be resolved. If there is time, off go a master copy and a duplicate set of galleys to the author, along with the edited manuscript. The author is requested to make necessary corrections on the galleys, referring to the edited manuscript whenever necessary. If time is short, the author receives unproofread galleys, which he or she reads while the proofreader is reading the master set against the manuscript. Remember, of course, that other houses may handle the copyediting and proofreading process differently.

Bill. As an author, I try to draft someone to read the galleys along with me. The most effective approach, though necessarily time consuming, is to have someone read exactly what appears in the edited manuscript while I hold and correct the galleys. Failing that, I read the galleys independently and try to persuade someone to do the same. When I proofread, I use a ruler to force myself to read line-by-line. At the galley stage and even more at the page proof stage, I am highly aware that the copyeditor keeps track of author's alterations, so I try to keep them to a minimum.

I flinch each time I come to something that cries out for updating, and must admit that I have been known to succumb to the temptation of attaching typed inserts, marked clearly as to their placement, on the galleys. I've learned not to be alarmed by the absence of artwork, for I know now that this is sent separately to authors. I no longer respond to an editor's queries ("belong here?") with an OK, because this just confuses everybody. The preferable response to "belong here?" is "belongs at end of this paragraph" or a similar explanation.

Pam. When the galleys are returned by the author, the copyeditor assembles all changes from all sources on the set of master galleys and sends them off to the typesetter, who breaks them into pages. They come back to the publishing house as page proofs. They may or may not be returned to the author for a last look.

Jack. Journals seldom send page proofs to authors. In our shop, we think galleys should suffice for authors' corrections. Indeed, some magazines do not even send galleys to their authors. The staff edits and sends the article to press. Following submission of the article, the author next sees his or her words in cold print.

Bill. Isn't that risky? The author has no opportunity to make changes.

Jack. I prefer sending galleys to authors; however, I understand the time pressures some journals face. In the conga line at the university printing establishment, the university president's pet project may take precedence over the journal.

Bill. Those authors who do receive page proofs of articles or books should read with special care any lines that have been reset by the compositor. In correcting errors on the galleys, typesetters have been known to introduce new errors into the lines that they reset. I place my duplicate set of galleys alongside the page proofs, and I identify the reset lines. Then I begin reading two or three lines above the reset material, and continue through the two or three lines that follow the resetting. If I find in page proofs some gross error, mine, or the editorial staff's, or the typesetter's, I try to make a correction that will involve resetting only a single line. Only torture on the rack is worse than deciding upon precisely which six-letter word can replace an offending six-letter word so that only one line need be reset.

Pam. At the page proof stage, we hope authors will look with particular care at cuts and captions in order to verify phrasing and placement. For the artwork, which earlier had been sent separately to the author for a recheck, is generally firmly in place in the page proofs. If it is not, at least the proper space and caption should be there. We also hope authors will insert page numbers into cross references or check those inserted by the proofreader (though we try to discourage the use of cross references to specific pages because of all the resetting involved). When specifically asked to, authors can also help in eliminating widows.

Bill. Eliminating widows? Sounds like genocide!

Pam. In the colorful language of typesetters, a widow is an incomplete line of type, usually ending a paragraph, that has been carried over to the top of the next page or column. The author's cooperation in cutting some words at the end of the paragraph can result in completion of the paragraph as a whole on the prior page and thus the elimination of the widow at the top of the new page. Cutting a few words can help; the widow is no longer left bereft and alone.

Bill. The copyeditor then takes the last look at page proofs.

Pam. After an author returns page proofs, there are no more changes by the writer. The author nervously waits for publication. Meanwhile, the anonymous, unsung copyeditor has turned the corrected page proofs back to the typesetter, and has moved on to a new project characterized by the same familiar copyediting chores.

Jack. Or has turned to copyediting articles scheduled for the next issue of the journal. Copyeditors have no past or present; they live in the future.

Bill. I have increased respect for the forgotten copyeditors. They make a substantial contribution to making or breaking the writer's brain child.

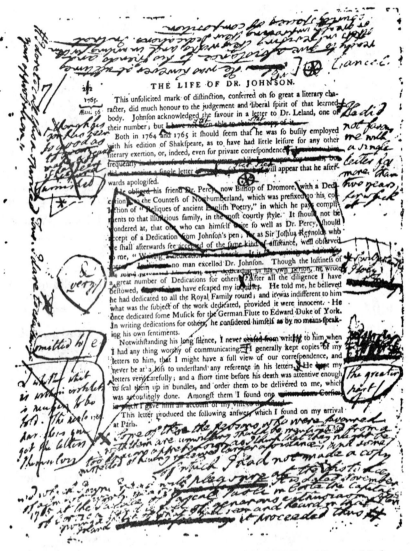

Figure 25–1 *Corrected Proof by James Boswell for* Life of Samuel Johnson. *Printed with permission of Yale University and the McGraw-Hill Book Company.*

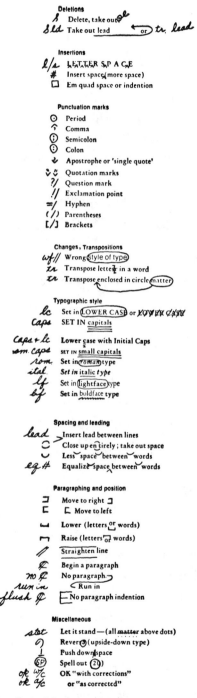

Figure 25–2 *Proofreader's Marks and What They Mean. Permission to reproduce this material from the 13th edition of* Pocket Pal® *was granted by International Paper Company.*

Proof with errors marked

cap THE PRACTICE OF TYPOGRAPHY, if it be followed faith-
fully, is hard work—full of detail, full petty restrictions full of drudgery, and not greatly rewqrded as
Men now count rewards: There are times when we
need to bring to it, all the history and art and feeling
that we can, to make it bearable.
But in the light of history and of art, and of knowledge and of mans achievement, it is as interesting a
work as exists—a broad and humanizingemployment
which can indeed be followed merely as a trade, but
which if perfected into an art, or even broadened into
a profession, will perpetually open new horizons to
eyes our and new opportunities to our hands.

—D. B. Updike

Proof after corrections have been made

THE PRACTICE OF TYPOGRAPHY, if it be followed faith-
fully, is hard work—full of detail, full of petty restrictions, full of drudgery, and not greatly rewarded
as men now count rewards. There are times when we
need to bring to it all the history and art and feeling
that we can, to make it bearable. But in the light of
history, and of art, and of knowledge and of man's
achievement, it is as interesting a work as exists—a
broad and humanizing employment which can indeed
be followed merely as a trade, but which if perfected
into an art, or even broadened into a profession, will
perpetually open new horizons to our eyes and new
opportunities to our hands. —D. B. UPDIKE

Figure 25–3 *Proofread Galley Proof. Permission to reproduce this material from the 13th edition of* Pocket Pal® *was granted by International Paper Company.*

26

The Production Process

Publishers and the new computer technology
Schedules for book production
Transmittal, copyediting, design
Typesetting, proofreading galleys, preparation of page proofs
From page proofs to the return of reproduction proofs
Repros, negatives, stripping, printing, binding
Bindery to warehouse to bookstore
Reasons for delays in publication

*At lunch, Pam, Bill, and Jack continue their discussion. Pam and Jack com-
pare and contrast what happens to a manuscript after acceptance by a book
publisher and by a journal editor. Bill is particularly interested in the steps
in the process. At the close, he is in danger of being overwhelmed by his
luncheon companions' knowledge of the production process.*

Bill. So far we've talked mostly about those aspects of developing a book in which the author is most closely involved—interacting
with the editor, responding to the reactions of manuscript reviewers,
and handling edited manuscript, galleys, and page proofs with the
copyeditor.

Pam. That's only part of the iceberg—more than the tip, yet certainly not the entire floe. Much goes on in the production process that
the author only dimly senses.

Bill. What should a writer know about other aspects of production of a book or article, those in which an author is less involved?

Pam. Shall I tell you about our present practices or about the processes we'll use in the future?

Bill. What do you mean?

Pam. Our company still publishes books in the standard manner.
But the new computer technology could revolutionize the book publishing industry.

Bill. For instance?

Pam. Here are several possible scenarios. Authors may write their
books on their word processors, then send them on floppy disks to pub-

lishers. The publishers would then put the disks into company computers and produce proofs for editing by the company and the authors. The company would then print the book.

However, a publisher could bypass printing the author's words by editing the disks and then feeding the result into the memories of computers owned personally by individuals or collectively by libraries, businesses, and so on. People could then read the resultant videotex on their computer screens or could store the material on disks or could print it out. Another possibility is that after editing, publishers could sell floppy disks directly to the consumers, the owners of computers.

Jack.   Who might then possibly reproduce the disks and sell them to their friends and neighbors—or even possibly market them to strangers?

Pam.   Piracy of software is at present among the unsolved problems of the sponsors of the new technology. Financial problems, including the highly important matter of profitability, still persist. So for a time at least, our company will continue to produce books in the customary way. Yet we'll stay alert to the new technology as it develops. Some publishing companies already have staff members assigned to exploring electronic possibilities.

Jack.   While we await the arrival of a new era in book publishing, what should today's authors expect as to the publication process after submission and acceptance of their manuscripts?

Pam.   Let's look at a schedule for publishing a book. I can't call it typical or representative because, in this industry, production time ranges from the few weeks of crash publishing that follow receipt of a first chapter about a highly newsworthy event, to the many years spent on the production of a dictionary or reference book. Take, however, a professor's book that is assumed to follow the pregnancy analogy, the traditional nine months from the final manuscript ready for production to a published book available in the bookstores. Bear in mind that a novel published by a trade book division might take less time, that a textbook published by a college division will probably take a longer time, and an el-hi book still longer.

Jack.   Why longer?

Pam.   Checking and rechecking. Concern about meeting the requirements of the market. The substantial amount of artwork. Scholarly caution of authors and editors.

Bill.   I assume that you are not including in the nine months of production the several months required to convert what the author thought was a "final" manuscript into a truly final manuscript from the publisher's point of view.

Pam.   That's right. The acquiring editor may still want reactions to a supposedly completed manuscript from several outside reviewers. The acquiring editor also hopes to give the finished manuscript a final unhurried reading. After all, he or she is the person in the house who originally backed the publication. The editor's reputation, and possibly even job, is on the line.

Now that the manuscript is genuinely final, should the sponsoring editor stand pat on original plans? Or must necessary modifications be made in the editorial plans for price, discount, page size, binding, size of first printing, date of publication, cost, and profit? Have all permissions been received and been checked? Has the author's questionnaire, a help in marketing the book, been received? Have various forms been completed, such as those for Library of Congress number, listing in *Books in Print*, paying for permissions, etc.?

Bill. Let's assume that the manuscript is now authentically and incontestably final. Lead off, Pam, on our hypothetical nine months of production. Please compare the process with journal publication, Jack.

Pam. The first stage is transmittal, copyediting the manuscript, and development of design. This takes about two months.

Early in the process, a launching or transmittal conference is scheduled. The acquiring editor will call a meeting that usually is attended by representatives from production, art, purchasing, and marketing, if the house includes all of these departments. The acquiring editor talks of matters to be taken into account in editing, illustrating, producing, and marketing the book. The sponsoring editor probably has a publication date in mind that has been communicated to the group. Those attending the conference, such as a managing editor, a production editor representing copyediting, a production supervisor, an art director, and a representative from marketing, have read the manuscript in part or in whole; all are specialists who have their own opinions and proposals. Through one or more such meetings the manuscript is transmitted to the several departments. Some houses have a scheduling editor who sets up the timetable. The manuscript is officially released for production.

Jack. In producing my journal, the managing editor absorbs that scheduling function. On a smaller journal, the jack-of-all-trades editor, who handles all the editing, assumes the scheduling responsibility. My version of the transmittal meeting is turning over the edited copy to my managing editor, who in turn passes it on to the copyeditor. After copyediting, the manuscripts go to the print shop.

Pam. In our establishment, a designer, a buyer, and a production editor are assigned to the book. (In some houses there is only a copyeditor rather than a production editor.) During the launching conference the entire schedule and manufacturing processes are mapped out.

Bill. What kinds of decisions are reached?

Pam. For instance, at a recent launching conference on a handbook for college administrators, we agreed to a double-column format. It was a long book, and the use of double columns reduced the length of the book and saved money. The managing editor had an important role in this decision.

The buyer was particularly concerned for coordination in scheduling of the total process. The designer talked about the book's interior design. The production editor anticipated some problems that would be encountered during copyediting. I tried to stay sensitive to the schedule and deadlines of the author. The managing editor and I pressed for completion of production by February, in time for the major conventions that college administrators attend.

Mostly we discussed schedule matters. If there had been serious problems in manuscript preparation, such as author delays, or permission foul-ups, or art problems, or failure by our staff somewhere along the line, the managing editor and I would have commented on changing, delaying, or even the highly unlikely possibility of scrapping the project.

We talked of the author's capabilities and reputation too, whether she would be punctual with galleys and page proofs and indexing, whether she would be conscientious in handling her responsibilities. Past experience indicated that she would be punctual and trustworthy. The book would require little artwork. We anticipated no delays. So, we set up a schedule in late June for publication in early February, a very tight and disciplined seven-and-a-half month schedule. After the launch, I receded, to some degree, into the background.

Bill. But you still maintained some relationship to the project?

Pam. Even after a launch, authors occasionally write to their acquisitions editor. Authors sometimes tell me about problems of editing or production. Eager beavers phone, usually collect.

While copyediting is going on, a duplicate manuscript is being used to come up with an estimate of total pages. Preparing such an estimate involves counting characters, including footnotes; assigning space for needed artwork; and taking into account space needed for chapter openings, heads and subheads, front matter, and blank pages.

At the same time a designer works on dimensions for the book; on the relationship among words and artwork and the page backgrounds on which they will appear; on the possible alternatives as to types to be used. Designers appreciate authors who distinguish every element of the manuscript from every other element; distinguishing among heads and subheads is especially important. A designer must fully understand the organization of the book.

Meanwhile, the art department is moving toward camera-ready copy through working on the author's rough diagrams of drawings and the author's suggestions for photographs or enclosures of prints for consideration. Captions must be written; artwork must be checked for accuracy; proposals for additional art may be dreamed up.

Bill. Some publishers merge the design and art functions into a single department. Who decides on the cover?

Pam. Arriving at the exterior design is a major operation with many surgeons in attendance. A cover is always needed, and sometimes a jacket. The art department provides a sketch that is circulated to the other departments and vigorously debated. After rejections or modifications, some exterior design is judged acceptable to most or all. Since specifications from production sources have confirmed the size of the exterior of the book, the cover design is developed and completed. Reproductions of the cover or jacket are often available for publicity weeks before the publication of the book, particularly in trade publishing.

Bill. As an author, I am often needled or complimented by friends concerning the covers of my books. They assume I have designed them or at least selected them! Needless to say, I haven't. Does the author have any say in exterior design?

Pam. Not if the editor can help it, and not unless the author has great clout with the publisher. Too many cooks are already adding to the exterior design broth. Yet authors often try to get into the act as to the nature of the cover or jacket. Sometimes, though, publishers do send sample pages to authors for their reactions and advice on interior design.

Jack. In journal publication, the editor estimates the space that each article, column, or editorial will occupy. He or she adds in the recurring pages devoted to table of contents and the masthead page listing editor, board, editorial policy, correspondence address, copyright, and so on. The journal editor makes judgments as to what will appear in the issue and, after copyediting, sends it all off to the typesetter. In our office, after galleys are received and corrected, and the printer makes the needed changes, the editor or the copyeditor pastes up pages for the printer. At about that point, the editor may have to rummage in the file for a good two-page article or one that is even longer in order to complete the issue!

Questions of cost are usually faced by the journal editor annually and not issue by issue. As to design, interior or exterior, this is reviewed annually by the editor with the editorial board and changed if and when needed. When a new editor with fresh ideas takes over a journal, readers can expect changes in the looks as well as the content of the publication.

Bill. Pam, after approximately two months of transmittal, copyediting of the manuscript, and design, what then?

Pam. Then two months or about ten weeks for typesetting, and for proofreading and corrections and changes in galleys by copyeditor and author. Meanwhile, work on art is continuing. Some publishers obtain photographs for books, in accordance with the suggestions of authors. Others require authors to obtain needed photographs without the publisher's help. This latter policy is hard on authors who live in the boondocks where picture resource files are unavailable; some rigid editors are remarkably unrealistic in their expectations.

Bill. So about three months after a manuscript is truly final, the author receives and corrects the galleys?

Pam. If that's in the plan—which it usually is—and if all goes well—which it often doesn't. Now, after a few weeks for proofreading, allow another two months or more for preparing of page proofs, for reading and correcting of page proofs by copyeditor and perhaps author, for typesetting corrections of the page proofs, and for the preparation of repro proofs and their checking and correction.

Jack. On our journal, we try to maintain a series of two-week steps in the production process. Take, for instance, the schedule for our first issue of the year, optimistically planned to appear September 1. Step one, on June 15, edited manuscripts are sent to the print shop for typesetting. Step two, on July 1, the print shop returns first galleys to the copyeditor. Step three, on July 15, the copyeditor returns corrections to the print shop. Step four, on August 1, the print shop returns galleys to the editor for paste-up. Step five, on August 15, the editor returns copy in final form for the camera operator. Step six, on September 1, the issue appears. Every professional periodical has its own pattern; that happens to be ours. In professional publication, it's not unusual for a journal to appear late.

Bill. Thanks, Jack. Since, as author, I departed from the picture after reading page proofs, Pam will have to tell me what repro proofs are.

Pam. Repros are reproduction proofs. These are camera-ready proofs that the typesetter sends back so that printing plates can eventually be made. Camera-ready drawings are pasted onto the repros. Then film negatives are made of the entire book by the printer.

Still with me?

Bill. Just about hanging in.

Pam. After that, negatives of the pages and the halftones (black and white photographs to you) are cut and taped in place in a process called stripping. A positive contact print known as a blue line is run off. When assembled page by page, the blue lines look like the book in its final form, save for color. Back go the blue lines to the production department, where they look for such things as whether some picture has been put upside down or a page inserted at the wrong place. Don't laugh; it has happened.

Back go the blue lines to the printer, who makes printing plates from the negatives. The publisher's purchasing department has long ago bought paper, which is sent to the printer's plant. The book is then printed by photo-offset. Letter press is only used for an occasional university press or small circulation book involving printing of less than a thousand copies.

The book comes off the press as large printed sheets that are sequences of eight, sixteen, or thirty-two pages. After being folded and trimmed, each sheet, now called a signature, becomes a section of the book. Incidentally, that's why the total number of pages in a book is almost always an amount divisible by eight.

The printing establishment may also include a bindery, or the book may be sent off to a firm specializing in binding. Books are almost always bound by glue, without the sewing of groups of sheets.

Bill.   I surrender. About how long does it take for all of these technological marvels?

Pam.   From receipt of camera copy to bound books, about one-and-a-half months. From the bindery into the warehouse, and from the warehouse to the bookstore, adds an additional month.

Bill.   Summarize, please.

Pam.   I will, only if you recognize that I am not taking into account Murphy's Law—if something can go wrong, it will. The schedule I have described from receipt of the author's final manuscript to book-store delivery is

> transmittal, copyediting, design—two months;
> typesetting, proofreading galleys—two-and-a-half months;
> preparation of page proofs, reading and correcting, return of reproduction proofs—two months;
> negatives, stripping, blue lines, printing, binding—one-and-a-half months; and
> bindery to warehouse to bookstore—one month.

The total is nine months. With increasing use of computers at several stages, production time will be reduced.

Bill.   But I shouldn't be surprised if the time amounted to fifteen months.

Pam.   You shouldn't be surprised at anything. Remember that I haven't taken into account strikes and the aberrations of management in assorted plants.

Jack.   Or delays in mail delivery followed by frantic use of express delivery services in the attempt to recoup lost time.

Bill.   Or a publication being "dumped" by house higher-ups in favor of a book given a higher priority.

Pam.   Or delays in return of galleys or page proofs by authors unavailable in the tropics, or attempting to rewrite their books in proof, or cantankerously remiss, or otherwise inexplicably slow.

Bill.   Or editors getting tied up with other manuscripts, or going on vacation at inconvenient times, or quarreling with co-workers, or getting promoted or fired, or having nervous breakdowns.

Pam. Or a hundred other causes of delays.

Bill. I'll no longer ask, "Why does it take so long?"

PRODUCTION SEQUENCE
FOR THE AVERAGE TEXTBOOK

Leading Educational Publishers since 1868

Allyn and Bacon, Inc.
7 Wells Avenue, Newton, MA 02159
617/964-5530

STAGE 1 (2-3 Weeks):
Manuscript (ms) released to production by series editor.
    Production editor, designer, and buyer assigned. Letter
    sent to author telling him/her who the production
    editor will be.
Production editor reads reviews and other background, checks
    for completeness and difficulty, design elements, and
    the like.
Designer works up initial specifications for composition of
    book's interior (typeface and size, chapter openings,
    headings, and other elements) and checks art for quantity,
    sizes, and production requirements.
Buyer assesses manufacturing method needed, scheduling re-
    quirements, etc.
Permissions editor checks status of permissions.
Launching conference held with series editor, production ed-
    itor, designer, buyer, senior production editor, and
    (sometimes) permissions editor, senior series editor,
    and salesperson. The entire schedule and manufacturing
    methods are mapped out at this conference, and each
    person's duties are determined.

STAGE 2 (6-12 Weeks):
Production editor or freelance copyeditor copyedits original
    manuscript. Edited ms sent to author for review.
Duplicate ms is typemarked and given to the buyer for com-
    position, printing, and binding estimates, including
    estimated final page count (castoff).
Designer sends art out for bids.
Bids received. Buyer determines compositor. Manufacturing
    costs computed for initial pricing of the book and for
    determining quantity to be printed. (Design adjustments
    may be made to keep costs down.) Paper stock ordered.
Sample ms pages sent to compositor for design check. Typeset
    sample pages are then approved by designer, series ed-
    itor, and production editor.
Edited ms returned from author. Production editor checks
    author's changes, makes final check of ms, figure numbers,
    chapter titles, and typemarking.
Ms released to compositor for typesetting. Art released to
    artist.

STAGE 3 (10-14 Weeks):
Manuscript typeset by compositor.
Galley proofs received from compositor. Production editor or
    freelance proofreader proofreads master galleys against
    edited ms.

Production editor sends galleys to author. Author reads
    galleys.
Art proofs received, checked, and sent to author for approval.
Galleys and art proofs returned from author. Production
    editor transfers author's changes to master galleys
    and master art proofs.
Art to artist for corrections and final rendering.

STAGE 4 (4-12 Weeks):
Option 1 (compositor lays out pages): Master galleys re-
    turned to compositor for corrections and paging. Pro-
    duction editor sends paging instructions, and marks
    final art sizes on galleys so that compositor will know
    how much space to leave for illustrations (if any).
Option 2 (dummy of pages prepared for compositor's guidance):
    Designer (occasionally production editor or freelancer)
    cuts and strips duplicate set of galleys into page lay-
    outs, leaving exact space for final art, photos, etc.
    (Sometimes art proofs are stripped on this dummy.)
    Dummy and master galleys sent to compositor for pages.
Compositor makes corrections and pages the galleys.

STAGE 5 (2-6 Weeks):
Page proofs from compositor. Production editor checks all
    corrections against master galleys, checks page makeup,
    page numbers, position of art, etc.
Page proofs (uncorrected) immediately sent to indexer (often
    this is the author).
Front matter (title page, preface, contents, copyright) to
    designer for specifications, and then to compositor for
    typesetting.
Final page count (to an even printed form) given to buyer for
    final printing and binding prices. Paper shipped to
    printer. Buyer determines final bulk (width of spine)
    for cover designer.
Page proofs sent to author to check corrections.
Front matter proofs received, proofread, and returned to
    compositor.
Final art checked. Permissions rechecked. Cover design
    approved by series editor.
Page proofs returned from author. Corrections transferred
    to master page proofs. Master pages sent to compositor
    by production editor.
Index ms received, edited by production editor, typemarked,
    and sent to compositor.

STAGE 6 (2-4 Weeks):
Camera copy prepared by compositor.
Camera copy received from compositor (entire book except in-
    dex). Production editor checks corrections, contents,
    art. If art is not already in place, production editor
    or designer writes positioning and sizing instructions
    on each piece of art (sometimes actually strips art on
    camera copy instead).
Index proofs received, checked, and returned for camera copy.
Instructions finalized for color, endpapers, or other special
    elements; proofs or samples of these may be needed.

STAGE 7 (4-6 Weeks):
Final printing and binding instructions written by buyer and
    checked by designer and production editor.
Index camera copy received and checked.
All camera copy (art, text, endpapers) to printer.
Printer does camera and stripping.
Printer's proofs ("blues") checked, approved, returned to
    printer.
Printer makes corrections; then prints, folds, and collates
    signatures.
Cover proofs checked, approved, sent to cover printer for
    printing.

STAGE 8 (2-6 Weeks):
Printed sheets (unbound) received from printer and checked by
    production editor.
Books bound by bindery.
Bound books (advance copies) received by buyer, checked by
    production editor and designer.

STAGE 9 (4-6 Weeks):
Printer ships balance of order to warehouse.
Warehouse ships to bookstores.

27

The Copyright Rules

During lunch, Bill keeps a promise he has made to himself to learn more about the rules of the copyright game. Fortunately, Jack has boned up on the "new" copyright law. Like many other editors of journals, Jack has revised forms sent to authors concerning the rights and responsibilities of journal authors and editors. Pam contributes too, from the viewpoint of a book editor.

Bill. Writers for professional publications are often confused about copyright. They hear talk and read releases from organizations of librarians and teachers about "the old law" and "the new law" (which isn't so "new" for it went into effect in 1978). The discussion seems to center on the legitimacy and extent of copying by librarians and teachers of copyrighted materials. The term "fair use" is bandied about. Authors of professional books, most of whom write as a sideline, ask, "What does this current debate mean to me?" What *should* they know about copyright in relation to their work?

Jack. Since "the new law" affects my editorial practices, I've learned all I can about copyrights. The confusion of the typical author of professional publications is ironic in light of the origins of copyrights. A copyright, by definition, is a right granted by statute to the authors of literary, artistic, and musical productions to control the use of their products for a limited period of time. The problem of who controls what rights dates back to the invention of printing from movable type in the fifteenth century. In sixteenth-century England, the common law protected authors against the publication of their works without the author's permission. However, when authors did sanction publication, their works passed completely from their control. The first English copyright act in the early eighteenth century allowed authors to copyright their work for fourteen years and to renew the copyright for an additional fourteen. They deposited copies of their works with the authorities, and their writing carried notices that the works were copyrighted.

The basic idea of a copyright was to protect authors in their control over their creations. Yet authors are often quite ignorant of copyright rules and regulations!

Pam. Most authors don't know or have forgotten that the rights of authors are written into the Constitution of the United States. This *Copyright Handbook* on my desk quotes Article I, Section VIII, as giving Congress the power "To promote the Progress of Science and useful Arts by securing for limited Times to Authors and Inventors the exclusive Right to their respective Writings and Discoveries."

Jack. The Founding Fathers said it well. But new technological developments and inventions have raised questions that they were understandably unable to foresee when the first American copyright statute was passed, soon after adoption of the U.S. Constitution. Especially in the twentieth century, technological developments in communications came on fast, including motion pictures, sound recordings, radio, and television. New information, storage, and retrieval techniques were developed. Communication satellites were launched. Many new techniques for reproducing and disseminating copyrighted works had developed since 1909, the date of what is today called "the old law." So in 1976, after years of debate, Congress passed what is referred to as "the new law." As pointed out, it went into effect in 1978.

Bill. You both certainly know more about copyright than I do. What are the differences between the 1909 copyright provisions and the 1976 provisions?

Jack. There are both similarities and differences, with many of the latter attributable to the copycat capacity of tape recorders, computers, and photocopiers. Similarities between the "old" and "new" acts include continuation of protection of original works of authors who have exclusive rights to use, and can authorize others to use, their original works. Users of copyright materials continue to have rights to make "fair use" of copyrighted works. A notice of copyright is ordinarily called for in published works. Copies of the work are deposited with the Copyright Office in Washington, D.C., and registered.

Yet there are differences, too. The old law provided for twenty-eight years of protection with a renewal, if applied for; the new law copyrights works for the author's lifetime, plus fifty years. Under the new law, ownership of a portion, rather than the totality of rights inherent in a copyright, may be transferred. The new law expands librarians' and teachers' rights to "fair use" of authors' copyrighted works without permission. Guidelines have been developed to aid people in interpreting what constitutes "fair use." Under the new law, a work is federally protected from the time it is set down in tangible form.

Bill. You mean that authors have copyright protection before publication of their work?

Jack. Yes. Perhaps the most important feature of the revised law is the provision of statutory copyright protecton just as soon as the author's work is fixed in tangible form. Under the new law, a person obtains a U.S. copyright by developing a work and setting it down in tangible form, such as by way of videotape or the typewriter or the word processor.

Bill. So a person doesn't have to publish a work to have federal copyright protection. A typewritten page is protected by copyright.

Jack. Correct. Publication is a less important factor than it was under the old rules.

Bill. That should reassure the unpublished writer.

Jack. Of course, theft and pirating are still possibilities, but there is legal recourse in cases of infringement of rights to either published or unpublished works. Since it is acceptable to put a copyright notice on a work that is not yet published, authors of unpublished writing who are cautious about their rights might indicate on the top sheet that this is an unpublished manuscript in which copyright subsists, and state the author's name and date. A careful soul might add that this copy is not for distribution to the public.

Still more cautious authors may wish to send one copy of their unpublished manuscript to the Copyright Office for official registration of their rights.

Bill. With all of this old and new copyright protection for authors, why should anybody, including all three of us, bother to register a copyright at all?

Jack. Registration provides extra protection. For instance, suppose your copyright was infringed. You can't actually begin a lawsuit for infringement of a copyright until you have registered a claim to the copyright. If you register a claim before the supposed infringement, you have a chance to collect attorneys' fees incurred in the lawsuit. If you hadn't registered your copyright, any attorney's expenses would be on you.

Bill. The average author should be particularly concerned about copyright when his or her work is published. Somebody should register the copyright, even if registration isn't mandatory. In your opinion, in whose name should the copyright be registered, that of the publication or that of the author?

Jack. In the case of a journal, the periodical almost always registers copyright. The notice of copyright for the entire issue protects the copyright of the individual's contribution. Occasionally the author registers the copyright for an individual article. If the periodical does not register the copyright and the author wants registration, the author should register the copyright.

Bill. Suppose a compiler wants to use the published article, copyrighted by the magazine, in an anthology. Or suppose another magazine wants to reprint the article. What then are the author's rights? Under the old law, authors sometimes copyrighted their work to have power over how their writing would be used. A writer might prefer that his or her work not appear in some particular outlet.

Jack. There is a provision in the new copyright law to the effect that a periodical registering the copyright on the collective work can reprint an article from one issue of the magazine in a later issue, but can't use the article in another magazine or a new anthology unless the writer has transferred full ownership to the original magazine through a written agreement.

Bill. Lacking such transfer, the magazine editor would have to turn to the author to share in giving permission for the author's work to appear in a new anthology or another magazine. In that case, the author might legitimately ask for compensation?

Jack. That's my understanding. But if the ownership of the article has been expressly transferred to the magazine by the author, the editor is free to decide independently on permission and payment.

Bill. Pam, who usually holds the copyright on books?

Pam. The author of a textbook frequently turns the registration of copyright over to the publisher. Almost all book contracts are written accordingly. Our authors seldom raise a question about this. When they do, we point out that we have a permissions department that saves them the headaches of individually responding to requests for quotations that are lengthy enough to require correspondence.

Bill. Many authors of trade books prefer to register copyrights of their own books. My impression is that an increasing number of authors of specialized books and textbooks are reserving, not assigning, their copyright. The Authors Guild and the Society of Authors' Representatives advise an author to register the copyright in the author's own name. The arguments for this include that the publisher could go bankrupt, or might engage in an unauthorized sale of rights, or might not be sufficiently active in bringing about a suit of infringement of rights.

Pam. Quite unlikely situations. Deal with a reputable publisher, such as our house, and let us handle the mechanics of registering copyrights, permission payments, and similar routines, while authors go about their proper business of writing.

Bill. There's much to be said on the pro and con of authors' reserving, not assigning, their copyrights. In the discussion that preceded the new copyright law, what were most of the arguments about?

Pam. The arguments were largely between the organizations of librarians and teachers, who wanted more liberal opportunities to copy and reproduce segments or the totality of copyrighted published works, and the representatives of authors and publishers, who wanted to safeguard their rights to unpublished and published material.

Bill. Basically, how was the conflict resolved?

Pam. By a substantial increase in opportunities for librarians, teachers, students, and scholars to photocopy. For instance, under the "fair use" doctrine, teachers have the right to make single photocopies of a chapter from a book, an article from a magazine, and a chart or picture from a book or magazine. Multiple photocopies can be made for classroom use by students, subject to restrictions. For example, excerpts from prose can be not more than 1,000 words or 10 percent of the work; completed articles can be used only if they are less than 2,500 words; and copying must be at the instance and inspiration of the individual teachers and thus spontaneous. In short, there should be "fair use" that would not substitute for anthologies or for the purchase of books and periodicals. The outcome was a compromise between the discussants. "Fair use" was constantly invoked.

Bill. In this connection, were the "fair use" sections of the law highly specific?

Pam. No, they were left quite vague. The statute supports copying "for purposes such as criticism, comment, news reporting, teaching (including multiple copies for classroom use), scholarship, or research" and regards these as "not an infringement of copyright."[1] According to the law, fair use depends on four factors "(1) the purpose and character of the use, including whether such use is of a commercial nature or is for nonprofit educational purposes; (2) the nature of the copyrighted work; (3) the amount and substantiality of the portion used . . . and (4) the effect of the use upon the potential market for or value of the copyrighted work."[2]

Bill. It looks as though there will be plenty of employment for lawyers as "fair use" is adjudicated.

Pam. Possibly so, but the major reason for the generality of the legislation is that no law can sufficiently cover the infinite variations that characterize contemporary publishing. What's fair in one situation is definitely foul in another.

Bill. Let me be sure that I understand the elements in a copyright notice for a published work.

Pam. On the reverse side of the title page the word *copyright* followed by © has usually appeared. Under the new law, placement of the notice is more flexible. The notice can appear "in such manner and

---

[1]Section 107, Copyright Revision Act of 1976, 90 stat. 2541 (Oct 19, 1976).
[2]Ibid.

location as to give reasonable notice as the claim to copyright."[3] Three elements are necessary in a notice: (1) the symbol ©, *or* Copyright *or* Copr; (2) year date of first publication; (3) name of owner of copyright.[4]

Two copies of the work bearing this notice are deposited with the Copyright Office at the Library of Congress in Washington, D.C., along with a copyright application form and a filing fee of $10. In the case of an unpublished work only one copy is needed, and the writer fills out the same application as for a published work. The year of creation must be included in applications for unpublished as well as published works. In unpublished works, the date and place of publication are simply left blank. After the work is published, a new copyright registration can be obtained. Correct, Jack?

Jack. Yes. Authors are frequently startled to recognize that placement of the copyright notice on the published work comes first, and is then followed up with registration of the copyright. It sounds topsy-turvy to them. Common sense tells them that registration with payment should come first, prior to putting a copyright notice on a work. However, some reflection on the physical impossibility of adding the copyright notice to a book or a magazine after publication should help them to understand the process.

Pam. After some personal experience with registering the copyright, authors have more appreciation and respect for the copyrights of others, and become more understanding of the necessity to secure permissions to use the writing of other authors in their own work. They can readily obtain from their editors information as to how many words from copyrighted materials may be legitimately quoted without permissions. Publishers vary in their prescriptions as to legitimate usage. Currently, the magic numbers of 250 words from a book, 5 percent of an article, and zero from poetry or songs are used by most publishers. Others depart from these figures, but not by much. Authors learn to write first to the copyright holder, whether author, or magazine, or publisher, for permissions in excess of those magic numbers. They find that they are sometimes asked by their editors to thank their brother and sister authors too, even though the authors may not hold the official copyright.

Jack. Authors seeking permission have kind things to say about the much-abused United States government when they learn that a work, however lengthy, prepared by an officer or employee of the United States government as part of that person's official duties, is not eligible for U.S. copyright protection.

Writers are sometimes surprised to find that a letter from a person cannot be quoted without that person's permission. Although most peo-

[3]Section 401(c), Copyright Revision Act of 1976, 90 stat. 2541 (Oct 19, 1976).

[4]Section 401(b), Copyright Revision Act of 1976, 90 stat. 2541 (Oct 19, 1976).

ple feel that they can quote from a letter they themselves wrote to another person, some authorities claim that it is also necessary to obtain the addressee's permission.

Bill. Authors might well consult *Copyright Handbook* by Donald F. Johnson, published by R. R. Bowker Company. The new edition interprets the new law and deals with court decisions and copyright procedures.

Jack. Since copyrighting a work may involve legal complications, authors who are in doubt should consult a lawyer rather than blame people like you and me who write or talk about copyrights. We shouldn't be held liable by readers or listeners if something goes wrong in the copyrighting of their publications. After all, editors and authors like us don't claim to be experts on legal matters.

Pam. Some writers are troubled that they can copyright only their words, not their ideas.

Bill. For myself, I am glad that writers can't copyright ideas. Scholarship involves standing on the shoulders of one's predecessors. Justice Oliver Wendell Holmes said it well: ''The ultimate good desired is better reached by free trade in ideas.''

PAGES FROM APPLICATION FOR
COPYRIGHT REGISTRATION

Filling Out Application Form TX

Detach and read these instructions before completing this form. Make sure all applicable spaces have been filled in before you return this form.

BASIC INFORMATION

When to Use This Form: Use Form TX for registration of published or unpublished non-dramatic literary works, excluding periodicals or serial issues. This class includes a wide variety of works: fiction, non-fiction, poetry, textbooks, reference works, directories, catalogs, advertising copy, compilations of information, and computer programs. For periodicals and serials, use Form SE.

Deposit to Accompany Application: An application for copyright registration must be accompanied by a deposit consisting of copies or phonorecords representing the entire work for which registration is to be made. The following are the general deposit requirements as set forth in the statute:

Unpublished Work: Deposit one complete copy (or phonorecord).

Published Work: Deposit two complete copies (or phonorecords) of the best edition.

Work First Published Outside the United States: Deposit one complete copy (or phonorecord) of the first foreign edition.

Contribution to a Collective Work: Deposit one complete copy (or phonorecord) of the best edition of the collective work.

The Copyright Notice: For published works, the law provides that a copyright notice in a specified form "shall be placed on all publicly distributed copies from which the work can be visually perceived." Use of the copyright notice is the responsibility of the copyright owner and does not require advance permission from the Copyright Office. The required form of the notice for copies generally consists of three elements: (1) the symbol "©", or the word "Copyright," or the abbreviation "Copr."; (2) the year of first publication; and (3) the name of the owner of copyright. For example: "© 1981 Constance Porter." The notice is to be affixed to the copies "in such manner and location as to give reasonable notice of the claim of copyright."

For further information about copyright registration, notice, or special questions relating to copyright problems, write:

Information and Publications Section, LM-455
Copyright Office
Library of Congress
Washington, D.C. 20559

LINE-BY-LINE INSTRUCTIONS

1 SPACE 1: Title

Title of This Work: Every work submitted for copyright registration must be given a title to identify that particular work. If the copies or phonorecords of the work bear a title (or an identifying phrase that could serve as a title), transcribe that wording *completely* and *exactly* on the application. Indexing of the registration and future identification of the work will depend on the information you give here.

Previous or Alternative Titles: Complete this space if there are any additional titles for the work under which someone searching for the registration might be likely to look, or under which a document pertaining to the work might be recorded.

Publication as a Contribution: If the work being registered is a contribution to a periodical, serial, or collection, give the title of the contribution in the "Title of this Work" space. Then, in the line headed "Publication as a Contribution," give information about the collective work in which the contribution appeared.

2 SPACE 2: Author(s)

General Instructions: After reading these instructions, decide who are the "authors" of this work for copyright purposes. Then, unless the work is a "collective work," give the requested information about every "author" who contributed any appreciable amount of copyrightable matter to this version of the work. If you need further space, request additional Continuation sheets. In the case of a collective work, such as an anthology, collection of essays, or encyclopedia, give information about the author of the collective work as a whole.

Name of Author: The fullest form of the author's name should be given. Unless the work was "made for hire," the individual who actually created the work is its "author." In the case of a work made for hire, the statute provides that "the employer or other person for whom the work was prepared is considered the author."

What is a "Work Made for Hire"? A "work made for hire" is defined as: (1) "a work prepared by an employee within the scope of his or her employment"; or (2) "a work specially ordered or commissioned for use as a contribution to a collective work, as a part of a motion picture or other audiovisual work, as a translation, as a supplementary work, as a compilation, as an instructional text, as a test, as answer material for a test, or as an atlas, if the parties expressly agree in a written instrument signed by them that the work shall be considered a work made for hire." If you have checked "Yes" to indicate that the work was "made for hire," you must give the full legal name of the employer (or other person for whom the work was prepared). You may also include the name of the employee along with the name of the employer (for example: "Elster Publishing Co., employer for hire of John Ferguson").

"Anonymous" or "Pseudonymous" Work: An author's contribution to a work is "anonymous" if that author is not identified on the copies or phonorecords of the work. An author's contribution to a work is "pseudonymous" if that author is identified on the copies or phonorecords under a fictitious name. If the work is "anonymous" you may: (1) leave the line blank; or (2) state " anonymous" on the line; or (3) reveal the author's identity. If the work is "pseudonymous" you may: (1) leave the line blank; or (2) give the pseudonym and identify it as such (for example: "Huntley Haverstock, pseudonym"); or (3) reveal the author's name, making clear which is the real name and which is the pseudonym (for example: "Judith Barton, whose pseudonym is Madeline Elster"). However, the citizenship or domicile of the author **must** be given in all cases.

Dates of Birth and Death: If the author is dead, the statute requires that the year of death be included in the application unless the work is anonymous or pseudonymous. The author's birth date is optional, but is useful as a form of identification. Leave this space blank if the author's contribution was a "work made for hire."

Author's Nationality or Domicile: Give the country of which the author is a citizen, or the country in which the author is domiciled. Nationality or domicile **must** be given in all cases.

Nature of Authorship: After the words "Nature of Authorship" give a brief general statement of the nature of this particular author's contribution to the work. Examples: "Entire text"; "Coauthor of entire text"; "Chapters 11–14"; "Editorial revisions"; "Compilation and English translation"; "New text."

3 SPACE 3: Creation and Publication

General Instructions: Do not confuse "creation" with "publication." Every application for copyright registration must state "the year in which creation of the work was completed." Give the date and nation of first publication only if the work has been published.

Creation: Under the statute, a work is "created" when it is fixed in a copy or phonorecord for the first time. Where a work has been prepared over a period of time, the part of the work existing in fixed form on a particular date constitutes the created work on that date. The date you give here should be the year in which the author completed the particular version for which registration is now being sought, even if other versions exist or if further changes or additions are planned.

Publication: The statute defines "publication" as "the distribution of copies or phonorecords of a work to the public by sale or other transfer of ownership, or by rental, lease, or lending"; a work is also "published" if there has been an "offering to distribute copies or phonorecords to a group of persons for purposes of further distribution, public performance, or public display." Give the full date (month, day, year) when, and the country where, publication first occurred. If first publication took place simultaneously in the United States and other countries, it is sufficient to state "U.S.A."

4 SPACE 4: Claimant(s)

Name(s) and Address(es) of Copyright Claimant(s): Give the name(s) and address(es) of the copyright claimant(s) in this work even if the claimant is the same as the author. Copyright in a work belongs initially to the author of the work (including, in the case of a work made for hire, the employer or other person for whom the work was prepared). The copyright claimant is either the author of the work or a person or organization to whom the copyright initially belonging to the author has been transferred.

Transfer: The statute provides that, if the copyright claimant is not the author, the application for registration must contain "a brief statement of how the claimant obtained ownership of the copyright." If any copyright claimant named in space 4 is not an author named in space 2, give a brief, general statement summarizing the means by which that claimant obtained ownership of the copyright. Examples: "By written contract"; "Transfer of all rights by author"; "Assignment"; "By will." Do not attach transfer documents or other attachments or riders.

a whole constitutes an original work of authorship." A "derivative work" is "a work based on one or more preexisting works." Examples of derivative works include translations, fictionalizations, abridgments, condensations, or "any other form in which a work may be recast, transformed, or adapted." Derivative works also include works "consisting of editorial revisions, annotations, or other modifications" if these changes, as a whole, represent an original work of authorship.

Preexisting Material (space 6a): For derivative works, complete this space and space 6b. In space 6a identify the preexisting work that has been recast, transformed, or adapted. An example of preexisting material might be: "Russian version of Goncharov's 'Oblomov.'" Do not complete space 6a for compilations.

Material Added to This Work (space 6b): Give a brief, general statement of the new material covered by the copyright claim for which registration is sought. Derivative work examples include: "Foreword, editing, critical annotations"; "Translation"; "Chapters 11-17." If the work is a compilation, describe both the compilation itself and the material that has been compiled. Example: "Compilation of certain 1917 Speeches by Woodrow Wilson." A work may be both a derivative work and compilation, in which case a sample statement might be: "Compilation and additional new material."

7 SPACE 7: Manufacturing Provisions

General Instructions: The copyright statute currently provides, as a general rule, that the copies of a published work "consisting preponderantly of nondramatic literary material in the English language" be manufactured in the United States or Canada in order to be lawfully imported and publicly distributed in the United States. If the work being registered is unpublished or not in English, leave this space blank. Complete this space if registration is sought for a published work "consisting preponderantly of nondramatic literary material that is in the English language." Identify those who manufactured the copies and where those manufacturing processes were performed. As an exception to the manufacturing provisions, the statute prescribes that, where manufacture has taken place outside the United States or Canada, a maximum of 2000 copies of the foreign edition may be imported into the United States without affecting the copyright owners' rights. For this purpose, the Copyright Office will issue an Import Statement upon request and payment of a fee of $3 at the time of registration or at any later time. For further information about import statements, write for Form IS.

5 SPACE 5: Previous Registration

General Instructions: The questions in space 5 are intended to find out whether an earlier registration has been made for this work and, if so, whether there is any basis for a new registration. As a general rule, only one basic copyright registration can be made for the same version of a particular work.

Same Version: If this version is substantially the same as the work covered by a previous registration, a second registration is not generally possible unless: (1) the work has been registered in unpublished form and a second registration is now being sought to cover this first published edition; or (2) someone other than the author is identified as copyright claimant in the earlier registration, and the author is now seeking registration in his or her own name. If either of these two exceptions apply, check the appropriate box and give the earlier registration number and date. Otherwise, do not submit Form TX; instead, write the Copyright Office for information about supplementary registration or recordation of transfers of copyright ownership.

Changed Version: If the work has been changed, and you are now seeking registration to cover the additions or revisions, check the last box in space 5, give the earlier registration number and date, and complete both parts of space 6 in accordance with the instructions below.

Previous Registration Number and Date: If more than one previous registration has been made for the work, give the number and date of the latest registration.

6 SPACE 6: Derivative Work or Compilation

General Instructions: Complete space 6 if this work is a "changed version," "compilation," or "derivative work," and if it incorporates one or more earlier works that have already been published or registered for copyright, or that have fallen into the public domain. A "compilation" is defined as "a work formed by the collection and assembling of preexisting materials or of data that are selected, coordinated, or arranged in such a way that the resulting work as

8 SPACE 8: Reproduction for Use of Blind or Physically Handicapped Individuals

General Instructions: One of the major programs of the Library of Congress is to provide Braille editions and special recordings of works for the exclusive use of the blind and physically handicapped. In an effort to simplify and speed up the copyright licensing procedures that are a necessary part of this program, section 710 of the copyright statute provides for the establishment of a voluntary licensing system to be tied in with copyright registration. Copyright Office regulations provide that you may grant a license for such reproduction and distribution solely for the use of persons who are certified by competent authority as unable to read normal printed material as a result of physical limitations. The license is entirely voluntary, nonexclusive, and may be terminated upon 90 days notice.

How to Grant the License: If you wish to grant it, check one of the three boxes in space 8. Your check in one of these boxes, together with your signature in space 10, will mean that the Library of Congress can proceed to reproduce and distribute under the license without further paperwork. For further information, write for Circular R63.

9,10,11 SPACE 9, 10, 11: Fee, Correspondence, Certification, Return Address

Deposit Account: If you maintain a Deposit Account in the Copyright Office, identify it in space 9. Otherwise leave the space blank and send the fee of $10 with your application and deposit.

Correspondence (space 9): This space should contain the name, address, area code, and telephone number of the person to be consulted if correspondence about this application becomes necessary.

Certification (space 10): The application can not be accepted unless it bears the date and the **handwritten signature** of the author or other copyright claimant, or of the owner of exclusive right(s), or of the duly authorized agent of author, claimant, or owner of exclusive right(s).

Address for Return of Certificate (space 11): The address box must be completed legibly since the certificate will be returned in a window envelope.

FORM TX

UNITED STATES COPYRIGHT OFFICE

REGISTRATION NUMBER

TX   TXU

EFFECTIVE DATE OF REGISTRATION

Month   Day   Year

DO NOT WRITE ABOVE THIS LINE. IF YOU NEED MORE SPACE, USE A SEPARATE CONTINUATION SHEET.

1

TITLE OF THIS WORK ▼

PREVIOUS OR ALTERNATIVE TITLES ▼

PUBLICATION AS A CONTRIBUTION If this work was published as a contribution to a periodical, serial, or collection, give information about the collective work in which the contribution appeared.   **Title of Collective Work ▼**

If published in a periodical or serial give: **Volume ▼**   **Number ▼**   **Issue Date ▼**   **On Pages ▼**

2

NAME OF AUTHOR ▼

a

DATES OF BIRTH AND DEATH
Year Born ▼   Year Died ▼

Was this contribution to the work a
"work made for hire"?
☐ Yes
☐ No

AUTHOR'S NATIONALITY OR DOMICILE
Name of Country
OR { Citizen of ▶
{ Domiciled in ▶

WAS THIS AUTHOR'S CONTRIBUTION TO THE WORK
Anonymous?   ☐ Yes ☐ No
Pseudonymous? ☐ Yes ☐ No

If the answer to either of these questions is "Yes," see detailed instructions.

NATURE OF AUTHORSHIP Briefly describe nature of the material created by this author in which copyright is claimed. ▼

NOTE

Under the law, the "author" of a "work made for hire" is generally the employer, not the employee (see instructions). For any part of this work that was "made for hire" check "Yes" in the space provided, give the employer (or other person for whom the work was prepared) as "Author" of that part, and leave the space for dates of birth and death blank.

NAME OF AUTHOR ▼

DATES OF BIRTH AND DEATH
Year Born ▼   Year Died ▼

Was this contribution to the work a "work made for hire"?
☐ Yes
☐ No

AUTHOR'S NATIONALITY OR DOMICILE
Name of country
OR { Citizen of ▶ _____
Domiciled in ▶ _____

WAS THIS AUTHOR'S CONTRIBUTION TO THE WORK
Anonymous?   ☐ Yes ☐ No
Pseudonymous?   ☐ Yes ☐ No
If the answer to either of these questions is "Yes," see detailed instructions.

NATURE OF AUTHORSHIP Briefly describe nature of the material created by this author in which copyright is claimed. ▼

NAME OF AUTHOR ▼

DATES OF BIRTH AND DEATH
Year Born ▼   Year Died ▼

Was this contribution to the work a "work made for hire"?
☐ Yes
☐ No

AUTHOR'S NATIONALITY OR DOMICILE
Name of Country
OR { Citizen of ▶ _____
Domiciled in ▶ _____

WAS THIS AUTHOR'S CONTRIBUTION TO THE WORK
Anonymous?   ☐ Yes ☐ No
Pseudonymous?   ☐ Yes ☐ No
If the answer to either of these questions is "Yes," see detailed instructions.

NATURE OF AUTHORSHIP Briefly describe nature of the material created by this author in which copyright is claimed. ▼

3 **YEAR IN WHICH CREATION OF THIS WORK WAS COMPLETED** This information must be given in all cases.
▲ Year

DATE AND NATION OF FIRST PUBLICATION OF THIS PARTICULAR WORK
Complete this information Month ▶ _____ Day ▶ _____ Year ▶ _____
ONLY if this work has been published.
◀ Nation

4 **COPYRIGHT CLAIMANT(S)** Name and address must be given even if the claimant is the same as the author given in space 2.▼

See instructions before completing this space.

TRANSFER If the claimant(s) named here in space 4 are different from the author(s) named in space 2, give a brief statement of how the claimant(s) obtained ownership of the copyright. ▼

DO NOT WRITE HERE
OFFICE USE ONLY

APPLICATION RECEIVED

ONE DEPOSIT RECEIVED

TWO DEPOSITS RECEIVED

REMITTANCE NUMBER AND DATE

MORE ON BACK ▶ • Complete all applicable spaces (numbers 5-11) on the reverse side of this page.
• See detailed instructions.   • Sign the form at line 10.

DO NOT WRITE HERE
Page 1 of _____ pages

FORM TX

EXAMINED BY

CHECKED BY

CORRESPONDENCE
Yes

DEPOSIT ACCOUNT
FUNDS USED

FOR
COPYRIGHT
OFFICE
USE
ONLY

DO NOT WRITE ABOVE THIS LINE. IF YOU NEED MORE SPACE, USE A SEPARATE CONTINUATION SHEET.

PREVIOUS REGISTRATION Has registration for this work, or for an earlier version of this work, already been made in the Copyright Office?
☐ **Yes** ☐ **No** If your answer is "Yes," why is another registration being sought? (Check appropriate box) ▼

☐ This is the first published edition of a work previously registered in unpublished form.

☐ This is the first application submitted by this author as copyright claimant.

☐ This is a changed version of the work, as shown by space 6 on this application.

If your answer is "Yes," give: **Previous Registration Number** ▼   **Year of Registration** ▼

5

DERIVATIVE WORK OR COMPILATION Complete both space 6a & 6b for a derivative work; complete only 6b for a compilation.
a. Preexisting Material Identify any preexisting work or works that this work is based on or incorporates. ▼

b. Material Added to This Work Give a brief, general statement of the material that has been been added to this work and in which copyright is claimed. ▼

6

See instructions
before completing
this space.

MANUFACTURERS AND LOCATIONS If this is a published work consisting preponderantly of nondramatic literary material in English, the law may require that the copies be manufactured in the United States or Canada for full protection. If so, the names of the manufacturers who performed certain processes, and the places where these processes were performed **must be given.** See instructions for details.
Names of Manufacturers ▼   **Places of Manufacture** ▼

7

8 REPRODUCTION FOR USE OF BLIND OR PHYSICALLY HANDICAPPED INDIVIDUALS   A signature on this form at space 10, and a check in one of the boxes here in space 8, constitutes a non-exclusive grant of permission to the Library of Congress to reproduce and distribute solely for the blind and physically handicapped and under the conditions and limitations prescribed by the regulations of the Copyright Office: (1) copies of the work identified in space 1 of this application in Braille (or similar tactile symbols); or (2) phonorecords embodying a fixation of a reading of that work; or (3) both.

a ☐ Copies and Phonorecords   b ☐ Copies Only   c ☐ Phonorecords Only

See instructions

9 DEPOSIT ACCOUNT   If the registration fee is to be charged to a Deposit Account established in the Copyright Office, give name and number of Account.

Name ▼   Account Number ▼

CORRESPONDENCE   Give name and address to which correspondence about this application should be sent.   Name/Address/Apt/City/State/Zip ▼

Area Code & Telephone Number ▶

10 Be sure to give your daytime phone ▶ number.

CERTIFICATION*   I, the undersigned, hereby certify that I am the

Check one ▶

☐ author
☐ other copyright claimant
☐ owner of exclusive right(s)
☐ authorized agent of _____
　　Name of author or other copyright claimant, or owner of exclusive right(s) ▲

of the work identified in this application and that the statements made by me in this application are correct to the best of my knowledge.

Typed or printed name and date ▼ If this is a published work, this date must be the same as or later than the date of publication given in space 3.

_____ date ▶ _____

Handwritten signature (X) ▼

11 MAIL CERTIFI- CATE TO

Name ▼

Number/Street/Apartment Number ▼

City/State/ZIP ▼

Certificate will be mailed in window envelope

Have you:
• Completed all necessary spaces?
• Signed your application in space 10?
• Enclosed check or money order for $10 payable to *Register of Copyrights?*
• Enclosed your deposit material with the application and fee?

MAIL TO: Register of Copyrights, Library of Congress, Washington, D.C. 20559.

☆ U.S. GOVERNMENT PRINTING OFFICE: 1984: 461-584/10,017

December 1984 — 100,000

28

The Economics
of Publishing

Volume of book industry sales
Breakdown of the publisher's dollar
Books by category published annually
Best sellers
Average textbook sales

On the return of the trio from lunch, Pam, Jack, and Bill are joined by a remarkable statistician. Keyne has a reputation at the publishing company for being a human computer. Publishing companies and their trade association jealously guard information about sales from the prying eyes of competitors. Keyne, however, does supply some generalized information on the economics of book publishing.

Pam. Bill, you told me you wanted some facts and figures on book publishing. So I asked our statistician to join us. Keyne keeps me conscious of the importance of bottom lines.

Keyne. If I didn't, Pam, the vice-presidents would.

Pam. Keyne, meet Bill and Jack. Bill is one of our authors. Jack edits a journal. Both of them teach in universities and write articles and books whenever they get around to it.

Keyne. Since I'm not a walking encyclopedia, I made some horseback guesses as to what an author might want to know, and I brought along some data. So, fire away.

Bill. Will book publishing in the years ahead be dominated by a half-dozen conglomerates that bring together varied media?

Keyne. Quite possibly. On the other hand, about half of the book publishers tallied by the Census of Manufactures employ only one to four people.[1]

Pam. An old quip in publishing is that all that you need to be a

---

[1]Bureau of the Census, *Census of Manufactures,* U.S. Department of Commerce, 1977.

book publisher is a desk and a supply of Tums, Rolaids, or Alka-Seltzer, according to your preference.

Jack. What can you tell us of the extent of the kinds of books professionals usually write—elementary and secondary school textbooks, college textbooks, and the variety of specialized books?

Keyne. A book trade compilation, the *Bowker Annual of Library and Book Trade Information,* is our best bet. My 1984 edition reports that, in 1982, book publishing sales of el-hi textbooks, expressed in dollars, amounted to $1,051 million. The sales of college textbooks amounted to $1,142 million. Along with textbooks, the industry sold $148 million worth of audio-visual and other media. Standardized tests, almost all at the el-hi level, weighed in at $70 million.[2] All figures are rounded off to the nearest million.

Bill. I admire the casualness of statisticians in rounding off millions. How about specialized books, many of which are "scholarly"?

Keyne. The book trade doesn't report a "scholarly" category, so you'll have to piece this grouping together. Though university presses occasionally publish other books, their heaviest contribution would be in your scholarly category. Their sales amounted to $92 million. Then there is a large category that the book trade lumps together as "professional." Included are technical/scientific, sales of $431 million; medical, $268 million; and business/other professional, $531 million.[3]

Jack. I imagine that trade books constitute a mighty large segment of sales?

Keyne. You might be surprised. Trade book sales were $1,355 million, even though trade includes both adult and juvenile hardbound and paperbound books; this is only somewhat more than college textbooks. However, in addition to the books included in the trade category, Bowker attributes book sales of $590 million to book clubs, $605 million to mail-order publications, and $823 million to mass-market paperbacks.[4]

Bill. Put it all together and we must come out with a healthy figure?

Keyne. If we add in religious books, including Bibles, $390 million; and subscription reference books, $397 million; and "other" books, $77 million; the estimated sales of the book publishing industry for 1982 amounted to $7,971,500,000.[5]

---

[2]*1984 Bowker Annual of Library and Book Trade Information* (New York: R. R. Bowker, 1984), pp. 420–21.

[3]Ibid.

[4]Ibid.

[5]Ibid.

Jack. Barrel in for a moment, Keyne, on textbooks, educational materials that are largely audio-visual, and standardized tests.

Keyne. Bowker tells us that el-hi textbooks, college textbooks, AV and other media, and standardized tests account for a great volume of the industry's sales—almost one-third[6] The college market, of course, also buys the technical-scientific-medical-business-other professional cluster that Bowker categorizes as "professional"; it also buys trade books, university press, book club, and mail-order publications. So the education market is a substantial part of the book business.

Bill. I prefer the term "specialized" for the technical-scientific-medical-business-other professional cluster, rather than the blanket term "professional." To me, textbooks, most university press and reference books, and many trade books are also professional publications. So are contributions to professional magazines and journals. But who am I to argue with book trade language?

Jack. Keyne, let's take just one of the categories you have mentioned, college textbooks. Have college textbook publishers ever broken down what happens to the typical dollar?

Keyne. The Faculty Relations Committee of the Association of American Publishers, Inc., did a small pamphlet, *Books and Bucks*, a few years ago that included figures concerning the economics of college textbook publishing. *Books and Bucks* broke the publisher's dollar down into six cents for editorial expenses, twenty-nine cents for costs to manufacture the book, fourteen cents for marketing, eighteen cents for general overhead, fifteen cents for royalties, eight cents for taxes, and ten cents for profits.[7]

Of course, there is variation from company to company. There are approximately 300 publishers selling to the college market. However, only about a dozen of them make 60 percent of the sales to colleges.

Bill. Keyne, I wouldn't trade you for the world's best computer. Tell me, please, how many new books and how many new editions are published in the United States each year?

Keyne. In 1982, 36,238 new books and 6,712 new editions constituted the American book title output of hardbound books and trade paperbacks, a total of 42,950. When all paperbound books are included, the figure rises to 46,935. Our total figure is based on the 1984 *Bowker Annual of Library and Book Trade Information*.[8] Want the figures for any particular category?

---

[6]Ibid., p. 381.

[7]Faculty Relations Committee, Association of American Publishers, *Books and Bucks*, Association of American Publishers, New York, undated, pp. 4–7.

[8]*1984 Annual of Library and Book Trade Information*, (New York: R. R. Bowker, 1984), p. 412.

Jack. Yes, for several of the professions. To simplify matters, give us just the title outputs, combining both new books and new editions.

Keyne. I'll start with the largest and work down. Sociology and economics, 7,449; medicine, 3,229; science, 3,124; technology, 2,328; history, 2,177; religion, 2,075; literature, 1,742; art, 1,722; philosophy and psychology, 1,465.[9]

Jack. Does the list separate these latter two strange bedfellows?

Keyne. No. Then follows law, 1,451; business, 1,327; sports and recreation, 1,191; home economics, 1,099; education, 1,046; language, 576; agriculture, 439; music, 346. I know that you are interested particularly in the professions, yet allow me to complete my listing with fiction, 5,419; juveniles, 3,049; biography, 1,752; general works, 2,398; poetry and drama, 1,049; travel, 482.[10]

Bill. Let's look at the matter of economics from the author's point of view. Authors are curious about how many copies books sell. In *The Guinness Book of World Records'* tradition, let's start with those magic words in the publishing lexicon, best sellers.

Keyne. You won't find many books by members of the various professions at the rarefied top of the best sellers list—with one conspicuous exception.

Bill. What's that?

Keyne. *Pocket Book of Baby and Child Care* by Benjamin Spock, M.D. This super seller was first published in 1946. Hackett and Burke's *80 Years of Best Sellers, 1895–1975* reported its sales as 23,285,000 copies.[11] (By 1983, sales had passed the 30,000,000 mark.) Other books high on the all-time best seller list are dictionaries, cookbooks, and atlases. Also, there are books on home and garden, world records, diet, sex, self-help, religion, health, birds, and comics.

Bill. Comics?

Keyne. Yes. Again and again compilations of comic strips by Charles M. Schulz appear on best seller lists. Yet even a book about Snoopy, Charlie Brown, and their friends can't compare in sales to some of the cookbooks. The otherwise sober authors of *80 Years of Best Sellers, 1895–1975,* comment that an ideal title for a best seller would be *Lincoln's Doctor's Dog's Favorite Recipes for Beginners.*[12]

Jack. Jim Davis's Garfield the Cat books have regularly appeared on best seller lists during the 1980s. Maybe ''*Cat's*'' should replace ''*Dog's*'' in that title.

---

[9]Ibid.

[10]Ibid.

[11]Alice Payne Hackett and James Henry Burke, *80 Years of Best Sellers, 1895–1975* (New York: R. R. Bowker, 1977), p. 10.

[12]Ibid., p. 22.

Bill. In his newspaper column, Jim Bishop once suggested that a sure-fire fiction best seller could be written "about a girl who is cloned and becomes the world champion jogger while on her secret diet between spasms of nymphomania."[13]

Jack. Some practitioners of the professions do appear on the best seller list of books read by the general public?

Keyne. For instance, Edith Hamilton, a classical scholar, began her writing career when she was sixty, after spending twenty-five years as Head Mistress of the Bryn Mawr School for Girls in Baltimore. Her *Mythology*, published in 1930, has sold 7,272,000 copies, proving that it's never too late to begin to write. Other professionals high on the best seller list are physicians Thomas Harris and D. C. Jarvis, social philosopher Alvin Toffler, psychologists Eric Berne and Haim G. Ginott, and law professor Charles A. Reich, with sales ranging between 2,460,000 and 6,005,000 copies of their best sellers.[14] Since Hackett and Burke's cutoff date of 1975, many other professionals have become best-selling authors, including astronomer Carl Sagan and educator Leo F. Buscaglia.

Pam. Gentlemen, may I bring you down to earth? It's all very well to dream about best sellers, but let's recognize realities. The same AAP pamphlet that Keyne quoted, *Books and Bucks*, says flatly that "the average textbook sells fewer than 5,000 copies in a year."[15]

Bill. I have a favorite quotation from Richard Balkin's *A Writer's Guide to Book Publishing*:

> Of all the major industries in the United States, surely book publishing is the most primitive, the most disorganized, and the most haphazard. Consider the following: What other industry would launch a national campaign for an untested product whose life span is usually less than a year and whose chances of recouping its investment are worse than one in three? What other industry would manufacture so many competing products with only the barest notion of which of them might succeed in the marketplace?[16]

Pam. Let's not get personal, or I'll tell you what editors, in their blacker moods, say about authors. Keep on dreaming, gentlemen, else publishers would go out of business.

Keyne. If you will excuse me now, I must get back to my computers.

[13]Jim Bishop, "Stuff in Books Too Rough to Digest," *Terre Haute Tribune*, July 7, 1979, p. 4.

[14]Hackett and Burke, pp. 10–20.

[15]*Books and Bucks*, p. 6.

[16]Richard Balkin, *A Writer's Guide to Book Publishing* (New York: Hawthorn Books, Inc., 1977), p. 137.

PAYMENT TO WRITERS

Writers

Just how many writers or would-be writers there are may be impossible to ascertain. Professional groups such as the Writers Guild and the Authors Guild, both of which require at least a modicum of success for membership, account for only 12,000 people. But other signs, such as the 100,000-plus circulation of *Writer's Digest* and the brisk sales of an annual publication called *Writer's Market*, indicate that a large number of people are looking for realistic, professional advice about how to make money as a writer. Many of them are, of course, disguised as secretaries and copy editors in publishing houses, or as accountants and housewives who keep their typewriters hidden in attics and basements. What they have in common, however, is the tenacity to pursue very demanding work without guarantee of reward. . . .

But the publicity given to multimillion dollar deals seriously distorts the public's view of the typical payments publishers offer and of the average income levels of most book authors. According to *The Columbia University Study of American Authors* (1981), only 5 percent of the 2,239 writers surveyed earned over $80,000 and only 10 percent over $45,000. The Columbia study, sponsored by The Authors Guild Foundation, is the first attempt to ascertain the economic rewards of writing. Here are some of its more interesting findings:

- The average author realized $4,775 from his or her writing.
- Of those authors who wrote for a living, only 28 percent earned $20,000 or more.
- 46 percent of the writers surveyed had full-time jobs in another field: 36 percent in university teaching, 11 percent in publishing, 5 percent in journalism, 5 percent in public relations, 4 percent in school teaching, and 20 percent in other professional occupations, including doctors, lawyers, and clergy.
- Genre fiction (romances, mysteries, Gothic) is the most lucrative kind of writing with 20 percent of its authors earning over $50,000 from their books and stories.
- 55 percent of authors earning less than $2,500 from writing were poets or those doing academically oriented non-fiction.
- Among authors who have had books on the best seller lists, 70 percent had at least five books to their credit, and 80 percent were full-time writers.

Representative Payments for Magazine Articles

Magazine	Payment
Advertising Age	$125–200
Antiques	10 cents per published word
Apartment Life	$250–400
Atlantic Monthly	$200 min.
Better Homes and Gardens	$300 per column
The Christian Century	$25 per *Century* page ($50–100 average)
Cosmopolitan	$200–500 for up to 3,000 words
	$750–1,500 for longer pieces
	$1,000 min. for short fiction
	$4,500 for condensed novel
Family Circle	$250–2,500 for nonfiction
	$500 min. for fiction
Good Housekeeping	$500–1,000 for average nonfiction
House Beautiful	$150–400 for 1,000 words
Los Angeles Magazine	$400–750
McCall's	$200 for nonfiction
	$1,250 min. for fiction
Mademoiselle	$100 min. for nonfiction
	$300 min. for fiction
Money	$1,000 for 1,000-word nonfiction article
Ms.	"Gazette" paragraph $25–100
	short review $150–250
	long feature $500–1,000
The Nation	$150 top
National Geographic	$3,000–6,000+
New Republic	10 cents per word
People	$200 for "Lookout" page
	$400–1,000 for two-page biography
Playboy	$1,000–2,000 per article
	much more for established writer
Quest	50 cents per word
Redbook	$500 for 1,000–2,000-word article
	$850–1,000 for fiction
Savvy	$500–700 per article
Smithsonian	$1,500 per article
Sports Illustrated	$400–750 for regional articles
	$1,000 min. for national
TV Guide	$1,500 per article
Travel and Leisure	$500–750 for 1,000–1,750 words
Vanity Fair	$3,000 for 750 words
Vogue	$300 min. for 2,000–2,500 words
The Washingtonian	10 cents per word for nonfiction, fiction, poetry

29

Marketing

Authors' fantasies on promotion and publicity
The realities of marketing a book by a professional
Advertising in magazines and journals
The importance of the author's questionnaire
The importance of book reviews to authors
Authors' relationship to marketing
Whether sales can be predicted

After Keyne's departure, Pam helps Bill and Jack to understand the marketing process. She stresses how important it is that authors conscientiously fill out the author's questionnaire. In the process, some dreams of super-promotion of professional books are fractured. Yet, as Pam points out, there are some marketing approaches in the real world of professional publication with which authors can cooperate.

Bill. What about publicity, promotion, advertising, distribution, sales—all that comes under the broad heading of marketing? When the book is published, how will the author participate in these areas?

Pam. Are you referring to the author's role in the real world? Or the author's fantasy about what the writer's role will be?

Bill. What do you mean?

Pam. People who write professional books conjure up fantasies about their forthcoming participation in promotion and publicity. Now, after all the travail of authorship, nationwide recognition of the book and, naturally, the author, develops. The author appears on *Good Morning America*; *The Today Show*; Phil Donahue's program; Public Broadcasting Service's book review programs; and begs off from appearing with Johnny on *The Tonight Show* because of the volume of other commitments. CBS considers making a mini-series of the book.

The author is in constant demand on the lecture circuit, and the author's agent grows weary of carrying bags from metropolis to metropolis. Bookstores hold autographing parties; later, at a reception, the author complains of writer's cramp from the demands of hordes of admiring purchasers.

The Sunday *New York Times Book Review* section features the book on the front page and runs a full-page advertisement. When tuning in a favorite prime-time television program, the writer is pleasantly surprised to hear a commercial for the book. Clipping services flood the author with favorable reviews, first from the press, then from the magazines.

There are intimations that Hollywood may be interested in the book if the writer would be willing to do the adaptation. Publishers jostle one another for paperback rights. The multimillion-circulation magazines make fabulous offers. The professional journals, which run full-page advertisements for the book issue after issue, implore the author to contribute lead articles and editorials, rather than neglect the demands of scholarship. National organizations in the writer's professional field plead for responses to their requests for lectures at future national conventions. The State Department phones, inquiring when the author will schedule a foreign tour.

Bill. I take it that you are saying "Forget it!" What's it like in the real world for the usual author of a professional book?

Pam. No TV interviews, triumphal lecture tours, autographing parties, glamorous receptions, *Times* reviews, ads, deluge of clippings, paperback printings, Hollywood offers, full-page journal ads, or international invitations.

Jack. My experience, Bill, is that if the author is diligent in self-promotion, the college newspaper and the author's alumni bulletin may break the news to the waiting world. Buried in the back pages of the local newspaper, an inch-high university press release announces that another professor has written a book.

Bill. They usually misspell the author's name.

Jack. Then the author gives most of the six publisher-supplied free copies to close relatives, who proudly place the book on their bookshelves with assurances that they intend to read it some day.

Bill. Not so. My relatives always read the dedication page.

Pam. I've heard that an author on vertebrate physiology dedicated his book to "all the cold-blooded fishes in the sea and to my wife."

Bill. Tell us, Pam, about the techniques relied on by publishers in marketing an average book by a professional.

Pam. Though the fantasies of razzle-dazzle best seller promotion won't materialize, the real world is not so bad. After all, publishers do want to sell books written by members of the professions.

When a book by an academic is published, the publisher's first responsibility is to familiarize prospective purchasers with the name of the book and the author. For a trade book, the publisher uses calls by salespeople on bookstores in the community, advertisements in magazines and sometimes newspapers, and review copies to periodicals. For a college book, the publisher uses calls on professors by travelers, convention displays and program ads, occasional advertisements in journals, and free copies to selected potential users and to those who request sample copies. Publishers conduct mail-order campaigns for books best sold by mail. For el-hi books, publicity and promotion may be somewhat splashier, sometimes including elaborate advertisements in selected magazines, flyers or brochures in color, convention displays and program advertisements, and even convention handouts such as buttons or pens, as well as the standard approaches of free sample copies and persuasion by sales representatives.

Each company has its own favorite mix of such approaches. Some depend heavily on sales representatives. Some lean toward advertisements in professional periodicals. Others stress order blanks accompanying mail advertisements.

One trend seems to be turning away from salespeople on the road and toward the use of mailing lists of members of organizations. The increase in energy costs is one reason for this shift in sales strategy. Another trend is away from advertising in journals. Few orders for books by professionals can be traced directly to journal ads.

Jack. I appoint myself counsel for the defense of journals. Direct results of journal advertising may be hard to trace, but they are nevertheless real. Journal advertising makes the profession conscious of the existence of the book. It contributes to highly valuable word-of-mouth mention in the profession. Journal ads pave the way for the sales representative; when he or she calls, the professor may say, "Yes, I've heard of that book, so tell me more."

Pam. Jack, you didn't mention that a page in some journals may cost a thousand dollars an issue, and bring only a half-dozen traceable requests for sample copies. Some publishers are growing skeptical of the supposed intangible benefits of journal advertising.

Jack. Authors unanimously urge that their books be advertised in selected journals.

Pam. That I know. They scream especially loudly in protest when their books are not advertised in the journals of their major organizations.

Bill. And understandably. An author urgently wants colleagues to know of the existence of the new book. Journal advertisements tie in with every motivation of the professional, whether it be hunger to communicate essential ideas or findings, desire to set one's colleagues straight on things, or earthy drives for recognition, consultation opportunities, salary, promotion, and tenure.

Pam. In book publishing, we recognize that. We'll sometimes advertise in journals to keep an author happy, even when we regard the sales outcome as negligible. If we don't and the book doesn't sell, the author is sure to tell us that the absence of advertisements in the professional journals was the cause. No author ever conceded the horrid possibility that the book simply wasn't good enough.

So a writer should provide a publisher with a carefully selected and well-justified list of magazines and journals for possible placement of advertisements. The author had best make the case for the selected periodicals vigorously. Marketing departments have their share of doubting Thomases.

Bill. Pam, is there much that the author of a professional book can really do to help in marketing?

Pam. Not a great deal, once the book is published. In advance, the author can make a solid contribution by giving substantial time and thought to the author's questionnaire. A sensible publisher repeatedly uses that questionnaire in sales meetings, and the sales staff uses suggestions from the questionnaire in the field. The author's suggestions are also useful in determining what to stress in advertising, in obtaining quotations from influentials, and in deciding where to place ads and review copies.

Bill. You folks in publishing houses do take the author's questionnaire seriously then? Professors are somewhat skeptical. We know of introductory books that have been advertised in high-level research journals rather than in the magazines emphasized by the authors in their questionnaire responses.

Jack. What's wrong with advertising a book in a research journal?

Bill. Nothing at all, if a book is a report on research that the professor may buy and/or require or recommend in courses. However, most serious readers of high-level research journals are professors teaching on the graduate level. They usually aren't the beginners in the field who are assigned to introductory courses. Advertising for an introductory book would be more effective if it appeared in a periodical with broader readership.

Pam. I won't deny occasional ineptness of publishers in promotion. In our house, though, we rely heavily on information from the author's questionnaire.

Bill. What do you especially value?

Pam. All suggestions from authors can be helpful in publicizing and selling the book. We especially value careful and comprehensive descriptions of the market and lists of individuals and organizations that only the author can provide.

Bill. Such as?

Pam. We want authors to tell us who specifically will buy the book. Students in which courses? Professors in which specializations? Librarians for what purposes? General readers with what backgrounds?

As to lists, we value the names of fellow professionals who might comment favorably on the book. Give us a dozen or two and we will follow up with galleys to professional leaders. A personal letter from the author to the potential endorsers would also be helpful. If the names of those who might provide testimonials are widely known, that is all the better. Supply us with an even longer list of the influentials whose word-of-mouth might contribute to the book's success, and we'll send some of them copies when the book is published.

Jack. You didn't mention lists of magazines and journals that might review the book.

Pam. Authors should supply that type of list too. Yet to be brutally honest, Jack, I don't think book reviews after publication are as important to sales as journal editors and authors commonly assume. Journals are slow in carrying reviews; sometimes they appear a year or two later, when the book is over the hill.

Bill. I doubt, Pam, that you could convince authors and journal editors that reviews aren't important influences on sales. They regard reviews as crucial both to distribution and the author's reputation. Whether they appear early or late, reviews are of high importance to any author who works in the professions. Naturally an author hopes the book will be reviewed early. Yet even if reviews appear late, they affect the author's standing in the profession.

If the reviewers of books by professionals were as caustic as drama and film critics and book reviewers of fiction, I suspect the suicide rate among professors would rise. However, reviews of academic publications are often tame—too often too tame.

Jack. You mentioned the book author's standing in the profession, Bill. That's a concern of the journal author, too. Our authors frequently order reprints of their articles from the printer. Their motivations are mixed. They want to communicate to those who should read their findings. They also want to improve their standing in the profession. They have no intention of contributing to marketing our journal, yet indirectly their reprints do call attention to us, as well as to their articles. They become our unconscious partners in marketing our journal, though they fill out no questionnaires.

Pam. When filling out a questionnaire, an author should bear in mind that not everyone involved in marketing the book will read the book. That's an understatement; the fact of life is that few who promote and advertise the book will read it. Given the number of books published by large and medium-sized publishers, and the specialized nature of the content of books by professionals, the most an author can expect from the marketing and sales staffs is sampling. Remember that the sampling on the part of marketing and sales personnel may come closer to nibbling than taking substantial bites.

So spell out in the questionnaire the strengths of the book. Stress the innovative ideas. Tell the questionnaire reader exactly how the book differs from the competition. Cite chapter and verse.

The author doesn't write the advertisements but can influence copy writers. An author doesn't peddle books but can put words into the travelers' mouths. So if page 42 is particularly brilliant or Chapter 12 especially innovative, let's hear about these specifics. If your company does direct mail advertising, tell the marketing director what you liked and disliked about mailing pieces for books by other authors.

Bill. You advise authors to get acquainted with marketing directors, sales managers, publicity directors, or whatever the title might be?

Pam. By all means. From an author's viewpoint, as a book moves into manufacturing, the acquisitions editor and copyeditor, once all-important to the author, begin to fade away like General MacArthur's old soldiers. Editors become busy with new projects. The key marketing person becomes an important person for the author to know. Getting the book into the hands of purchasers becomes the target.

Bill. How else can an author help in marketing?

Pam. Gently encouraging colleagues to use the book in their classes. Personally sending out some flyers. Bringing copies of the book to conventions and conferences and consultations. Mentioning the book to program chairpersons, so the title will be mentioned on occasions when the author speaks to audiences. The possibilities are limited only by the author's ingenuity.

Jack. And position on the continuum between modesty and aggressiveness.

Bill. And much depends upon the publisher's enterprise and skills.

Jack. Does anyone really know what makes a book sell?

Bill. As to trade books, I heard a good answer when my first book, a travel book, was being edited. At Scribner's, they told me one of the many legends about Maxwell Perkins, the editor's editor, and Papa Scribner, the publisher's publisher. In his early days as an editor, Maxwell Perkins was given several manuscripts to read and report on at a forthcoming editorial conference. He did his homework diligently and brought reports on the books to the editorial conference. They were masterpieces of intellectual analysis. Then Papa Scribner asked him how many copies of each recommended book the company should print. Flabbergasted, Perkins said, "My God, sir, I haven't the faintest idea." Papa Scribner is reported to have said, "After a lifetime in publishing, I haven't any idea either. But I thought one of you young fellows might know."

Pam. In the field of publishing college and el-hi textbooks and professional reference books, we're somewhat better off. Thanks to research fed into the computer and to people like Keyne, we can estimate the market. But no one can be confident of what share of that market will go to a specific book.

Bill. A philosopher under whom I once studied, Boyd H. Bode, said, "The gods give no guarantees."

Pam. He missed his calling. He should have been in the field of book publishing.

AUTHOR'S SUGGESTIONS
FOR ADVERTISING AND SALES

Leading Educational Publishers since 1868

Allyn and Bacon, Inc.
7 Wells Avenue, Newton, MA 02159
617/964-5530

Title of Your Book: _____

Your Name: _____

Birthdate: Authors' birthdates are requested by the Library
of Congress's new Cataloging in Publication (CIP) Program.
This information is customarily printed on the copyright page.
You may enter your birthdate in the space provided below;
however, if for any reason you do not want this date to appear
in your book, please place an "X" in the following box <u>instead</u>:

☐

Birthdate: _____ _____ _____
           (date)   (month)   (year)

If the book is co-authored, list below the proper order of
names (including your name) as they should appear in the book
and in advertising:

    1. _____

    2. _____

    3. _____

Please be specific. Supply complete information. Use extra
sheets if necessary.

PERSONAL HISTORY

EDUCATION   <u>College</u>   <u>Year</u>   <u>Field</u>

B.A. _____

M.A. _____

Ph.D. _____

Other Degrees _____

PRESENT AFFILIATION AND OFFICIAL TITLE (As it should appear
in our advertising):

_____

_____

BIOGRAPHICAL SKETCH: (Emphasize accomplishments which establish the authoritative character of your book.) Use extra sheets if necessary.

DESCRIPTION AND OUTSTANDING FEATURES
GIVE A BRIEF DESCRIPTION OF YOUR BOOK IN 200 WORDS OR LESS. (Please be specific. Refer to chapters, sections or pages in your book.)

ASIDE FROM NEWNESS, WHAT ARE THE OUTSTANDING FEATURES OF YOUR BOOK? (Cite specific points at which these features can be found in your book.)

EXAMPLES
The following are typical examples of features found in most textbooks. Please describe in detail those or others which apply to your book:
Original Approach
Organization
Special Research
Wealth of Problems
Flexibility
No Prerequisites
Graphic Illustrations
Tested Material
Simplicity
Comprehensiveness

OTHER BOOKS IN THE FIELD
Published or revised in the last five years.

Title	Author	Publisher
A.		
B.		
C.		
D.		
E.		

ASIDE FROM NEWNESS, HOW DOES YOUR BOOK DIFFER FROM EACH OF THESE? HOW IS IT SUPERIOR? (Be specific - illustrate if possible by referring to specific sections and/or pages of above books.)

A. _____

B. _____

C. _____

D. _____

E. _____

TEACHING AIDS

DOES YOUR BOOK CONTAIN (please check appropriate answers):

Problems............( ) By chapter............( ) Back of book( )
Questions...........( ) By chapter............( ) Back of book( )
Answers.............( ) For students..........( )
Worked-out solutions( ) For students..........( )
Line drawings.......( ) Halftone illustrations( ) Graphs......( )
Tables..............( ) Bibliographies........( ) Charts......( )
Footnotes...........( )   Summaries...( )
Appendixes (Particular type) _____

PLEASE LIST PROBABLE CHAPTER HEADINGS FOR YOUR BOOK

<u>Journal Information</u>

Please list the two or three most appropriate academic journals
to be considered for advertising purposes.

Please list most appropriate academic journals that regularly
review textbooks. (Please give name of book review editor,
if known.)

List most appropriate conventions at which your book should
be displayed.

List titles of appropriate courses for which your book could
be used:

_____

Author's signature

SALES LETTERS FOR TEXTBOOKS

Leading Educational Publishers since 1868

Allyn and Bacon, Inc.
7 Wells Avenue, Newton, MA 02159
617/964-5530

Your local sales representative, Jack Mc Canna, has reserved a copy for you of the upcoming fourth edition of TEACHING THEM TO READ by Dolores Durkin. Shortly after its April publication, you'll have this examination copy in hand. And I urge you to review it carefully.

I'm confident you'll find this new edition's extensive coverage and unique focal point -- comprehension -- make it the best choice for a first course in Reading Methods at the undergraduate or graduate level. And, I think you'll agree with the author, that comprehension is the point to be emphasized at any grade level. Durkin has devoted two full chapters to this topic as well as relating it to all aspects of reading instruction throughout the text.

Durkin has retained her clear writing style in this edition, along with her noted organizational format, i.e. preview and review sections, chapter outlines and summaries, and effective questions to promote understanding.

After you review this new edition, I think you'll find it well worth the wait. So hold off on your text decision until you've seen TEACHING THEM TO READ, FOURTH EDITION by Dolores Durkin. And, if you require further assistance, please feel free to contact your sales rep, Jack Mc Canna, at (317) 984-5711.

Cordially,

Hiram Howard
Managing Editor
Longwood Division

P.S. After you receive your copy of Durkin's new edition, I'd appreciate your comments on the text. Just drop me a note on the reverse side of this letter and mail in the enclosed prepaid envelope.

Leading Educational Publishers since 1868

Allyn and Bacon, Inc.
7 Wells Avenue, Newton, MA 02159
617/964-5530

We recently sent you a copy of DIAGNOSIS AND REMEDIATION OF THE DISABLED READER, SECOND EDITION by Ekwall and Shanker, and I urge you to look at this new text closely.

The book retains the highly successful, original format and teacher/practitioner orientation so popular in the first edition. Now you'll also find two brand new chapters -- Chapter 9, Diagnosis and Remediation of Severe Reading Disabilities, and Chapter 13, A More Efficient Path to Diagnosis. In this edition, the authors include: the very latest research on reading diagnosis and remediation (particularly in the areas of decoding and comprehension skills); expanded coverage of the role of the reading specialist; more techniques and strategies; more in-depth directions and samples; four extremely useful Appendices, and more. Really, I believe a close look at this practical new edition will confirm that the best text in the field is now even better.

An important reminder! An outstanding Instructor's Manual to accompany this new edition will be published in early June. In it you'll find a wealth of valuable material -- chapter outlines, discussion questions, transparency masters, black-line masters for quizzes and practice tests, plus phonetic and linguistic tests. Contact your local Allyn and Bacon sales representative, Nancy Birdsong, at (817) 567-3514 if you would like a copy sent to you upon publication.

In closing, I sincerely hope you'll consider adopting DIAGNOSIS AND REMEDIATION OF THE DISABLED READER, SECOND EDITION by Ekwall and Shanker...I guarantee it's a superior book backed by superior customer service. We look forward to serving you.

Cordially,

Hiram Howard
Managing Editor
Longwood Division

P.S. I'm very interested in your reaction to Ekwall and Shanker... would you mind taking a minute to jot your thoughts down on the back of this letter and return it to me in the enclosed postage-paid reply envelope? Thanks so much.

Leading Educational Publishers since 1868

Allyn and Bacon, Inc.
7 Wells Avenue, Newton, MA 02159
617/964-5530

Professor John A. Sample
Department of Psychology
The Sample University
Anywhere, U.S.A. 00000

Dear Professor Sample:

Dave Faherty has asked me to share some thoughts with you regarding our innovative new introductory text by Neil Carlson, PSYCHOLOGY: THE SCIENCE OF BEHAVIOR. As Psychology Editor for Allyn and Bacon, I have worked with Neil for six years on this project and feel we have developed a book that makes good psychology accessible to all students. In addition to the text, which is rapidly securing adoptions daily (see list), several other components work in concert to provide an integrated learning system unique to the introductory marketplace. Here's how the system works:

1) <u>Learning Objectives</u>: Each chapter alerts the student to the essential information in each chapter; reinforcement takes place when the objectives are "called out" in the chapters by the use of a printer's symbol such as the one on page 4.

2) <u>Breaking down the text into smaller, more digestible units</u>: This is accomplished by Neil's use of interim summaries throughout the text, rather than just rehashing content at the end of each chapter. This feature is carried through in the study guide, <u>Discovering Psychology</u>, which uses the objectives as its organizational basis and which breaks each chapter down in three or four smaller units. Students - especially average ones - love this feature.

3) <u>Test Items</u>: Our items are directly linked to the learning objectives, and each item is identified by type: Conceptual, Factual, Applied and Empirical. A student <u>cannot</u> be tested on material

extraneous to the objectives, and each
objective has a corresponding test item.
Your students are the winners here,
especially since so many texts have such
horrible test files.

4) <u>Superior</u> <u>Graphics</u>: We have the best graphics
of any book on the market; and we have lengthened the text to increase their size so that
students can comprehend them better. We even
list the key figures along with key terms at
the end of each chapter. Good graphics are
accessible to all students.

5) <u>Neil</u> <u>Carlson's</u> <u>Writing</u> <u>Style</u>: Neil's personal
way of addressing students is much appreciated
by them. Show students some of the "Discoveries"
in Chapter Seven (they're set off by brackets)
to elicit their reaction.

These are a few features, but the important thing is that the
students get one of the best textbooks to be written in years. For
that, they will be thankful that they haven't been talked down to
again (see attached article from <u>Publisher's</u> <u>Weekly</u>).

Convinced? If not, let the students decide; I'm confident
that the pedagogy of Carlson in the form of this integrated learning
system will serve to enhance student understanding of Neil's book.
Let them "discover" Carlson. Give us a shot.

Sincerely,

Bill Barke
Managing Editor

Enclosure

PART IV

HOW ABOUT . . . ?

30

A Miscellany of Questions and Answers

Though the dialogues in this book have answered many questions asked by those who write for professional publication, some questions inevitably remain. The questions taken up in this final chapter are derived verbatim from participants in Writing for Professional Publication workshops taught by the author throughout the country. A sampling of such questions, along with the answers attempted by the author, closes this book.

Question. If my first-choice scholarly journal rejects my article, should I revise the manuscript to suit the editorial style of my second-choice journal before mailing it off?

Answer. Yes. Your chances of publication will be enhanced. See the advice in Chapters 4 and 5 on adapting your writing to particular audiences and editorial practices.

Question. If I submit a completed article, would it be ethical and reasonable to state in a cover letter that if I receive no reply by a specified date, I will assume the article is rejected and will submit the identical article to another publication for consideration?

Answer. Although there is nothing unethical or unreasonable about your approach, it may not be wise. You risk at least raised eyebrows and quite possibly irritation on the part of editors. A rigid editor might respond that the journal would not review any article submitted with restrictions or conditions attached. Editors are accustomed to assigning deadlines to writers; unfortunately, they are not accustomed to writers assigning deadlines to editors.

The time span you specified might be briefer than the periodical's customary period of consideration prior to acceptance or rejection. So if you do decide to name a date, you should consult the authors' guides to magazines and journals named in Chapter 5. Take into account the possibility that readers for refereed journals might be late in responding to editors. Otherwise you might receive insufficient consideration and an overly hasty rejection.

Question. You read to keep abreast of your field, and you conduct research based upon the best knowledge that you have. The publications go on and on. But how do you *really* know that you have a good grasp on the *entire* field? How do you know when you have reviewed the literature sufficiently?

Answer. All the evidence is never in. The publications do go on and on, and a grasp on the *entire* field eludes even the celebrated authorities. As in the first swim of the season, you must at some point take a deep breath and plunge in. With your high degree of conscientiousness, the greater danger will not be an insufficient review of the literature, but rather your own rationalization that you are never ready. Qualify your findings with the caution of a good scholar. Yet be heard by your colleagues in your field. Proceed on the best knowledge that you have and recognize that there will be other opportunities for additions and modifications—and even admission that new developments have superseded what you knew earlier.

Question. Do you have any information as to the general success of blacks in the area of publishing articles? Is there discrimination as to race?

Answer. Racism is an unfortunate reality in American life. However, a growing number of black authors are achieving publication of their articles and books through a variety of outlets. The overwhelming majority of editors of professional publications with whom I am personally acquainted welcome contributions from black authors and from members of a variety of ethnic groups.

In general, writing for professional publication represents a good opportunity for people of all races and nationality backgrounds to compete. Editors of professional publications do not ask for ethnic identification of authors of manuscripts. Editors usually have no way of identifying an author by race when a manuscript is being considered. Scholarly journals and book publishers often use reviewing procedures that call for manuscripts to be read ''blind''—all identifying information regarding the author is deleted. (You might respond that editors could possibly determine racial background from the institutional identification of the author of a manuscript. Yet in a time of integrated faculties, institutional identification is now no longer the guide to racial background that it once was.)

In the field of professional publications, editors who can identify the racial/ethnic backgrounds of authors through self-descriptions by the writers or other indications are usually favorable to inclusion of authors of varied backgrounds in their publication programs. Today, many motivations contribute to their valuing the representation of multicultural groups in professional publications.

Question. My first articles were published under my initials to deemphasize the fact that I am a woman. Is it safe to use my full name now?

Answer. While no one can claim that sexism has been completely eliminated from the professions, I would certainly advise use of your full name. In doing so, you support the concept of sex equality and show confidence and pride in your identity as a woman.

For every obsolete editor still practicing sex discrimination, there exist many more editors who repudiate discrimination. Indeed, as affirmative action campaigns proceed in the professions, many editors want to include more writing by women in their periodicals or on their publication lists. Writing about contemporary views on publications by women, Audrey Roberts says in the Winter 1980 issue of the *Journal of General Education:* "The attitudes of the younger generation of scholars and editors are perhaps less traditionbound, less threatened, more open to interdisciplinarity, more aware of their own biases, their own struggles to achieve, and their own politics."

Universities searching for able female staff members would not identify you as a possibility if you signed yourself J. B. Author. Move confidently into your rightful place in a better world for women.

Question. Can you assume that the leaders of your university will respect your freedom of expression?

Answer. Usually yes, and occasionally no. Freedom of speech is guaranteed in the United States Constitution. Yet, distinguishing between liberty and license perennially presents problems. Justice Oliver Wendell Holmes said, "The most stringent protection of free speech would not protect a man in falsely shouting fire in a theater and causing a panic. . . . The question in every case is whether the words used are used in such circumstances and are of such a nature as to create a clear and present danger that they bring about the substantive evils that Congress has a right to prevent." Undeniably, university administrators have sometimes taken upon themselves, rather than left to the law and the legislators, the awesome responsibility of deciding that "a clear and present danger" existed, and that faculty members were "falsely shouting fire in a theater and causing a panic." So, freedom of expression cases have occurred and will continue to occur. Constitutional guarantees were violated in the witch hunts of the early 1950s, and they could be violated again.

Supportive of freedom of expression are American libertarian principles, the doctrine of academic freedom, and the programs of such organizations as the American Association of University Professors and

338 *How About . . . ?*

the American Civil Liberties Union. Turn to them if your freedom of expression is actually violated. Assume that the leaders of your university will respect your freedom of expression until their behavior proves you wrong. Self-censorship may be a greater threat to professors than censorship by vice-presidents in charge of academic affairs.

Question. I am teaching a two-course overload and also teaching summer school. My wife works full-time and my son starts at a private college next fall. I just took on a weekend job to pay my oil, gasoline, and tax bills. When am I supposed to write a book?

Answer. You can't. The situation you describe has forced many professionals off their campuses to seek greener pastures. I can only wish you luck.

Question. How do you view the publishing of dissertation results with the adviser's name on the article? Often first?

Answer. A dissertation belongs to the scholar who writes it. A scholar should be free to publish dissertation results independently or equally free to collaborate with whomever the scholar wishes, including the adviser. The crux of the matter is that the scholar should not be coerced into collaboration with the major professor.

I confess to gagging a bit when a report on a dissertation appears with the adviser's name first, followed by that of the creator of the dissertation. I believe that for an article reporting dissertation results, academic protocol and common fairness suggest that the name of the dissertation writer should come first, regardless of age or status of the two collaborators.

Scientific papers are frequently developed through laboratories and involve multiple authorship that sometimes presents sticky problems. But even here the modern tendency is "to define the *first* author as the senior author and primary progenitor of the work being reported. Even when the first author is a graduate student, and the second (third, fourth) author is head of the laboratory, perhaps even a Nobel Laureate, it is now accepted form to refer to the first author as the 'senior author' and to assume that he did most or all of the research."[1]

Question. Will any publisher take a stab at publishing creative nonorganized but germinal data?

Answer. None that I have met. Although publishers admire creativity and have nothing against seeds, neither they nor their readers can find a use for nonorganized data. The writer had better organize the data if publication is anticipated.

Question. Since writing one's ideas has a way of making the ideas

[1]Robert A. Day, *How to Write and Publish a Scientific Paper* (Philadelphia: iSi Press, 1979), p. 15.

permanent, I am somewhat frightened about publishing. How does one get over this fright?

Answer. Very many writers, both beginners and veterans, have experienced and do experience this fright. Cold print is permanent, errors and omissions do occur, and writers often have second thoughts. Console yourself with the recognition that nobody is perfect and with the knowledge that psychiatrists recognize that demanding perfection of oneself is psychologically unhealthy.

Yes, your work may be criticized, even attacked. Yet anticipated criticisms are usually phantoms of your own mind. Your severest critic is usually you yourself.

So, as advised in Chapter 21, check your data, develop your manuscript to the best of your ability, read your galleys and proofs with care, and stop worrying. Recognize that others are under no obligation to agree with you. Abraham Lincoln's comment was perceptive, "If I were to try to read, much less answer, all the attacks made on me, this shop might as well be closed for any other business. I do the very best I know how—the very best I can; and I mean to keep doing so until the end."

If you find that your personality structure is such that you are racked by any criticism, avoid the controversial and stay with the safe. A later president than Lincoln also had good advice. Harry S Truman said, "If you can't stand the heat, get out of the kitchen." But don't let ghosts drive you from the kitchen. It may be only your imagination that is heated.

Though unacknowledged and seldom even discussed, writers' fright is real. You are not alone.

Question. Please comment on the advisability of publishing a work as a monograph prior to submitting it to a periodical for possible publication.

Answer. Dictionaries define monograph as "a learned treatise on a particular subject which may take the form of a scholarly book, article, or pamphlet." The monograph differs from more general and wide-ranging publications, such as trade books for the general reader or textbooks for the student, in that the monograph is on a specific and usually limited subject. Since sales-conscious commercial publishing is wary of the distribution potential of scholarly treatises on specific and limited subjects, monographs in book form are often submitted to university presses or to publishers who specialize in monographs, as Chapter 12 indicates. You might take this route with your monograph. You might also consider the possibility of publication of your monograph as a pamphlet through a professional organization, or as a sustained article in a scholarly journal.

Few journals will publish your monograph as an article after it has appeared elsewhere, presumably as a book or pamphlet. The journal editor may reason that your work has already appeared in print or may be unable to include a book-length or pamphlet-sized study in the journal. You might attempt to overcome such reluctance through substantial adaptation and compression of your study, reworking the monograph into a distinctive and different article.

Question. Should a manuscript (supplemental text) displaying "raw talent" and thought to be a "marketable" product, but needing refining or even redeveloping, be submitted to prospective publishers, or should attempts to revamp the contents take place prior to contacting the publisher?

Answer. Be encouraged that someone, presumably a colleague, thought that the manuscript showed "raw talent" and was "marketable." But if the material needs refining or even redeveloping, do not submit the crude first draft of an unsolicited manuscript to a prospective publisher. Query first. Interact with a publisher on the nature of the manuscript. Write and rewrite. Refined, redeveloped, and revamped content will have a better chance of acceptance.

Question. A young author works very hard on a team of three—herself and two frequently published authors—to write an article. The two recommend an experienced faculty member to review the first draft. He reviews it, and the young author takes the article back to the team for revision. In the meantime, the experienced professor writes on his own an article very close in content and submits it for publication. The young writer's coauthors show her the article by the experienced faculty member and say, "Welcome to academia."

Question 1: Should you write alone or with others? Question 2: How do you choose whom to ask to review an article when new on a faculty or just arriving out of the isolation of developing a Ph.D. dissertation?

Answer. Your teammates sound like good people. I'm surprised they weren't aware and wary of the ways of the pilfering professor. Don't abandon the team approach or reject the process of collaboration, the pros and cons of which are weighed in Chapter 4, because of this single unpleasant experience. Happily, pilfering professors are rare.

Clearly, you don't choose as reviewers faculty members such as the one who stole your article. Under the new copyright law, you might sue for infringement of rights to your unpublished material, but, for obvious reasons, you probably prefer to avoid the hassle. Confront the dishonest professor, or bring the matter to the attention of the administration as a team or an individual, only if you have carefully weighed the consequences and are ready and willing to do battle. In this particular situation, you should omit any future local reviewing of your articles until you are personally more certain about whom you can trust. After all, local reviewing is not a necessary prerequisite for publication.

Question. What might be the problems in breaking into fields in which one does not have academic degrees but to which one has devoted extensive study?

Answer. Not as many problems as you apparently think. The major headaches of the world cannot be confined tightly within disciplinary boundaries. Specialists in a particular discipline sometimes cross disciplinary lines or engage in interdisciplinary work, as Chapter 11 demonstrates. Naturally, narrow specialists view this with alarm, but the public at large may view the venturesome with approval and call the best of them universal scholars. Editors seldom inquire into degree specializations or doctoral dissertation topics; the title "doctor" suffices, for editors recognize that people do grow and develop new scholarly interests.

If you have devoted extensive study to another field, feel free to join the scholarly discussion in that area. Obviously, this advice can be run into the ground. For instance, a specialist on classical languages has no business submitting amateur treatises on genetics to scholarly journals just because the individual happens to be prejudiced against blacks. Consciously deceiving an editor about the field in which one took a doctorate is equally unconscionable.

Question. Should you do anything other than swallow hard when you receive a journal rejection accompanied by reviews that are inaccurate, have missed the point of your article, raise questions outside the scope of your article, etc.?

Answer. A little profanity might help. Yet if several reviewers missed the point or raised additional questions, it is possible that the article requires revision or rewriting.

Question. How does one go about submitting articles to popular wide-circulation magazines read by the general public? If at first you don't succeed, is there any point in trying again?

Answer. I presume you are referring both to the giants, typified by *TV Guide, Reader's Digest, National Geographic, Modern Maturity, Better Homes and Gardens, Family Circle, Woman's Day,* and *McCall's,* each with a circulation of more than six million; and the relatively smaller magazines such as *The New Yorker, Home Magazine, Forum,* with circulations in the 500,000 range. From two to six million people read *Playboy, American Legion, Sports Illustrated, Southern Living,* and *Field and Stream.* From one to two million read *Smithsonian, Popular Science, Workbasket, Boys' Life, Ebony, Money, Psychology Today,* and *Golf Digest.* You must ask yourself, "What do I know from my work in my profession that would genuinely interest the readers of this specific magazine?"

If you hope to publish in the leading general public magazines, Van Til's First Law, "Query, always query," must be observed, as Chapter 2 advises. Unsolicited over-the-transom articles on professional topics appear in popular wide-circulation magazines as frequently as diamonds occur in your backyard. Your query must be both painstaking and provocative, for it must compete with the proposals of freelancers who, unlike yourself, make their living through writing articles and books. Certainly, if at first you don't succeed, try again with a differentiated query to another magazine, or with a brand-new proposal to still another.

People who are professionals in fields other than writing can, do, and indeed should write for popular magazines. What better way is there of informing the general public about our particular professions? More power to those in the professions who occasionally do publish in general magazines!

Question. I would like to revise a textbook that I admire very much but is now outdated. How does one go about initiating a project like this?

Answer. Try a letter directed to the textbook author. Stress your admiration for the book, the kinds of changes now needed, the contribution you could make to the book, your qualifications and credentials. The author, perhaps busy with other matters, would surely appreciate your admiration and might welcome your collaboration.

If you prefer to approach the publisher directly rather than the author, be especially tactful. You wouldn't want to be mistaken for the young actress in *All About Eve*, who began with admiration for a star, opportunistically schemed to win her confidence, and ended by replacing her in the Hollywood heavens.

If the author happens to be deceased, write directly to the publisher.

Question. If I have a four-part article, should I chop it up and get four publications instead of one? My tenure committee is playing the numbers game.

Answer. If what you have written is really one article, publish your material as one article rather than trying any dirty tricks. If the article is for a scholarly journal with limited circulation, you might also consider popularizing it in a more widely read outlet, or vice versa. But don't artificially multiply the same article in a variety of outlets. Intelligent people on a tenure committee can readily spot a thinly disguised series of nearly identical articles.

Question. Suppose I—a university faculty member in elementary education—choose to write an article on a subject rather far removed from that field. As a university professor, would I be penalized for publishing in a non-education periodical on a non-education subject?

Answer. Some colleagues might mutter, "Shoemaker, stick to your last," while other colleagues might admire your versatility. Stephen Leacock became one of the world's best-known humorists while teaching economics at McGill University. Eric Segal, while a classical scholar at Yale, won fame and fortune through the book and movie version of *Love Story*.

However, don't expect to be rewarded with tenure or salary increments or scholarly prestige for your article in "a non-education periodical on a non-education subject." That article is irrelevant to matters of rank and pay.

You might be penalized if you dally so long in other fields that your own garden goes untended. If you continue to cultivate your garden, your foray into a tempting daisy field might well be admired.

Question. If a book needs color plates to make a substantial contribution, should I even consider undertaking authorship?

Answer. Color plates or any other expensive artwork should never deter a prospective author from querying. Play fair with the prospective publisher by facing the issue of color plates squarely. Estimate their extent and justify their necessity understandably and carefully. Comment on the inferior quality of any alternatives that you think might occur to the editor. If the publisher can't afford or can't justify color plates or similar expensive features, you will soon have a response to that effect.

The same advice and procedure applies to authors whose works require many halftones, cartoons, maps, graphs, charts, and the like.

Question. What do you do when all the journals in your field say they are filled for the next three years—even though they comment that your article is good?

Answer. Suspect yourself of undue pessimism. *All* the journals in your field? Or two? Or even five? Check carefully with the comprehensive *Directory of Publishing Opportunities in Journals and Periodicals*, described in Chapter 5, to determine whether you have overlooked any possibilities. Check further in specialized guides to journals in your field, also discussed in Chapter 5.

Consider the possibility of publishing your article in a related field. For instance, in the field of philosophy, Joseph L. Esposito, recognizing that philosophers justly complain of difficulties in finding an outlet for their writings, prepared a *Directory of Periodicals Relevant to Philosophy* that lists sources not indexed by *The Philosopher's Index*. His directory suggests outlets for articles by philosophers in journals of philosophy of the natural sciences; philosophy of the social and life sciences; ethics, religion, law; mathematics; linguistics; aesthetics; semiotics; history of ideas; and interdisciplinary journals. Use similar ingenuity in regard to journals in fields somewhat related to your own discipline.

Question. What do you think of the great proliferation of journals? Does that encourage poor writing? Do they exist to provide publication opportunities for assistant professors having difficulties in getting published?

Answer. I doubt that journals are established with the welfare of assistant professors in mind. A proliferation of journals exists because knowledge is exploding in our complex technological society. As we move into what sociologist Daniel Bell calls a post-industrial society, the knowledge industry becomes increasingly important. Despite any increase in the number of journals, the volume of knowledge outstrips publication opportunities. The difficulty of sharing ideas and knowledge is aggravated when university libraries and scholars themselves must curtail their purchases of periodicals in times of high inflation or of recession. Academic writers facing high rejection rates usually complain of too few available journals rather than an excess of outlets.

As to poor writing, the volume of journals does not encourage inept prose. The problem rests with a visually oriented society stressing communication through television and movies, and with insufficient attention to skillful writing at all levels of education, including the graduate level.

Question. What about teaching activities that I've created? What possibilities exist for having personal classroom experiences published? In what possible ways can I organize these, and where might I try to get them published?

Answer. In the educational profession, opportunities to publish teaching activities and personal classroom experiences in book form are rare. Books on methods in a teaching field or at a particular level afford the best of the few opportunities. A publisher will occasionally release a how-to book on some new educational development, such as learning centers or action learning.

Articles in the more general professional magazines afford the best opportunities for reporting classroom experiences and teaching activities developed by the creative teacher. If you choose to write for the grassroots teacher rather than the cloistered scholar, recognize that some of your colleagues may look down their noses at publication in outlets that seem to them pedestrian.

Question. With the difficult review procedure that a book has to go through for publication, how do you account for the really bad books that get into print?

Answer. Being human, people sometimes make bad movies, bad marriages, bad fielding plays, and bad foreign policies. We make mistakes in writing and publishing too. They are frequently related to the love of money.

Question. In regard to writing, many members of professions are not self-starters. Is there some kind of situation you could suggest that would stimulate the initiation and continuation of professional writing as a developing activity in one's department or division or institution?

Answer. Persuade the powers-that-be to sponsor a workshop or seminar on writing for professional publication for those staff members who wish to attend. The duration may be from a single day to a weekend, to several summer weeks, to a semester course enrolling both faculty and graduate students.

Follow up this initiation with regular informal meetings of those participants who wish to continue to read and criticize one another's queries and manuscripts. Utilize the leadership that has emerged from the initial seminar or workshop. Dragoon no one into attendance, but keep the door open for participation by those who become newly interested in the writing group.

Such an approach is infinitely preferable to administrative exhortation on the desirability of more writing and research by the faculty. The ancients have perceptively pointed out that people cannot make bricks without straw.

Question. Have you written a book on writing for professional publication?

Answer. Yes. This is it.

Index